REGIONAL DEVELOPMENT AND SPATIAL PLANNING IN AN ENLARGED EUROPEAN UNION

Urban and Regional Planning and Development Series

Series Editors: Professor Peter Roberts and Professor Graham Haughton

The Urban and Regional Planning and Development Series has developed a strong profile since it was launched in 1995. It is internationally recognised for its high quality research monographs. The emphasis is on presenting original research findings which are informed by theoretical sophistication and methodological rigour. It is avowedly global in its outlook, with contributions welcomed from around the world. The series is open to contributions from a wide variety of disciplines, including planning, geography, sociology, political science, public administration and economics.

Other titles in the series

Rethinking European Spatial Policy as a Hologram
Actions, Institutions, Discourses
Edited by Luigi Doria, Valeria Fedeli and Carla Tedesco
ISBN 0 7546 4548 7

The Dublin-Belfast Development Corridor: Ireland's Mega-City Region?
Edited by John Yarwood
ISBN 0 7546 4702 1

Evaluation in Planning
Evolution and Prospects
Edited by E.R. Alexander
ISBN 0 7546 4586 X

Spatial Planning and Urban Development in the New EU Member States
From Adjustment to Reinvention
Edited by Uwe Altrock, Simon Güntner, Sandra Huning and Deike Peters
ISBN 0 7546 4684 X

Regionalism Contested
Institution, Society and Governance
Edited by Iwona Sagan and Henrik Halkier
ISBN 0 7546 4361 1

Regional Development and Spatial Planning in an Enlarged European Union

Edited by

NEIL ADAMS
London South Bank University, UK

JEREMY ALDEN
Cardiff University, UK

NEIL HARRIS
Cardiff University, UK

ASHGATE

Published by
Ashgate Publishing Limited
Gower House
Croft Road
Aldershot
Hampshire GU11 3HR
England

Ashgate Publishing Company
Suite 420
101 Cherry Street
Burlington, VT 05401-4405
USA

Ashgate website: http://www.ashgate.com

British Library Cataloguing in Publication Data
Regional development and spatial planning in an enlarged
  European Union. - (Urban and regional planning and
  development series)
  1.Regional planning - European Union countries
  I.Adams, Neil II.Alden, Jeremy III.Harris, Neil
  307.1'2'094

Library of Congress Cataloging-in-Publication Data
Regional development and spatial planning in an enlarged European Union / edited by
Neil Adams, Jeremy Alden, and Neil Harris.
     p. cm. -- (Urban and regional planning and development series)
   ISBN-13: 978-0-7546-4714-0
   ISBN-10: 0-7546-4714-5
    1. Regional planning--European Union countries. 2. Regional disparities--European
Union countries. 3. European Union countries--Economic conditions--Regional
disparities. 4. European Union countries--Economic policy. I. Adams, Neil. II.
Alden, Jeremy. III. Harris, Neil, 1973- IV. Series: Urban and regional planning and
development.

HT395.E85R44 2006
307.1'2094--dc22

                                                                    2006017126

ISBN-13: 978 0 7546 4714 0
ISBN-10: 0 7546 4714 5

Printed and bound in Great Britain by Antony Rowe Ltd, Chippenham, Wiltshire.

Contents

List of Figures

Notes on Contributors

Neil Adams is Senior Lecturer in Spatial Planning at London South Bank University and his main interests are European spatial planning at the supra-national, national and regional level. He was previously employed as a consultant based in Brussels and has extensive experience of regional development and spatial planning at national, regional and local levels in the Baltic States. Neil was also Project Co-ordinator for the INTERREG IIIC GRIDS project that provided the inspiration for this book.

Jeremy Alden is Professor of International Planning Studies in the School of City and Regional Planning at Cardiff University, Wales, United Kingdom. He is Lead Partner for the INTERREG IIIC project on regional development and spatial planning sponsored by the European Commission during 2004 and 2005. He has published widely on regional development and spatial planning issues in the European Union.

Neil Harris is Lecturer in Planning at the School of City and Regional Planning in Cardiff University. His interests cover the statutory planning system and new approaches to the development of spatial plans in Britain at the national and regional scales. He has advised the Welsh Assembly Government on its approach to the preparation of a national spatial planning framework.

Klaus Kunzmann is Jean-Monnet Professor of European Spatial Planning at the Institute of Spatial Planning at the University of Dortmund in Germany. He has been closely involved with the development of the European Spatial Development Perspective since its publication in 1999. He has an international reputation for his research and practice in urban and regional development.

Joris Scheers is Head of the Monuments and Landscape Division of the Ministry of the Flemish Community and was previously centrally involved in the preparation of the Flemish Structure Plan. He is also Professor in Spatial Planning at the University of Leuven in Belgium and is currently President of the Flemish Association of Spatial Planners.

Graeme Purves is Principal Planner in the Development Department of the Planning Division of the Scottish Executive, and was a central figure in the preparation of the Scottish National Planning Framework. He has a particular interest in regional development and spatial planning in the Celtic and Baltic countries.

Finian Matthews is in the Spatial Policy Section of the Irish Department of the Environment, Heritage and Local Government. He is part of the team which has had responsibility for the implementation of the Irish National Spatial Strategy. The Strategy has attracted particular interest within the enlarged European Union given Ireland's recent economic success.

Anders Paalzow is Rector of the Stockholm School of Economics in Riga, Latvia. He is also Chairman of the Board for the Baltic International Centre for Economic Policy Studies. He has expertise on a wide range of economic and social issues facing the Baltic States within an enlarged European Union.

Sandra Ezmale has worked in the Latgale Regional Development Agency in Latvia since 2000. She has been centrally involved in the preparation of the Latgale development and planning documents. Prior to her work with the Latgale RDA, she worked for Rezekne District Council on spatial planning issues. She is currently Head of the North Latgale office for the RDA, and is responsible for spatial planning within the Agency.

Gaile Dagiliene is the Undersecretary of the Ministry of the Interior of the Republic of Lithuania. Prior to taking this position, she was Director of the Regional Policy Department. She is also an Honorary Research Fellow at the School of City and Regional Planning at Cardiff University. Among others, her responsibilities include developing and implementing national regional policy, participating in EU Structural Funds, acting as the Managing Authority for INTERREG IIIA programme LT-PL-RU as well as co-ordinating INTERREG IIIB and IIIC programmes in Lithuania.

Lowie Steenwegen is a Freelance Spatial Planner in Flanders and has worked for a number of years on international capacity building and research projects in the field of regional development. He has extensive experience of practice in central and eastern Europe including the Baltic States. He has also served as a Member of Parliament in the Flemish Parliament and has a particular interest in the Flemish Structure Plan.

Foreword

The Best Practice Guidelines for Regional Development Strategies project (GRIDS) can definitely be considered as an exemplary initiative for the INTERREG IIIC programme (the European Community Initiative designed to promote inter-regional co-operation). I am very happy that this publication has been directly inspired by this operation. Indeed, when we consider its characteristics, while the vast majority of INTERREG IIIC running operations are focusing on a specific sector or policy, GRIDS is one of the few that deals directly with the elaboration of regional strategies and policies, and, in this respect, with the whole scope of EU regional policy. Therefore, it is by nature totally relevant to the INTERREG IIIC programme whose aim is to contribute to the improvement of regional policies. In addition, GRIDS builds on the experience of its partners who exchange know-how and experience in order to enrich their own approaches. Its aim is not to reinvent the wheel but rather to look for innovative practices that were successful in the different regions. This is also fully in line with the programme's principles. Finally, the strong involvement of a New Member State partner is of added-value as it contributes to the expansion of the effects of Structural Fund programmes in new EU Regions.

The INTERREG IIIC programme places particular importance on the dissemination of operations results. GRIDS has already been a successful initiative in the sense that the strategies and policies of most of the participating Regions have been influenced by the activities undertaken within the operation. Thanks to this book, these benefits will not only remain within the existing partnership; while contributing directly to the sustainability of the operation's results, it is hoped that it will be of use to many other regional/local authorities in Europe. This emphasises the importance of this publication.

As strategic planning concerns all fields in the public sphere, I have no doubt that this publication will contribute sound methodology practices to the development of interregional co-operation planned within the Lisbon and Gothenburg priorities in the future!

Michel Lamblin
Programme Manager
INTERREG IIIC West Secretariat

Acknowledgements

The preparation of this book has been inspired by a project funded by the European Union under its INTERREG IIIC programme. The GRIDS project – designed to identify and disseminate good practice guidelines for regional development and spatial planning – has involved partners and associates from eight different European countries. Such projects inevitably involve a very wide range of people and it would be practically impossible to acknowledge all of them here.

Thank you to the contributors who have supplied and revised materials in accordance with our guidance – we are especially grateful to our practice-based contributors for taking on additional work in sharing their experiences with wider, academic audiences. Several of the contributors to the book have supported the project in a number of other ways, providing presentations at key events and acting as 'critical friends' to the project.

Additionally, we would like to thank all of the following people who have been involved in the book or the wider project in one way or another: Rene van der Lecq, Julie Bynens, Dimitri Meesen and Koen Vermoesen (Ministry of the Flemish Community, Belgium), Joris de Clercq (Aalst Borough Council), Mark Tewdwr-Jones (University College London), Vincent Nadin (University of West of England), Uldis Kirsteins and Igors Graurs (Riga City Council), Alf Vanags (Baltic Institute Centre for Economic Policy Studies), Sue Essex, Grant Duncan and Neil Hemington (Welsh Assembly Government), John Laffan, Brian Kenny, David Ryan and Tom Ferris (Ministry of Environment and Department of Transport, Republic of Ireland), Dirk Lauwers and Sirka Ludtke (iris consulting), Juri Lass (Ministry of Environment, Estonia), Ilze Kukute, Nina Linde and Ilze Kjahjare (Ministry of Regional Development and Local Government, Latvia), Tudor Davies, Phil Davy, Victoria Phillips and Jan Bennett (Caerphilly County Borough Council), Gareth Hall (Welsh Development Agency), Aled Thomas, Rachel Jowitt and Kevin Bishop (Welsh Local Government Association), Richard Essex (Royal Institute of Chartered Surveyors), Anne Azam-Pradeilles (DATAR), Artur da Rosa Pires (Aveiro University), Paul Lewis (Scottish Enterprise), Stephen Crow (Cardiff University), Maris Bozoviks and Mark Benn (Latgale Regional Development Agency), Michel Lamblin (INTERREG), Alexandras Gordevicius (Ministry of Environment, Lithuania), Algirdas Astrauskas (Ministry of Regional Development, Lithuania).

We would particularly like to thank Margaret Roberts for both her excellent support in making arrangements for the numerous project meetings and for helping to assemble the manuscript. Thanks also to Janice Edwards, Andrew Edwards and Tom Garne for their technical and graphic support, and to Cynthia Trevett for assistance in manuscript preparation. Cerys Phillips managed the project's financial regulations extremely well and liaised closely with Partners and the INTERREG office in Lille.

Val Rose, Carolyn Court and Nicola Nieuwoudt at Ashgate Publishing helped us at key stages with various questions and in preparing the book for publication.

Neil Adams, Jeremy Alden and Neil Harris
London and Cardiff
March 2006

PART I

New Approaches to Regional Development and Spatial Planning

Chapter 1

Introduction: Regional Development and Spatial Planning in an Enlarged European Union

Neil Adams, Jeremy Alden and Neil Harris

Introduction: Regional Development and Spatial Planning

Experience across the various regions within Europe suggests a rapidly changing context for undertaking regional development and regional planning activities. Governments have increasingly had to recognise the open nature of their economies as a consequence of globalisation, and the inevitable interdependencies this creates between different parts of Europe and other spaces that are connected into the global economy. Domestic government funding for regional policy has in many cases been curtailed, further limiting the ability to address regional imbalances through targeted policy measures. In many cases, decades of regional policy measures and targeted interventions have failed to redress the difficulties or problems that they have been designed to resolve. This has in turn led to recognition of the deep-seated and persistent nature of many regional development problems and, in response, the need to develop new and innovative measures as alternatives to traditional regional policy activities. One of the fields in which there has been innovation in public policies over the past decade is in spatial planning. There has been an increase in spatial strategy-making in Europe at various different scales, from the European scale through to transnational, national and regional scales (Albrechts, 2001; Healey, 2004; Healey *et al.*, 1999). In some contexts, such as the peripheral countries of north-west Europe, the embrace of spatial planning has been particularly marked (see Hammond, 2002; Vigar *et al.*, 2000; see also Chapters 5, 6 and 7). The activities of spatial planning and regional development are reviewed further in later chapters, especially in the following chapter. However, some of the more important characteristics need outlining here. This is particularly the case for readers who are not based in some of the contexts or countries where spatial planning has emerged with any significant clarity or profile.

Spatial planning can be understood and defined in a variety of different ways (see Tewdwr-Jones, 2004; Harris *et al.*, 2002). Indeed, it is an activity that may take different forms in different contexts, depending on institutional and legal context, or variations in planning cultures and traditions (Healey, 1997). The intention here is not to evaluate these competing or differing definitions of spatial planning, but to simply try and provide some sense of spatial planning as an activity by summarising some of its common characteristics. Spatial planning is a particular form of public policy, one that claims to be focused on the spatial dimensions of a wide range of other sectoral policies, from economic development, transportation and environmental protection through to health, culture and language. This claim has two important dimensions that will be explored here as a basis for understanding recent attention to spatial planning: (1) the 'spatial' dimension and (2) the 'breadth' of sectoral policy coverage. On the first of these, spatial plans or strategies offer a means of reintroducing the significance of place or geography to public policy. They have an important role in relating public policies to particular places and demonstrating that policies, and national-level policies in particular, do not play out evenly or uniformly across a territory. The outcome and effectiveness of any policy is derived from the interaction of that policy with the particular qualities and characteristics of the area to which they are applied. Spatial plans can help policy-makers to understand this and even anticipate where certain policies will be effective and where they will not, or where they may take on a particular form in implementation. Expressed simply, spatial planning injects the question of 'where?' into all policy sectors. A related element to this particular aspect of spatial plans is their potential as place-making tools. Such plans can be important vehicles for expressing, or even bringing into effect, a territory or defined physical and political space. The second dimension relates to the breadth of policies and different policy sectors embraced in the activity of spatial planning. Spatial plans are therefore usually defined very widely in terms of their sectoral scope or policy coverage. Not only do spatial plans typically embrace these various different policy fields, but claims are also made for the capacity of spatial planning and spatial strategies to synthesise or integrate these various policies. This particular quality of spatial plans – their supposed capacity for integration of a range of different policies – is one that perhaps best explains their recent popularity, especially in contexts where a suite of different policies exists or has developed recently, such as in the devolved countries of the United Kingdom (Lloyd and McCarthy, 2002). These and other issues are addressed in the final chapter of the book, where some of the claims made for the activity of spatial planning will be assessed, particularly with reference to regional development.

Spatial planning is often presented as an activity that can be undertaken at any scale, from the supranational to the national, regional or local. Examples can be provided of spatial planning initiatives at each of these scales. However, the focus of this book is on spatial planning at the 'regional' level, a scale at which spatial planning is said to be particularly focused and pertinent. The use of the term regional needs some qualification here. The term is interpreted in different ways depending on institutional and historical context, including the formation of the nation state. Its use in this book is a fairly inclusive one and aligns fairly well with the definition for European statistical purposes as NUTS I and NUTS II levels with populations of between 3 million and 7 million people (NUTS I) and between 800,000 and 3 million people (NUTS II). The various case study chapters on selected countries in the Baltics and the Celtic periphery rest comfortably within this understanding of a region, even though they clearly can be identified in other ways too, including as independent states. The region remains a meaningful concept for both analysis and research, as well as for policy intervention. Indeed, the European Union's present emphasis on cohesion policy – designed to reduce disparities in output, productivity and employment and thereby promote greater economic, social and territorial cohesion – has a particular focus on regions, regional policy and the role of regional development. The commitment to regions at the EU level is illustrated by the fact that EU regional policy and cohesion policy now have the second largest budget of all EU policy areas after the Common Agricultural Policy.

Enlargement and the Changing Geography of Europe

The European Union has been an important force in promoting the concept and practice of spatial planning within Europe as a whole, and also within individual member states. A key part of this has been the publication in 1999 of the European Spatial Development Perspective, an initiative which features in several of the chapters and case studies that follow in the book (see also Faludi and Waterhout, 2002; see also Chapters 2 and 3 of this volume). However, several important changes with implications for the activities of regional development and spatial planning have taken place since the publication of the European Spatial Development Perspective. These include the additional significance afforded to cohesion policy and, of course, the enlargement of the European Union in 2004 with the accession of ten central and eastern European countries (see Pallagst, 2006). The enlargement of the European Union, with the admission of countries such as Hungary, Poland and Slovakia as well as the Baltic states of Estonia, Latvia and Lithuania, has potentially far-reaching effects for a whole range of different policies of relevance to spatial planning and regional development. Some of these issues are elaborated upon in Chapters 8 to 11 where the experiences in some of the new member states are relayed, although some key points are of wider significance and deserve consideration here too. Firstly, the admission of the new members in 2004 further increases the historical and cultural diversity that exists within the European Union. This diversity can be understood at various levels, for example in terms of how historical and cultural diversity impacts on the design of political institutions, including how it frames the general activities of government and its relationships with citizens. This is especially significant for those countries which were until the early 1990s part of the Soviet Union. This can then be translated into more specific implications for the activities of regional development and spatial planning, as tools of government, which shape how those activities are undertaken and understood. Studying spatial planning and regional development within the context of these different cultures is itself a revealing and interesting activity, helping us to better understand our own familiar systems in new and interesting ways. The final chapter in the book comes back to address some of these issues. Secondly, and perhaps of most significance for regional development, the accession of the new member countries results in a Europe of increased social and economic disparities. Accession signified a different socio-economic geography for Europe with implications in particular for future design of the Structural Funds. The selection of case studies in this book is of special interest here, for it juxtaposes some of the new member states with earlier European Union member countries that face the greatest risks, at least in terms of receipt of Structural Funds, from the admission of countries with weak socio-economic profiles. So, as the socio-economic geography of Europe changes, we can also expect patterns of spending of European Union funds to change. Finally, and of special relevance to spatial planning, the 'geography' of Europe also changes in other ways. Europe in an expanded form changes its centre of gravity, meaning that different countries come to occupy changed positions within it. Some regions already considered peripheral, for example, may become more so. The relevance of this to spatial planning is how different countries or regions may utilise their spatial plans or strategies to 'position' themselves strategically within Europe. Again, some of the case study chapters provide an insight into how the selected countries and regions have anticipated the effects of enlargement of the European Union and are responding to these.

The Purpose and Structure of the Book

This book is one of the products arising from an international project funded by the European Union as part of its INTERREG IIIC programme. The INTERREG IIIC programme is designed to help Europe's regions form partnerships to work together on common projects. The programme assists the regions involved in their attempts to develop new solutions to economic, social and environmental challenges. The particular project that has brought together the various contributors to this book specifically focused on developing a series of good practice guidelines for instruments of regional development and spatial planning. The GRIDS project, as it became known, included various partners from Ireland, Wales, Flanders, Latvia and Lithuania, and also involved a range of other external participants from Scotland, England, Estonia, Portugal, Germany and even China. The immediate project outputs, a series of good practice guidelines, are targeted at those engaged in preparing regional development strategies and spatial plans across Europe (Adams and Harris, 2005). It was soon recognised that, while such outputs were likely to be of value to their intended audience, the project had generated a great deal of learning and material that could be shared more widely and also have appeal to other audiences. This book is therefore an attempt to provide a more in-depth and reflective account of how spatial planning and regional development activities are evolving in some of Europe's smaller countries.

The book is structured in five separate parts. Part I attempts to clarify the terms regional development and spatial planning as the basis for analysing the various case studies presented in the following sections. Part II then focuses on the evolving European context for regional development and spatial planning, highlighting the key developments that have occurred in recent years and are likely to happen in the near future. Part III provides a collection of case studies of regional development and spatial planning in three of the Celtic countries of north-west Europe, covering Ireland, Scotland and Wales. This section brings together contributions from academics and policy makers, some of whom have been responsible for or closely involved in the preparation of spatial strategies in their countries over the past five years. It complements an increasing literature focused on reviewing the progress of spatial planning activity in particular in the periphery of north-west Europe. Part IV is perhaps one of the most valuable in this edited volume, providing case studies of regional development and spatial planning in the Baltic states of Latvia, Lithuania and Estonia. Again, the contributions are written by practitioners, policy-makers and academics and therefore provide a detailed insight into how the particular regional and spatial planning challenges are being addressed within the context of the Baltics. The chapters provide a particularly valuable addition to the literature on spatial planning in Europe, a literature that is well-developed in relation to certain parts of the European territory (see Healey *et al.*, 1997), but will require further development through case studies on spatial planning in a wider range of new European countries, including the Baltic states. Expanding this literature, both in terms of geography and scope, is a necessary part of taking forward the wider agenda of European spatial planning, both within and across member states. The final part of the book attempts to draw together the key lessons and common themes arising from the individual case studies, with a particular emphasis on the theme of sustainable development.

The fact that the contributors to the book are drawn from across Europe and have a range of different backgrounds has already been referred to. They include senior policy-makers and civil servants from Western Europe and the Baltics, as well as independent consultants, those who are politically active and also those engaged in academic work. The assembled contents prepared by both academics and practitioners are one of the strengths of this book. The contributions by practitioners are especially welcome, given the acknowledgement that few practitioners write for academic as well as practitioner audiences. Yet, the challenging circumstances in which they write need to be acknowledged. There is the difficulty of finding time to write material, as well as the challenges of accessing academic materials and being able to objectively review some of the work that they are responsible for on a day-to-day basis. The book is richer for their involvement and the various different contributions by practitioners and others provide an incredibly valuable overview of regional development and spatial planning activity across Europe.

Part I: New Approaches to Regional Development and Spatial Planning

The first chapter following this introduction reflects on the apparent increase of interest in spatial planning and its particular development at the regional level. Jeremy Alden paints a positive portrait of spatial planning, pointing to its renaissance during the past decade. In doing so, he tries to define the practice of spatial planning in order to provide a platform for the chapters that follow in the remainder of the book. The term is not one that is understood in the same manner across Europe, yet it is possible in most contexts to identify activities that could be regarded as spatial planning activities, even if they are not so described in their domestic context. Alden defines a series of key features or principles of spatial planning, focusing on its strategic character, long-term perspective and integrative qualities. He concludes his chapter with what emerges as one of the most significant challenges in an expanded European Union – the prosperity gap that exists between the Union's richest and poorest countries and how to address the development of the recently-joined members.

Part II: The Evolving European Union Context for Regional Development and Spatial Planning

Klaus Kunzmann's chapter addresses what is described as the Europeanisation of spatial planning. His account emphasises how the concept and practice of spatial planning has emerged within the context of Europe, with historical roots in the more traditional and widely understood practice of regional planning. His perspective on the importance of spatial planning is a relatively pessimistic one, claiming that spatial planning has a weak or even marginal role and influence on spatial development. So, while planners themselves may be positive about the value of their activities, Kunzmann argues that wider society does not share such a view. Certainly, his chapter highlights that the practice of spatial planning faces many different challenges across the different parts of Europe, from rapid economic growth, to stemming decline and dealing with the less desirable aspects of deindustrialisation. Not all of these provide favourable conditions in which the activity of spatial planning can flourish. Yet there is a strand of optimism in Kunzmann's account based on the claim that there has been an 'unexpected renaissance' in spatial planning in Europe. This has been brought about by debates on territorial cohesion, a central policy objective framed within debates on the European Union constitution. The objective of territorial cohesion, with its emphasis on what one might regard as the geographic or spatial coherence of the European territory, clearly relates to the potential of spatial planning as an activity. The chapter's overview of spatial planning in Europe also demonstrates that a considerable institutional and organisational framework has built up around the practice of spatial planning, from research and data collection bodies to collaborative networks and key policy documents. Yet, despite the existence of such a framework, Kunzmann points to the lack of hard instruments and mechanisms in spatial planning, particularly when compared with related fields, and argues that this explains in large part the weaknesses and shortcomings of spatial planning. One of the more tangible outcomes of the European spatial planning renaissance is the European Spatial Development Perspective. The impact of the ESDP process has been extensive, not necessarily in terms of the specific contents of the document, but certainly in terms of what Faludi (2004) refers to as shaping minds. There has been speculation about how the significant achievements in arriving at the production of the ESDP will be taken forward, particularly in view of the recent expansion in 2004 of the European

Union to include some ten new Member States. Kunzmann provides an insight into the future of the ESDP, relating its future development to the agenda of territorial cohesion. The reader is likely to feel that Kunzmann's account leaves them with an almost contradictory sense that spatial planning has considerable potential to contribute towards the goal of territorial cohesion, yet that potential will be difficult to realise and communicate to policy and decision makers.

The experience of devising a new planning framework in the form of the Structure Plan for Flanders is relayed by Joris Scheers in Chapter 4. Flanders represents one of the more prosperous regions of the European Union, yet one that is still subject to the challenges posed by globalisation and internationalisation of industry. In addition, it is a region that has identified strategic spatial planning as a potentially valuable framework through which to manage these and other challenges, including the protection of open space. As a case study, it is of particular interest for how a spatial planning framework or strategy occupies a negotiated position within a complex set of governance arrangements and practices. Of significance in the Flemish context is the principle of subsidiarity of decision-making and ensuring decisions are taken at the appropriate administrative level. Its contribution also lies in the story of how a particular system achieves the transition from traditional, regulatory forms of land-use planning to the more strategic, flexible and dynamic processes of spatial planning with their emphasis on vision, partnership and stakeholder engagement. His evaluation of Structure Planning in Flanders to date reveals a mixed picture. Scheers points to its value in creating improved opportunities for more integrated spatial solutions, but that it has also lacked some of the necessary instruments for particular themes, including increasing car-dependence and managing urban sprawl. The case study of Flanders is relevant due to the relative maturity of the Structure Plan and the fact that discussions are currently ongoing in Flanders about what form the revised document should take.

Part III: Regional Development and Spatial Planning in the Celtic Periphery

In Chapter 5, Neil Harris, in looking at regional development and spatial planning in Wales, highlights some enduring problems faced by those engaged in regional development. His account stresses that Wales' classic regional development challenges continue to define the parameters of regional development policy in Wales. The principal policy challenges facing Wales are raising productivity through increasing participation rates and ensuring a more even distribution of prosperity across Wales. The decline of manufacturing and extractive industries has left a permanent scar on the Welsh economic landscape. Sustained policy interventions have perhaps prevented Wales being subject to some of the worst consequences of economic restructuring. However, the underlying structural characteristics of Welsh society and the economy have proven resilient and demonstrate the particularly long-term periods over which resolving interregional disparities must be undertaken. This is a point that will not be lost on the Baltic states. The principal lesson for others from this case study is that successful regional development must be worked towards in a sustained manner, and that the creation of a regional development infrastructure and the allocation of funding for regional development are not the only ingredients for success. Harris's case study is, like many others in this volume, one in which complex governance changes have redefined the context for both regional development and spatial planning. Devolution and the establishment of the National Assembly for Wales have created a context in which new and revised policy frameworks are being attempted. In particular, the Assembly's preparation of the Wales Spatial Plan, a form of national spatial strategy, is one of the more interesting innovations to emerge from Wales' new governance landscape. Notwithstanding such developments, and the fact that the process in relation to the Wales Spatial Plan has been widely acclaimed, the case study of Wales is not entirely optimistic, and the challenges facing policy-makers in Wales continue to appear very real and demanding.

The experience of the Scottish Executive in preparing the first national spatial strategy for Scotland is relayed in Graeme Purves' chapter. The National Planning Framework, published in 2004, represents the continuation of a strong tradition of regional and strategic planning that has become of one the defining characteristics of planning in Scotland. Consequently, Scotland also has an extensive institutional framework to support regional development and strategic planning initiatives. The National Planning Framework is reported to have been received positively by the wide range of stakeholders that have been involved in its preparation. The value of the framework in addressing some of the key challenges facing Scotland, with its distinctive settlement pattern, significant economic disparities and challenging geographic context, is yet to be demonstrated. However, Purves' account suggests that it has made a positive start and is assisting with various objectives, including providing an improved means of relating Scotland to the wider European territory and accessing European funding programmes and related actions. It has also focused attention on the significance of Scotland's cities as drivers of the economy, with the resulting emphasis on improving infrastructure between the cities and their associated regions. This finds its expression in the themes of 'quality and connectivity'. Purves' case study of the National Planning Framework for Scotland is of particular interest for its insight into how EU Directive 2001/42/EC (known in the United Kingdom as the Strategic Environmental Assessment directive) may be applied to and in turn challenge some of the policies in strategic spatial plans or strategies. The capacity of spatial plans or strategies to integrate different policy spheres is one of their attractive and defining qualities, yet it also means they become arenas for addressing perceived conflicts between economic development, social progress and environmental protection. As Purves notes in his account, facing up to the environmental consequences or implications of certain development trajectories may force policy makers to engage in serious re-evaluation of their strategies in the longer-term.

Any collection of papers examining recent practice in regional development and spatial planning in the European Union would be incomplete without the inclusion of a case study focusing on Ireland. Finian Matthews and Jeremy Alden start their chapter with a statement of Ireland's closing of the prosperity gap between Ireland and the EU average within a generation. This, of course, is the reason why Ireland has attracted so much interest in regional development circles from those, including the Baltic states, wishing to emulate the success of the Irish economy. The chapter acknowledges some of the factors explaining the phenomenon of the 'Celtic Tiger', including demographic change, success in inward investment projects, and effective use of European Union funding mechanisms. The approach is, and remains, one that is based on identifying the critical factors for success and ensuring that they are set in place. Yet, as their account identifies, such economic success has resulted in the exacerbation of spatial disparities across Ireland. The economic and social profile of the various regions within Ireland is therefore markedly different and requires tailored approaches to dealing with economic and planning issues. Of clear significance has been the expansion of the Greater Dublin Area in terms of population and economic influence. The Government's response to addressing such patterns of spatial imbalance is, in part, expressed in the preparation of a National Spatial Strategy. Like many similar approaches elsewhere, the preparation of the Strategy has focused on developing public awareness and consensus. Its overall objective of achieving more balanced development across Ireland focuses on a relatively well-developed spatial strategy, identifying a range of gateways, hubs and other urban centres that are to act as counter-points to some of the attractions of the Greater Dublin Area. As a case study, the National Spatial Strategy provides one of the more advanced examples of a spatial strategy, in terms of both content and the time that the Strategy has been in preparation and engaged in implementation. Consequently, interest in Ireland's National Spatial Strategy is likely to continue.

Part IV: Regional Development and Spatial Planning in the Baltics

The Baltic States of Estonia, Latvia and Lithuania face a range of important challenges as post-Soviet countries and new Member States of the European Union. Neil Adams addresses the three Baltic States together in how they are adapting to further structural change, having already undergone significant restructuring during the previous decade and since independence in the early nineties. Adams is keen to emphasise the cultural, historic and economic differences between Estonia, Latvia and Lithuania, focusing on the complex relationships that each country has with various different parts of Europe. As with any country, but particularly pertinent in the case of the Baltic states, with their ongoing Soviet legacy, is the challenge of reconciling the past with ambitions for the future. Each country has reasons to be optimistic on the future facing some of their regions, most notably the comparatively buoyant capital regions, yet limited prosperity and weak accessibility continue to drive worrying demographic trends in the countries as a whole and their more peripheral regions in particular. These economic and social challenges are juxtaposed with the significant natural environmental assets and resources in the various regions of the three countries. Adams' perspective on regional development and spatial planning in the Baltic States concludes that attaining more balanced regional development is fraught with difficulties, but remains an important and necessary goal.

Following Neil Adams' portrait of the Baltic States, Anders Paalzow focuses on regional development and spatial planning activities in Latvia. Paalzow's address of barriers to regional development in Latvia commences with a reminder of the peculiar circumstances that Latvia faces as a country formerly a part of the Soviet Union and facing the challenges of integration into the European Union. The impact of being located at the outer periphery of the European Union rather than close to the gravity centre of the former Soviet Union is examined and Paalzow makes clear that the legacy of the Soviet period will continue to frame the country's development for many years to come. Despite restructuring over the past 15 years, the programmes and actions carried out in the Soviet era still cast long shadows over the economic and social landscape, not least in terms of ethnic diversity and citizenship. An important point made at the outset of the chapter is that the Soviet legacy is not only evident in the physical infrastructure of the country, but also frames the institutional context for regional development and spatial planning policies and initiatives. Economic and spatial disparities feature as one of the most concerning aspects of the development of the economy since independence, and Paalzow's account highlights how such disparities are likely to increase leading to an exacerbated core-periphery model. This is one of the factors explaining the growth in regional development activity in Latvia, including in Latgale region which forms the focus of the following chapter by Sandra Ezmale, Anders Paalzow and Neil Adams. Latgale region has the misfortune of being characterised as one of the poorest regions of the European Union. It faces particular difficulties in dealing with its post-Soviet legacy following the decline of many of the manufacturing industries located in its urban centres that were historically oriented to the Soviet system. High unemployment and limited participation in economic activities present some of the starker challenges for Latgale. However, the region's rich culture and extensive natural environment provide important assets and form part of the region's development strategy. It is also seeking to capitalise on its Soviet past and make use of its high proportion of Russian residents, presenting itself as in a valuable position to act as a bridge between Europe and Russia.

Regional policy has escalated in political and public profile in recent years in Lithuania. However, Gaile Dagiliene paints a mixed picture in her portrayal of regional development in Lithuania, highlighting varying interpretations over the scope and aims of regional development policy. Of particular interest in her account of regional disparities in the country is the legacy of Soviet planning of the economy, whereby certain regions specialised in the production of certain products under a planned economy and system of production. Independence resulted, as it did too for Latvia, in a rapid period of economic transformation as the planned economy gave way to the market. As one would expect, some places fared better than others in adapting to changed economic circumstances, resulting in increased economic and social disparities. Dagiliene reminds us that in the fifteen years or so since independence was regained, only in the past eight years has any serious attention been directed to addressing the regional policy challenges of post-Soviet economic restructuring processes. Interestingly, the European Commission has been an important driver in the preparation of regional policy to address spatial disparities, with policy targeting 'lagging regions', and its influence continued in the period leading to access to the European Union. The chapter provides an interesting insight into the challenges of relating domestic regional policy objectives to those of the European Commission, although Dagiliene concludes that different regional policies can co-exist. Regional disparities are shown in the chapter, as they are in other accounts in the book, to be some of the most enduring and problematic aspects of regional development. In an account that will be familiar in different parts of the European Union, the case study of Lithuania makes clear that promoting development of the national economy does not always rest comfortably with the securing of more balanced economic and spatial development across a territory.

Part V: Key Challenges for the Future

The penultimate chapter of the book focuses on one of the issues that a spatial planning approach arguably does introduce more clearly to regional development and regional policy – the pursuit of sustainable development. Lowie Steenwegen traces the evolution of sustainable development as an objective of regional development policy and reviews what it can offer in challenging 'business as usual'. His account acknowledges that the term 'sustainable development' risks becoming meaningless and that aiming for more sustainable forms of development can all too readily be traded off against more immediate, economic concerns. Steenwegen identifies an apparent paradox – greater planning and regulation appear necessary to meet the challenges posed by sustainable development, yet many of the programmes evident in regional policy promote deregulation and liberalisation as regions compete to secure investment. His case for promoting improved integration between regional development and spatial planning, using sustainable development as the vehicle to do so, will be welcomed by like-minded academics and policy-makers. The key and ever-present challenge, however, will be to ensure that the attractive qualities of a greater relationship between these two activities is not compromised for short-term, economic advantage or political expediency.

The final chapter provides the opportunity to look across the various contextual chapters and individual case studies of spatial planning and regional development practice. In particular, it permits an assessment or overview of the various approaches in the Celtic periphery and in the Baltics. The analysis identifies important commonalities in the various approaches to spatial planning, leading to discussion on how a particular form and style of spatial planning has emerged over the past half decade. The case studies illustrate and inform an understanding of the principal features of spatial strategy-making in the smaller countries of the European Union. The review also enables some conclusions to be made and further questions to be asked on the effectiveness of spatial planning and regional development. These questions must include whether spatial planning can genuinely promote integrated policy delivery and 'joined-up governance' and whether it can be a truly effective instrument for dealing with wicked issues. As many of the case studies illustrate, many spatial plans or strategies act as 'frameworks for dialogue'. An important part of our concluding discussions therefore centres on whether spatial plans and strategies are likely to inform and influence difficult policy decisions – including addressing increasing disparities and the challenge of balanced regional development – while preserving their qualities as important frameworks for discussion and debate on the future of places.

References

Adams, N. and Harris, N. (2005), *Best Practice Guidelines for Regional Development Strategies*, Cardiff: Cardiff University.

Albrechts, L. (2001), 'In Pursuit of New Approaches to Strategic Spatial Planning', A European Perspective, *International Planning Studies*, vol. 6, no. 3, pp. 293–310.

Faludi, A. (2004), 'Spatial Planning Traditions in Europe: Their Role in the ESDP Process', *International Planning Studies*, vol. 9, nos. 2/3, pp. 155–172.

Faludi, A. and Waterhout, B. (2002), *The Making of the European Spatial Development Perspective – No Masterplan*, London: Routledge.

Hammond, C. (2002), 'New Approaches to Regional Spatial Planning?', In: Rydin, Y. and Thornley, A. (eds) *Planning in the UK: Agendas for the new millennium*, Aldershot: Ashgate, pp. 131–155.

Harris, N., Hooper, A. and Bishop, K.D. (2002), 'Constructing the Practice of "Spatial Planning": A National Spatial Planning Framework for Wales', *Environment and Planning C: Government and Policy*, vol. 20, no. 4, pp. 555–572.

Healey, P. (1997), 'The Revival of Strategic Spatial Planning in Europe', In: Healey, P., Khakee, A., Motte, A. and Needham, B. (eds), *Making Strategic Spatial Plans: Innovation in Europe*, London: UCL Press, pp. 3–19.

Healey, P. (2004), 'The Treatment of Space and Place in the New Strategic Spatial Planning in Europe', *International Journal of Urban and Regional Research*, vol. 28, no. 1, pp. 45–67.

Healey, P., Khakee, A., Motte, A. and Needham, B. (eds) (1997), *Making Strategic Spatial Plans: Innovation in Europe*, London: UCL Press.

Healey, P., Khakee, A., Motte, A. and Needham, B. (1999), 'European Developments in Strategic Spatial Planning', *European Planning Studies*, vol. 7, no. 3, pp. 339–355.

Jørgenson, I. (1998), '"What's love got to do with it?" The European Spatial Development Perspective and Some Ideas for Researching it', in: Bengs, C. and Böhme, K. (eds), *The Progress of European Spatial Planning*, Stockholm: Nordregio, pp. 11–23.

Lloyd, G. and McCarthy, J. (2002), 'Asymmetrical Devolution, Institutional Capacity and Spatial Planning Innovation', in: Rydin, Y. and Thornley, A. (eds), *Planning in the UK: Agendas for the New Millennium*, Aldershot: Ashgate, pp. 103–117.

Pallagst, K. (2006), 'European Spatial Planning Reloaded: Considering EU Enlargement in Theory and Practice', *European Planning Studies*, vol. 14, no. 2, pp. 253–272.

Tewdwr-Jones, M. (2004), 'Spatial Planning: Principles, Practices and Cultures', *Journal of Planning and Environment Law*, May, pp. 560–569.

Vigar, G., Healey, P., Hull, A. and Davoudi, S. (2000), *Planning, Governance and Spatial Strategy: An Institutionalist Analysis*, London: Macmillan.

Chapter 2

Regional Development and Spatial Planning

Jeremy Alden

Introduction: The Current Interest in Regional Development and Spatial Planning

Introduction

This chapter examines the increasing interest in regional development and spatial planning which has taken place within the EU in recent years. It has been particularly informed by the completion of the INTERREG IIIC GRIDS project (i.e.: 'best practice guidelines for instruments of regional development and spatial planning in an enlarged EU') at the end of 2005.

The INTERREG IIIC Newsletter of June 2005 summarised the many challenges facing Europe and its regions in the years ahead. These include a doubling of socio-economic disparities following EU enlargement, an acceleration in economic restructuring as a result of globalisation, the effects of the technical revolution, the development of the knowledge-based economy and society, an ageing population, and a demographic downturn for some Member States whilst a growth in immigration for others.

It was within this context that in March 2000, at the meeting of heads of Government in Lisbon, a strategy was agreed to make Europe 'the most competitive and dynamic knowledge-based economy in the world'. At the Gothenburg European Council in 2001, the strategy was widened to encompass environmental issues to achieve a more sustainable pattern of development.

This chapter begins by examining the extent of economic and social disparities across the enlarged EU, at both national and regional level. Successful regional development requires tackling these regional disparities. The current interest in regional development and spatial planning across the EU has arisen by developing new paradigms of regional development and regional planning which can help improve both national and regional prosperity. These new paradigms are examined here in terms of their two main types i.e.: firstly, substantive regional development theory which addresses substantive issues like regional competitiveness and sustainable development, and secondly, procedural regional planning theory which addresses plan-making methodologies and best practice issues in preparing regional development strategies. Only a brief review can be made here of what amounts to a very large body of literature which is seeking to assist planners and policy makers at all spatial levels to increase regional economic performance and reduce regional disparities.

This review of substantive regional development paradigms and procedural regional planning paradigms is followed by an explanation of the terms 'regional development' and 'spatial planning'. What is spatial planning? What are its main features? How different is spatial planning from traditional land-use planning? Why has spatial planning generated so much interest in the field of regional development?

The chapter concludes by looking at some recent examples of regional development strategies and spatial plans within the Celtic and Baltic nations. This includes some comments on how far the new concepts and paradigms associated with regional development and spatial planning have informed such strategies and plans. Finally, some observations are made on possible future directions in this field of activity.

Reducing the Prosperity Gap within the Enlarged EU

The EU's Regional Policy, based on the Structural Funds programme (previously 2000–2006 and now 2007–2013), has risen to the top of the EU's policy agenda. According to data published by the Statistical Office of the European Communities (Eurostat) in 2005, disparities in Gross Domestic Product per capita (GDP per capita) between the new EU25 Member States have increased markedly, as shown in Figure 2.1. The disparities range from Latvia with a GDP per capita in 2002 at 38.9 per cent of the EU average to 212.6 per cent for Luxembourg (a special case as a city state), followed by 132.6 per cent for Ireland. Figure 2.1 illustrates that many of the richer EU15 nations improved their GDP per capita figure of the EU25 average with enlargement by some ten percentage points. The focus of the EU's Regional Policy has necessarily shifted to the new Member States, and particularly those in the former Soviet block countries such as the Baltic States.

In January 2005 Eurostat published new regional GDP per capita data for the 254 NUTS II level regions of the EU25. In 2002, GDP per capita, expressed in terms of purchasing power standards, in the EU25's 254 NUTS II level regions ranged from 32 per cent of the EU25 average in the region of Lubelskie in Poland, to 315 per cent of the average in Inner London in the UK i.e.: a disparity of 10:1 between the highest and lowest scoring regions of the EU. For purposes of Structural Fund support, both Latvia and Lithuania are classified as NUTS II level regions. The ten highest and ten lowest GDP per capita NUTS II level regions in the EU25 are shown in Figure 2.2. The Eurostat data showed that one in every seven of the NUTS II regions had a GDP per capita exceeding 125 per cent of the EU25 average. At the opposite end of the scale, a quarter of regions had GDP per capita of 75 per cent or less of the EU 25 average. This figure of 75 per cent was the eligibility criteria limit for Objective 1 funding in the 2000–2006 Structural Funds programming period. Spatial planning

Figure 2.1 Gross domestic product per capita: EU25 (and comparison with EU15)

	Purchasing Power Parities			EU25 = 100			EU15 = 100		
	2000	2001	2002	2000	2001	2002	2000	2001	2002
EU25	19,748	20,455	21,172	100.0	100.0	100.0	91.0	91.3	91.4
EU15	21,696	22,412	23,164	109.9	109.6	109.4	100.0	100.0	100.0
Austria	25,248	25,453	25,979	127.9	124.4	122.7	116.4	113.6	112.2
Belgium	23,079	23,994	24,711	116.9	117.3	116.7	106.4	107.1	106.7
Cyprus	16,937	18,164	17,553	85.8	88.8	82.9	78.1	81.0	75.8
Czech Republic	12,806	13,526	14,315	64.8	66.1	67.6	59.0	60.4	61.8
Denmark	25,042	25,841	25,929	126.8	126.3	122.5	115.4	115.3	111.9
Estonia	8,582	9,155	9,868	43.5	44.8	46.6	39.6	40.8	42.6
Finland	22,572	23,332	24,001	114.3	114.1	113.4	104.0	104.1	103.6
France	22,509	23,480	23,909	114.0	114.8	112.9	103.7	104.8	103.2
Germany	22,120	22,513	23,005	112.0	110.1	108.7	102.0	100.5	99.3
Greece	14,312	15,088	16,457	72.5	73.8	77.7	66.0	67.3	71.0
Hungary	10,561	11,546	12,398	53.5	56.4	58.6	48.7	51.5	53.5
Ireland	25,001	26,486	28,081	126.6	129.5	132.6	115.2	118.2	121.2
Italy	21,970	22,420	23,073	111.2	109.6	109.0	101.3	100.0	99.6
Latvia	7,005	7,656	8,246	35.5	37.4	38.9	32.3	34.2	35.6
Lithuania	7,606	8,338	8,975	38.5	40.8	42.4	35.1	37.2	38.7
Luxembourg	43,162	43,634	45,014	218.6	213.3	212.6	198.9	194.7	194.3
Malta	15,521	15,342	15,723	78.6	75.0	74.3	71.5	68.5	67.9
Netherlands	24,015	25,401	25,840	121.6	124.2	122.1	110.7	113.3	111.6
Poland	9,045	9,383	9,661	45.8	45.9	45.6	41.7	41.9	41.7
Portugal	15,267	15,782	16,243	77.3	77.2	76.7	70.4	70.4	70.1
Slovakia	9,461	10,006	10,854	47.9	48.9	51.3	43.6	44.6	46.9
Slovenia	14,466	15,290	15,937	73.3	74.8	75.3	66.7	68.2	68.8
Spain	18,107	18,887	20,020	91.7	92.3	94.6	83.5	84.3	86.4
Sweden	23,656	23,818	24,298	119.8	116.4	114.8	109.0	106.3	104.9
UK	22,522	23,544	24,938	114.0	115.1	117.8	103.8	105.1	107.7

Source: Eurostat 2005

and regional development have a key role to play in raising both national and regional levels of prosperity and reducing prosperity gaps between localities within regions. The prosperity gaps illustrated in Figure 2.2 are clearly a major challenge facing EU spatial policies and those of Member States.

Figure 2.2   Regional GDP per capital in the EU25 in 2002

In PPS, EU25 = 100					
The ten highest (in per cent)			**The ten lowest (in per cent)**		
1	Inner London (UK)	315	1	Lubelskie (PL)	32
2	Bruxelles-Capitale (BE)	234	2	Podkarpackie (PL)	33
3	Luxembourg	213	3	Warmińsko-Mazurskie (PL)	34
4	Hamburg (DE)	188	4	Podlaskie (PL)	35
5	Île de France (FR)	176	5	Świętokrzyskie (PL)	36
6	Wien (AT)	174	6	Észak Magyároszag (HU)	37
7	Berkshire, Buckinghamshire and Oxfordshire (UK)	162	7	Opolskie (PL)	37
			8	Eszag-Alföld (HU)	38
8	Provincia Automoma Bolzano (T)	160	9	Východné Solvensko (SK)	39
9	Stockholm (SE)	158	10	Latvia	39
10	Oberbayern (DE)	158			

Source: Eurostat News Release: 25 January 2005

The Third Report on Economic and Social Cohesion published by the European Commission in February 2004 set out the Commission's vision for the future of Europe's policy to reduce disparities and to promote greater economic, social and territorial cohesion. The Third Cohesion Report refers to the contribution made by the INTERREG IIC programmes of 1994–1999 period, with cooperation on regional and spatial planning, and to the 2000–2006 INTERREG IIIC programme which favoured cooperation and exchange of experiences between regions. Proposals for a reformed cohesion policy for the enlarged EU in the 2007–2013 programme period include the focus on reducing regional disparities being reinforced. There will be a new architecture for EU cohesion policy after 2006. The three Community priorities which will provide the future generation of programmes will be grouped under the headings (a) convergence (b) regional competitiveness and (c) territorial cooperation. The Third Cohesion Report stresses the need to concentrate resources on the poorest Member States and regions, with an emphasis on the new Member States.

Paradigms of Regional Development

Economic and social disparities have substantially increased in the enlarged EU made up of 254 NUTS II level regions. The INTERREG IIIC programme recognises the strong link between the EU's competitiveness and the regions' capacities to design and implement clear growth strategies. The EU's regional policy, focussed on the Structural Funds, is facing major change for the next programming period 2007–2013, with a sharper focus on the Lisbon and Gothenburg agendas with their emphasis on the three requirements of competitiveness, employment and sustainable development.

The regional development and spatial planning agenda has been closely linked to regional planning theory which has sought to explain the causes and consequences of regional economic disparities and regional competitiveness. Regional development strategies must address why regional disparities occur and why they persist (Taylor 1991). There has been a growing interest and academic literature in recent years in developing new paradigms of regional development to inform new ways of tackling longstanding regional problems. In 2003 the Regional Studies journal published a special issue on the current state of regional development theory with its new focus on a knowledge-driven, service-oriented, information or post-industrial globalized economy, which has ushered in a new age of regions. The editorial comments also included reference to the increasing multi-disciplinary research being undertaken, with economists taking geography, location and space as seriously as geographers in addressing regional problems.

The first part of the 2003 special issue contained articles on the economic performance of regions, including the role of innovation, knowledge creation and labour flexibility. Scott and Storper (2003) in their article concluded by saying that conventional economic theories of development and trade have largely ignored questions of economic geography. This was also a continuing theme of the second part of the special issue on the contribution of the 'new economic geography' to the conceptualization of regional economies. For example, McCann and Sheppard (2003) outlined possible future directions along which location theory might develop. The article which perhaps attracted most attention was in the final part of the special issue, written by Markusen (2003), which made some provocative and critical comments regarding the recent debates and research on conceptualising regional studies. The title of her article 'Fuzzy Concepts, Scant Evidence, Policy Distance: The Case for Rigour and Policy Relevance in Critical Regional Studies' has resonated with many researchers in the field of regional development theory working on a wide range of topic areas, ranging from regional competitiveness, social capital, knowledge economies, flexible specialisation etc. Markusen emphasised the need to address the current state of much regional analysis which is often characterised by fuzzy concepts that lack clarity and are difficult to test or operationalise. These comments have sharpened the minds of academics and policy makers alike in addressing regional development problems.

The new paradigms of regional development are well illustrated by the European Commission's 5th Framework Programme which has funded a research project on city regions as intelligent territories i.e.: knowledge has become the most essential resource for urban and regional competitiveness. The findings of this project (whose acronym is CRITICAL) were presented at a conference in Berlin in December 2005

(Kunzmann 2005). This project has developed some of the concepts examined by Morgan (1997) in his influential article on the 'learning region'. This examined some of the theoretical and policy implications of combining the two hitherto distinct fields of innovation studies and economic geography and referred to as the network or associational paradigm.

New regional development paradigms have been progressed to overcome some of the shortcomings of the more classical paradigms, which continue to exert considerable influence on regional development strategies and spatial planning. The concept that nations and regions contain a hierarchy of places and spaces has been developed by many writers. Alden and Morgan (1974) have reviewed the contributions of Christaller (1933) in developing central place theory, Perroux (1955) in presenting his growth pole theory, and the contributions of Myrdal (1957) and Hirschman (1958) who developed a core-periphery model of spatial economic development. Both Myrdal and Hirschmann distinguished two types of transmission effects from the core to the periphery, the one favourable and the other unfavourable. The favourable effects consist of the flow of investment activities from the core into the periphery. These favourable flows are termed spread effects by Myrdal and trickling down effects by Hirschman, and they give rise to new core regions in the periphery. The unfavourable effects consist of the flow of people and capital out of the periphery who seek more secure returns in the core. Myrdal termed these effects backwash and Hirschman termed them polarization. These have found new currency in recent years within the context of balanced polycentric regional development and regional spatial strategies.

These earlier regional development paradigms have since become the subject of intensive research. Cooke (2002) has traced the evolutionary approach which has taken place to learning clusters and regional economic development. This has included both the classical and equilibrium approach which examined concepts of centrality and agglomeration, and the disequilibrium approach adopted by the neo-classical writers like Schumpeter, Perroux, Myrdal and Hirschman. From these roots has emerged the current interest in knowledge economies and learning regions, and the concept of intelligent cities and regions linked to economic competitiveness. Innovation, location and competitiveness are central themes in the inter-linkage between knowledge, space and economic development (Bryson, Daniels, Henry and Pollard 2000). There has also been considerable interest in innovation clusters and interregional competition (Brocker, Dohse and Soltwedel 2003). Indeed, at the end of the 1990s, innovation was seen by many observers as the most important factor for regional competitive advantage. Many stakeholders in regional development, and especially the Regional Development Agencies (across Europe) prepared Regional Technology Plans and a substantial literature emerged (see for example Braczyk, Cooke and Heidenreich 1999). Even with the emergence of new paradigms of regional development in recent years, innovation still occupies an important place on the regional development strategy and spatial planning agenda and continues to inform the new paradigms. As Kitson, Martin and Tyler (2004) have illustrated, there is now widespread agreement that we are seeing the resurgence of regions as a key locus and spatial unit in the organisation and governance of economic growth. Regional competitiveness has become a key concept for both academics and policy-makers although there is still no generally accepted definition or theory of regional competitiveness. It remains, however, a key concept for policy-makers at all spatial levels i.e. regional competitiveness contributes to both national and local economic growth and prosperity as well as of the regions themselves. Kitson, Martin and Tyler refer to the regional competitiveness debate as 'the competitiveness fad' i.e. 'economists and experts everywhere have elevated competitiveness to the status of a natural law of the modern capitalist economy' (Kitson, Martin and Tyler, 2004, p. 991). However, the authors concluded that the notion of regional competitiveness requires informed debate. This seems to have been the case in the field of regional development. The new EU Regional Policy and Structural Funds programme for the 2007–2013 period has embedded regional competitiveness as one of its basic goals, based on the Lisbon and Gothenburg strategies. It was also a pre-requisite for the Irish Government in the transformation of their economy, which has made them the success story of the EU in recent times (illustrated later in this chapter and more fully in Chapter 7). Reference is also made later in this chapter to the important contribution of the European Spatial Development Perspective (ESDP 1999) which promoted the potentially conflicting concepts of both competition and cohesion between regions and within regional policy.

Other new paradigms of regional development have emerged in recent years of which 'social capital' has attracted considerable attention (see special issue of *Regional Studies* journal, Vol 39(8) 2005, which followed a special issue on 'regional competitiveness' in Vol 38(9) 2004). There is a growing literature on the links between social capital, economic, growth and regional development. Differences in social capital between regions have been examined in fifty-four Western European regions by Beugelsdijk and Schaik (2005), although the authors have concluded it is too premature to provide clear policy implications. As social capital can provide public goods, foster social communications and trust, and promote cooperative behaviour, institutions and culture have become important variables in such new paradigms of regional development. These new paradigms have also attracted an inter-disciplinary approach by social scientists. It is also interesting that one of the results of these paradigmatic developments in regional development has been the emergence of social and cultural explanations for regional economic performance as well as more traditional economic ones.

This brief review of some old and new paradigms of regional development has illustrated the new and widespread interest in this subject which has attracted the attention of academics and policy-makers alike. Paradigms of regional development resonate in many ways with the practitioners and policy-makers who prepare regional development strategies and spatial plans. The paradigms contain concepts which have helped to shape both national and regional spatial plans across the EU. Nowhere is this more the case than with the European Spatial Development Perspective (ESDP 1999) which has dominated the regional development and spatial planning agenda in recent years in many EU Member States. However, it should be recognised that the take-up of the ESDP and its principles of balanced polycentric regional development has been variable across different countries. For example, the fragile foundations of European Spatial Planning in Portugal have been explored by Pires (2005). He has concluded that for Portugal, a country with a population of 10 million and one of the poorer member States in the EU15, the European Spatial Development Perspective (ESDP) is far from occupying a prominent position on the current planning agenda. His article suggests that spatial planning may be called upon to play a more significant role in Portugal in the future. Whilst there is clearly some diversity across the EU in pursuing regional development objectives through the preparation of regional spatial strategies, the pace of change in favour of this new method of approach over the past five years has been immense.

Added impetus to the usefulness of regional development paradigms has been provided by the newly emerging future of interregional co-operation and Structural Fund support contained in the 2007–2013 programming period. The strong focus of the Lisbon and Gothenburg agendas has ensured a continued interest in the concept of regional competitiveness and job creation in regional development.

Making Spatial Plans: The Europeanisation of Planning as a New Planning Paradigm

Interest in spatial planning within the European Union (EU) has never been greater, and particularly interest in the activity of planning at the regional level. It is fair to say that regional planning, regional development, and spatial planning have been elusive concepts for many people. As Albrechts, Alden and Pires (2001) concluded in their book on the changing institutional landscape of planning, there has been a renaissance of interest in planning at all spatial levels, and this has been reflected in its institutional framework, particularly at a regional level. Planning as an activity, both statutory and non-statutory, has enhanced its position in recent years within many member countries of the EU. 'Regional planning is an idea whose time has come' is an accurate message for the activity of planning in the first decade of the twenty-first century. The regional dimension has been strengthened within both nations and the EU as a whole (now EU25).

Nowhere has this been more the case than in the UK, where a new planning framework has emerged over the past ten years (Alden 2001). One of the main features of planning in Britain has been its strong base in local government, and its centralised nature with central government preparing national guidance, and via regional planning guidance to be taken into account by local planning authorities preparing development plans and in decisions on individual planning applications. For a hundred years, from the first Town Planning Act of 1909 to the end of the 1990s, regional planning was regarded as a rather ambiguous concept and an activity undertaken on a non-statutory and voluntary basis.

The New Labour Government of 1997 in the UK has been associated with several major changes in the spatial planning system, and particularly (a) constitutional reform in devolving decision making and governance to the regional level, and (b) strengthening the European context for planning in the UK. These developments included the creation of 'regional' governments with the Scottish Parliament, Welsh Assembly, and the Northern Ireland Assembly. The Regional Development Agencies in 1999, and the new Greater London Authority and Regional Chambers in the English regions in 2000 also strengthened the regional level of governance (although they are not regional governments). This new institutional framework at regional level has produced new, exciting spatial plans to provide roadmaps for the future development of their regions/nations. The regional spatial strategies for Northern Ireland (2001), Ireland (2002), Scotland (2004), London (2004) and Wales (2004) provide good examples of new approaches to regional development through the activity of spatial planning. Moreover, the 2004 Planning and Compulsory Purchase Act has created statutory regional development planning with a requirement that the English regions must prepare Regional Spatial Strategies, having legal status for the first time in the UK. The 2004 Planning and Compulsory Purchase Act also places a duty on the Welsh Assembly Government to prepare a Wales Spatial Plan. The UK statutory planning system, which has stood out within the European planning paradigm for both its centralised nature, and for its discretionary rather than regulatory approach, is a very different activity today from that which emerged in the early years of the twentieth century and lasted until very recently. As Alden (1999, 2003) has observed, this raises the question as to what are the alternative scenarios for the planning system in the UK? How far will the focus on 'regions' and 'Europe' be taken?

As Alden (2001b) has noted, the current system of regional planning in the UK is a considerable advance from hitherto, and the new system created by the 2004 legislation is producing some exciting examples of regional planning which focus upon more strategic thinking on the achievement of sustainable economic development and greater spatial equality in prosperity within regions, as well as between them. The membership of the 10 new countries in an enlarged EU25 in 2004 has enhanced the regional focus of both governance and planning within Member countries and the EU as a whole. Both low national and regional levels of GDP per capita and wide regional disparities in prosperity within the new Member countries, and particularly the Baltic States, have given a new impetus and urgency to create new approaches to regional development and spatial planning. The new EU25 faced the difficult task in 2005 in agreeing a new budget for the 2007–2013 programming period but this was completed.

Whilst there has been an explosion in activity in preparing both national and regional spatial strategies for promoting regional development in recent years within EU countries, it should not be forgotten that 'regionalism' is not a new idea. It rather continues interest first generated in the early years of the twentieth century when regionalism was linked to regions and local government. In the UK, publications like those of P. Geddes (1913) 'Cities in Evolution' and C.B. Fawcett (1919) 'Provinces of England', emphasised the need for a regional approach to local government to meet the needs of a city-region style of life, and the need to devolve power from central government to the regions. In the 1990s regionalism became linked to regions and Europe, and many EU countries made the transition from traditional land use planning to strategic spatial planning (see Alden 2003).

Indeed, the 1990s saw an increasing Europeanization of planning amongst the EU15 countries, which then attracted wider interest amongst the EU25 with enlargement in 2004. The former East European states have begun to focus on new style spatial planning and away from old style master-planning and traditional land use planning. This transition from traditional land use planning and/or master planning to spatial planning at an EU level began with the European Commission's policy document on regional development and spatial planning, i.e.: Europe 2000+ published in 1994. Alden (1996) has documented how this publication emphasised the emergence of a European dimension in planning policies of Member States, an increasingly important regional dimension of European policies, and an enhanced role for regional development strategies in achieving the objectives of nations, regions and localities in an enlarged EU. The European Commission's regional development strategy contained in Europe 2000+ paid particular attention to three main objectives i.e.: (a) increased economic competitiveness of areas in an increasingly competitive global economy; (b) a move towards more sustainable economic development; and (c) the reduction of regional disparities and need for greater economic and social cohesion.

The revival of strategic spatial planning, particularly in the 1990s, in Europe has been described as an 'innovation in Europe' by Healey (1997) in her review of this activity. Her article on the treatment of space and place in the new strategic spatial planning in Europe (2004) emphasised again the resurgence of spatial planning in a European context, supported by Europe's planning policy communities and actively promoted by EU initiatives.

In addition to looking at the significance of the ESDP (1999) as an influential advocacy document, Healey examined the experience of three examples, i.e.: (a) Netherlands Fifth National Policy Document on Spatial Planning 2000–2020; (b) Shaping our Future: The Regional Development Strategy of Northern Ireland 2025; and (c) Restructuring Greater Milan: Framework Document for Municipal Planning Policies 2000. These cases were chosen to illustrate the way in which strategic spatial planning had created new ways of thinking and new ways of doing things, compared to more traditional planning approaches. They are examples which 'illustrate deliberate attempts to transform the spatial vocabulary used in planning practices and to mould a new kind of planning politics' (Healey, 2004, p. 51).

However, it has been the European Spatial Development Perspective (ESDP 1999) which has dominated the regional development and spatial planning agenda and debate in recent years. Shaw and Sykes (2004) have illustrated the extent to which the ESDP and its concept of balanced and sustainable polycentric development has become not only one of the hallmarks of the emerging field of European spatial planning, but also the most frequently debated topic amongst planning academics and those engaged in spatial development making at different scales in Europe.

In terms of regional development and spatial planning the ESDP made a significant contribution in terms of a new planning methodology paradigm. It addressed issues of both cohesion and competitiveness. It re-defined the core-periphery model paradigm and addressed the excessive economic and demographic concentration in the congested core areas of the EU. This particularly resonated with the Celtic and Baltic countries, and other smaller Member States, where a dominant capital city flourished alongside a poor periphery, and particularly smaller towns and rural areas. As both Shaw and Sykes (2004) and the INTERREG IIIC GRIDS Project final Guidelines Report (Adams and Harris 2005) on best practice in preparing regional development strategies have noted, Wales, Scotland and Ireland are examples of regions/countries which have adopted the ideas of the ESDP, including the polycentricity principles, to a considerable extent in shaping their new regional/national spatial strategies. These examples are discussed further below. It is interesting that Shaw and Sykes (2004) conclude their comprehensive review of the concept of polycentricity in European spatial planning by saying that it is open to multiple interpretations, i.e.: it can mean different things to different people. To this extent the ESDP and its concept of polycentricity as a new plan making paradigm, shares the features of many of the substantive regional development paradigms reviewed earlier in this chapter.

A related appealing concept related to the ESDP and regional development strategies is that of the Polycentric Urban Region (PUR). In his review of the recent debate on the PUR, Parr (2004) concluded that while the apparent success of particular PURs has attracted the attention of the planner and policy maker, the validity of the concept has yet to be confirmed. Notwithstanding this caution, many observers see the promotion of PURs as a means of solving a number of regional development problems, and a form of action which fits comfortably within the wider concept of balanced and sustainable polycentric development.

The prospects for a more dynamic, innovative and proactive role for regional development planning in the EU, through the activity of spatial planning, have never looked more promising. This raises the question, what is the difference between the new style spatial planning and the old style, traditional land use planning, in the preparation of regional development strategies?

What is Spatial Planning? Key Features

Tewdwr-Jones (2001) has documented very well how the term 'spatial planning' has come into widespread use only since the early-mid 1990s. Reference has already been made to the contributions of the European Commission's documents Europe 2000+ (1994) and the ESDP (Potsdam 1999). The traditional approach to town and country planning often comprised a planning system that was intended to facilitate development, regulate land-use, and distinguish between urban and rural dimensions. However, the pace of change during the past ten years has produced a planning system far more complex and with the new label of spatial planning.

It is generally recognised that spatial planning is a much wider concept and activity than the more narrowly focused activity of land-use planning which was, for example, the hallmark of Britain's traditional planning system. The term spatial planning is a direct translation of German and Dutch planning terminology ('raumordnung', 'ruimtelijke planning') and a close proximation to the French concept 'aménagement du territoire' (Williams 1996). The main characteristic of spatial planning is that the activity of land-use/physical planning is closely linked to economic, social and environmental development policies. The nature, definition, purpose and remit of planning has undergone considerable change within all Member States of the EU25. The number of stakeholders involved in the planning process has increased markedly. Whilst spatial planning can operate at all spatial scales i.e.: global, national, regional, sub-regional and local, it is the regional level which has perhaps attracted most attention.

Why is this? The new focus on regions and the Europeanisation of planning has been a response to the challenges and opportunities provided by the EU's regional policy, i.e.: Structural Funds to assist the poorer regions and reduce regional income disparities within the EU. The scale of regional development problems and issues within the EU25 has been matched by the size of Structural Funds aid. Of the 2003 EU budget of €102 billion, €34 billion went for regional aid, second only to the Common Agricultural Policy funding of €47.4 billion. The €200 billion structural fund monies for the 2000–2006 period have been a powerful instrument for regional development, especially for the priority Objective 1 regions. There has been intense debate and considerable tensions within the EU over the Structural Funds allocation for the 2007–2013 period, which will see another €200 billion being spent specifically to support regional development for the poorer Member States and regions. The concept of balanced and sustainable polycentric development, which emerged from the ESDP, has become one of the hallmarks of the emerging field of European spatial planning (Shaw and Sykes 2004).

During the course of the INTERREG IIIC GRIDS project it became very clear that the phrase 'spatial planning' meant different things to different Member States and actors/stakeholders within them. The diversity of concepts and definitions surrounding terms such as regional development, regional planning and spatial planning, have the potential to cause confusion as they can be interpreted in a variety of ways.

Figure 2.3 provides some insight to the substance of 'spatial planning' within the context of the British planning system. After nearly one hundred years of traditional land-use planning in the UK since the first Housing and Town Planning Act 1909, and inspired by documents like the ESDP (1999), the activity of planning has been widened well beyond land-use planning/physical planning. The more passive, technical exercise of land-use planning with its focus on development plans and development control/regulation has widened to a far more dynamic and proactive approach to guiding spatial change. The new activity of planning, formerly known as town and country planning or land-use planning has been given a new label of spatial planning. One of its major beneficial outcomes has been that it has opened up new agendas for all those involved in the activity of planning. Whilst the term is applicable to all spatial scales, it is at the regional level that spatial planning has made its greatest impact. In the UK the momentum behind the switch to spatial planning has come from many sources e.g.: devolution and decentralisation, the new 2004 Planning and Compulsory Purchase Act requiring the preparation of regional spatial strategies, EU initiatives on regional development and spatial planning and all regional stakeholders adopting more strategic approaches to development issues.

Figure 2.3   The transition to spatial planning in the UK

- 100 years of traditional land-use planning in UK?;
- spatial planning driven by EU initiatives etc.;
- spatial planning wider than land-use planning;
- in UK 'Spatial Planning' replaces 'Town and Country Planning';
- 2004 Planning Act creates statutory regional planning;
- land-use planning focuses on development plans and control;
- spatial planning is a dynamic and pro-active approach to guiding spatial change;
- spatial planning has opened up new agendas;
- regional spatial strategies are frameworks to guide future development;
- professional body RTPI responds to spatial planning.

Source: Compiled by the author

The impact of the new activity of spatial planning has been particularly great in the UK, and nowhere more so than amongst the planning profession itself. The Royal Town Planning Institute is the professional body for planners in the UK and has a membership of nearly 20,000. In response to the widening role of planning, the RTPI has published a 'New Vision for Planning', which is built around four core ideas i.e.: (a) spatial (b) sustainable (c) integrative and (d) inclusive (recognising the wide range of people now involved in planning). Moreover, the RTPI has revised its Charter and Byelaws to state its primary objective as being 'the objects of the Chartered Institute shall be to advance the science and art of planning (including town and country and spatial planning) for the benefit of the public' (i.e.: the term spatial planning was inserted in 2003). The RTPI's 'New Vision for Planning' has been accompanied by a comprehensive review of its governmental structure and all aspects of planning education.

The key features of spatial planning are shown in Figure 2.4, and they can be found in many regional spatial strategies produced across the EU in recent years which have sought to adopt good practice in their plan preparation. A regional spatial strategy which adopts good practice would be expected to exhibit the attributes/features displayed in Figure 2.4. Of particular importance are the concepts of strategic approach, long term perspective, joined-up government, integration of public and private sectors, land-use planning linked to all mainstream policies and programmes, embrace the concept of balanced and sustainable polycentric development, emphasise the importance of space and place and spatial issues within the region, identify the spatial impact of national policies, and address 'wicked' issues. This means confront difficult issues rather than avoid them which was often a feature of old style land-use plans, Structure Plans and also the Regional Development Strategies produced in the English regions during the 1990s. By 2000 however, the newer-style regional spatial strategies had sought to adopt the principles of good/best practice expected of spatial planning/regional development.

Figure 2.4   Key features of spatial planning

- strategic framework for resource allocation and investment;
- long term perspective, usually 20 years;
- joins-up and integrates public and private sector policies;
- links land-use planning with economic development policy and other policies;
- explains spatial dimension of national policies;
- achieves more balanced distribution of economic development;
- embraces the concept of balanced and sustainable polycentric development;
- identifies and addresses 'wicked' issues;
- strengthens regional/local governance capacity;
- puts focus on space, place and issues of spatial distribution;
- the region is a focus for spatial planning;
- spatial planning provides roadmap for future regional development;
- evidence-based rigorous monitoring and review.

Source: Compiled by the author

Some Recent Examples of Regional Development Strategies/Spatial Planning

The Celtic countries provide a number of recent examples of regional spatial strategies being produced to provide a roadmap for regional development over a twenty year time period. Regional spatial strategies were published for Northern Ireland in 2001, Ireland in 2003, Scotland in 2004 and Wales in 2004. The London Plan 2004 and the North East Regional Spatial Strategy 2004 were also good examples of regional spatial strategies in so far as they sought to adopt the features of 'good practice' in spatial planning illustrated in Figure 2.4. All these documents were also produced ahead of the implementation of the 2004 Planning and Compulsory Purchase Act in the UK which required the UK regions to prepare regional spatial strategies, which had statutory status for the first time in the UK. Ireland (3.9 million population) Scotland (5.0 million population) and Wales (2.9 million population) are small nations within the EU, and share many common features with the Baltic countries, such as Lithuania (3.5 million population) and Latvia (2.3 million population). All these nations/regions have sought to adopt good practice principles of spatial planning in preparing regional development strategies, which have addressed similar challenges. These common challenges include a priority to increase GDP per capita and personal incomes, focus on job creation and reducing unemployment, address both urban and rural issues, protect and enhance high quality natural and built environments, safeguard language and culture, utilise the potential of foreign direct investment and tourism, and also of the EU Structural Funds. The EU INTERREG IIIC programme in general, and the GRIDS project in particular, illustrate very well the benefits to all nations and regions of looking at the experience of other nations and regions.

Whilst Ireland was not the first EU nation to produce a new style National Spatial Strategy with its 2002 document, it has attracted the greatest interest, largely because of its recent economic success. Many smaller (and larger) nations and regions in the EU25 have looked closely at Ireland's 'economic miracle' and reasons for its success, including the Baltic countries. In 1986 Ireland had a GDP per capita 64 per cent of the EU15 average: by 1998 i.e.: just twelve years later it had reached parity with the EU15 average i.e.: 100 per cent. Eurostat GDP per capita data for 2002, published in January 2005, showed that by 2002 Ireland had then reached 120 per cent of the EU15 average and over 132 per cent of the EU25 average. Whilst the Baltic nations have been matching Ireland's 7 per cent economic growth rate in recent years, justifying the label of 'tiger economies' for Lithuania and Latvia as well as Ireland, raising their still low levels of GDP per capita (Lithuania 42 per cent and Latvia 39 per cent of EU25 average respectively) remains a top priority. For nations/regions of the EU25 seeking to close the prosperity gap between themselves and the more prosperous regions, Ireland's success story is of considerable interest.

The reasons for Ireland's success in the 1990s and into the twenty-first century include a number of factors including adopting a strategic approach with single-mindedness, focusing on economic competitiveness, providing a stable macro-economic environment, low company taxation, attracting foreign direct investment, attracting high value added economic activity plus indigenous growth, infrastructure investment, promoting an ICT information technology, and good management of EU Structural Funds (Ireland secured £8.7 billion for Objective 1 areas 1994–1999). Regional competitiveness is certainly a regional development concept and paradigm which resonates with Irish policy matters and the academic literature. Ireland truly moved from 'potato chips' with the 1840s potato famine to a 'computer chips' economy by the end of the 1990s. The economic and social impact of Ireland's rapid economic growth has been considerable and no more so than in strengthening Ireland's demographic profile. Figures from the 2002 Census of Population illustrate that Ireland's population increased from 3.5 million in 1991 to 3.9 million by 2002, the highest figure in more than a hundred years. A 4.0 million population figure is expected for 2005 and 5.0 million predicted by 2030. This is in marked contrast to the population losses experienced by Lithuania and Latvia in recent years. From being a large exporter of people, Ireland is now a net importer. It is now the former Soviet block states of Eastern Europe which are losing population to Western Europe, and particularly Ireland and the UK which have built strong economies in recent years. Latvia has estimated a loss of some 50,000–100,000 a year in 2004 and 2005, with a quarter of those working in Ireland. Latvia fears that the current exodus is destroying the country's social fabric. A similar picture has been reported in the British Press regarding 'the new Baltic State of East Anglia', i.e.: a largely rural area in Eastern England which now has 80,000 migrant workers, with two thirds of them from Lithuania, Latvia and Estonia (Sunday Times, 18 December 2005). Lithuania estimates that more than 100,000 or 3 per cent of its population, has gone abroad to work since it joined the EU. Demography remains an important challenge facing many EU nations and regions: for example, both Scotland and Wales in the UK are concerned to maintain their population levels at a time of increasing population in London and South East England.

Ireland's economic success brought particular growth for the Greater Dublin area, which by 2000 contained 40 per cent of the nation's population. Many other Celtic and Baltic countries are small nations with dominant capital cities (e.g.: Riga contains 40 per cent of Latvia's population). Ireland published its National Spatial Strategy in 2002, embracing the principles of the ESDP (1999), determined to achieve more balanced and sustainable polycentric development for its seven regions. The National Spatial Strategy contained strong endorsements from Ireland's Prime Minister and its Minister for the Environment and Local Government, whose Department prepared the spatial strategy. Both their statements in the document illustrate their commitment to adopting good practice principles of spatial planning to achieve more balanced, sustainable polycentric development throughout national space. Ireland's National Spatial Strategy was national, spatial and strategic in approach; it provided regional strategies for the development of each of its seven regions; and it put into practice the key concepts of the ESDP and spatial planning of potential, critical mass, gateways, hubs, corridors, complementary roles and linkages, as being important instruments of successful regional development. The purpose of the National Spatial Strategy was clearly set out in Section 1 of the NSS document, and its main points are illustrated in Figure 2.5.

The issue of regional development is clearly very topical in Ireland at the present time. The challenges to Irish policymakers at local, regional and national levels to address the increasing disparities in living standards that have emerged between the Irish regions have been discussed by O'Leary (2003). In his review of regional development and spatial policy he has identified a new agenda for regional development which has become closely associated with the activity of spatial planning.

Figure 2.5   Main points of Ireland's national spatial strategy 2002–2020

- The strategy is a 20 year planning framework designed to deliver more balanced economic, social and physical development between regions;

- Ireland's economic success in recent years has been accompanied by spatial patterns of development which have seen employment opportunities becoming more concentrated in some areas, while economic weaknesses remain in others;

- A commitment to prepare a spatial strategy to plan at national level for the country's future spatial development was included in the National Development Plan 2000–2006;

- Balanced regional development requires that the full potential of each region to contribute to the overall performance of the State be developed;

- The strategy sets out how all areas of the country will have the opportunity to develop to their potential;

- The strategy will provide strategic planning guidance for a range of Government policies and regional and local plans;

- In conjunction with the Regional Development Strategy for Northern Ireland's 'Shaping Our Future', the NSS addresses spatial issues for the island of Ireland as a whole;

- The NSS is national, spatial and strategic in approach;

- The rate at which the NSS can be implemented will be subject to overall macro-economic and budgetary considerations.

Source: Compiled by the author from Ireland's National Spatial Strategy: 'People, Places and Potential' (2002)

Within the UK the Welsh Assembly Government (WAG) has been particularly proactive in its preparation, launch and follow-up to its Wales Spatial Plan. The Welsh Assembly Government produced a final draft of its Wales Spatial Plan, 'People, Places, Futures' in 2004 and it was adopted by the WAG on 17 November 2004. At its launch, the Minister responsible for the Wales Spatial Plan emphasised that the WSP was not a land use plan nor a Structure Plan, but rather a strategic framework to guide future development throughout Wales. The Minister responsible for Spatial

Planning in Wales therefore recognised the inter-connectivity between the terms regional development/regional planning/spatial planning. Just as the EU's ESDP (1999) proved to be one of its best selling documents with over 70,000 distributed/ sold in eleven languages, the Wales Spatial Plan also attracted much interest in Wales and has become one of its most widely distributed and discussed documents. Like the Irish National Spatial Strategy, the Wales Spatial Plan (WSP) contained a strong commitment by the First Minister that the WSP was a key part of the WAG's strategic agenda. It sets out a 20 year horizon for setting an agenda to produce a more prosperous and inclusive Wales. The Foreword to the WSP which contains the First Minister's statement, also contains the photographs of the WAG's eight Cabinet Members to illustrate the strong support within the WAG for the WSP. The process undertaken by the WAG in preparing the WSP, including wide consultation with all stakeholders, and follow-up area workshops to progress implementation of the WSP, has been widely recognised in Wales as a major strength of this new exercise in spatial planning.

The Minister responsible for producing and progressing the Wales Spatial Plan has emphasised that the WSP is not just a document for planners, but rather a document for all stakeholders. The Minister has also emphasised that the WSP goes well beyond the remit of previous Structure Plans or Land-Use Plans by providing a strategic framework to guide future development across the whole of Wales. It is expected that implementation and monitoring of the Wales Spatial Plan will take place between 2005–2008, including the publication of annual performance indicators.

It is also worth noting that the Wales Spatial Plan addressed the question 'what is spatial planning?' The WSP defined Spatial Planning as follows:

> Spatial planning is the consideration of what can and should happen where. It investigates the interaction of different policies and practices across regional space, and sets the role of places in a wider context. It goes well beyond 'traditional' land-use planning and sets out a strategic framework to guide future development and policy interventions, whether or not these relate to formal land use planning control.
>
> (Welsh Assembly Government, 2005, Wales Spatial Plan, page 5)

The role of the Wales Spatial Plan was explicitly stated in the document as being:

a. to ensure the WAG and its partners and agents develop policy in ways which take account of the different challenges and opportunities in the different parts of Wales;

b. to provide a basis and momentum for working together on a shared agenda locally, so that different parts of Wales can establish their own distinctive approaches to meet the objectives set out in the WSP and other strategic policy documents of the WAG;

c. provide a clear framework for future collaborative action involving the WAG and its agencies, local authorities, the private and voluntary sectors to achieve the priorities it sets out nationally and regionally;

d. influence the location of expenditure by the WAG and its agencies;
e. influence the mix and balance of public sector delivery agencies' programmes in different areas;
f. set the context for local and community planning;
g. provide a clear evidence base for the public, private and voluntary sectors to develop policy and action.

Finally, in this review of the Wales Spatial Plan as an instrument of regional development, mention must be made of the 'gateway test'. The Minister responsible for the WSP has ensured that all WAG policies and programmes have to pass the 'WSP gateway test' i.e.: what are the spatial implications, i.e.: the 'where' dimension of WAG policies and expenditure? Devolution and creation of the WAG, and the spatial planning exercise related to the WSP, have sharpened Government thinking and policy in Wales and produced a more effective spatial planning approach for promoting regional development. The WAG 'gateway test' in relation to all WAG strategic policies and programmes further illustrates the extent of the Europeanisation of planning in Member States.

The National Planning Framework for Scotland ('Quality and Connectivity') was published by the Scottish Executive in 2004. The framework is intended to guide the spatial development of Scotland to 2025, and exhibits the essential elements of a Spatial Planning approach to regional development. However, the framework document does not illustrate who is championing the spatial strategy or the strength of commitment within the Scottish Executive in the same way as illustrated in the Irish and Welsh Spatial Plans e.g.: no statements or endorsements by Ministers in the document. However, a very positive response to the National Planning Framework has prompted Ministers to accord it a key strategic policy role in Scotland's recent White Paper 'Modernising the Planning System' (2005). The National Planning Framework for Scotland is a robust document and sets out a vision for Scotland in which other plans and programmes can share and to which they can contribute. The document is not intended to be an economic development strategy but complements the Executive's 'Framework for Economic Development in Scotland', in a similar way to the Welsh Assembly Government's Wales Spatial Plan complements the WAG's National Economic Development Strategy 'A Winning Wales'. The National Planning Framework for Scotland is not intended to be a prescriptive blueprint, but will be a material consideration in framing planning policy and making decisions on planning applications and appeals. The Executive intends to review the National Planning Framework in 2008, and emphasises that strategic spatial planning must be evidence-based to ensure that resources are targeted where they can achieve most. Rigorous monitoring and review should be a key feature of the spatial planning process for regional development.

The London Plan (2004) deserves some mention here as it won an award by the Planning Officers' Society in the UK for best practice in spatial strategies. Published in February 2004, the London Plan is the first statutory strategic plan for London to be adopted in the past twenty years. The previous attempt to produce a city-wide strategy for the capital i.e.: Greater London Development Plan 1944, took a decade to produce and was largely out of date by the time it was published (as was the fate of many subsequent Structure Plans in the UK). By contrast, The London Plan was produced in only three years, and had the full support of the Mayor Ken Livingston's office behind it. It clearly states that it is the first of a new type of strategy, moving beyond land-use and transport issues to co-ordinate the spatial dimensions of all strategic policy. The plan, like other recent regional spatial strategies, is based on partnership and has wide support across central and local government as well as the private and voluntary sectors. This spatial strategy for Greater London has taken on greater significance given the awarding of the 2012 Olympic Games to London.

The Preamble to The London Plan report illustrates the robust spatial planning approach adopted throughout its process of preparation. The Greater London Authority (GLA) was established in 2000 and covers the 32 London Boroughs and the Corporation of London. In 2003 London's population was 7.3 million, well below its peak of 8.6 million in 1939 (caused largely by policies of decentralization). The London Plan has a key role to play in helping London achieve its estimated population of 8.1 million by 2016.

The Mayor is responsible for strategic planning in London and has a wide range of duties and powers. His duties include producing a Spatial Development Strategy for London, called 'The London Plan'. The Greater London Authority (GLA) Act 1999 requires that The London Plan deals only with matters that are of strategic importance to Greater London. The GLA Act also requires that the London Plan takes account of three crosscutting themes i.e.: (a) the health of Londoners (b) equality of opportunity and (c) its contribution to sustainable development in the UK. The London Plan is the strategic plan setting out an integrated social, economic and environmental framework (i.e.: the hallmark of spatial planning) for the future development of London, looking forward 15–20 years. It also integrates the physical and geographical dimensions of the Mayor's other strategies. It sets the policy framework for the Mayor's involvement in major planning decisions in London, and sets out proposals for implementation and funding. The London Plan is also seen as London's response to European guidance on spatial planning and a link to European Structural Funds. Indeed, the London Plan is required to take account of the European Spatial Development Perspective (ESDP) and other EU directives.

Many other examples of regional spatial strategies which have been produced as instruments of regional development in the EU25 could be cited. In the brief space of some five years the 'science and art' of spatial planning has advanced rapidly. The Baltic States are no exception here, as they too have embraced spatial planning and regional development. In Lithuania, for example, the Government is determined to address regional disparities in prosperity between its ten counties, and will be seeking to make more targeted use of EU Structural Funds in the 2007–2013 programme period. A national Regional Policy Strategy and a National Spatial Plan were both approved in 2002 and the Government is seeking to produce more balanced and sustainable polycentric regional development in the future. The focus of its regional development strategy and spatial planning approach is a growth centre strategy being implemented within a hierarchy of urban centres and places, and again based on principles embedded in the EU's ESDP. The Ministry of Interior (responsible for regional policy) and the Ministry of Environment (responsible for spatial planning and regional development) are key actors in adopting a joined-up government approach to addressing spatial issues in Lithuania.

Nowhere is the challenge of 'more balanced sustainable polycentric development' greater within the EU than in Latvia. Latvia is the poorest nation within the EU25 in terms of GDP per capita as illustrated earlier in Figure 2.1. In 2002, Latvia had a GDP per capita (Purchasing Power Parities) of 38.9 per cent of the EU25 average (followed closely by Lithuania with a figure of 42.4 per cent). Within Latvia there are wide regional disparities in prosperity, ranging from the increasingly prosperous capital city of Riga to poorer rural regions like that of Latgale. As noted earlier in this chapter, like Greater Dublin in Ireland, the Riga City region contains 40 per cent of the nation's population. The Latvian Government is currently preparing a National Development Plan for the period 2007–2013, and the Ministry of Regional Development and Local Government is scheduled to complete its National Spatial Plan for Latvia by the end of 2006.

Conclusions

The current interest in regional development and spatial planning across the EU has never been greater and can be expected to gain even further momentum than it has to date. Whilst most nations and regions have been touched by the Europeanization of Planning, and particularly at the regional level, its impact and intensity has varied. The adoption of a spatial planning approach has been marked in countries like Ireland, UK (Wales, Scotland and Northern Ireland are good examples), Netherlands, and the Baltic States of Lithuania, Latvia and Estonia.

The INTERREG IIIC GRIDS project final report 'best practice guidelines for regional development strategies' (Adams and Harris 2005) illustrates the diversity of approaches adopted by the Celtic and Baltic nations in the preparation and implementation of regional development strategies. The report illustrated that one size does not fit all. However, the important achievement of spatial planning and regional development strategies has been in providing new ways of thinking and new ways of addressing longstanding problems. Spatial planning has also enabled planners to set new agendas, and engage stakeholders outside planning. It has also galvanised people to deliver change. Planning has therefore become much more than just a regulatory and bureaucratic process and much more a core activity of government.

In the field of regional development theory and paradigms there has also been an explosion of interest in exploring the causes and consequences of regional disparities. However, the article by Markusen (2003) has reminded all those involved in regional development of the need for policy-related, evidence-based and rigorously undertaken research.

The enlargement of the EU in 2004 has led to a large number of Member States sharing their experiences in addressing common challenges in the field of regional development and spatial planning. The concept of more balanced and sustainable polycentric development has resonated with many Member States who are seeking to reduce prosperity gaps both between and within their regions. Together with the agendas and strategies of the Lisbon and Gothenburg summits, the next EU programming period of 2007–2013 promises to be one where the focus on regions and regional welfare disparities will remain as strong as in recent years.

References

Adams, N. and Harris, N. (2005), *Best Practice Guidelines for Regional Development Strategies*, INTERREG IIIC Project, Cardiff University, Cardiff.

Albrechts, L., Alden, J. and Pires, A. da Rosa (2001), 'Conclusions', in Albrechts L., Alden, J. and Pires, A. da Rosa (eds), *The Changing Institutional Landscape of Planning*, Ashgate Publishing Ltd, Aldershot, pp. 257–267.

Alden, J. (1999), 'Scenarios for the Future of the British Planning System: The Need for a National Spatial Planning Framework', *Town Planning Review*, vol. 70, no. 3, pp. 385–407.

Alden J. (2001a), A New Planning Framework for the UK, in Albrechts, L., Alden, J., and Pires, A. da Rosa (eds), *The Changing Institutional Landscape of Planning*, Ashgate Publishing Ltd, Aldershot, pp. 55–82.

Alden, J. (2001b), Devolution since Kilbrandon and Scenarios for the Future of Spatial Planning in the United Kingdom and European Union, *International Planning Studies*, vol. 6, no. 2, pp. 117–132.

Alden, J. (2002), Chapter 3, Scenarios for the Future of Regional Planning within UK/EU Spatial Planning, in Marshall, T., Glasson, J. and Headicar, P. (eds), *Contemporary Issues in Regional Planning*, Ashgate Publishing Ltd, Aldershot, pp. 35–53.

Alden, J. and Boland, P. (eds) (1996), Regional Development Strategies: *A European Perspective*, Jessica Kingsley Publishers, London.

Alden, J. and Morgan, R. (1974), The Development of Regional Planning, in *Regional Planning: A Comprehensive View*, Leonard Hill Books, Leighton Buzzard, Hertfordshire.

Beugelsdijk, S. and Schaik, T.V. (2005), Differences in Social Capital between 54 Western European Regions, *Regional Studies*, vol. 39, no. 8, Nov. 2005, Special Issue on Social Capital, pp. 1053–1064.

Braczyk, H.J., Cooke, P. and Heidenreich, M. (eds) (1998), *Regional Innovation Systems*, UCL Press, London.

Brocker, J. Dohse, D. and Soltwedel, R. (eds) (2003), *Innovation Clusters and Interregional Competition*, Springer-Vering, Berlin.

Bryson, J., Daniels, P., Henry, N. and Pollard, J. (eds) (2000), *Knowledge Space, Economy*, Routledge, London.

Christaller, W. (1933), *Die Zentrislen Ork in Süddeutschland*, Jena: Gustav Fischer, translated (in part) by Baskin, C.W. (1966) as Central Places in Southern Germany, Prentice Hall.

Cooke, P. (2002), *Knowledge Economies: Clusters, Learning and Cooperative Advantage*, Routledge, London.

Department of the Environment and Local Government (2002), *The National Spatial Strategy for Ireland 2002–2020: People, Places and Potential*, Irish Government Publications, Dublin, Ireland.

European Commission's 5th Framework Programme (2005), *Conference held in Berlin on 8 December 2005 to present findings of three year research programme on Intelligent Territories*, organised by University of Dortmund and chaired by K. Kunzmann.

European Commission (2005), *Interreg IIIC Newsletter No. 6*, June 2005, www.interreg3c.net.

European Commission (2005), *Eurostat News Release: Regional GDP per Capita in the EU25*, Eurostat, 25 January 2005.

European Commission (2004), *A New Partnership for Cohesion: Convergence and Competitiveness Co-operation*, Third Report on Economic and Social Cohesion, February 2004.

European Spatial Development Perspective (1999), Final Draft, *Towards a Balanced and Sustainable Development of the Territory of the EU*, Potsdam, May.

Greater London Authority (2004), *The London Plan: Spatial Development Strategy for Greater London*, Greater London Authority, February 2004, London.

Healey, P. (1997), The Revival of Strategic Spatial Planning in Europe, Chapter 1, in Healey, P., Khakee, A., Motte, A. and Needham, B. (eds), *Making Strategic Spatial Plans: Innovation in Europe*, UCL Press, London.

Healey, P. (2004), The Treatment of Space and Place in the New Strategic Spatial Planning in Europe, *International Journal of Urban and Regional Research*, vol. 28, no. 1, pp. 45–67, March 2004.

Kitson, M., Martin, R. and Tyler, P. (2004), Regional Competitiveness: An Elusive yet Key Concept?, *Regional Studies*, vol. 38, no. 9, pp. 991–999, December 2004, Special Issue on Regional Competitiveness.

Markusen, A. (2003), Fuzzy Concepts, Scanty Evidence, Policy Distance: The Case for Rigour and Policy Relevance in Critical Regional Studies, *Regional Studies*, vol. 37, nos 6 and 7, pp. 701–717, August/October 2003.

McCann, P. and Sheppard, S. (2003), The Rise, Fall and Rise Again of Industrial Location Theory, *Regional Studies*, vol. 37, nos 6 and 7, pp. 644 and 663, August/October 2003.

Morgan, K. (1997), The Learning Region: Institutions, Innovation and Regional Renewal, *Regional Studies*, vol. 31, no. 5, pp. 491–453, July 1997.

Myrdal, G. (1957), *Economic Theory and Underdeveloped Regions*, Methuen.

O'Leary, E. (2003), *Irish Regional Development: A New Agenda*, The Liffey Press, Dublin, Ireland.

Parr, J.B. (2004), The Polycentric Urban Region: A Closer Inspection, *Regional Studies*, vol. 38, no. 3, May 2004, pp. 231–240.

Perroux, F. (1955), *Note sur la Notion de la Pole de Croissance, Economic Appliance*, vol. 8: translated from the French in Livingstone, I. (ed.), Economic Policy for Development, Penguin, 1971.

Pires, A. da Rosa (2005), The Fragile Foundations of European Spatial Planning in Portugal, *European Planning Studies*, vol. 13, no. 2, March 2005, pp. 237–251.

Scott, A.J. and Storper, M. (2003), Regions, Globalization, Development, *Regional Studies*, vol. 37, nos 6 and 7, pp. 579–593, August/October 2003.

Scottish Executive (2004), *National Planning Framework for Scotland*, Edinburgh, Scotland.

Shaw, D. and Sykes, O. (2004), The Concept of Polycentricity in European Spatial Planning: Reflections on its Interpretation and Application in the Practice of Spatial Planning, *International Planning Studies*, vol. 9, no. 4, pp. 283–306, November 2004.

Taylor, J. (1991), Chapter 2, Regional Economic Disparities: Causes and Consequences, in Bowen, A. and Mayhem, K. (eds), *Reducing Regional Inequalities*, Kogan Page Ltd, London, pp. 70–108.

Tewdwr-Jones, M. (2001), Complexity and Interdependency in a Kaleidoscopic Spatial Planning Landscape for Europe, in Albrechts, L., Alden, J. and Pires, A. da Rosa (eds), *The Changing Institutional Landscape of Planning*, Ashgate Publishing Ltd, Aldershot, pp. 8–34.

Welsh Assembly Government (2005), *The Wales Spatial Plan: People, Places, Futures*, Cardiff, Wales.

Williams, R.H. (1998), *European Union Spatial Policy and Planning*, Paul Chapman Publishing, London.

PART II

The Evolving European Union Context for Regional Development and Spatial Planning

Chapter 3

The Europeanization of Spatial Planning

Klaus Kunzmann

Spatial Planning: A Bridge to Europe

Spatial Planning has become a new hope for territorial cohesion in Europe. Though urban and regional planning have a long tradition in Europe, albeit under continuously changing policy environments and planning cultures, the Euro-English buzz term 'spatial planning' seems to have caused a renaissance of regional planning across regions and nations in Europe. This term was almost unknown in Europe until a decade ago. Since the beginning of the twenty-first century spatial planning has become prominent among academic and professional planners in the anglophone world of Europe, as a term which points to a new approach for guiding spatial development. It describes space-related planning at mainly three tiers of planning and decision-making, at the European tier, the national tier, and various forms of regional tiers. Occasionally the term is now even applied to strategic planning at the city region or the local level.

The community of practice in planning across Europe, however, is still far away from agreeing on a unanimously accepted definition. In essence, there is not much difference. Regional planning as well as spatial planning aim at integrating and coordinating all space-consuming activities in a territory. In the past, planning at the regional level often ended up as mere regional land use planning, assigning potential uses to space and protecting land from urban sprawl and undesirable development. In contrast to the traditional term regional planning, spatial planning seems to reflect a more ambitious, holistic approach to territorial development, incorporating all actors in a region to follow a joint vision for the development of a geographically-defined territory.

Regional/spatial planning never got much political support in national policy arenas across Europe with just two exceptions: in France *aménagement du territoire* has been a comparatively strong instrument in the hands of the powerful French centralist State, and in the Netherlands, where the need to protect the territory from flooding has brought about a long tradition of *ruimteliike ordeningen*. In market-driven Germany, *Raumordnung* (the German concept of spatial planning at the Federal or lander level) has lost its former influence. Despite its unholy alliance with the political power in Hitler's Third Reich, the policy field had played a considerable role in reconstructing the country after World War II, though the term 'Raum' (space) was clearly a political legacy (Schloegel, 2006: 32). Turning central place theory into a normative spatial concept, regional (spatial) planning under the responsibility of planners in the eleven Federal States of (West-) Germany has had a key role in guiding the development of regional infrastructure. Three decades later, in the 1990s, after re-unification, though only for a short time period, spatial planning contributed to the spatial reframing of the run-down socialist territory of East Germany. At present, in the beginning of the twenty-first century the influence of *Raumordnung und Landesplanung* on territorial development is modest, if not marginal, probably mainly due to the obvious crisis of the welfare state, which rather concerns about shrinking than about growth, usually the rationale for spatial planning. The crucial role of spatial planning under conditions of decline has not yet received much theoretical attention and professional consideration.

This chapter aims to describe the status and importance of European spatial planning. It will sketch the evolution of spatial planning in Europe as a distinct policy at the European tier of planning and decision-making, and it will explore a possible future of European spatial development as a means to achieve territorial cohesion across the continent. Addressing the difficult relationship of spatial planning, regional economic development and ecologically defined sustainable development in this wider European context, the chapter also presents the virtues of spatial planning to bridge the Lisbon and Gothenburg goals of territorial development in Europe.

The Evolution of Spatial Planning in Europe

The history of spatial planning in Europe is young, though political territorial concepts of Europe reach back to the times of the Roman Empire. For centuries emperors, kings and ambitious generals have fought for territorial power, sacrificing the lives of multiple generations of soldiers and civilians. Emperors and dictators aimed to draw and redraw maps of Europe. Geopolitics has been their passion. Their approach to spatial development was dictated by power considerations. While urban planning played a role in developing feudal headquarters and new towns, regional planning was not seen to be of any relevance.

The modern history of spatial planning in Europe started only a few years after the end of World War II. In 1950, Walter Christaller, the author of the influential central place theory, published a map on the system of central places in Europe (Christaller 1950, Dickinson 1967, Kunzmann 1992). In his map the renowned German geographer suggested a hierarchy of European cities, based on his personal perception of the continent. This map, though it was not based on real empirical investigations, is one of the first efforts to address Europe in its spatial dimension. Not surprisingly, given the Cold War environment which evolved in Europe at that time, the map had no impact on European politics at the time of publication.

Prior to 1964, when the Council of Europe published its first Report on *Regional Planning a European Problem* (CoE 1968), the European territory as a whole had not been a major concern of politicians and planners. This report, published in three languages, aimed to promote regional planning as the appropriate means to guide spatial development in the territories of its members countries, and, even more important, of the European territory as a whole. And, indeed, this report set a mark. It brought European regional planning on the political agenda. European regional planning had become a European concern, though it took three more decades until a spatial plan for Europe had been approved.

It took, however, another 15 years until a first initiative was launched by the Parliamentary Assembly to the Council of Europe to establish regional planning in Europe as a policy field. The famous Resolution 289 of 1964 called for an initiative to explore the prospects of regional/spatial planning in Europe (CoE 1968). Subsequently a study was commissioned and in 1967 the Council of Europe published the results in a report, written in German, English and French with the English title *Regional Planning: A European Problem*. The Euro-English term spatial planning was not yet in use at that time. This report triggered off a debate about the need and the aims of transnational regional planning in Europe (see Mudrich 1980, CoE 1984). A few years later, in 1970, the German Federal Ministry of Interior, where *Raumordnung* was formally located at that time, invited ministers responsible for Regional Planning to Bonn. This meeting has started a tradition of conferences, which form under the label of CEMAT (*Conference Européenne de Ministers Responsable pour L'aménagement du Territoire*). These annual conferences address topical themes of spatial planning of transnational importance and many of their documents seem to be timeless accounts of concerns of our time.

An institution which acted as the driving engine of regional/spatial planning during the 1970s was the Council of Europe. Under the active secretariat of Guenther Mudrich the European institution promoted a series of conferences and seminars on various aspects of European spatial planning, bringing together planners and researchers mainly from France, Great Britain, Germany and the Netherlands. The outcome has been a series of English and French documents on 'Aménagement du Territoire Européen', published during 1976 to 1980, which fed the debates at these events (Mudrich 1980, CoE 1991). These documents covered a broad range of themes, from planning in border regions to balanced regional development; from transportation to urban regeneration. One of these documents suggested a *First Concept for European Regional Planning* (Kunzmann *et al.*, 1977) and identified policy areas for guiding spatial development in Europe. Later, when the Council of Europe, mainly due to internal personal re-organization, lost its interest in spatial planning, the European Parliament and the European Commission took over the initiative.

In 1975, the European Commission established the European Regional Development Fund implementing an idea of the British government, which joined the European Project in 1972. This fund was seen as an instrument to support European regions lagging behind. It is in these days that the now much appraised Irish success story had its beginning. In practice, the ERDF, a brainchild of European regional policy advisors, had not much to do with spatial planning. Up to today regional policy in the form of regional economic development and spatial planning are policy fields of two quite different communities of practice, though in day-to-day business and pursuing similar goals they overlap considerably.

It is another event which gave spatial planning in Europe a new momentum. At the CEMAT conference in Torremolinos/Spain, in 1983, the ministers unanimously adopted a European Charter of Regional/Spatial Planning. (Kunzmann 1978, CoE 1984). This charter, most probably the first official document using the term *spatial planning*, is a concise document listing a set of 'fundamental objectives' for territorial development in Europe. It says: 'Regional/spatial planning seeks at one and the same time to achieve, balanced socio-economic development of the regions, improvement of the quality of life, responsible management of natural resources and protection of the environment, and rational use of land', stating that 'the achievement of regional/spatial planning objectives is essentially a political matter' (CoE 1984).

In 1983, the European Parliament, upon the initiative of its Belgium MP, *Paul-Henry Gendebien*, advocated a European Planning Scheme and after his report had been submitted to the Parliament, the CEMAT conference in Liege in 1993 decided to embark on the elaboration of a European Spatial Concept. During the late 1980s and the early 1990s, the European Commission shifted its interest to the role of cities in regional development. A first study initiated by *Paul Wäldchen*, explored *Urban Problems in Western Europe* (Ceshire and Hay 1989). And not much later, resulting from a number of studies undertaken by a large group of consultants all over Europe, the document *Europe 2000* was published (CEC 1991). This document focused on the conditions of spatial development in Europe and supported the launch of the INTERREG programmes, which were seen as a means to promote the interregional discourse on spatial development in Europe. One of the supporting documents to this landmark document has been a small study on *Urbanisation in Europe 1960 to 1990* which gave a concise description of the European urban system in the outgoing twentieth century (Kunzmann/ Wegener 1990). *Europe 2000+*, a follow-up report to the first document of the European Commission on spatial development in Europe, further deepened the institutional commitment to European space (CEC 1994).

It took another few years and a number of CEMAT conferences to end up, in 1999, with the publication of the first official European Spatial Development Perspective (CEC 1999). This document became a kind of a Mao bible of the spatial planning community in Europe. Apart from being responsible for the ESPON initiative, this document had even triggered off an academic discourse on large scale spatial development in the United States (Faludi 2002a, b and c). Few planners in the 1960s or 1970s of the last century would have anticipated that the Council of Ministers responsible for Regional Planning would ever adopt a common document such as the European Spatial Development Perspective (CEC 1999). Since then this document has become a non-controversial piece of reference, widely used by spatial planners all over Europe, in both planning agencies and universities to support their arguments and give their regional or national territorial development concepts a wider European dimension. While regional policy is one of the key policy areas of the European Commission to narrow regional disparities in Europe, spatial planning, contradicting the subsidiarity principle, has never been a legitimized policy arena of the European Commission. However via its new label of 'territorial cohesion' the all embracing goal of European regional policy, spatial planning has found a kind of back door entrance to the European constitution (Faludi 2005, 2005a). Although the ambitious constitutional project has failed to win popular support in two European referenda, territorial cohesion in Europe will remain a symbolic political aim, and spatial planning, knowing the complexity of space better than any other institution, can offer its services to prepare the territory for cohesion.

Over the years a community of practice has emerged favourable to the idea that European Spatial Planning makes sense (Faludi 2002c; Bengs and Böhme 2004; Jensen and Richardson, 2004). And despite all skepticism, European spatial planning has got a modest place in the European political arena, not just because of the generous financial commitment to INTERREG programmes, which are verbally linked to the ESDP, but because it has triggered-off a Europe wide discourse on the future of European space in times of globalisation and new communication technologies. A follow-up initiative to the ESDP is under preparation (CEMAT 2005). It will be launched under the German presidency in 2007 and it aims to benefit from the momentum and unexpected attention European spatial planning has experienced over the last decade.

The Europeanization of Spatial Planning

This brief chronology has shown that, over the last three decades, spatial planning has grown up from local and national arenas to a wider European dimension (Williams 1999). Though its political acceptance and power remains far behind the unrealistic expectations of the community of planners across Europe, spatial planning has become an arena of political concern, of growing professional and academic interest. Apart from the CEMAT, the politico-administrative arm of national agencies responsible for spatial planning, a growing community of spatial planners, organized in professional or academic networks, such as the ECTP or ISOCARP, has evolved over the decades. Thereby INTERREG, ESPON and AESOP are the key catalysts for the promotion of spatial planning in Europe.

INTERREG: Undoubtedly INTERREG has become the driving engine of the Europeanisation of spatial planning. Regions in Eastern Europe benefited particularly from the programme. With an enormous financial budget, the initiative has spun an impressive spatial planning network across Europe. This trans-European network is a net of institutions eager to get projects financed; a set of connections of individual planners in the regions who are curious to learn about planning practices in other countries. These are supported by professional consultants, who contribute their international management experience, or academic advisors, who link their research experience to professional practice. Although the substantial outcome of the projects may occasionally be dubious or even marginal, and certainly below expectations, the participants learn how to communicate across national regulatory systems and established spatial planning cultures. This learning process could be characterized as 'learning by bridge building'. Thereby learning means accepting other planning cultures and project management approaches, communicating with a limited vocabulary in another language. In such international project environments a younger generation of flexible, curious and communicative planners grows up and qualifies for the territorial challenges in Europe ahead.

ESPON: The need for comparative data on urban and regional development was already felt when the European Commission initiated the first report of spatial development in Europe (COM 1990). EUROSTAT could only provide very basic demographic and socio-economic data, and almost nothing on the spatial dimensions of urban and regional development. When the project to launch a European Spatial Development Perspective was in the making, the lack of comparative data had become a major concern of those who had to analyse European spatial problems and trends. Finally, in 2002, with the support of the Luxemburg Government and the INTERREG Programme, the ESPON project was initiated to establish a European data-base for spatial planning. The very existence of this network and its secretariat in Luxembourg, although not yet fully secured for the years to come, is conspicuous proof of the progressing Europeanisation of spatial planning. Future spatial research will benefit much from the efforts of the network to compile space-relevant comparative data (ESPON 2005).

AESOP: The Association of European Schools of Planning was established in Dortmund in 1987 to bring an international dimension to planning schools (Kunzmann 1998; Stiftel and Watson 2005). Today the organization has 103 full and 35 associate member schools in 21 countries of Europe (AESOP 2004). The annual AESOP Congresses have become an important event in the calendar of spatial planners across Europe. The congresses are seen as an inspiring cosmopolitan platform for communication and information exchange. The transnational PhD workshops organised in the context of the annual events have become a favourite place for young academics to learn about cutting edge developments in the discipline. Moreover, every fifth year, the members of the various Associations of the world's mega regions come together globally. The existence of the dense network of academic teachers has made it much easier for the community to organise the popular ERASMUS and SOCRATES exchange programmes, personal Jean Monnet Chairs of European Spatial Planning and Marie Curie fellowships. Swedish, German, Dutch and Italian and Portuguese students enjoy being for a term in the planning school of another European country. There is some evidence that planning schools have developed one of the most active academic exchange cultures in Europe, and contributed much to a better awareness of the need of a European Union. The planning schools will additionally benefit from the ongoing Bologna process, which has been initiated to facilitate student mobility within Europe and beyond.

In addition to these arenas, which support the gradual Europeanisation of spatial planning, there are many other signs of growing interest in the European dimension of spatial planning. In the Netherlands, in France, in Italy, in Germany and in the Nordic countries, programmes to explore the future of national territories in a wider European context have been an obvious component of national initiatives. The German Academy of Spatial Research and Regional Planning (ARL), for example, has developed a series of initiatives to overcome their inward looking image (ARL 1984, ARL/DATAR 1992). Already in the late 1980s working groups have been commissioned to explore the European dimension of spatial planning (ARL 1990). Similar activities can be identified in most other national arenas, in Britain as well as in Italy. Other support for the Europeanisation of spatial planning comes from the Research Programmes of the European Commission, which offered financial opportunities to European research networks to do comparative studies.

Which Spatial Vision for Europe: Banana or a Bunch of Grapes?

The interest in European spatial planning has caused a surprising boom of efforts to create spatial scenarios and spatial images of future spatial development in Europe (Kunzmann 1993, Duehr 2003, Baudelle 2005). This boom has been triggered off by a French comparative study of European Cities (Brunet 1989), which, rooted in French geopolitical tradition, summarized its complex findings in a single map. This map shows a strong *dorsale* from London to Milan. This spatial image, which reflects a very superficial and partially even incorrect perception of the spatial concentration of economic power before the fall of the iron curtain – one third of the surface of the dorsale represents declining or peripheral regions in the heart of Europe. Notwithstanding, this image triggered off a still ongoing discourse, mainly among geographers, about the power of images in spatial planning.

The purely analytical image of RECLUS, which intended to signal to the French government that the agglomeration of Paris is not quite a part of this dorsal, which was labelled 'blue banana', was soon mistaken as a normative or at least suggestive image. It conveyed fuzzy messages to mayors, city marketing managers and the real estate community The bunch of grapes, a normative regionalist image of a Europe of metropolitan regions soon became the counter-metaphor to the banana image (Kunzmann 2001). This spatial metaphor aimed at promoting a more balanced spatial development in Europe.

These early efforts to create scenario maps of future European space triggered off quite a number of similar maps which confirmed or corrected the banana image by using similar, simplistic symbols. Given the appeal of these images to the spatial planning community and their audiences, however, it is not surprising that the fathers of the ESDP, respectively the CEMAT Conference in Nordwijik in 1998, abstained from offering any clear spatial vision, using abstract pictograms instead. The whole message of the ESDP is a balanced Europe, and a balanced Europe is difficult to draw on a map.

The ESDP: A Paradigm for Spatial Planning in Europe

Despite all criticism and shortcomings, the ESDP, approved in 1999 in Potsdam by the member states of the European Union (CEC 1999), has become an important policy document for spatial development in Europe. Spatial planning is holistic and communicative. It is an essential means to preserve identity and it relies on local and regional endogenous cultures and potentials. The holistic feature of spatial planning results from its cross-disciplinary nature, linking social and economic, as well as cultural and environmental dimensions of urban and regional development. And only by continuous dialogue across regions in Europe and intensive communication between the various European sector institutions, national governments and regional representatives, can spatial planning can achieve a wise use of European territory. The European identity is very much based on the cultural and physical diversity of urban and regional spaces. To preserve this diversity is one of the key aims and tasks of European spatial planning. It is diversity of endogenous cultures and traditions, of natural and urban landscapes which is the territorial capital of future socio-economic development in times of regional competitiveness and globalization.

Though spatial planning, as a rule, has limited political power and lacks efficient tools for implementation, it is a perfect arena for regional dialogue and learning. What is the importance of the ESDP document? First, the ESDP sets European-wide normative goals and principles of spatial planning at regional and national levels. Particularly, balanced spatial development and polycentricity are promoted as key concerns of spatial development. Based on experience in Germany and the Netherlands, where polycentric development has been a dominant feature since spatial planning has become a policy field after the Second World War, the ESDP is aiming to transfer such experience to the whole of Europe. It is an effort to contain uncontrolled metropolization and counteract short-sighted market driven concentration processes. Referring to the ongoing process of spatial concentration in Europe, however, one could easily argue that the ambitions as postulated in the ESDP contradict mainstream policies in the European Union, which, following the Lisbon agenda and market forces, prioritize macro-economic competitiveness over social and environmental goals. Indeed, most European sector policies, whether it is competition policy, transport policy or even urban policies favour, though not explicitly, the concentration of economic activities in a limited number of metropolitan regions. Obviously, this has considerable impact on European rural regions in the periphery of the continent and beyond the immediate hinterland of European metropolitan regions. Particularly, countries in Eastern Europe will experience the concentration effects of such policies.

Second, the existence of the ESDP underlines the importance of the spatial dimension in sectoral planning. Given the weak position of spatial planning as a future oriented policy field in most European countries, the document is at least a manifesto which stresses the role of space in sectoral policies such as transport, agriculture or energy. Only few institutions engaged in such sectoral policies will in the end use the document to check and eventually review the spatial implications of their activities and programmes.

Third, the ESDP demonstrates the considerable communication power of the European Union. The document is one of the most circulated documents on spatial planning in Europe. It is available in all languages of the member states of the European Union, except those of the new members in Central and Eastern Europe. As a consequence, the ESDP has become a powerful Pan-European source of information on principles of spatial development. It has the quality of a textbook of how spatial planning at regional and national should be done.

Fourth, without the ESDP, the European Spatial Planning Observatory Network (ESPON) would never have been initiated. When working on the document it soon became apparent that reliable, comparative space-related data in Europe were not available. While Eurostat could provide economic and social data, the collection of spatial and urban data had been neglected. In order to obtain such data the member states had agreed to establish and finance a network of national observatories with a small co-ordinating office in Luxembourg. This network has been asked to compile comparative information on spatial development trends in Europe and to commission transnational studies in areas where appropriate spatial information was not available (Davoudi, 2005).

Fifth, the ESDP contributed much to the justification of the various INTERREG programmes, which became a key instrument of the European Commission to promote interregional communication and exchange. Over the years the INTERREG programmes have attracted much local and regional interest. The many interregional projects which have been supported by the Commission under the INTERREG label have contributed much to highlight the importance of the spatial dimension of regional development. They have brought together hundreds of regional planners, managers and policy makers across regions and nations, learning from each other and promoting a sustainable Europe as a common project (Schäfer 2003).

Sixth, the ESDP, apart from being a significant employment initiative for internationally-minded planners, has been very instrumental to bring together European planners beyond their respective national academic and professional milieus and a few international networks. The document has triggered off multiple debates in the international planning community on the nature and the rationale of spatial planning. More than once, such debates led to the formation of transnational research teams and networks who joined their forces for applications to European basic and applied research programs. In addition, the ESDP inspired journal and book editors to initiate special volumes on planning issues of European importance.

Last, but not least, one could argue that the ESDP legitimizes the role of the public sector in guiding spatial development with all its underlying social, cultural and environmental ambitions and concerns, which market forces tend to neglect. Although this has never been expressed explicitly, it is an essential dimension of territorial policies. Without a strong and efficient public administration, initiating continuous discourses on spatial development, influencing spatial policies by guiding private investment to appropriate locations, spatial cohesion in Europe cannot be achieved.

In the absence of the availability of hard instruments, spatial planning by nature, and compared with policy fields such as agriculture or transport, is a rather weak policy area. In the post-industrial information society, however, spatial planning could be a valuable agenda-setting policy arena for sustainable development. The reasons are:

- The European space with all its cultural and scenic assets will be a key to the future economy of the continent. Spatially relevant policies, with all their knowledge of spatial conditions are crucial in defending amenities against uncontrolled economic growth and uncoordinated, non-sustainable infrastructure development;
- With its information and communication power and its strong concern for cities and regions, spatial planning reaches citizens all over Europe as it addresses problems of regional identity, cultural traditions and quality of life;
- The process of formulating a follow-up document to the ESDP is an important catalytic element to foster a European wide discourse on a sustainable Europe. In no other policy arena, the multiple dimensions of sustainable development will be discussed in such a comprehensive way;
- The discourse on spatial planning at the European level will have some influence on European sectoral policies, such as agriculture, transport or competition policies. In the absence of any spatial framework and principles, sector policies tend to neglect the likely spatial implications on cities and regions;
- Spatial planning promoted at the European level will encourage national governments to follow; either to elaborate and provide national concepts before the European Commission is launching European wide proposals, or to react to European proposals from a national position. Both require strong national and regional spatial perspectives;
- Spatial planning efforts at the European level will require more up-to-date information on spatial development trends in Europe and on the requirements for spatial guidance and intervention. Consequently more transnational and comparative spatial research is necessary.

Such reasons suggest that the ambitious goals of the Potsdam document should be followed-up in one way or the other, preferably in the form of a new ESDP initiative (Faludi 2002, Kunzmann 2005a and b, Schoen 2005).

Towards a New ESDP for Europe?

At present, it seems, there is little enthusiasm and willingness at European and national levels to invest much effort, time and money into European spatial planning. Apart from a clear commitment to continue the INTERREG Programme beyond 2006, no explicit efforts are being undertaken to up-date or cover the territories of Central Eastern Europe. As a matter of fairness at least, the contents, aims and principles of the ESDP should be communicated to the planners and decision-makers of the new member states in their respective native language. Regrettably, there is little political commitment to produce precisely such a follow-up document, at least not one with such a denomination.

What is in the pipeline is the preparation of a document, which has been launched by the EU Ministers for Spatial Development for 2007, when Germany holds the Presidency of the European Union. It will be a document labelled *Territorial State and Perspectives of the European Union*, building explicitly on the ESDP, though replacing space with territory (Schoen 2005). In this forthcoming document, *territorial capital, territorial cohesion* and *territorial development policies* will be the politico-administrative buzz words. Space, it seems has been replaced by territory, probably following along the lines of the OECD, which has carried out a number of model territorial reviews for regions or nations to demonstrate how to link regional economic, social and spatial development.

Future academic research will have to explore whether there are notable substantial differences between spatial planning and territorial planning, between spatial development and territorial development, beyond the different linguistic traditions in the Anglophone and the Roman worlds.

The Ministers responsible for Regional Planning in the member states of the European Union, together with the European Commission, have already endorsed a scoping document and a summary of political messages for *an assessment of the Territorial State and Perspectives of the European Union towards a stronger territorial cohesion in the light of the Lisbon and Gothenburg ambitions* (Conference of EU Ministers of Spatial Planning 2005). Three policy objectives for strengthening territorial cohesion will be elaborated in this document: *improving the strength and diversity/identity of urban centres/networks as motors for territorial development in Europe; improving accessibility and territorial integration in the Union, preserving and developing the quality and safety of Europe's natural and cultural values and developing sustainable urban rural-linkages. A special challenge in this respect is*, as the scoping document states, *to strengthen the territorial capital of areas with a weak economic structure or physical or geographical handicaps in an EU perspective, including their links to the potentially strong EU areas.*

These are great ambitions and the 2007 document may become another impressive account of spatial planning rhetoric. How the ambitious goals articulated in the document can be implemented, or at least infiltrated into partially contradicting sectoral policies will still have to be seen. One requirement will certainly be fulfilled.

The forthcoming document will cover all 25 states of the European Union and hence include the new accession countries in Central and Eastern Europe.

One problem will remain: from what can be guessed from the scoping document is that the new territorial cohesion report will address the full complexity of territorial cohesion in Europe. This may lead to a document full of spatial/territorial development rhetoric. Unless communicated to key decisions-makers, this ambitious new document may easily become another paper tiger. Even if the focus is on 'territorial capital', it will certainly not argue that the development of the territorial capital of Paris or Munich will have to be slowed down in order to promote the territorial capital of cities in peripheral or *in-between-regions* in Central or Eastern Europe.

What could be a way out of the dilemma? While maintaining the European dimension, it could make sense to first agree on reducing the complexity of the future documents to make it more down-to earth and more readable for policy makers, who are not familiar with the specialised jargon of spatial planners. The reduction of complexity could be done by focussing on selected spatial themes, themes which either reflect important European challenges or spatially relevant political concerns, such as knowledge industries, immigration or peripheral border regions, *in-between-regions*, medium sized cities, or regions with second home development pressure.

There is one additional rationale of reducing the complexity of the new document by cutting its agenda into better digestible pieces. It will then be much easier to enrich the thematic documents by illustrative maps. In contrast to earlier versions of the ESDP, and as a consequence of some resistance by individual member states, the final document did not contain scenario maps, illustrating the catalogue of policy objectives. However, a European territorial development perspective, where space is reduced to symbolic pictograms, is not really convincing. It does not use the power of images (Baudelle 2005, Duehr 2005). As the totally overrated though very popular 'Blue Banana' map has demonstrated, simple cartographic images are a good means of triggering-off dialogues, particularly in multi-lingual policy environments. Words cannot substitute maps – space or territory has a geographical dimension.

The next step is to address the most urgent challenges of European spatial development in Europe. This would require to seek consensus about those challenges, even if the perspective may differ from South to East from West to North. One thematic area which may soon find political acceptance is the future development of those regions in Europe, where accessibility is poor and basic infrastructure is eroding, where, due to the absence of scenic beauty or cultural assets, even tourism and second homes development is not flourishing. Such regions are mainly situated in the periphery of Europe or in between the Metropolitan European growth zones. Although no one would openly dare to speak it out, such regions are relative 'loser regions' of globalization, structural change and European spatial integration. However, to remain realistic, these regions can only be the target of compensation policies cushioning the negative impacts of regional decline by guaranteeing a minimum of basic public infrastructure. Whether Europe as a whole or national governments will have to maintain such basic infrastructure will be the outcome of political negotiations. A future territorial document dealing with this theme can only present a few success stories of spatial development, although all over Europe efforts are being made to identify effective ways to address the challenges of demographic and economic decline in such regions.

In the forthcoming document one could also focus on the spatial impacts of immigration on cities and border regions, as one significant and highly sensitive policy field of urban development in Europe. Or one could address the spatial interrelationships and spatial implications of European transport development. Given their political sensitivity and controversies, such themes, however, may not be helpful to demonstrate the necessity and efficiency of European spatial development in media-dominated political environments. In contrast, one could explore less controversial spatial policy arenas which more likely validate spatial planning as a policy field. Water protection and flood control could be such themes, or tourism and coastal development. In these policy fields success stories are easier to find and better to communicate than failures, unless one relies on the effects of threats and disasters, which the mass media tend to communicate with fervour.

In the end the choice of themes will depend on the Council of Ministers of Spatial Planning and on the Commission in Brussels, who have to jointly decide on the future of territorial policies in Europe. They have to agree on which theme the future document should focus within its ambitious and complex policy agenda. Given the power of the Structural Funds, the Commission can easily define thematic priorities. It remains important to promote spatial planning or/and territorial development as an instrument to sustain public discourse on the future of space in Europe, and to find political commitment beyond election campaigns.

Concerns on the Future Path of Spatial Planning in Europe

No doubt, the progress of Europeanisation in spatial planning over the last 50 years has been impressive. When the interest in the future of the European territory was first articulated, few would have imagined the broad interest which spatial planning receives today, even beyond the community of spatial planners. What could be seen as a striking success story, however, may also have some undesired repercussions, which should not be neglected.

The more the discourse on spatial planning in Europe is gaining ground, and the more it is promoted and dominated by the European Commission with the help of a generous budget for interregional communication, the more national and regional institutions rely on European funding for local and regional initiatives. It is not a secret that many INTERREG projects would not take place without European co-funding. Undoubtedly many regional initiatives would look different, if they would just have to rely on local financial contributions. And this would not just change the scope of local projects. Most likely it would also change the approach chosen, if European project management, contract and assessment rules do not have to be met. Weighing advantages and disadvantages of the strong hand of the European

Commission in such projects, to ensure transparency and quality, the positive aspects will certainly prevail. Such European screening, however, does not leave much space for local approaches. The consequence may be a policy environment, where all regional problems are treated with the same standard European medicine, just because the region is keen to get European funding.

There are voices across Europe which promote unitary European spatial planning legislation to unite spatial planning approaches across the European Union. The benefits of such legislation are not clear. The experience with environmental legislation at the European level has shown that the centralization of legislation, though it may have some positive implications, is not positive per se. What would be the likely benefits of having a European wide regulation in the field of a Spatial Planning Act? Such regulation may rather tend to wipe out regional differences, thus contradicting the aim of regional diversity and regional territorial capital, embedded in regional planning cultures and traditions. European planning regulation is not helpful to promote European spatial planning, rather the contrary.

Another, though more threatening fact is that English becomes the prevailing working language of communication in European spatial planning. In the absence of an appropriate translation technology (though this may change in the long run), the consequences for local and regional communication are enormous (Kunzmann 2005). The distance between the local community and the international discourse will widen, parallel worlds of spatial planning discourses will evolve, where only a few interpreters and professional moderators can bridge the gap between the international discourse and the local concerns. The scientific community will fully rely on English as the means of communication and publication to further the theoretical knowledge of the discipline, while the local community of practice has to use the local idiom to involve local opinion leaders and decision-makers, who, as a rule are not bi-lingual. There is not much to do about it, apart from just being aware of such concerns in order not to fall into the trap of unreflective internationalism.

Strengthening regional spatial planning cultures in the light of European experience should, therefore, be a prime concern of Europe minded spatial planners. Otherwise, resistance and opposition to the Europeanisation of spatial planning will gain momentum at a time, when the discipline has just been successful to surmount national boundaries.

What are the Virtues of Spatial Planning in Europe?

Despite all these signs of progress and success at the European level, however, spatial planning as a policy field is still weak in Europe, when compared to other policy areas, such as competition policy, agricultural policy, transport policy or regional policy. This is similarly true for spatial planning at national or regional tiers in the member states of the European Union. This weakness has many reasons. They reach from the systemic differences in communicating the concept and the need for spatial planning to a wider public, to the lack of instruments and funds available to implement spatial planning. The complexity of spatial planning is certainly a major barrier to understand the need for spatial intervention into territorial development. And its widely negative image as a public sector instrument to intervene into market led economic development is yet another reason for its poor popularity among opinion leaders and decision-makers. Moreover, the media, seemingly for the same reasons, do not consider spatial planning to be an exciting theme which needs to be exploited (Kunzmann, 1999). Hence spatial planning at the European, national or regional tier has remained an arena for a small community of practicing planners.

As a rule spatial planning as a policy arena at the national level has little political and co-ordinating power, and no instruments for implementation. It cannot command where private investment has to be done, nor can it decree to line ministries where to act, and where not. Consequently, spatial planning may contribute little to regional economic development. In contrast to institutions established to promote regional economic development, the institutional power of spatial planning at national or regional tiers of planning and decision-making, is quite weak all over Europe, even in centralist France or Britain.

The power of spatial planning is the power of discourse, and as evidence shows all over Europe, with only few exceptions in smaller countries such as the Netherlands or Denmark, at the regional level. Britain has not produced a national spatial plan, nor has Italy or Spain such a document. Germany is in a process to elaborate a new spatial 'Leitbild' (spatial perspective) for the country, though not as a means to guide economic development, but to nourish the ongoing national political discourse on the future of German regions between growth and decline.

Much of the opposition to spatial planning as an important public sector action field is based on prejudice, lack of information, or just unwillingness to accept the leading role of the public sector on territorial development. Spatial planning has no strategic alliances. As a rule, the private sector considers spatial planning as a hindrance to economic development, and spatial planning is not taught in business schools or schools of economics. For the majority of actors and interest groups in the economic world, spatial planning is rather a public sector apparatus which should be deregulated to facilitate economic development. Developers know of the essential role urban planning has for shaping locations for their investments and projects, though they maintain a reserved attitude towards spatial planning in general. Citizens, in contrast, complain about the power of technocratic planners, when it comes to airport extensions or motorways. For them the complexity of spatial planning is difficult to grasp. Also most media all across Europe consider spatial planning a negligible topic, when it comes to cover national or regional policies.

With the exception of Poland, the situation may be different in the countries of Eastern Europe, where infrastructure development is a prime political concern and a major task. Additionally favoured by the manageable size of their national territories, spatial planning in these countries is laying the foundations for balanced spatial development. This is done by providing appropriate information on the physical and socio-economic conditions of spatial development, by exploring the territorial potential for development and by elaborating spatial visions, which open the dialogue among local and regional and national stakeholders, and guide the development process.

Consequently those who wish to strengthen the role of spatial planning in our society have to promote its hidden strength and redefine its role in economic development. This role is easy to define. Spatial planning can:

- provide spatial knowledge to policy makers at all four or five tiers of planning and decision-making;
- prepare the ground and show directions for infrastructure development;
- develop spatial visions;
- protect the environment and regional resources;
- bridge, not command sector policies;
- strengthen local and regional institutions;
- moderate territorial learning;
- monitor spatial change; and
- involve citizens in regional communication processes.

The tools and instruments available for doing all that are rather tools of information handling and communication, imagining and monitoring tools, which usually are neither the interest nor the competence of traditional line ministries, such as economics or transportation. Spatial planning institutions can offer appropriate and up-to-date spatial information, tailored to the comprehension of target groups and communicated to whom it may concern in the cities and regions of Europe. For such activities they benefit from their competence in cartography and visualization. Spatial planning institutions can create opportunities to meet and communicate in order to express concerns, requirements and wishes. They can also moderate processes to seek compromises and to enhance civic commitment. Obviously, such functions require a new political assignment, a different understanding of the role of spatial planning beyond statutory rules, and, above all, a differently trained manpower which is able to manage such processes.

In the post-industrial information and knowledge society only such a significantly different approach to spatial planning is a great opportunity for the established institutions to contribute to the shaping of sustainable life spaces, and to overcome the traditional frustration of spatial planners complaining of their limited power and resources (Blotevogel 2000, Kunzmann 2000, Tewdwr-Jones, 2005).

Outlook: Spatial Planning and Territorial Cohesion

Europe is still far from being a territorial entity. It will take more than half a century until the territories of a Europe of 25 or soon 27 member states will grow together. This Europe is still divided by quite different policy cultures and value systems stemming from ideologically quite different socio-political environments. In a global economy, where the struggle for limited resources is dominating geo-political strategies, this

Europe is forced to compete with other macro-regions for investments, markets and the better brains. The continent, which has been the cradle of industrialisation in the eighteenth century, is suffering from rapid de-industrialization, the consequence of both technological change and fierce competition from newly industrialising countries. For cities and regions in 'old' Europe the spatial consequences of this global competition are enormous. At least for a while, these consequences quite differ in Western and in Eastern Europe. Only a concerted approach of top-down and bottom-up approaches to territorial development, involving all five tiers of spatial planning and decision-making in Europe; the European; the national, the regional, the sub regional and the local tier of spatial planning, will bring about confidence to policy arena, which is so essential for sustainable territorial development in Europe.

Under conditions of globalization and technological change, the integration of regional and national economies into the competitive European market will cause considerable territorial implications. It will require long term public action in the states of Western, as well as of Central and Eastern Europe. National policy makers will have to address the challenges: growing interregional social and spatial polarization, structural change and industrial modernization, agricultural divergence, insufficient transport infrastructure, environmental protection, conservation of the cultural heritage, and last but not least, the brain drain of qualified labor force.

In 1957, in Rome, when Europe was established as an ambitious peace project, one could certainly not imagine how this project would look like in 2006. Nobody could expect that, only 16 years after the fall of the wall in Berlin, most Central and Eastern European countries would already have joined the ambitious European project. Although there has been a backlash in 2005, when the European constitution was rejected by the people in France and the Netherlands, the future looks bright. This backlash has already caused political as well as intellectual opinion leaders between Lisbon and Helsinki to explore more appropriate corridors in order to continue the process of European political integration and territorial cohesion. Spatial planning can very much contribute to that goal. However, it has to raise its voice, avoid rhetoric and clear out its language, build bridges across regions and stakeholders, and search for strategic alliances in the media-dominated world.

References

AESOP (2005), AESOP Yearbook 2004, Oxford Brooks University.

ARL (Akademie für Raumforschung und Landesplanung Hannover), Hrsg., *Ansätze zu einer Europäischen Raumordnung: Forschungs-und Sitzungsberichte*, Bd. 155, Hanover.

ARL/DATAR (eds) (1992), *Perspektiven einer Europäischen Raumordnung*, Hanover.

Baudelle, G. (2005), *Figures d'Europe: Une Question d'Ìmage(s)*, Norois: Environnement, Aménagement, Société, vol. 1, nr. 194, pp. 27–48.

Bengs, C. and Böhme, K. (eds) (1998), 'The Progress of European Spatial Planning', *Nordregio*, 1.

Blotevogel, H. (2000), 'Rationality and Discourse in (Post) Modern Spatial Planning', in: Salet, W. und Faludi, A. (eds), *The Revival of Strategic Spatial Planning*, Royal Netherlands Academy of Arts and Sciences, Amsterdam, pp. 121–134.

Brunet, R. (1989), *Les villes Européennes: Report pour la DATAR*, Paris, La Documentation Francaise.

Commission of the European Communities, (CEC), (1991), Europe 2000, *Les perspectives de développement du territoire communautaire*, Office des publications officielles des Communautés européennes, Luxembourg.

CEC (1994), *Europe 2000 + Coopération pour l'aménagement du territoire européen*, Office des publications officielles des Communautés européennes, Luxembourg.

CEC (1995), 'Cohesion and the Development Challenge Facing the Lagging Regions', *Regional Development Studies*, no. 24, Luxembourg.

CEC (1999), *European Spatial Development Perspective: Towards Balanced and Sustainable Development of the Territory of the EU (ESDP)*, Luxembourg.

CEC (2000), *Spatial Perspectives for the Enlargement of the European Union*, *Regional Development Studies*, no. 36, Luxembourg.

CEC (2004), *A New Partnership for Cohesion: Convergence,Competitiveness, Cooperation, Third Report on Economic and Social Cohesion*, Luxembourg.

CEC (2005), Cohesion Policy in Support of Growth and Jobs, *Community strategic guidelines 2007–2013*, Luxembourg.

CEMAT (Conference of EU Ministers of Spatial Planning) (2005), *Scoping document and summary of political messages for an assessment of the Territorial State and Perspectives of the European Union towards a stronger European territorial cohesion in the light of the Lisbon and Gothenburg ambition*, 20/21 May 2005, Luxembourg.

Ceshire, P. and Hay, D.G. (1989), *Urban Problems in Western Europe*, London: Unwin.

Christaller, W. (1950), 'Das Grundgerüst der Räumlichen Ordnung in Europa', *Frankfurter geographische Hefte*.

CoE (Conseil de l' Europe) (1968), *Regional Planning a European Problem*, *Report of the Consultative Assembly*, Strasbourg.

CoE (Conseil de l'Europe) (1984), *Recommendation R 84/2 Du Comité des Mnistres aux États Membres Relative a La Charte Européenne de l'Amènagement du Territoire*, Adoptée par le Comité des Délégués des Ministres le 25 Janvier, Strasbourg.

CoE (Conseil de l' Europe), (ed.) (1991), *Schema Européen d'Aménagement du Territoire*, présenté par Nicolas Momper a l'occasion dur 8 ieme session de la CEMAT à Lausanne 1988, Strasbourg/Luxembourg.

Dabinett , G. and Richardson, T. (2005), 'The Europeanisation of Spatial Strategy: Shaping Regions and Spatial Justice through Governmental Ideas', *International Planning Studies*, vol.10, no. 3–4, pp. 201–218.

Damette, F. (1997), 'Wie steht es um das Europäische Raumentwicklungskonzept?', *EUREG-Europäische Zeitschrift für Regionalentwicklung*, vol. 6, pp. 17–21.

David, C. (2005), 'Zur Konvergenz der nationalen Raumordnungspolitiken Frankreichs und Deutschlands im Post-EUREK Process', *Raumforschung und Raumordnung*, vol. 63, no. 1, pp. 11–20.

Davoudi, S. (2005), 'ESPON-Past, Present, and Future', *Town and Country Planning*, vol. 74, no. 3, Special Issue on European Spatial Planning, pp. 100–102.

Dickinson, R.E. (1967), *The City Region in Western Europe*, London: Routledge.

Doucet, P. (2005), *Territorial Cohesion of Tomorrow: A Path to Co-operation or Competition*, Paper presented to the AESOP-Conference in Vienna.

Duehr, S. (2003), 'Illustrating Spatial Policies in Europe', *European Planning Studies*, vol. 11, no. 8, pp. 929–948.

Duehr, S. and Nadin, V. (2005), 'The European Agenda and Spatial Planning in the UK, *Town and Country Planning*', vol. 74, no. 3, Special Issue on European Spatial Planning, pp. 83–85.

Faludi, A. (2000), 'The European Spatial Development Perspective – What next?', *European Planning Studies*, vol. 8, no. 2, pp. 237–250.

Faludi, A. (2001), 'The Application of the European Spatial Development Perspective: Evidence from the North-West Metropolitan Area', *European Planning Studies*, vol. 9, no. 5, pp. 663–675.

Faludi, A. (ed.) (2002a), *European Spatial Planning*, Lincoln Institute for Land Policy, Cambridge: MA.

Faludi, A. (2002b), 'Positioning European Spatial Planning', *European Planning Studies*, vol. 10, no. 7, pp. 897–909.

Faludi, A. and Waterhout, B. (2002c), *The Making of the European Spatial Development Perspective: No Masterplan*, (The RTPI Library Series), London: Routledge.

Faludi, A. (2004), 'The Open Method of Co-ordination and "Post-regulatory" Territorial Policy', *European Planning Studies*, vol. 12, no. 7, pp. 1019–1033.

Faludi, A., (2005a), 'Territorial cohesion; an unidentified political objective', Town Planning Review vol. 76, No.1, 1–13.

Fauldi, A. (2005b), 'Polycentric territorial cohesion policy', *Town Planning Review*, vol. 76, no. 1, pp. 107–118.

Jensen, O. B. and Richardson, T. (2004), *Making European Space: Mobility Power and Territorial Identity*, London: Routledge.

Klein, R., Kunzmann, K.R., Frhr von Malchus, V., Tönnies, G. und Wolf, K., 'Comments on the Draft of a European Spatial Development perspective (ESFP)', *EUREG-Europäische Zeitschrift für Regionalentwicklung*, vol. 6, pp. 37–41.

Krätke, S. (2001), 'Strengthening the Polycentric Urban System in Europe: Conclusions from the ESDP', *European Planning Studies*, vol. 9, no. 1, pp. 105–116.

Kunzmann, K.R., Jenssen, B., Lemke, M. und Rojahn, G. (1977), 'A Concept for a European Region Policy Council of Europe', *European Regional Study Series*, 3, Strasbourg.

Kunzmann, K.R. (1978), 'Anmerkungen zur Erstellung einer Charta der Europäischen Raumordnung, Informationen zur Raumentwicklung', *Bonn-Bad Godesberg*, vol. 11/12, pp. 939–948.

Kunzmann, K.R. (1982), 'The European Regional Planning Concept', *Ekistics*, vol. 49, no. 294, pp. 217–222.

Kunzmann, K.R., (1984), 'The European Regional Planning Concept', Council of European, Regional Planning Study Series, No. 45 (Appendix), Straßburg 1983, 28–39.

Kunzmann, Klaus R. (1984a), 'Eine Raumordnungskonzeption für Europa? Methodische und inhaltliche Annäherungen', in: *Akademie für Raumforschung und Landesplanung (Hg.)*, Ansätze zu einer europäischen Raumordnung, Forschungs-und Sitzungsberichte, Bd. 155, Hannover, pp. 53–72.

Kunzmann, K.R.(1984b), 'Gedanken zur Erstellung eines Raumordnungskonzeptes für Europa', *Berichte zur Raumforschung und Raumplanung (Wien)*, vol. 28, no. 1, pp. 3–10.

Kunzmann, K.R. und Wegener, M. (1991), 'The Pattern of Urbanisation in Western Europe 1960–1990', Report for the Directorate General XVI of the Commission of the European Communities as part of the study 'Urbanisation and the Function of Cities in the European Community', *Schriften des Instituts für Raumplanung*, vol. 28, pp. 1–67.

Kunzmann, K.R. (1992), 'Zur Entwicklung der Stadtsysteme in Europa', *Mitteilungen der Österreichischen Geographischen Gesellschaft, Wien*, vol. 134, pp. 25–50.

Kunzmann, K.R. (1993), 'Geodesign: Chance oder Gefahr?', *Informationen zur Raumentwicklung*, no. 7, pp. 389–396.

Kunzmann, K.R. (1994), 'Defending the National Territory: Spatial Development Policies in Europe', in: F. Knipping Hg. (1994) *Federal Conceptions in EU Member States: Traditions and Perspectives*, Nomos, Baden-Baden, pp. 300–315.

Kunzmann, K.R. (1998), 'Planning for Spatial Equity in Europe', *International Planning Studies*, vol. 3, no. 1, pp. 101–120.

Kunzmann, K.R. (1998a), 'AESOP: Raumplanung in Europe vernetzt', in: *Vereinigung für Stadt-, Regional- und Landesplanung (SRL) e.V. Hg. (1998) Stadtplanung und Städtebau: Positionen finden – Überzeugungen vermitteln*, Festschrift für Dieter Frick, SRL Schriftenreihe 43, Berlin, pp. 197–208.

Kunzmann, K.R. (1998b), 'Spatial Development Perspectives for Europe 1972–1997', in Christer, B. and Böhme, K. (eds), *The Progress of European Spatial Planning, Nordregio*, vol. 1, pp. 49–59.

Kunzmann, K.R. (2001), 'Aménagement du Territoire en Allemagne: Le Pouvoir de Persuasion', Echos du Conseil Général des Ponts et Chaussées, 32: 7.

Kunzmann, K.R. (2001a), *La 'Banane bleue 'est morte! Vive la 'Grappe européenne '! Les Cahiers du Conseil*, Numéro spécial 'Espace Européen & Politique Française des Transports', (Conseil Général des Ponts et Chaussées, Ministère de l'Equipement des Transports et du Logement), Paris, vol. 2, pp. 38–41.

Kunzmann, K.R. (2000), 'Strategic Spatial Development through Information and Communication', in: Salet, W. and Faludi, A. (eds) *The Revival of Strategic Spatial Planning*, Royal Netherlands Academy of Arts and Sciences, Amsterdam, pp. 259–266.

Kunzmann, K.R. (2005a), 'Unconditional Surrender: The Gradual Demise of European Diversity in Planning', in: *AESOP Yearbook 2004*, Oxford: Brookes University, pp. 17–26.

Kunzmann, K.R. (2005b), *Does Europe really need another ESDP? And if yes, how should such an ESDP + look like*, Manuscript of a lecture, given at the Dipartimento Archittetura e Pianificazione, Politecnico di Milano, 10 December 2003, (in print).

Kunzmann, K.R. (2006), 'Which Future for the European Spatial Development Perspective?' (Power Point Presentation) Seminar, Regional Policy and Spatial Planning, Background and Prospects, Brussels, DG Regio, 16 January 2006.

Mudrich, G. (1980), 'Europäische Raumordnung: Aktuelle Probleme und Auifgabenfelder', ARL Arbeitsmaterialien, 44, Hanover.

Schäfer, N. (2003), 'Ansätze einer Europäischen Raumentwicklung durch Förderpolitik-das Beispiel INTERREG', *Schriften zur Raumordnung und Landesplanung*, Bd. 14, Augsburg, Kaiserslautern.

Schlögel, K. (2006), 'Im Raume lesen wir die Zeit: Über Zivilisationsgeschichte und Geopolitik', Frankfurt, Fischer Taschenbuch Verlag.

Schoen, P. (2005), 'Territorial Cohesion in Europe?', *Planning Theory and Practice*, vol. 6, no. 3, pp. 389–399.

Stiftel, B. and Watson, V. (2005), 'Building global integration in planning scholarship', in: *Dialogues in Urban and Regional Planning*, London: Routledge, pp. 1–14.

Sykes, O. and Shaw, D. (2005), 'Tracing the Influence of the ESDP on Planning in the UK', *Town and Country Planning*, vol. 74, no. 3, Special Issue on European Spatial Planning, pp. 108–110.

Tewdwr-Jones, M. (2005), *Spatial Planning: Creating the conditions for distinctive places*, (Power point manuscript), London: Bartlett School of Planning.

Williams, R.H. (1996), *European Spatial Policy and Planning*, London: Chapman.

Chapter 4

Spatial Planning in the Economic Core of Europe: The Transition from Land-use Planning to Spatial Structure Planning in Flanders

Joris Scheers

Introduction

Flanders, located in northern Belgium, is positioned at the centre of the economic core of the European Union. The region is one of the most prosperous and affluent in Europe. The region's spatial and economic position is clearly positive, yet it gives rise to a series of particularly demanding spatial challenges. Flanders also records a high figure for Gross Domestic Product per capita, estimated in 2004 to be approximately 26,000 Euros (see Planbureau, 2005). However, sustaining such high living standards in the future is far from being assured. Policy-makers are faced with a series of complex issues, including high rates of tax and increasing labour costs, as well as unemployment rates measuring 8.7 per cent in 2005. In addition, many of the traditionally important economic activities for the region, such as car manufacturing and textile production, have relocated to some of the new, developing economies of Europe as well as to Asia. Economic restructuring has also been accompanied by an increasing number of environmental challenges, such as increasing energy consumption and pollution arising from traffic congestion. These various factors raise important questions on the future of the region and the various kinds of policy interventions that can address these complex, multifaceted issues. The region, like many other parts of Europe, witnessed a growing societal awareness of environmental issues during the 1990s. Pressures on the environment and the importance of environmental quality are recognised very clearly within the context of the region's densely populated settlements, with the region experiencing population densities of 443 inhabitants per square kilometre. It became clear that a rather neo-liberal spatial policy, effected by a traditional land-use planning system based on regulation via a building permit system, was not sufficient as a means of addressing the complex spatial challenges facing the region. It simply did not provide either the appropriate instruments for managing change or offer effective solutions. The Flemish Government therefore embarked in the early 1990s on a process of reorienting the system towards strategic spatial planning, known in Flanders as spatial structure planning. An established legal framework for spatial structure planning has since been put into place. A considerable body of experience has now also been built up in Flanders of implementing such plans at the regional and local levels. The new system of spatial structure planning is a significant departure from the earlier land-use planning system, and previous practices now appear retrospectively as rather historic and antiquated.

The experience in Flanders of developing and implementing a new form of strategic spatial planning over more than a decade is one of the key reasons for its inclusion here as an example of spatial planning practice. Clearly, many of the challenges faced in Flanders are different to those faced in many other parts of the European Union, especially in the new member states in the Baltics and in the Celtic periphery. Nevertheless, there are important methodological lessons that can be learnt from experience in Flanders and that have far wider relevance. This chapter uncovers these through firstly identifying the background to the emergence of spatial structure planning in the region. The context for the transition to the new form of planning is outlined before addressing the process by which the spatial structure plan was prepared, as well as the plan's content. The account then focuses on the achievements of the spatial structure plan and the lessons that can be drawn on the implementation of the plan. This is arguably the area in which a case study of planning in Flanders can make the most significant contribution to the study of spatial planning more generally. The chapter concludes with some consideration of the forthcoming revision of the Flemish spatial structure plan 'Ruimtelijk Structuurplan Vlaanderen'.

Political and Institutional Context

Belgium has since the beginning of the 1970s been engaged in significant processes of state transformation in which a nineteenth century 'nation state' concept has given way to a fully-fledged federal state system. For certain issues, this operates as a de facto confederal state. Two distinct types of sub-national identities have formed around a series of complex linguistic and cultural differences. First, a range of important regional territorial issues such as urban renewal, transport, regional economic development and environment were transferred to three regions. These regions – the Flemish region, the Walloon region and the Brussels Capital region – are each fully responsible for the above range of functions. Second, a range of 'person-bound' issues, such as education and culture, were transferred to three communities: the Flemish, the French-speaking and German-speaking communities. This resulted in a complex set of governance arrangements as a consequence of Belgian state reform. Five new governments and parliaments were created, in addition to the national government, to accommodate the six new sub-national identities. One of the consequences of these state and institutional reforms is that spatial planning has become a fully autonomous competence of the region, with the national level now having no specific competence in spatial planning (see Van der Lecq (2002) and Kerremans and Beyers (1998)).

The Genesis of Structure Planning in Flanders

It is against the complex background of state reform in Belgium that the Flemish government started to think about introducing a new spatial planning act. The Flemish government had inherited a Belgian act of 1962 that set out a very traditional form of land-use planning. This was felt to be deficient in addressing the visions, challenges and priorities facing the Flemish government. The introduction of a new form of spatial structure planning was preceded by some methodological studies and experiments carried out by universities in Leuven and Gent, selected private consultants and a wide range of local governments. Based on these studies, a group of professional planners was commissioned in 1992 to develop a Flemish Structure Plan. A Spatial Planning Decree was later voted for in July 1996 and the Spatial Structure Plan for Flanders was approved in September 1997. In doing so, the Flemish region replaced the previous system of planning with a new, action-oriented strategic planning methodology known as structure planning.

The emergence of structure planning took considerable time, with some sixteen years between the granting of specific competencies in spatial planning to the Flanders region and the adoption of the Flemish Spatial Planning Decree. Yet the various spatial planning challenges that had emerged in Flanders during that time established a pressing context for the Structure Plan. Some of the more important planning challenges facing the region include:

- the changing use of and pressures on rural areas, with subsequent loss of certain landscape qualities and economic potentials;
- increasing levels of traffic and consequent congestion and pollution difficulties;
- decline of both physical and social fabric in urban areas;
- and the various difficulties created by ad hoc decision making in the absence of clear strategy for securing new investment initiatives.

These various issues combined to push the Flemish authorities towards the development of a clear, long-term vision for the future spatial development of Flanders. The planning process was guided by a clear set of aims established early on in the process. These included the desire to shift from a relatively passive form of planning towards a more action-oriented style of planning. These aims also included moving towards a more sustainable approach to planning, as well as ensuring planning was undertaken with a much more positive attitude. These aims could not, if was felt, be easily achieved with the existing range of planning instruments. New, innovative and more adequate spatial instruments were considered necessary to develop solutions to the various spatial demands of sectors such as housing, the economy, nature and environmental protection and so on, and to respond effectively to these within the context of fierce international competition (see Albrechts, 1998).

The Design and Organisation of the Structure Planning System

Structure planning introduces a 'three-times-two tier system' in which three different tiers (national/regional, provincial and municipal) each prepare a structure plan and a series of implementation plans (see Figure 4.1). Specific planning competencies are granted to each of the three levels. Each level is responsible for the two basic tools in order to implement its spatial policies. The spatial structure plan is a document that addresses the wider area and is then developed through a set of spatial implementation plans for area-specific developments. The spatial implementation plans can only be developed following the approval of the spatial structure plan. The spatial structure plan incorporates a clear analysis of the existing spatial structure and a set of prognoses, as well as a long-term spatial vision and a set of strategic objectives. The long-term vision presented in the structure plan is envisaged as covering a period of 10 years. This is intended to ensure that the vision engages at least two government terms in office and enjoys some stability in the face of ad hoc pressures to alter or adapt the agreed vision. However, no less than four Flemish governments were engaged in the preparation of the Flemish structure plan approved for the period 1997–2007. The process of preparing the structure plan was initiated by the government in office between 1991 and 1995, which outlined the framework and developed it as part of its political agenda in the period leading up to elections. The second government in office between 1995 and 1999 made many of the significant political decisions on the structure plan and approved it, while a further government (1999–2004) effectively carried out the plan and its implementation. The present government, (2004–2009), the fourth in the evolution of the Flemish structure plan, will continue to implement the plan through to 2007 and also oversee the revision of the first plan.

Figure 4.1   Three-times-two tier system

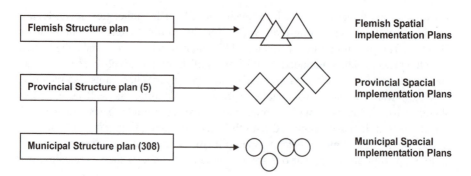

The strategic objectives expressed in the Spatial Structure Plan are especially important as they are legally binding on public authorities and are subject to clear and specified procedures. The strategic objectives may be regarded as the core planning decisions or issues that the government is politically required to realize and give effect to. These must be expressed in a manner that makes them realistic and capable of clear interpretation and implementation. They cannot be expressed in vague, non-specific or overly ambitious terms. However, while the strategic objectives are legally binding on public authorities, they are not legally binding on individual citizens. In addition, the strategic objectives cannot be used when evaluating an application for a building permit or an investor's proposals or plan. This is the role of a spatial implementation plan that needs to be prepared for a specific area. The contents of a spatial implementation plan may include traditional land-use prescriptions, but could also incorporate spatial management and planning issues as well as time-related conditions. The most important characteristic of the spatial implementation plans is their direct link with the structure plan. The implementation plans can only implement the clearly stated spatial vision contained in the structure plan.

Subsidiarity as a Guiding Principle for Spatial Planning

Subsidiarity is one of the most important principles framing the system of spatial structure planning. In the system outlined above, in which each of the three political-administrative levels prepares a structure plan and associated implementation plans, subsidiarity has an important role in determining the allocation of responsibilities and functions between the three levels. Each level is able to develop its own vision and draw up area-specific implementation plans for those sites they wish to promote for development, taking into account the issues that are at stake at that level. The concept of subsidiarity has been promoted in various different contexts, including in the development of Canon law (see Scheers and Vega, 2001). However, subsidiarity is most commonly understood as a principle in relation to the development of the powers of the European Union, including its relationships to and division of responsibilities with individual nation states. The concept has always been implicit in European Union discourse as is evident from basic legislation emanating from the 1950s, and has also been reflected in environmental legislation during the 1980s. Nevertheless, the concept of subsidiarity was made central and more explicit with the 1991 Maastrict Conference on the Political Union. Some commentators have highlighted how the subsidiarity principle enabled the transfer from the European Economic Community to the European Union (see Cass, 1992; Schilling, 1995).

The subsidiarity principle is defined in article 3b(2) of the Maastrict Treaty as meaning that the Community shall take action only *if and so far as the objectives of the proposed action cannot be sufficiently achieved by the Member States and therefore, by reason of the scale or effect of the proposed action, be better achieved by the Community* (cited in Schilling, 1995). The definition is framed in a way that relates to two different political-administrative levels. Toth (1994) sees the subsidiarity principle as a 'double-edged sword' that prevents both the higher and the lower levels taking an action in areas properly falling within each other's respective sphere of action. The definition is however, within the preamble to the Maastricht Treaty, broadened to include relationships between society and state and between actors within the same level, indicating that *decisions are to taken as closely as possible to the citizen*. Some aspects of the concept of subsidiarity were formalised at the meetings of the European Councils held in Birmingham and Edinburgh during the second half of 1992. The meetings developed a protocol on the application of the concept of subsidiarity. Some of the most important aspects of the protocol were: firstly, the notion of subsidiarity as a dynamic concept, adaptable to changing functions and circumstances; and secondly, the clear determination of the competencies of higher-levels in order to avoid or overcome fears of dominance by higher administrative or political levels (see Scheers and Vega, 2001). It is in the combination of both definitions that the subsidiarity principle becomes even more clearly a means of protecting or maintaining the advantages of the lowest political and administrative level. Interpreted in this way, it protects the use of powers by the level of government best able to achieve a certain objective against the encroachment of another level (see also Schilling, 1995).

The principle of subsidiarity clearly has a juridical, administrative-organizational background. It was initially used within organisations wanting to deal with complex and changing issues, and in turn affecting their overall internal organisation and the relationships between their different organisational levels (see Scheers and Vega, 2001). The concept provides an important guideline for managing political decision-making processes and procedures, including the relationship between different levels of government. As an instrument, it is capable of delimiting the different spheres of competence between the individuals, organisations and institutions that make up any particular society. A vertical expanding structure can be constructed from the most basic levels and ascending to more complex communities, based on criteria such as efficiency, equilibrium and need, that helps to determine the most appropriate level for decision-making. Spatial planning is an activity that deals with a wide range of complex issues, with each of them affecting the use of space within a particular territory. There is also a very clearly established link between spatial planning and decision-making processes, as well as with technical and political organisation and general administration within such territories. It is therefore not at all surprising that the concept of subsidiarity has been a necessary and useful one in acting as a guiding principle for spatial planning. The concept is one that is adaptable to specific situations or operational objectives, and it has been adapted to spatial planning in new ways and subsequently re-interpreted.

Spatial planning is about setting substantive and procedural frameworks and principles to guide the location and quality of development and physical infrastructure. It consists of a set of governance practices for conceiving, developing, implementing and monitoring strategies, plans, policies and projects, and for regulating the location, timing, type and form of development (see Healey, 1997). Planning is indivisibly part of social reality and cannot be understood solely as a technical activity, separate and divorced from its ethical implications (Albrechts, 1997). The planner, when engaged in defining terms such as 'optimal', 'better', 'efficient' or 'sufficient' within the context of the principle of subsidiarity is inextricably involved in the determination of who gets what, when and how. This is equally the case in applying such terms and concepts to the activity of spatial planning. Spatial planning in the context of sustainable development means focusing on the pursuit of welfare and social justice, taking account of power, inequalities, economic relations and modes of capitalist production, as well as the cultural production of gender, race and ethnicity. In other words, it is about a complexity of multiple structuring forces (see Swyngedouw, 2000 and Healey, 1997b). This complexity actively shapes space, and so the spatial planner has to be aware of all of these elements as well as aware of the direction and impact of 'technical' solutions proposed by him or her in this field. Subsidiarity might be conceived in this context as a multifunctional and complementary element of the political-territorial organisation of a state.

The Flemish Structure Plan, the highest level in the structure planning framework, operationalises the principle of subsidiarity by specifically indicating the planning elements that are at stake at each of the three levels. Firstly, it identifies as the responsibility of the Flemish government those aspects of the spatial structure that it considers appropriate to the national/regional level. Responsibilities for different aspects of spatial planning are made more transparent and credible by this process, and provincial and local level responsibilities are also made clear. The identification of new regional economic development zones, for example, is clearly identified as a responsibility of the Flemish government. They may be located only in a specified and listed number of urban areas and economic nodes or networks. This will include specification of a fixed number of hectares for the entire planning period and indicate a number of different functions or types. Local governments, on the other hand, can identify and develop new economic development areas up to 5 hectares, so long as they are related functionally to their immediate surroundings, located close to an existing centre and are constituted of small parcel lots. Additional land or identified areas for housing are typically located in close relation to existing urban areas in an attempt to prevent continued urban sprawl. To facilitate this, the Flemish structure plan categorises 56 urban areas, quantifies global housing needs and specifies a minimum percentage of all housing, currently standing at 60 per cent, to be located in existing urban areas. The Flemish authorities take responsibility for the 13 largest urban areas, with the remaining 43 being the responsibility of the provincial authorities.

The dynamic and negotiated nature of the concept of subsidiarity, as well as the situational differences arising in relation to different planning issues, together mean that standard or pre-defined solutions are not possible. The starting point for applying the principle of subsidiary in spatial planning must therefore be a managerial one. However, the managerial starting point is not one understood in terms of the public administration's efficiency or the qualitative organisation of the planning process. Instead, the managerial approach should be one based on the characteristics of the planning issue itself. This means that from the outset the issue itself will determine who will be best placed to take decisions, how the process of decision-making will be organised and how decisions will be implemented at the various scales. A planning issue can only be dealt with in this way if it is considered within an integrated approach and based on a consensus between the different decision-making levels.

The Importance of Process: '*A Structure Plan is Never but a Plan, A Structure Plan is Always a Process*'

Spatial developments over the past century have been guided by a series of traditional planning approaches. These are often typified as comprising several specified steps, including the conduct of a comprehensive survey and use of standardised planning concepts, in order to produce some form of masterplan that represented some desired end state to be realised via the planning process. Implementation of such 'blueprint' plans was often organised in a relatively technocratic manner, and sometimes neglecting to take into account or respond to social, budgetary or political changes occurring during the implementation phase. Strategic spatial planning as practised in the form of structure planning in Flanders aims to avoid many of the implicit criticisms of traditional planning approaches as outlined above. For example, strategic structure planning combines a long-term vision with a series of short-term actions. By doing this, it incorporates some flexibility into the plan in order to cope with and respond to new and emerging challenges. It can simultaneously deal with complexity and sustainability, while also involving important stakeholders in both the public and private sectors (see Healey, 1997b; Faludi, 1997, Albrechts 1997, 2001 and Van den Broeck, 1996). It starts with the recognition of space as an integrating framework. Space embraces peoples' social, economic, political, cultural and activities in a given time setting and deals with the countless relationships between them (Scheers, 2002). Spatial structures, as expressions of the interplay between these many relationships, therefore play a central role when planning the future development of an area, city or region. It is such a perspective that helps to explain the use of the term 'structure' planning (Ministerie Vlaamse Gemeenschap, 1997, p. 563).

In the Flanders context, for example, an already densely structured medieval urban network formed around navigable rivers was overlaid by an eighteenth century stone road network, a nineteenth century rail network and then a twentieth century highways network. This successive development of networks over time created a vast and dense network of nodes that in turn generated urban sprawl with resultant loss of environmental, landscape and quality of life features. Even the so-called Flemish Diamond, a core area that has traditionally functioned well in spatial terms, came increasingly under threat. This precipitated a spatial policy aimed at restructuring space, focused on identifying clearly defined urban areas and still predominantly open spaces. This policy became one of the main objectives of the Flemish structure plan.

A three-track methodology has been applied in a number of local structure plans in Flanders since the late 1970s (see 4.2). Each one has been adapted to its specific context, although the three main tracks are discernible in each of the cases. The tracks are as follows:

- Track 1: a process resulting in the establishment of a *long-term vision*, including the specification of general objectives, spatial concepts and an intended spatial structure. This track produces the long-term framework for policies with a spatial impact.
- Track 2: a series of stages focused on the development of *action-oriented decisions*. This track includes in-the-field management of opportunities and threats, including (often very) short-term implementation of sector projects, as well as urgent and strategic interventions.
- Track 3: a series of processes and actions focused on the *engagement and active participation* of all relevant actors at key stages of planning and decision-making.

The three-track methodology was developed to reflect the fact that preparing the local structure plans demanded a wide range of different and complementary planning skills at various stages of the plan-making process. The process was also different to traditional masterplanning approaches, particularly in how it emphasised a continuous, circular process of plan preparation rather than a linear one. The three tracks – long-term vision; action-oriented decisions; and participation and engagement – run in parallel rather than sequentially.

Figure 4.2   The three track process

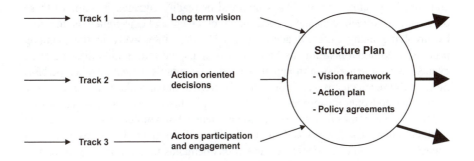

The three tracks, taken together, result in the production of a final spatial structure plan containing a long-term spatial vision that acts as a framework, an action plan and several different policy agreements. The first component acts as a frame of reference, almost acting as compass or strategic roadmap during the difficult and sometimes lengthy process of policy-making. Zonneveld and Faludi (1997, p. 7) define visioning and framing as 'a way of selecting, organising, interpreting and making sense of a complex reality so as to provide guideposts for knowing, analysing, persuading and acting'. People need a common dynamic and a set of clear objectives in order to recognise themselves as an individual, family or cultural entity. Visions and concepts,

Van den Broeck (2004) argues, create an image of a dynamic future and give meaning to isolated issues, measures and components. In Flanders, consensus on and support for the plan was secured based on the objective of safeguarding the high social and economic quality of life that was increasingly under threat. The second component is the more tangible one to all of the actors involved. It is a set of measures, actions and promises to be taken by the approving authority, directly related to the available resources and subject to political accountability. In the Flemish structure plan they took the form of clear categories of urban areas and roads in terms of their desired spatial function. This was complemented by a series of binding measures, such as the location of new housing areas, the identification of green areas where minimal economic growth is expected and other areas where significant economic growth in agricultural or economic sectors is planned. The final element is the inclusion of a number of signed policy agreements that commit the contracting partners to agreed actions or the financing of agreed investments. These arrangements often impact also on the various different sectors involved where partners, authority administrations and management are usually organised. In this way, implementation in accordance with the spatial vision is given effect. In Flanders, agreements were signed between the Flemish government and 13 of the largest urban areas and, in some cases, also involving the nationwide public transport company.

One of the main distinguishing characteristics of structure planning is its emphasis on a participatory approach to plan preparation. The concepts, structures and solutions proposed by planners and politicians are subjected at various stages to public scrutiny or issued for consultation. It is clear that 'the general public' and specific groups are not always involved or readily engaged in some of these processes. An effective means of securing involvement and engagement is therefore by involving many different actors or stakeholders intensively in the planning process. Traditional instruments such as workshops and information dissemination events have a role to play, although they need to be complemented by other, perhaps more useful mechanisms. Additional effort is needed in particular to achieve a more permanent and ongoing process of engagement. This involves providing various different opportunities for citizens and government to build mutual understanding and trust, empower stakeholders and citizens and help them to build their resources and capacity (see Albrechts, 1997). As stated, this demands that multiple opportunities for involvement need to be staged throughout the plan-making process. The task of dealing with space using a structure planning methodology requires all actors to participate in continuous democratic process aimed at achieving sustainable and quality places in which to work, travel and engage in recreation. It is worth emphasising again within the context of engagement of stakeholders, as one of the central principles of structure planning, that processes and approaches are designed around and inspired by the planning issue itself, rather than say the particular administrative, political or institutional requirements of the organisation steering it.

Planning Concepts and Metaphors in Structure Planning

The Structure Plan was conceived of and promoted as a strong policy tool able to respond with appropriate solutions to the various spatial challenges previously identified in relation to various sectors, including the economy, housing, protection of the natural environment, and the provision of infrastructure. The government coalition managed to convene the most important players who supported its own objectives of designing a different configuration of policies, plans and programmes that combined concerns for sustainability with international competitiveness. The government, with the support of a group of professional planners, devised a series of four spatial planning concepts as a means of focusing the attention and interest of the variety of stakeholders. This approach of selecting a limited number of key spatial planning concepts proved to be successful. It was successful both in terms of the provision of effective policies, and also in terms of communicating information and ideas. The selection of these key spatial concepts ensured the public could readily understand the need for a spatial structure plan and the complex issues that it addressed. The various partners on the coalition were also able to identify and understand the central policy issues being addressed in the plan. The four key spatial concepts on which the structure plan was based are:

- 'Deconcentrated clustering' acted as a first spatial planning concept. Deconcentration referred to the highly fragmented existing spatial structure, while clustering represented the essence of the new policy aimed at concentrating growth. The ongoing trend of sprawl had to be re-oriented to a more economic and qualitative use of space. The concept was based on the specific situation facing Flanders, in which high densities and concentrations of functions within a limited space is recognised as inhibiting the effective functioning of economic activities, efficient mobility and ecological protection.
- Ecological networks form another of the guiding spatial principles in the structure plan. These networks are formed around the existing river valleys, open areas and corridors and provide an articulating and ordering system for spatial development. The networks include a series of small and very small nature areas, although these are recognised as having particular significance within an otherwise very densely populated and highly developed urban context. Actions are required to integrate and strengthen this ecological network.
- Linear infrastructures and their role in structuring spatial development are identified as the third spatial concept. More sustainable forms of mobility network are achieved by the clustering of different modes of infrastructure, as well as through the establishment of investment priorities, the categorization of different networks and the upgrading of multi modal nodes.
- The fourth and final spatial concept is that of gates as motors for development. The different gates of national and international mobility networks are

reinforced as motors for development, keeping their historically developed functions and performances, and acting as important connections between Flanders, the north western European and the wider world.

These spatial concepts were complemented by a related metaphor. The planning team involved in preparing the structure plan for Flanders conceived the image of a 'Flemish Diamond'. The metaphor served a number of very important purposes. Firstly, it valorised the central position of Flanders in Europe and therefore provided Flanders with one of the necessary instruments to position itself within the context of fierce international competition and wider European strategic spatial planning exercises. Secondly, it provided a framework within which different cities like Antwerp, Ghent, Leuven and Brussels could be encouraged to work towards cooperation and collaboration, rather than see themselves as in competition with each other. By combining the complementary contributions of a network of Flemish cities, it was argued, the Flanders region could compete more effectively for inward investment against nearby urban networks like the Randstad, the Rhine-Ruhr and the Lille-Roubaix-Tourcoing area (Albrechts, Healey and Kunzmann, 2003). The rhetorical but powerful and 'bright' image of the Flemish Diamond signifies and reinforces the existing potentials of the Flanders region and provides the new spatial policy with a clearly recognisable and memorable image.

Evaluating Progress on the Flanders Structure Plan: 1995–2005

The Spatial Structure Plan for Flanders has had an enormous impact over the past decade on planning practice at all levels within the region. All policy decisions that affect the use of space are now carried out with reference to a clear and explicit spatial vision and its related spatial concepts. Policies and policy decisions that do not do so are no longer accepted. The spatial structure planning exercise has instigated a necessary change in attitudes towards planning, and has also promoted greater public involvement and political debate on spatial development issues. An entirely new planning methodology has been fully implemented at all levels and the principle of subsidiarity, so central to the reforms, has been accepted and is working. Real and substantial progress has been made. Some 131 out of a total of 308 municipalities had by the end of 2005 prepared an approved structure plan in either final or provisional form. A further 132 municipalities have started their planning process. More than 280 municipalities have installed a municipal spatial planning commission and more than 200 of them have employed qualified spatial planners to undertake the task of preparing structure and implementation plans. Dozens of municipal spatial implementation plans have been approved and more than 250 plans are currently in process. They all are being developed based on the long term vision, as outlined in the structure plan, and contain innovative spatial action-oriented instruments. These instruments differ from the old-fashioned layout

Figure 4.3   Spatial strategy diagram of the *Ruimtelijk Structuurplan, Vlaanderen* ('Spatial structure plan for Flanders')

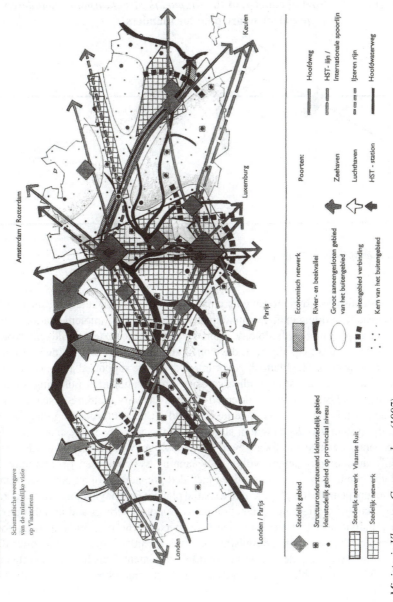

Kaart 1

Schematische weergave
van de ruimtelijke visie
op Vlaanderen

Amsterdam / Rotterdam

Keulen

Luxemburg

Parijs

Londen / Parijs

Londen

Steedelijk gebied

Structuurondersteunend kleinstedelijk gebied

kleinstedelijk gebied op provinciaal niveau

Stedelijk netwerk Vlaamse Ruit

Stedelijk netwerk

Economisch netwerk

Rivier- en beekvallei

Groot aaneengesloten gebied
van het buitengebied

Buitengebied verbinding

Kern van het buitengebied

Poorten:

Zeehaven

Luchthaven

HST - station

Hoofdweg

HST- lijn /
Internationale spoorlijn

IJzeren rijn

Hoofdwaterweg

Source: Ministerie Vlaamse Gemeenschap (1997)

plans and provide evidence that the move towards spatial structure planning has been successful at all stages, from vision through to implementation.

Figure 4.4   Spatial concept of the *Ruimtelijk Structuurplan Vlaanderen* ('Spatial structure plan for Flanders')

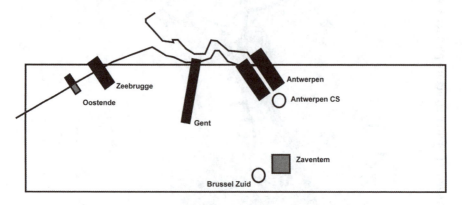

Source: Ministerie Vlaamse Gemeenschap (1997)

The Flemish government recognised that it would need to make significant investments in capacity building in many municipalities to support the implementation of the new structure planning methodology. It understood that the system could only work if the local levels were equally well developed and capable of organising and managing the new system. The Flemish government therefore supported a number of relevant activities, from assisting with organising consultations, to financing studies and projects and other activities oriented towards capacity building in spatial planning. Much of this activity was undertaken based on the understanding that the success of the system was dependent in large part on the capacity and responsibility for real decision power at the local level. Municipalities were guided towards becoming fully autonomous actors within the planning system based on attaining certain stated conditions. These conditions included preparation of an approved municipal structure plan, the employment of a spatial planner, and having three fully operational registers (of spatial implementation plans, building permits and un-built plots) that any individual can consult on-line or in person. The first municipalities formally became autonomous in administrative terms in 2005, some six years after the new integrated planning decree was passed by parliament. This has enabled them to act as a fully responsible and accepted actor in the planning system vis-à-vis the Flemish level.

Structure planning at the intermediate provincial level has also become fully mature. All five provinces now have an approved provincial structure plan. They have also expanded their planning department and installed spatial planning commissions. Each province has also started designing spatial implementation plans in order to realise the objectives stated in the spatial structure plan. Major changes have taken place to both the provinces' policies as well as their administrative organisation. For example, one of the important tasks for the past 150 years, the management of provincial roads connecting the main cities and sub-regions, has been completely revised and integrated in specific subsidiarity agreements. The different existing (and in some cases new) roads are no longer approached from an historical, administrative or technical point of view, but categorized according to their spatial function: to connect origin-destination areas, to gather or distribute traffic within these areas or to provide access to individual lots. These functions are equally applied to the surrounding national and international territories, and provincial, sub-local and local areas. This form of categorisation enables an appropriate design to be proposed, as well as providing indications for lower planning levels. The way in which the principle of subsidiarity has been applied illustrates that a form of planning and organisation that starts with the planning issue itself as the central factor can be successful. It allows that issue to be considered and decided upon at the right decision-making level, whether that means centralisation or decentralisation of decision-making capacity. Moreover, it shows that the principle of subsidiarity does not necessarily have to be interpreted as being applied in a top-down or bottom-up manner, but simply one that assigns a function to the most appropriate and effective level. In the Flemish case, for example, the international and regional connecting functions cannot be handled by local or sub-local levels. Similarly, it is not necessary or appropriate for the regional level to identify how issues of local road access should be addressed. Another example is provided by recreation and tourism policies, where the provincial level has integrated the established sector approach into its own spatial policies. This does not mean, however, that the different levels are not included whatsoever in the design or implementation of infrastructure. The subsidiarity principle has not always been applied rigidly across various planning practices in Flanders. Many examples illustrate provincial or Flemish spatial implementation plans taking up purely local issues, such as the change of a small industrial plot into a housing area for example, when conforming to the approved municipal structure plan. So, in conclusion, spatial structure planning demonstrates a series of successes in how it has become embedded as a key part of the planning system and in terms of its implementation. The merits of the spatial structure planning approach cannot, of course, be fully compared with a situation without structure planning. Nevertheless, it is clear and certain that a more integrated, less ad hoc and more consensus oriented approach has offered more opportunities for qualitative spatial solutions. These opportunities are not always fully taken into account when it comes to translating rather general sustainable spatial concepts and principles into practice. More effective and continuous monitoring still has an important contribution to make in this important respect.

Towards a Second Spatial Structure Plan for Flanders?

The structure planning approach demands that a regular evaluation be undertaken of the spatial policies that are produced. Regular review of spatial policies allows them to be amended or adjusted if necessary to account for new spatial patterns and trends within society, as well as providing opportunity to respond to new spatial demands or challenges with new visions and approaches. The planning legislation or decree introducing spatial planning within Flanders was designed to contain an enforced evaluation every five years. The 1999–2004 government, based on a series of political discussions and agreements, felt that revision of the spatial assignments for industrial zones and housing was necessary. In addition, a general administrative evaluation with respect to the process of making the structure plan was set up. This evaluation included an examination of the different policy options and the formulation of an 'action list' for further elaboration. The exercise concluded that the first political agreement was no longer felt to be valid. The preparation of a new Structure plan was also envisioned to cover the period 2007–2014, providing a series of complementary opportunities to review the spatial structure plan. The various decisions surrounding the spatial structure plan were brought into focus in a series of interesting political discussions during the formation of the new Flemish government in 2004. These resulted in an increased emphasis on the implementation of the 1997 Flemish structure plan, thereby confirming the various political options presented in the plan. An important document guiding this discussion was an independent external evaluation conducted by consultants (WES, 2003). The principal objective of this independent evaluation was to collect expert views on the long term developments, trends and challenges of relevance to the development of future spatial policy. A selection of 30 prominent experts from different domains was involved in a Delphi method piece of research. The general conclusion to the exercise was that the existing policy framework would remain both relevant and applicable for at least the short to medium term. The basic philosophy of structure planning and the Flemish SP itself were still broadly supported. However, when it came to specific and concrete solutions on-the-ground, the SP was found to lack specific instruments for a number of important themes, including the following:

- Preventing the further sprawl of urban activities and the resulting damage to the quality of open spaces;
- Providing a supply of accessible economic areas in proximity to urban regions;
- The relationship between sea harbours and their hinterland areas;
- Addressing the changing economic dynamics of areas outside of urban areas and the need for tailored approaches to address this; and
- The ongoing dominance of car-mobility.

The current Flemish government – elected for the period 2004–2009 and the fourth consecutive government to be involved in the structure planning process – was prompted to prepare a replacement plan for the period after 2007. Several background factors, including the limited period remaining of the 1997–2007 time horizon of the first structure plan, precipitated this decision. The Flemish government had decided already to continue in the meantime with the implementation of the existing structure plan. The review, rather than being a complete re-design of a totally new structure plan, was based on consolidating the principles of the current plan but subjecting it to a thorough evaluation. The new plan will include three separate components. Firstly, it will include a content evaluation of the validity of the policy statements established previously in 1997. It will also include an evaluation of the performance of the plan that analyses and takes into account the various points of view of the different actors involved. Special attention is being paid to the development of a 'partnership model' in order to secure the increased involvement of actors and stakeholders. Emphasis is also increasingly being placed on the sharing of information and knowledge between government and a wider array of stakeholders. A quantitative evaluation of the spatial structure plan, focused on establishing whether stated targets are actually being met, also forms part of the review of the plan. Finally, the 1997 data and information upon which the original Flemish structure plan was based are to be revisited and updated. This will involve analysing the wider European context for spatial planning activity, and include assessment of emerging trends and patterns of relevance to effective spatial planning and development. The Flemish government's position is one where it has decided to allow the structure planning methodology to further embed itself and mature at all administrative levels, rather than introduce another vision and restructuring of the planning system. The time horizon or scope for the new structure plan extends to the year 2020. Consequently, the discussion on the 2020 planning concepts will be held in the period leading up to the 2009 government elections.

Conclusions

The transition from a traditional land-use planning system to an alternative framework of spatial structure planning has clearly changed the way politicians and professionals approach and manage space in Flanders. A traditional land use approach, regulating private developments and proposing what are essentially infrastructural solutions to societal challenges, has been displaced by a more proactive approach to planning based on an explicit vision for spatial development that is shared by a wide range of stakeholders. Land use plans still form one of the instruments available for managing spatial change and regulating development. However, they are one among a range of different instruments that assist with the implementation of a spatial development strategy that is based on a political and social consensus and expressed in the form of a spatial vision for the region. This apparent shift away from simply regulating development is an important one. The new spatial structure planning approach works not by directing what various parties should do, but by framing all stakeholders' activities in order to address shared concerns on and achieve common aims for the future spatial development of Flanders (Albrechts, Healey and Kunzmann, 2003). The spatial vision and concepts are being promoted across a range of different actions at various levels. The implications and consequences of the Flemish structure plan cannot be neglected by local and regional authorities, government departments and private actors. These actors need to take account of the structure plan if they want to be able to achieve their social or economic goals. In short, they have to play the new rules of the game. This wide range of different stakeholders have successfully adopted the new structure planning methodology, as required by the planning laws of 1996 and 1999, and have also responded with a more professional attitude towards the activity of planning in order to cope with their new responsibilities. Figures identify that all regional authorities, and 85 per cent of local government administrations, have now embedded the new structure planning approach in their practices. The governance arrangements within the Flanders region are one of the more significant issues in relaying the case of the emergence of spatial structure planning. Subsidiarity is an important and carefully articulated concept in relation to the new structure planning approach. Different forms of governance can be developed at different levels using common spatial concepts, a shared vision and an established methodology. This new form of innovative, territorially-integrated spatial policy enables Flanders, as a region, to express and promote its spatial position and future development within Europe. Yet, at the same time, the structure planning approach also provides a framework for local and regional development. In the Flanders context, local and regional administrations assume full responsibility for the spatial development of their area, framed within the wider spatial vision for the region.

The effects of introducing the new approach to planning in Flanders are of course long term and therefore difficult to measure. Spatial planning in Flanders at all levels has certainly become more mature and will continue to do so. The process has made more apparent and explicit some of the hidden costs of urban sprawl, including the loss of productive land and quality open space, or the predominant and increasing emphasis on car mobility, for example. This in turn has led to changing perceptions of spatial policy priorities. The new system becoming mature also means that there needs to be a willingness to engage in continuous processes of evaluation and review – including responding to new situations and opportunities by altering or adapting the strategy – without losing sight of the long term vision and agreed sustainability objectives. The discussions in Flanders, following a decade of experience in managing the new system of spatial structure planning, illustrate the importance of devising new policy instruments and the dangers of adhering to the status quo. Accepted and applied strategic spatial concepts constitute important policy tools in 'framing' investments and developments. It is consequently necessary to monitor them continuously in order to guide the regional spatial vision over time through an uncertain and dispersed political context. The past decade's experience of strategic structure planning in Flanders offers interesting lessons for other regions in Europe, particularly in how spatial strategies take into account their specific spatial cultural, socio-economic, political and environmental contexts.

References

Albrechts, L. 1997, 'Genesis of a Western European Spatial Policy?', *Journal of Planning Education and Research*, vol. 17, pp. 158–167.

Albrechts, L. 1998, 'The Flemish Diamond: Precious Gem and Virgin Area', *European Planning Studies*, 6(4), pp. 411–424.

Albrechts, L. 2001, 'From Traditional Land Use Planning to Strategic Spatial Planning', in: Albrechts, L., Alden, J. and da Rosa Pires, A. (eds), *The Changing Institutional Landscape of Planning*, Aldershot: Ashgate, pp. 83–108.

Albrechts, L. 2002, 'The planning community reflects on enhancing public involvement: Views from academics and practitioners', *Planning Theory and Practice*, vol. 3, no. 3, pp. 331–347.

Albrechts, L., Healey, P. and Kunzmann, K. 2003, 'Strategic Spatial Planning and Regional Governance in Europe', *Journal of the American Planning Association*, vol. 69, no. 2, pp. 113–129.

Albrechts, L. and Swyngedouw, E. 1989, 'The challenges for regional policy under a flexible regime of accumulation', in: Albrechts, L., *et al.* (eds), *Regional policy at the crossroads, New perspectives for regional planning and development policies for the 1990s*, London: Jessica Kingsley, pp. 67–87.

Cass, D.Z. 1992, *The Word that saved Maastricht? The Principle of Subsidiarity and the Division of Powers within the European Community*, in CMLRev, 1107.

European Union/TERRA 1998, *Adopción de 14 proyectos de Ordenación regional/ especial*, http//cue.tsai.es/nco5.htm, Europa, (Digital Document).

Healey, P. 1997a, *Collaborative Planning, Shaping Places in Fragmented Societies*, London: Macmillan Press.

Healey, P. 1997b, 'An institutionalist approach to spatial planning', in: Healey, P., Khakee, A., Motte, A. and Needham, B. (eds), *Making Strategic Spatial Plans: Innovation in Europe*, London: UCL Press, pp. 21–36.

Kerremans, B. and Beyers, J. 1998, Belgium: 'The dilemma between cohesion and autonomy', in: Hanf, K. and Soetendorp, B. (eds), *Adapting to European Integration: Small States and the European Union*, London: Longman, pp. 14–35.

Loeckx, A., Shannon, K., Tuts, R. and Verschure, H. 2004 (eds), *Urban Trialogues: Visions, projects, co-productions, Localising Agenda 21*, UN-Habitat and PGCHS-KULeuven, Kenya.

Ministerie van de Vlaamse Gemeenschap, 1997, *Ruimtelijk Structuurplan Vlaanderen*, MVG.

Scheers, J. 1993, *El crecimiento urbanístico acelerado de Guayaquil y la necesidad de un marco referencial teórico para la planificación espacial en el Ecuador*, ISRO-KULeuven, Working papers Guayaquil, 1.

Scheers, J. and Vega, S. 2001, *Subsidiarity and Spatial Planning: An evaluation concept for Bolivia*, CEPLAG working paper 1, UMSS, Cochabamba.

Scheers, J. 2002, *Koffie en het Aroma van de stad*, PhD, KULeuven.

Schilling, T. 1995, *Subsidiarity as a Rule and a Principle*, or: *Taking Subsidiarity Seriously*, Harvard Law School, Working Paper.

Swyngedouw, E. 2000, 'Authoritarian governance, power and the politics of rescaling', *Environment and Planning D: Society and Space*, vol. 18, no. 1, pp. 63–76.

Toth, A.G. 1994, 'Is subsidiarity Justiciable?', *ELRev* 268, 19.

Van den Broeck, J. 1996, *Pursuit of a collective urban pact between partners*, Paper presented to the 31st ISOCARP International Congress, Sydney, Australia, September 1996.

Van der Lecq, R. 2002, 'Belgium in the ESDP', *Built Environment*, vol. 27, no. 4, pp. 278–286.

WES 2003, *Evaluatie RSV*, Document available at Ministerie Vlaamse Gemeenschap, Brussels.

Zonneveld, W. and Faludi, A. 1997, 'Vanishing Borders: The Second Benelux Structural Outline: Introduction (special issue)', *Built Environment*, vol. 23, no. 1, pp. 5–81.

Websites

www.planbureau.be.

PART III

Regional Development and Spatial Planning in the Celtic Periphery

Chapter 5

Increasing and Spreading Prosperity: Regional Development, Spatial Planning and the Enduring 'Prosperity Gap' in Wales

Neil Harris

Introduction

Wales provides an important case study of regional development and spatial planning. In the case of regional development, it is a region that has been a long-standing recipient of regional development aid and assistance stretching back over some 70 years or more. It is a testament to the difficulties of overcoming past dependence on extractive industries and heavy manufacturing and managing the process of economic restructuring over the best part of a century. In addition, its process of economic restructuring and the difficulties of its economic position have produced a dedicated organisational landscape – the most widely known element of which is the Welsh Development Agency established in 1976 – that has been emulated elsewhere. Wales has for some time had a regional system of economic governance of the kind that has found favour recently as Government policy and been extended to the English regions (see Lovering, 2001). Similarly, and more recently, Wales has provided one of the first British examples of the emerging activity of spatial planning. These factors, complemented by the recent establishment of a new democratic institution in the form of the National Assembly for Wales, make Wales a clearly justified case study in the field of regional development and spatial planning.

This introductory part of the chapter outlines the institutional context for regional development and spatial planning in Wales, focusing on the establishment of the National Assembly for Wales in 1999. It highlights the Assembly as an important actor in driving forward regional policy and spatial planning, building on the agenda crafted by the Welsh Development Agency over the past 30 years. It then provides a brief portrait of the region by way of context, highlighting the particular characteristic of high quality environment co-existent with acute economic problems. Finally, it outlines the key challenges for regional development and spatial planning in Wales, many of which arise from its economic past and the particular spatial distribution of activities this has resulted in. The main part of the chapter elaborates on the economic and regional development issues facing Wales, focusing on the difficulties faced in closing the 'prosperity gap' and ensuring a more even distribution of prosperity across Wales. The case study makes clear that while some successes can be claimed for regional development in Wales, other problems have persisted and remain prominently on the regional development agenda. Two particular policy responses by the National Assembly for Wales are discussed, namely the Assembly's National Economic Development Strategy *A Winning Wales* and its more recent spatial plan *People, Places, Futures*. The chapter's concluding section extracts the most important lessons that the case study provides for wider regional development and spatial planning activity, and highlights the future challenges for Wales in the context of regional development.

The Institutional Context for Regional Development and Spatial Planning

The single most important development in Wales' institutional context of the past 30 years has been the establishment of the National Assembly for Wales. The Assembly was established by the Government of Wales Act 1998 and marked a key point in the process of democratic devolution to Wales. A process of administrative devolution to Wales has occurred since 1964 with the establishment of the Welsh Office. The Welsh Office was established as a department of the United Kingdom government, designed to oversee government policies and programmes as they applied in Wales. In the 30 years following the establishment of the Welsh Office it became increasingly apparent that a 'democratic deficit' existed in Wales (Morgan and Rees, 2000, p. 136). This became particularly apparent from the early 1980s as the policies of successive Conservative governments, administered through the Welsh Office, failed to resonate with the traditionally Labour-voting population of Wales and industrial south Wales in particular. The policy-making process was for many perceived to be distant and remote, with the Welsh population able to exert little influence over the character and content of policies that applied to it (Morgan and Rees, 2000). The full story of the struggle to achieve democratic devolution for Wales is told elsewhere (see Morgan and Mungham, 2000). However, a few key points are essential by way of introduction. The decision as to whether to establish a National Assembly for Wales was determined by a referendum in 1997 in which a 'yes' vote was secured by an incredibly small margin and on an overall limited turn-out by the electorate. So, while this was sufficient to establish the Assembly it fell short of a clear and resounding vote of confidence in the notion of democratic devolution. Some have commented that this conferred limited legitimacy on the Assembly and signalled that significant policy success was necessary for the Assembly to convince the Welsh population of its worth (Morgan and Rees, 2000, p. 140). Finally, the establishment of the Assembly is closely connected to the prevailing economic context in Wales. This interrelationship is so close that one key politician – Ron Davies, who was soon to become the first Labour Secretary of State for Wales for some 18 years and acknowledged as the 'architect' of Welsh devolution – is cited as arguing that:

The case for a Welsh Assembly is as much about economic renewal as it is about political
renewal.   (Ron Davies, 1996, cited in Chaney *et al.*, 2000, p. 9)

In practical terms, the Assembly is a democratically elected body of some 60
Assembly Members that secure their seats through a combination of direct election
and proportional representation. Assembly Members may therefore represent either
local or regional constituencies. The leading political party has established, either
alone or through coalition, a Government that has adopted a cabinet format. The
Assembly is of particular interest as a political organisation in a British context for
its recent experience in coalition government and its hybrid combination of a cabinet
system of government and a committee system that is more characteristic of British
local government. In terms of its powers, the Assembly has had transferred to it the
various powers previously exercised by the Secretary of State for Wales through
the Welsh Office. This provides the Assembly with significant powers in respect
of policy formulation (including health policy, economic development, spatial
planning, environment, transport and so on), the making of secondary legislation
and the determination of its own spending priorities within its budget of almost £13
billion. However, the Assembly has no powers to make primary legislation and has
no tax-raising or tax-varying powers. Devolution to Wales has therefore been partial,
particularly when compared to that for Scotland, yet there is significant scope for the
Assembly to determine and act on its own priorities in spite of the constraints of its
devolution settlement.

Wales has a long-established institutional framework for the activity of regional
development. It has been fortunate in having a dedicated institutional infrastructure
for regional development for some 30 years in the shape of the Welsh Development
Agency (see below). Organised regional development activity in Wales stretches
back even further to the 1920s and 1930s when a crisis in unemployment first
emerged as a consequence of decline in the extractive industries – coal mining
and the extraction of materials for iron production – that the region was so heavily
reliant upon. The south Wales region became eligible for special assistance and the
early period of the twentieth century marked the start of its continuing profile as a
region in need of some form of regional aid or support. The Welsh Development
Agency is the primary organisation within an extensive organisational landscape
that has built up around the activity of regional development. It is complemented by
a large number of other organisations either on an all-Wales or local basis that have
complementary functions, including those focused on education and training, skills
development and business support. Given that the institutional context in Wales is
so well developed and established in the field of regional development, there is little
demand for the further establishment of institutions. Nevertheless, the key issue
in such institutionally 'thick' contexts becomes the co-ordination of the various
organisations and ensuring that end-users are not confronted with so complex an
array of organisations that knowing where to secure support and advice becomes
difficult. This has been countered through various attempts to provide 'one-stop
shop' initiatives and the Welsh Development Agency has been key to these.

The Welsh Development Agency – 'one of the oldest and largest regional development agencies in Europe' (Morgan,1998, p. 231) – features as a key part of the institutional landscape in Wales. The Agency – established by an Act of Parliament in 1975 – has a remit in both economic renewal and environmental improvement across Wales. Since its establishment in 1976, it has enjoyed a positive reputation for its extensive work within Wales. It has, however, been subject to various bouts of criticism in Wales, including for its governance arrangements and its perceived accountability (see Morgan, 1998, p. 233). The Agency has had to respond to such criticisms and other important changes in its context over its almost 30 year history. For example, its traditional approach was focused firmly on what Cooke and Morgan (1998, p. 152) describe as 'hard' infrastructure based 'on the triad of land reclamation, factory building, and inward investment'. The Agency has been criticised for elements of its traditional approach, particularly its disproportionate emphasis in the past on attracting foreign direct investment (Morgan and Rees, 2000, p. 134). Yet such an approach could not be sustained in the context of increasing budget constraints through the late 1980s and early 1990s and its present role is claimed to be more along the lines of a regional animateur (see Henderson and Thomas, 1999). This adjustment to the prevailing context has witnessed a greater focus during the past decade on facilitating innovation, supporting supply chain development and enhancing skills in the workforce – all important elements of what is referred to as the associational economy (see Cooke and Morgan, 1998). In addition, the Agency is claimed to have resolved during the latter part of the 1990s many of the earlier concerns on its accountability. However, this has occurred at the expense of some of its entrepreneurial edge as it has become more risk averse (Morgan and Rees, 2000, p. 153). One of the key roles that the Agency has played is as a surrogate for private business. It has come to adopt such a role as the business community itself is identified as having played a limited role in the formulation of regional development policies in Wales, both generally and specifically in relation to Objective 1 activities (see Morgan and Rees, 2000 and Royles, 2003 respectively). The Agency will be absorbed into the Assembly in 2006, marking an end to 30 years of relative independence as an organisation, with a view to delivering greater coordination of economic and regional development activities across Wales. This may deliver improved policy coordination and facilitate implementation of the Assembly's economic development framework, yet it also risks further diminishing some of the entrepreneurial aspects of the Agency's work.

The final key player in respect of the institutional context in Wales is local government. Wales has since 1996 had a system of unitary local government. The previous two-tier system of local government was dismantled in order to avoid duplication of services and clarify responsibility for the range of different services distributed across the two tiers. Each unitary authority – of which there are 22 covering Wales – is responsible for the full range of functions and services in its area from social services and education to transport, planning and environmental protection. The establishment of the Assembly has witnessed a renewed relationship with local government in Wales. The Assembly is now perceived to be closer and more accessible to local government than the former Welsh Office. In addition, the Assembly is reliant on a whole series of partnerships with local government for the implementation of its policies and the delivery of services.

Economy, Society and Environment: A Portrait of the Region

Wales – like several of the case studies in this text – is a country with a relatively small population and a dominant capital. It has a population of some 2.9 million people and also has a low population density when compared to neighbouring England. These characteristics attract comparison in particular with some of the Baltic countries. Its population is largely concentrated in the urbanised areas of south Wales and the smaller pockets of urban development in north-east Wales. The former has traditionally been the focus for urban development and incorporates the country's capital, Cardiff, a settlement of some 300,000 population. Cardiff, like all of the now significant urban centres in Wales, owes its existence to the significant industrialisation of south Wales in the nineteenth century. This pattern of urbanisation reflects the rapid transformation of parts of Wales from an agricultural economy to one based on heavy extractive and manufacturing industries that have since spiralled into decline.

Figure 5.1   Main features of the Welsh economy

- Expanding services sector;
- Declining employment in heavy industry;
- Over 40 per cent of UK steel production;
- Substantial investment by foreign companies;
- Second lowest UK regional GDP per head;
- Relatively low average earnings;
- Relatively low economic activity rates.

(*Extracted from Digital Europe, 2003, p. 1*)

Past trends and activity patterns have therefore left Wales with a distinctive economic profile and spatial distribution of activities. It has a series of distinguishing characteristics that provide a challenging context for undertaking the twin activities of regional development and spatial planning (see Figure 5.1). Central to painting a picture of the region are the inherent tensions that exist between Wales as a country with a relatively weak economic profile and one that also has extensive areas of protected landscape and countryside. Some 20 per cent of the region is designated as a National Park, with extensive areas of land subject to some other form of protective designation for landscape or other environmental purpose, such as heritage coast designation or various designations under European legislation. The recognised environmental quality of much of Wales' landscape and countryside provides the backcloth for significant economic and social problems. Statistical publications paint a disconcerting picture of Wales. It has the lowest educational attainment in A-levels in the United Kingdom, has one of the lowest employment rates in the United Kingdom, and has a population that draws more heavily on health services than any other region in the United Kingdom (Causer and Virdee, 2004, p. 21).

The Key Challenges for Regional Development and Spatial Planning

There exists a reasonable degree of consensus among both academics and policy-makers on what constitute the main challenges facing regional development in Wales. These include:

* Increasing economic prosperity;
* Raising economic activity rates and participation in the workforce;
* Improving both educational attainment and workforce skills;
* Continuing with the diversification of the Welsh economy as a response to continued economic restructuring.

Several of these are elaborated upon in the sections that follow. The principal challenges for spatial planning are not so readily apparent and are not the subject of the same degree of consensus. This is a reflection of the comparatively recent emergence of the practice of spatial planning at national level in Wales, particularly when contrasted with the well-established discourse on regional economic development that has emerged over a period of 30 years or more. Nevertheless, some key challenges for spatial planning are emerging. One of the central challenges relates closely to those on regional development more generally, and that is the necessity of ensuring a more even distribution of economic and other activities across Wales, alongside spreading prosperity. This in itself is dependent on a range of other spatial planning challenges, including improving the accessibility of particular parts of the Welsh territory. The particular challenges facing the activity of spatial planning in Wales are returned to in more detail in the following section.

Regional Development and Spatial Planning in Wales: The Key Issues

Introduction

Some of the key issues facing regional development and spatial planning in Wales have been introduced in the previous section. This section develops some of these and focuses first on the enduring 'prosperity gap' between Wales and other regions of the United Kingdom. Wales remains one of the poorest regions of the United

Kingdom and redressing this and its underlying causes have become the primary focus of regional development policy in Wales. The section then addresses one of perhaps the most significant testimonies to Wales' limited prosperity, not only within the context of the United Kingdom but also Europe – its eligibility for Objective 1 funding under the European Union Structural Funds. The importance of capitalising on Objective 1 funding in the period 2000–2006 is underlined in the Assembly's national economic development strategy, *A Winning Wales*, which has experienced a controversial and difficult history. The strategy is considered alongside progress towards the ambitious targets and outcomes that are expressed in the strategy. Finally, the section outlines the development of the Wales Spatial Plan, a new and innovative approach to addressing the spatial dimension of the Assembly's various policies and strategies.

Wales and the Enduring 'Prosperity Gap'

Various commentators documented the range of regional development challenges facing the Assembly on its inception. Hill *et al.* (1998) highlighted the important skills development challenges in Wales, pointing to the record in Wales of high economic inactivity rates, poor educational attainment and limited qualifications, coupled with poor numeracy and literacy skills among sections of the population. They pointed out too that increasing activity rates through a range of measures, including increased skills training, was central to addressing what is proving to be one of the most resilient features of the Welsh economy – the 'prosperity gap' between Wales and other regions of the United Kingdom. Wales has arguably achieved a series of successes, including attracting significant levels of foreign direct investment and reducing levels of unemployment to at or below the United Kingdom average over the past decade. However, even the most optimistic accounts of the transformation of the Welsh economy acknowledge the enduring nature of the prosperity gap between Wales and other regions of the United Kingdom (see Alden, 1996, p. 130). The figure for GDP/capita in Wales has remained fairly consistently within the region of 85 per cent of the UK average, although the Assembly's economic development strategy published in 2002 recorded Welsh GDP as standing at 80 per cent of the UK average. Others have put the issue even more succinctly and point to the long-term difficulty in raising prosperity in Wales:

> despite a decade of inward investment success, infrastructure improvement and structural changes, the regional economy entered the 1990s, as it had the 1980s, as the poorest region of the UK in terms of key indicators of personal economic well-being (Brand *et al.*, 1997, p. 219).

This situation, unfortunately, remains pretty much unchanged half way through the first decade of the twenty-first century. Indeed, the trend pattern for GDP/capita in Wales has been falling as a percentage of the UK average. Yet while GDP/capita figures decline, the political significance of the issue increases. One commentary written at the time of the establishment of the Assembly made fundamentally clear the political significance of the prosperity gap:

> Of all the measures by which the National Assembly will be judged none will as important as the challenge of raising the level of economic well-being ...
>
> (Morgan and Morgan, 1998, p. 163).

Improvements in manufacturing productivity, growth in the service sector in Wales and significant achievements in attracting foreign direct investment have not been translated into increased GDP/capita. This enduring prosperity gap is attributed to a range of factors and there are a number of different takes on the matter. One perspective, most clearly exhibited by Lovering (1999, 2001), is to question the claimed 'successes' of economic and regional development policy as applied in Wales, arguing that the attraction of FDI and the promotion of a competitive regional economy simply fail to understand the fundamentals of regional economic welfare. Indeed, Lovering (1999) describes the various policy options pursued in Wales (and elsewhere) as 'fictions', based on neither careful theoretical work nor empirical study. Other explanations are more pragmatic and identify the characteristic profile of the Welsh economy as the principal cause of the enduring prosperity gap. Brand *et al.* (1997, pp. 226–228), for example, point to the fact that the Welsh economy is underrepresented in fast-growing and high value-adding sectors, has low activity rates and workers experience comparatively low rates of pay.

Objective 1

European Union monies in the form of the Structural Funds have become increasingly significant in addressing regional development issues in the United Kingdom as domestic funding has been curtailed as a consequence of budget restrictions (Bristow and Blewitt, 2001, p. 1085). Securing European funding has therefore become an essential part of funding regional development initiatives in Wales as elsewhere. Wales has been a recipient of various European funding packages for some time, including funding through the European Regional Development Fund and the European Social Fund. Nevertheless, GDP/capita in West Wales and the Valleys in the late 1990s fell below the 75 per cent of the European Union average required for the award of Objective 1 funding. The securing of Objective 1 status for Wales for the period 2000–2006 has been variously described as 'a mixed blessing' (Morgan and Mungham, 2000, p. 207) and as 'a dubious privilege' (Munday *et al.*, 2001, p. 52). Hill (2000a, p. 1) likewise points to the differing interpretations that may be placed on Wales' Objective 1 status, regarding it as either 'a badge of failure' or 'as a new opportunity'.

Figure 5.2   Promoting a sustainable economy

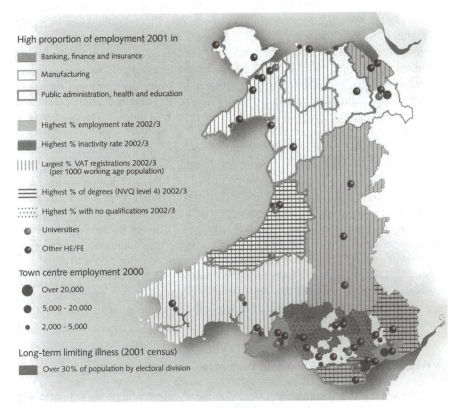

High proportion of employment 2001 in

▨ Banking, finance and insurance

☐ Manufacturing

☐ Public administration, health and education

▨ Highest % employment rate 2002/3

▨ Highest % inactivity rate 2002/3

||||| Largest % VAT registrations 2002/3
        (per 1000 working age population)

≡ Highest % of degrees (NVQ level 4) 2002/3

⋯ Highest % with no qualifications 2002/3

● Universities

● Other HE/FE

Town centre employment 2000

● Over 20,000

● 5,000 - 20,000

• 2,000 - 5,000

Long-term limiting illness (2001 census)

▨ Over 30% of population by electoral division

(Reproduced from the Wales Spatial Plan (2004)).
The map identifies the main centres of employment in Wales, as well as concentrations of inactivity.
In particular, it highlights some of the multiple challenges facing the former coalfield areas
in south Wales, focusing on high inactivity rates and lower levels of educational attainment.

Yet, Wales has not had a positive record of success in all previous funding packages, with underspend occurring or there being failure to fully capitalise on programmes due to inadequate match-funding or insufficient number of quality proposals (Morgan and Mungham, 2000, p. 207). Royles (2003, pp. 132–135) identifies how the early period of the Objective 1 funding period was similarly marred by a series of concerns, including limited involvement by the private sector, struggles among various interests to secure influence and a lack of organisational capacity. A long shadow was also cast over the awarding of Objective 1 status to west Wales and the Valleys by debate on securing match funding. One of the key questions was whether this had to be found within the Assembly's limited budget rather than by securing of funding from central government at Westminster and resulted in significant political debate (Bristow and Blewitt, 2000). Critical evaluations of the delivery and implementation of Objective 1 in Wales, one of the foremost of which is provided by Boland (2004), have not painted a picture of success. Boland (2004), for example, highlights how Wales appears not to have learnt the lessons from other regions' previous experiences of Objective 1 funding. Undertaking a review of Objective 1 at mid-point of the programme period, his account identifies 'significant shortcomings in both the design and delivery of Objective 1 in Wales' (p. 268) and questions the 'successes' claimed using official statistics. These concerns become even more pressing as the funding under Objective 1 is thought to be a 'one-off opportunity' with the accession of the new east European countries to the European Union (Royles, 2003, p. 131). The key question is whether this one-off opportunity has been seized upon and the 1.5 billion Euros of Structural Funds, along with match funding, has been used effectively. Eurostat figures published in 2005 and demonstrating GDP data averaged for the years 2000–2002 identify the NUTS II region of West Wales and the Valleys (aligning with the area in receipt of Objective 1 funding) as having a GDP/capita figure of 67 per cent of that for the EU15. Even with enlargement and accession of countries in Eastern Europe, that figure only increases to just below 74 per cent of the EU25, being below the 75 per cent threshold used to determine eligibility. The experience of Objective 1 funding in Wales therefore provides a number of important lessons for new member countries of the European Union, ranging from administering the funds to the real challenges of achieving structural change in the economy.

'A Winning Wales' – The National Economic Development Strategy

The Assembly, when it was established, was faced with finding a balance between securing some 'quick wins' in the field of economic development and addressing the obviously longer-term, structural weaknesses of the Welsh economy (Morgan and Morgan, 1998, p. 163). Its balance between these short-term and long-term issues is found in its national economic development strategy, *A Winning Wales*. The National Economic Development Strategy has been described as 'the most important and most politically contentious issue that has confronted the Assembly during the second session' (Storer and Cole, 2002, p. 113). Much of the controversy surrounding the strategy focused on its early consultation draft which was being prepared during the initial stages of the 2000–2006 Objective 1 programming period. Storer and Cole (2002, p. 117–118) report how the draft of the NEDS was criticised for its sketchy economic analysis, its general ambiguity and the establishment of targets for increasing GDP/capita that were deemed unachievable, leading to the rejection of the draft NEDS by the Assembly's economic development committee. The final strategy was issued early in 2002. It was based on an analysis of the Welsh economy published in 2001 and has since been subject to annual monitoring reports. A refresh of the strategy in early 2004 witnessed an adjustment of some of its key targets, while a further consultation exercise on the strategy was issued late in 2005.

The strategy, which adopts a 10 year time horizon, describes itself as one designed to deliver economic prosperity in Wales. It highlights the fact that while some limited parts of north-east and south-east Wales exhibit GDP/capita figures similar to the UK average, Welsh GDP/capita stands at 80 per cent of the UK average. Due to its persistent character, it will come as no surprise that addressing the prosperity gap 'has become the dominant focus of economic policy in Wales' (Hill, 2000a, 6). It therefore features prominently in the National Economic Development Strategy. *A Winning Wales* states:

> The Assembly Government's aspiration is that, within a generation, the standard of living in Wales will match that of the UK as a whole. Wales will become more prosperous and that prosperity will be sustainable and more evenly spread.
>
> (Welsh Assembly Government, 2002, p. 1)

This overall aim is supplemented by a series of targets relating to employment levels and participation rates, business start-ups, education and training and job creation. The strategy describes 'success' in achieving its aim as 'Welsh GDP per person rising from 80 per cent to 90 per cent of the UK average over the next decade – with the ultimate aim of achieving parity' (2002, p. 20). For comparison, Wales' GDP/capita figure presently stands at around 90 per cent of that for the EU25, with the UK figure almost 118 per cent (see also Chapter 2). Other targets stated in the strategy are acknowledged as being high-level, and some have been amended to become even more ambitious such as that for raising total employment, amended from a figure of 135,000 to 175,000 in order to achieve the desired closing of the prosperity gap. Annual monitoring statements for the strategy indicate a mixed picture, illustrating considerable success against some targets but not against others (National Assembly for Wales, 2003, 2004a). Successes arising out of the early stages of implementing the strategy relate mainly to the labour market in Wales, with valuable contributions being made to raising total employment and increasing labour market participation rates. However, other targets, such as those relating to exports and economic growth, were less positive and in some cases demonstrated a backwards step compared to the baseline figures for the year 2001. Much of this was attributed to prevailing conditions in the European and global economies, with the Assembly highlighting that 'The launch of A Winning Wales coincided with a difficult period in the global economy' (2004b, p. 21). So, overall, the Assembly's strategy is delivering some success, most notably in the labour market, yet it will need to deliver significant additional successes if it is to make progress towards its headline objectives of narrowing and ultimately closing the prosperity gap.

The Assembly has very recently issued a consultation document, titled *Wales: A Vibrant Economy*, designed to replace *A Winning Wales* as the Assembly's strategic framework for economic development (Welsh Assembly Government, 2005). This again highlights a series of successes in improving economic development in Wales, most notably in increasing total levels of employment and reducing levels of unemployment to at or below the average for the United Kingdom. The Assembly's priorities remain focused on increasing employment and raising the quality of jobs, while ensuring that increasing skills levels and improving education attainment support these objectives. Improving the quality of jobs in Wales is seen as a necessary part of addressing what is defined as a 'skewed' occupational profile in Wales, with senior positions being underrepresented. The consultation document also makes great efforts to play down the relevance of GDP/capita as a measure of economic performance, arguing that employment and earnings figures are more appropriate as measures of economic well-being, measures on which Wales compares more favourably.

Figure 5.3   Jobs and GVA by region

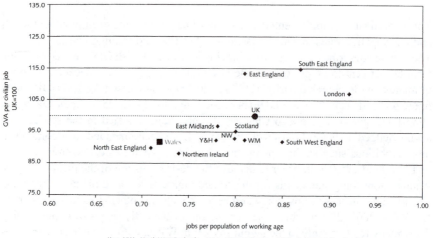

(*Reproduced from the Wales Spatial Plan* (*2004*))

People, Places, Futures: The Wales Spatial Plan

The preceding sections identified the aim of not only increasing prosperity, but also ensuring that it is spread more evenly. Ensuring that prosperity is spread more evenly has both social and spatial dimensions, with the latter in particular implying the need for some form of spatial strategy. The National Assembly for Wales has engaged since the year 2000 in the preparation of the Wales Spatial Plan following the making of a commitment in its first strategic plan to the preparation of a national spatial planning framework. This commitment represented an innovation in the context of the British planning system, a context which had increasingly been criticised for being despatialised, lacking in strategic capacity and with limited attendance to important issues of place (see Vigar *et al.*, 2000, Healey, 1998, 2001).

The Assembly is not the only devolved administration in Britain that has engaged in the preparation of a national strategic spatial plan (see, for example, the case study on Scotland in this volume), and the initiative on Ireland's National Spatial Strategy has had a marked influence on that in Wales. Nevertheless, the early and clear commitment of the Assembly to prepare a national spatial planning framework was widely welcomed among planning interests in Wales. The proposed document was seen to be, among other things, a potential solution to the limited strategic planning capacity that existed in Wales following the reorganisation of local government in 1996. Some 25 local planning authorities across Wales have been responsible for land use planning in Wales since reorganisation, with this giving rise to concerns that strategic issues, such as significant transport projects and the identification of major inward investment sites, were not being addressed in a joined-up manner. The framework was therefore eagerly anticipated as an instrument that could restore some strategic capacity to the land use planning system in Wales.

The initial concept of a national spatial planning framework for Wales was one that aligned very much with the statutory planning system. The national spatial planning framework would act as an important complement to the already existing policy documents that frame the preparation of development plans at the local level and set the parameters for the determination of planning applications. However, one of the most remarkable aspects of the Wales Spatial Plan (National Assembly for Wales, 2004c) is how it has developed from this initial concept of a primarily land-use planning instrument to a crosscutting, corporate policy instrument of the Assembly. The Plan has increased dramatically in its profile and political significance in the four years in which the plan was in preparation. It is now regarded as one of the principal policy documents of the Assembly and has been promoted as a document to which the whole range of cabinet ministers are signed up to. Several factors help to explain the profile now enjoyed by the Wales Spatial Plan. However, perhaps the most compelling explanation is that the Wales Spatial Plan has an integrative potential. The broad-ranging scope of spatial planning instruments is one of their defining characteristics, with most spatial planning instruments taking into account a plethora of different sectors and policy spheres. Their scope is not limited to particular policy spheres – so long as there are explicit or even implicit spatial dimensions to a particular policy area or sector, then a spatial plan may legitimately address and express it (see Harris and Hooper, 2004). The significance of this quality in a Welsh context becomes readily apparent when one recognises the very rapid development of a range of different sectoral policies that occurred with the establishment of the National Assembly for Wales. Morgan and Rees (2000, p. 168) speculated in the period following the creation of the Assembly that 'there is a real danger that Wales may overdose on a plethora of ill-considered strategies which have little or no synergy'. Indeed, in its first two years of existence the Assembly issued a range of draft and final versions of national strategies and programmes in relation to sustainability, economic development, culture, information and communication technologies, housing, waste, rural development, renewable energy and transport. Such an extensive raft of policies and strategies requires some form of co-ordination, and while the Assembly had a form of business or corporate planning in place, the Wales Spatial Plan offered the possibility of *spatial* as well as sectoral co-ordination. The general institutional and policy context prevailing in Wales in recent years has therefore been a particularly supportive and positive one for the activity of spatial planning.

An additional potential that derives from the characteristic feature of spatial plans to attend to policy matters in an explicitly spatial manner is the avoidance of seeing a territory as a homogeneous entity. A spatial plan can not only give expression to the diversity that exists in economic, social and environmental terms, but also highlight how national policies play out differently across space and the territory. In economic development terms, for example, past policies have impacted differentially across Wales. The headline figures for improvements or otherwise in various indicators of prosperity of economic performance can mask markedly different circumstances within localities. Morgan (1998, p. 248) has drawn attention to this and highlights the issue of 'divergent development' in Wales where economic success has not always taken place where it is needed the most. In addition to Wales as a whole recording a low and worsening figure for GDP/capita when compared to the UK average, it is also characterised by significant variation in GDP/capita across its own regions (see Brand *et al.*, 1997). In the words of Hill (2000a, p. 9), when measured by GDP/capita it becomes clear that 'there are many Waleses'. This is replicated across a range of other measures related to economic development. For example, economic inactivity rates in parts of the south Wales Valleys are double that of some of the more rural parts of mid Wales. The same Valleys communities also have double the proportion of people with no qualifications than some of Wales' more affluent communities. There is nothing particularly unusual in the existence of these differences. However, it is the fact that it is often the same communities demonstrating the weakest profile against these measures, leading to particular concentrations of economic and social disadvantage, most notably in the south Wales Valleys and former coalfield areas. The Wales Spatial Plan has the potential to help tailor policies and develop actions that are appropriate to each of the different parts of Wales. Indeed, there is evidence of an increasing synergy between the Assembly's economic development framework and its spatial planning initiative. Its most recent consultation document on the revision of its economic development framework recognises that some specific parts of Wales have enjoyed economic success or revival, while others have failed to replicate the success of those areas (Welsh Assembly Government, 2005). It also recognises a particularly spatial context for this, arguing that there is a need to try and somehow emulate in Wales the characteristics of urban, metropolitan areas in how they achieve agglomeration economies. There are, therefore, some positive signs that the preparation of the Wales Spatial Plan is encouraging a more 'spatial' approach to and understanding of particular policies in different sectors.

Figure 5.4   The 'spatial vision' as illustrated in the Wales spatial plan

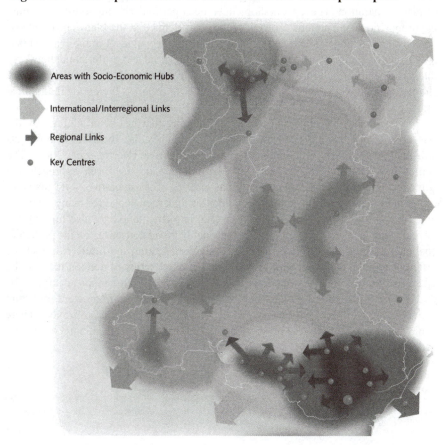

(*Welsh Assembly Government, 2004*).
It identifies 'socio-economic hubs' in each of the different areas of Wales outlined in the Plan, as well as a network of 'key centres'. The illustration of the spatial vision is not as specific or as well-developed as in some other spatial strategies, and is instead defined by 'fuzzy' boundaries and general depiction of linkages.

The process by which the Wales Spatial Plan has been prepared is one of its defining characteristics as a case study example of spatial planning. It can genuinely claim to be a document that is based on extensive consultation with a wide range of stakeholders across Wales. The Plan has been subject to formal consultation opportunities in the form of a consultation draft of the Plan and earlier opportunity to comment on the form and content of the Plan as well as the approach to preparing it. Consultation with stakeholders and the public is embedded in the Assembly's approach and it has been no different with the Wales Spatial Plan. In addition to such formal consultation opportunities, the Assembly has also undertaken a series of regional workshops across Wales designed to foster direct participation in the process of plan preparation. These workshops have been particularly important in refining the propositions and actions for each of the areas defined in the Plan. The emphasis on consultation, engagement and collaboration is clearly evident in the Plan. This is now being carried forward through a series of ministerial and professional networks that have been formed in each of the six areas or sub-regions across Wales. These sub-regional networks are now working together to progress the national and local priority actions established in the Wales Spatial Plan.

In conclusion, the approach to spatial planning that has been adopted by the Assembly is one that has been informed by approaches elsewhere but also reflects a distinctive approach to the preparation of a spatial plan (Harris *et al.*, 2002). The approach is characterised by extensive consultation on the form, approach and content of the plan. The Plan certainly has a series of shortcomings – it falls short of outlining many specific actions, its content is underdeveloped for many interests' expectations and its provisions with respect to implementation are also limited. Yet its real value is in having established a reasonably broad consensus on the particular challenges facing the different parts of Wales, suggesting the future role that the different regions may play and identifying a limited series of actions that can be taken to progress in that direction. The Wales Spatial Plan cannot accurately be described as a plan, but is perhaps best understood as a general framework for future collaborative work or, in it own words, it establishes 'a direction of travel'. There is now evidence that work is progressing within that framework of agreed, priority actions.

Conclusions

Learning the Lessons

This Chapter commenced with the claim that Wales provides an interesting and valuable case study in respect of the activities of both regional development and spatial planning. As a case study on regional development, Wales provides some very important lessons. Firstly, experience in Wales makes clear that many of the problems and difficulties facing peripheral or lagging regions, especially those engaged in processes of economic restructuring, are deeply embedded and can prove resistant to even sustained policy intervention over considerable periods of time. Secondly, a series of lessons for other regions can be drawn from Wales' experience of securing Objective 1 funding. Royles (2003, p. 133–4) claims that Wales was neither ready nor well-equipped for the notification of securing Objective 1 funding, citing inadequate staffing, the absence of an economic development strategy and the general difficulties arising from the recent establishment of the National Assembly for Wales. The securing of Objective 1 status for West Wales and the Valleys, as for any region, is clearly 'not a cause for celebration' (Brooksbank and Pickernell, 2000, p. 113). Nevertheless, it provides an important opportunity to specifically address what stands out as Wales' enduring regional development problem, the closing of the prosperity gap. The key lesson, then, is that the institutional and policy context that prevails in any region at a particular time can impact significantly on the capacity of that region to capitalise on the securing of European funding.

The lessons that may be learned from a case study of Wales in respect of spatial planning are several. The first is that spatial planning can demonstrate significant potential to political audiences in meeting the challenges of joined-up government and regional development. Certainly, it is too soon to provide evidence of the success of the Wales Spatial Plan in delivering on many of the Assembly's aims, objectives and targets. Nevertheless, the potential of the Plan is evident in the increased political and professional profile that the plan has enjoyed in the past three years. The fact that a spatial plan can become one of the most important corporate policy documents of a government administration is a very positive lesson to be drawn from the Welsh experience. The second lesson is that the activity of spatial planning can be tailored to its particular context. The Wales Spatial Plan is a particular form of spatial plan. The approach adopted by the Assembly and the document itself are distinct from those selected in other parts of the United Kingdom and elsewhere. It is an approach that reflects the institutional context in Wales, most notably the relationship between the Assembly and local government, and also some of the broad principles by which the Assembly operates, including a commitment to partnership working. The Plan – as stated above – is best viewed as a framework for future collaborative action or the development of a shared and agreed agenda for change, rather than a plan designed to prescribe a series of future actions.

Facing the Future

The story of Wales' economic history and its present economic and social circumstances make it difficult to be overtly optimistic on the immediate future prospects for Wales. Devolution and the establishment of the National Assembly for Wales – arguably the most important developments in the governance landscape in Wales in the last 20 years – give some limited cause for fresh optimism as policy needs are identified close to home and within a democratic context. Yet Morgan (2001, p. 345) concludes that the new devolved governance systems preside over a 'socio-economic landscape [that] has a depressingly familiar look to it'. The fact remains that significant regional development funding has been directed at Wales over a considerable period of time, yet this has not resulted in increased economic prosperity (Munday *et al.*, 2001, p. 51). Substantially closing the prosperity gap by 2011 will require Wales' GDP to increase by 1 per cent or more per annum than the rate of increase in that for the United Kingdom as a whole (Hill, 2000b, p. 132). These targets have been the objects of much criticism. Some commentators, drawing on analyses of the structure of the Welsh economy and related forecasting exercises, have even predicted that no significant inroads into the prosperity gap are likely before 2010 (Hill, 2000a, p. 5). The challenge of not only increasing economic prosperity in Wales but also ensuring a more even distribution of economic prosperity looks set to remain central to policy-makers' concerns for some time to come. The former Secretary of State for Wales Ron Davies coined a phrase that has proven to be an enduring and popular one within Wales – 'devolution is a process and not an event'. Economic restructuring and achieving increased prosperity might also be emphasised as particularly length and complex processes in which Wales continues to be engaged. The future for spatial planning in Wales, on the other hand, appears to be a positive one. The immediate future will be one of delivering on the promised potential of spatial planning. Delivering spatial change, like economic change, is a longer-term process and it will be difficult to judge the success of the Wales Spatial Plan in the short-term. The challenges for spatial planning will be in ensuring the future sustainable development of Wales and achieving an appropriate balance between economic development, social progress and environmental protection. This chapter has attempted to convey the political significance that achieving increased economic prosperity has within Wales. One of the key concerns must be that achieving ambitious medium-term targets in respect of increasing GDP/capita and other economic indicators does not compromise the longer-term sustainable development of Wales (see also Hull, 2004).

References

Alden, J.D. 1996, 'The Transfer from a Problem to Powerful Region: The Experience of Wales', in: Alden, J. and Boland, P. (eds), *Regional Development Strategies: A European Perspective*, London: Jessica Kingsley, pp. 129–158.

Boland, P. 2004, 'Wales and Obective 1 Status: Learning the Lessons or Emulating the Errors?', *European Planning Studies*, vol. 12(2), pp. 249–270.

Brand, S., Hill, S., Munday, M. and Roberts, A. 1997, 'Why Isn't Wales Richer? Economic Change and GDP/capita', *Local Economy*, pp. 219–233.

Bristow, G. and Blewitt, N. 2001, 'The Structural Funds and Additionality in Wales: Devolution and Multilevel Governance', *Environment and Planning A*, vol. 33, no. 6, pp. 1083–1099.

Brooksbank, D. and Pickernell, D. 2000, 'Making the Most of it: Objective 1 Status, Assisted Area Status and the Valleys', in: Bryan, J. and Jones, C. (eds), *Wales in the 21st Century: An Economic Future*, London: Macmillan, pp. 101–114.

Causer, P. and Virdee, D. (eds) 2004, *Regional Trends*, London: The Stationery Office.

Chaney, P, Hall, T. and Pithouse, A. 2000, 'New Governance – New Democracy?' in: Chaney, P, Hall, T. and Pithouse, A. (eds), *New governance – new democracy? Post-devolution Wales*, Cardiff: University of Wales Press, pp. 1–17.

Cooke, P. and Morgan, K. 1998, 'The Associational Economy. Firms, Regions and Innovation', Oxford: Oxford University Press.

Digital Europe, 2003, *Regional development in Wales: Case study summary*, downloaded from www.digital-eu.org, 16 June 2005.

Harris, N., Hooper, A. and Bishop, K.D. 2002, 'Constructing the practice of "Spatial Planning": A National Spatial Planning Framework for Wales', *Environment and Planning C: Government and Policy*, vol. 20, pp. 555–572.

Harris, N. and Hooper, A. 2004, 'Rediscovering the "spatial" in Public Policy and Planning: An Examination of the Spatial Content of Sectoral Policy Documents', *Planning Theory and Practice*, vol. 5, no. 2, pp. 147–169.

Haughton, G. and Counsell, D. 2004, *Regions, Spatial Strategies and Sustainable Development*, London: Routledge.

Healey, P. 1998, 'Collaborative Planning in a Stakeholder Society', *Town Planning Review*, vol. 69, no.1, pp. 1–21.

Healey, P. 2001, 'Towards a More Place-focused Planning System in Britain', in: Madanipour, A., Hull, A. and Healey, P. (eds), *The Governance of Place: Space and Planning Processes*, Aldershot: Ashgate, pp. 265–286.

Henderson, D. and Thomas, M. 1999, 'Learning through Strategy-making: The RTP in Wales', in: Morgan, K. and Nauwelaers, C. (eds) *Regional Innovation Strategies: The Challenge for Less-favoured Regions*, London, Routledge, pp. 80–95.

Hill, S. 2000a, 'Wales in Transition', in: Bryan, J. and Jones, C. (eds), *Wales in the 21st Century: An Economic Future*, London: Macmillan, pp. 1–9.

Hill, S. 2000b, Shaping the Future, in: Bryan, J. and Jones, C. (eds), *Wales in the 21st Century: An Economic Future*, London: Macmillan, pp. 131–138.

Hill, S., Roberts, A. and Miller, N. 1998, 'The Welsh Workforce', in: Osmond, J. (ed.), *The National Assembly Agenda: A Handbook for the First Four Years*, Cardiff, Institute of Welsh Affairs, pp. 217–229.

Hull, A. 2004, '"A Winning Wales": Integrated Strategy for Sustainable Economic Development?', *Planning Practice and Research*, vol. 19, no. 3, pp. 329–343.

Lovering, J. 1999, 'Theory Led by Policy: The Inadequacies of the 'New Regionalism' (illustrated from the case of Wales)', *International Journal of Urban and Regional Research*, vol. 23, pp. 379–395.

Lovering, J. 2001, 'The Coming Regional Crisis (and how to avoid it)', *Regional Studies*, vol. 35, no. 4, pp. 349–354.

Morgan, B. and Morgan, K. 1998, 'Economic Development', in: Osmond, J. (ed.), *The National Assembly Agenda: A Handbook for the First Four Years*, Cardiff: Institute of Welsh Affairs, pp. 163–178.

Morgan, K. 1998, 'Regional Renewal: The Development Agency as Animateur', in: Halkier, H., Dawson, M. and Damborg, C. (eds), *Regional Development Agencies in Europe*, London, Jessica Kingsley, pp. 229–252.

Morgan, K. 2001, 'The New Territorial Politics: Rivalry and Justice in Post-devolution Britain', *Regional Studies*, vol. 35, no. 4, pp. 343–348.

Morgan, K. and Rees, G. 2000, 'Learning by Doing: Devolution and the Governance of Economic Development in Wales', in: Chaney, P, Hall, T. and Pithouse, A. (eds), *New Governance – New Democracy? Post-devolution Wales*, Cardiff, University of Wales Press, pp. 126–171.

Munday, M., Pickernell, D. and Roberts, A. 2001, 'Regional Policy Effectiveness and Local Governance Issues: Some Welsh Perspectives', *Policy Studies*, vol. 22, no. 1, pp. 52–60.

National Assembly for Wales, 2002, *A Winning Wales: The National Economic Development Strategy of the Welsh Assembly Government*, Cardiff, National Assembly for Wales.

National Assembly for Wales, 2003, *A Winning Wales: Annual Report 2002–2003*, Cardiff, National Assembly for Wales.

National Assembly for Wales, 2004a, *A Winning Wales: Annual Report 2003–2004*, Cardiff, National Assembly for Wales.

National Assembly for Wales, 2004b. *A Winning Wales: Refresh*, Cardiff, National Assembly for Wales.

National Assembly for Wales, 2004c, *People, Places, Futures: The Wales Spatial Plan*, Cardiff, National Assembly for Wales.

Royles, E. 2003, 'Objective 1', in: Osmond, J. and Jones, B.J. (eds), *Birth of Welsh Democracy: The First Term of the National Assembly for Wales*, Cardiff, Institute for Welsh Affairs, pp. 131–148.

Storer, A. and Cole, A. 2002, 'Politics as Normal, The Economic Development Committee', in: Jones, B.J. and Osmond, J. (eds), *Building a Civic Culture: Institutional Change, Policy Development and Political Dynamics in the National Assembly for Wales*, Cardiff, Institute for Welsh Affairs, pp. 113–124.

Vigar, G., Healey, P., Hull, A. and Davoudi, S. 2000, *Planning, Governance and Spatial Strategy in Britain: An Institutionalist Analysis*, London: Macmillan.

Welsh Assembly Government. 2005, *Wales: A Vibrant Economy: The Welsh Assembly Government's Strategic Framework for Economic Development, Consultation document*, Cardiff, Welsh Assembly Government.

Chapter 6

Quality and Connectivity: The Continuing Tradition of Strategic Spatial Planning in Scotland

Graeme Purves

Introduction

This chapter outlines Scotland's tradition of strategic planning and regional development, commenting on its strengths and weaknesses. Like the Welsh Assembly Government, the Scottish Executive, Scotland's devolved administration, made an early commitment to drawing up a national spatial strategy. In describing the preparation of Scotland's first National Planning Framework, the chapter highlights the approach adopted to stakeholder engagement and comments on Scotland's experience of applying Strategic Environmental Assessment at the national level. It describes how the Framework has sought to pursue the objective of balanced and sustainable economic development through a strategy which places emphasis on environmental quality and improved connectivity. It comments on lessons learned, implementation mechanisms, arrangements for monitoring and review and issues for the future.

The Institutional Context for Spatial Planning and Economic Development

Scotland has the status of a devolved administration within the United Kingdom. The Scottish Parliament, which was re-established in 1999, has legislative powers over domestic matters, including planning. The Scottish planning system reflects the land use planning traditions of the United Kingdom, though it is subject to separate legislation (The Town and Country Planning (Scotland) Act 1997) and has developed some distinctive features in response to the particular needs of the country. At national level, the Scottish Executive is responsible for the development of national planning policy and the dissemination of advice on good practice. Responsibility for the preparation of development plans and determining applications for planning permission lies with 32 local authorities.

One characteristic which differentiates Scotland from Ireland and Wales is that it has a strong tradition of strategic planning at the regional level (Hayton 1996, Lloyd 1997, Rowan-Robinson 1997). In the 1940s, Scotland's wartime administration initiated the preparation of three major regional plans covering the most populous parts of the country to guide post-war reconstruction. The regional planning tradition established at that time has persisted through successive reforms of local government under Governments of different political complexions, with a particularly strong strand of continuity in Glasgow and the Clyde Valley (Wannop, 1986). The current instrument of regional strategic planning is the structure plan. Structure plans are prepared by local authorities and require approval by Ministers. At present there are 17 structure plan areas, providing all-Scotland coverage. There are six areas where the structure plan is prepared jointly by groups of local authorities. In the remaining 11 areas – mainly the more rural areas – the structure plan is prepared by a single local authority.

Responsibility for the promotion of economic development rests with two publicly-funded agencies, Scottish Enterprise and Highlands and Islands Enterprise (see Goodwin *et al.*, 2002). These are responsible for the delivery of the national economic development strategy via a network of 22 local enterprise companies. The institutional frameworks for land use planning and economic development are therefore separate and they have different operational cultures. Planning authorities are concerned with strategy and process, whereas local enterprise companies tend to focus on the shorter time horizons of individual projects. While its predecessor, the Scottish Development Agency, once played a key role in areas such as land renewal and urban regeneration, in the 1990s the focus of Scottish Enterprise moved away from land and place-based issues towards support targeted on the knowledge economy business sectors seen as key to Scotland's future. However, planning authorities and the enterprise network do collaborate on matters of common interest. In the late 1990s, they worked together in Glasgow and the Clyde Valley as the Glasgow and Clyde Valley Structure Plan Joint Committee (1999) on the identification and safeguarding of sites for strategic inward investment and agreed a common economic development perspective (see also Goodstadt, 2001 and Kumar and Paddison, 2000).

Economy, Society and Environment

Scotland is a small country of some 5 million people in the far North-West of Europe and has the lowest birth rate in the United Kingdom. Like many areas outside the European core, Scotland has a declining and aging population. The 2001 Census showed an 18 per cent decrease in those aged under 15 and a 29 per cent increase in those aged over 75. There are also marked differences in population change between different parts of the country, with growth in the East and decline in some rural areas. Scotland also has a distinctive and well-developed settlement structure, still largely based on the pattern of burgh settlement begun in the twelfth century, modified by industrialisation and the depopulation of rural areas in the eighteenth and nineteenth centuries, and supplemented by four twentieth century New Towns. Most of the population is distributed between six relatively small cities and a range of medium-sized and small towns. Almost two-thirds of the population is concentrated in the Central Belt, over a quarter in the four main cities, and there are large parts of the country which are very sparsely populated indeed. The concept of balanced polycentric development is somewhat problematic in a country where land form is such an assertive determinant of settlement patterns (see Bailey and Turok, 2001). Certainly, the pattern does not appear particularly 'balanced' when compared with countries like Denmark or Germany. The distribution of settlements in Scotland is probably more akin to that in Norway, Sweden and Finland than to that of countries closer to the European core. However, settlement is arguably more polycentric than in many small countries in Europe. While the capital is Edinburgh, with a population of around 500,000, the largest city is Glasgow, with a population of nearly 600,000. The East Coast cities of Aberdeen and Dundee have populations of 200,000 and 150,000 respectively. The two newest cities, Inverness and Stirling, are much smaller, with populations of less than 50,000. The country has some very high quality urban environments, with Edinburgh and Glasgow being two of the leading tourist destinations in the United Kingdom. The distinctive and concentrated settlement pattern also means that Scotland has large areas of high environmental quality in terms of landscape and wildlife. Over a quarter of the land area is covered by environmental designations and there are two National Parks.

In common with much of the developed world, Scotland is experiencing a long-term decline of traditional industries and a growth in service-based activity. Services are now the dominant sector of the economy. Manufacturing is strongly export-oriented and accounts for around 20 per cent of GDP. The economy has clear strengths in tourism, financial services, electronics, whisky, oil and gas. GDP per head is 115 per cent of the EU25 average, although performance lags well behind the most successful small European economies. There have also been important structural changes in the rural economy over the last 20 years. The continuing decline of the primary industries of farming and fishing has been accompanied by an expansion of the service sector, diversification into new activities and the growth of the leisure economy. The fortunes of parts of the Highlands have turned round dramatically, but the South-West and the remoter islands continue to experience decline.

The Key Challenges for Regional Development and Strategic Planning

The key challenges facing Scotland in the early twenty-first century are the building of a competitive knowledge economy, the strengthening and renewing of infrastructure, the promotion of urban and rural regeneration and the management of demographic change. The Scottish Executive sees the cities as having a key role in the modernisation and development of the economy. It is keen to spread the benefits of economic activity more evenly by linking areas of deprivation to new economic opportunities. It is committed to safeguarding the environment and ensuring that development is sustainable. Fortunately, Scotland has a particularly strong tradition of strategic or regional planning that equip it better than many countries in facing these challenges. Where it works well, the strengths of regional planning in Scotland include a capacity for strategic thinking and a willingness to work together, good relationships and close liaison between local authorities and central government, and a commitment to active engagement with a wider constituency of stakeholders. However, a number of weaknesses have also been identified. Project management can be poor and it frequently takes too long to prepare plans. Plans that are prepared often lack strategic content and spatial focus. Plans also tend to be over-comprehensive and too long and there is often insufficient emphasis on implementation and delivery. Yet, despite some of these shortcomings, a capacity and tradition in strategic planning stands out as one of the hallmarks of the Scottish planning system.

In the late 1990s, concern began to be expressed that the local government reorganisation of 1996, which abolished the regional tier of local government, had resulted in the erosion of the strategic capacity of the Scottish planning system (Lloyd 1999). During the first term of Scotland's new Parliament, the Scottish Executive therefore undertook a review of the strategic planning system to ensure that it was fit for purpose. The review reached two key conclusions (2002a). The first was that there was a need for a national spatial strategy to provide a context for development planning. The second was that strategic development plans should only be prepared for the four largest city-regions. To address the latter conclusion, Scottish Ministers intend to introduce legislation to establish a new development plan framework. It is intended that City Region Plans should be prepared jointly by local authorities in the city regions of Edinburgh, Glasgow, Aberdeen and Dundee. These plans will be spatial development strategies with a 20-year horizon. They will focus on land and infrastructure issues and will be supported by action programmes to ensure an emphasis on delivery.

Quality and Connectivity: The National Planning Framework for Scotland

The Decision to Prepare a National Spatial Strategy for Scotland

While strategic planning at the regional level is well-established, Scotland has never previously had a single, over-arching national plan or strategy. In the late 1940s an attempt was made to draw together the three major post-war regional plans as the first stage in the development of a national plan (Purves 1988). Later, in 1963, the Scottish Office published a strategy for the Central Belt in the White Paper, *Central Scotland: A Programme for Development and Growth*. The 1966 White Paper, *The Scottish Economy 1965–1970: A Plan for Expansion* looked beyond the Central Belt, setting an economic development strategy for each of eight statistical and planning regions. However, subsequent administrations have been disinclined to attempt national planning exercises of this kind. Yet interest in a national spatial strategy reawakened after the re-establishment of Scotland's Parliament (see Tewdwr-Jones, 2002, pp. 259–261). In a paper published by the Royal Town Planning Institute in Scotland in 2000 a number of planning academics and practitioners called for the preparation of a national planning framework for Scotland (Lloyd *et al.* 2000). Other academic commentators revived the case for a more specific focus on the Central

Belt (Turok & Bailey 2002). One of the more significant influences steering the Scottish Executive towards the preparation of a national spatial strategy was the European Spatial Development Perspective (ESDP) (CEC, 1999). The Executive was aware that the European Commission was encouraging the preparation of spatial planning frameworks to provide a context for resource allocation in an enlarged EU, and that such frameworks could be a significant factor in EU regional policy after 2006. It was also alert to the fact that, while Europe's economic centre of gravity and the focus of structural funding support were moving East as a result of enlargement, Scotland's position on the north-western edge of Europe was fixed. The national spatial framework was seen as a vehicle for addressing the implications of Scotland's geographical position in Europe and the opportunities and challenges which that presented within the context of devolved government, European enlargement and the global economy. Therefore, as one of the outcomes of the review of strategic planning, Scottish Ministers announced in June 2002 that the Scottish Executive would prepare a national spatial strategy, to be known as the National Planning Framework. The Framework was to be a key element in a wider package of reforms to modernise the Scottish planning system, including measures to strengthen community involvement in planning and speed up plan preparation and decision-making (see Tewdwr-Jones, 2001, 2002 and Allmendinger, 2001, 2002). The Scottish Cabinet agreed the establishment of an Ad Hoc Group of Ministers to steer the preparation of the Framework. The team preparing the Framework was keen to learn from experience elsewhere, given that a range of other regions and countries were engaged previously or simultaneously in the preparation of strategic, spatial plans. Influences included the spatial planning exercises being undertaken in Wales, the Republic of Ireland and Northern Ireland, the strong spatial planning traditions of Scandinavia and the Netherlands, and Estonia's National Spatial Plan (2001).

There was a strong commitment to ensuring stakeholder involvement in the preparation of the Framework and it was considered important that it should identify development opportunities for each part of the country. During September 2002, a series of seminars was held in towns throughout Scotland to seek views on the status of the framework, the process of preparation and the issues which it should address. Throughout the preparation process, meetings were held with key public agencies and private sector interests. Divisions of the Executive concerned with transport, economic development and the environment were closely involved, as were Scottish Enterprise and Highlands and Islands Enterprise. Presentations were made to Members of the Scottish Parliament (MSPs), the Parliament's Transport and the Environment Committee, local authority councillors and environmental and professional organisations. The Executive undertook a number of additional measures to encourage participation by organisations and individuals in the preparation of the Framework. A regularly-updated web site was established, news releases were issued at key stages of the preparation process and articles were placed in the Scottish Executive's *Planning Bulletin*. In June 2003, a second round of regional seminars was held to share emerging thinking with stakeholders and seek views on the key messages the framework should be conveying for each part of Scotland. The broad consensus which emerged from engagement with stakeholders was that the Framework should focus on a limited number of key spatial issues of genuine national importance (Purves, 2002). The issues which emerged most strongly as central to the Framework were strategic transport infrastructure; the spatial aspects of economic development strategy; and energy, water and telecommunications infrastructure. It was felt that there was a need to take a holistic view of the Central Belt and address the important changes taking place in the rural economy.

Demographic Change and Economic Development: Key Challenges for the National Planning Framework

Scotland's first National Planning Framework was published in April 2004. It is intended to guide the spatial development of Scotland in the period to 2025. Like the ESDP, it is a perspective, not a prescriptive masterplan. It analyses development trends, identifies key areas of change and highlights the challenges Scotland faces. It provides a national context for development plans and planning decisions and will inform the ongoing programmes of the Scottish Executive, public agencies and local authorities. It is one of the factors the Executive will take into account in reaching decisions on policy and spending priorities. The National Planning Framework complements other top-level strategy documents such as the *Framework for Economic Development in Scotland* (2004b), highlighting the importance of place and identifying priorities for investment in infrastructure to support the realisation of the Executive's objectives for economic development and area regeneration. It is concerned with Scotland in its wider context and does not address local issues. Given Scotland's relatively strong tradition of regional planning, the Scottish Executive has been careful not to stray into matters which are best addressed by local authorities, the enterprise network or other local agencies.

The Framework identifies demographic trends as a key issue. There is concern that the population is projected to fall below 5 million in 2017. The Scottish Executive has therefore launched a *Fresh Talent* initiative, to encourage more Scots to remain in Scotland and promote Scotland abroad as an attractive place in which to live and work. The greater freedom of movement resulting from EU enlargement is seen as offering opportunities to attract people with the skills and abilities needed to develop key sectors of the economy. Although the overall population is falling, the trend towards smaller households means that the number of households is still growing, creating a continuing demand for new housing and infrastructure (Pacione, 2005).

Growing the economy is the Scottish Executive's top priority and the strategy set out in the National Planning Framework is based on the recognition that people and investment gravitate towards cities and regions which offer a variety of economic opportunities, a stimulating environment, amenities for a wide range of lifestyles and good connections to other high quality places. The themes of quality and connectivity are therefore central to the successful development of a modern knowledge economy. The Framework emphasises the key role of the cities as drivers of the Scottish economy (see Cooke and Clifton, 2005); the need to support the development of knowledge economy clusters; the scope for spreading the benefits of economic activity by addressing issues of quality and connectivity; and the need to link area regeneration and economic development.

Since the 1970s, the development of North Sea oil and gas fields has made an important contribution to the economy, underpinning prosperity in the North East. The oil and gas industry currently provides 100,000 jobs directly or indirectly, around 41,000 of these in the North East. North Sea oil production is expected to peak between 2005 and 2010. As the North Sea fields have matured, many of the companies established in Aberdeen have retained the city as a base for headquarters functions and international operations. There has also been substantial foreign investment in the Scottish economy over the last 30 years. West Central Scotland, which was badly affected by the decline of heavy industries in the 1970s and 80s, recovered strongly in the 1990s as a result of inward investment, primarily in the electronics sector. The boost to the economy provided by mobile international capital is now less than it was in the 1980s. Currently there are more than 1,000 inward investors in Scotland, employing some 80,000 people. While American and Far Eastern companies were dominant players in the past, Europe is an important source of new investment.

Scotland has areas of real economic vibrancy and some world class urban environments. In other areas, however, past industrial activity, economic change and poor land and urban management have left a legacy of social and environmental problems. The number of people in employment has been increasing, but there are marked differences across the country. Employment has increased in Edinburgh and Glasgow and in Eastern Scotland and the Highlands. However, employment has declined in Aberdeen, Dundee, the South West and the islands. Unemployment is at its lowest levels for decades and lower than in many European countries. Many of the more buoyant areas have skills shortages. The highest levels of unemployment are in parts of West Central Scotland, Dundee and the Western Isles. There are still significant disparities in wealth and economic activity, with concentrations of disadvantage in the old industrial areas of West Central Scotland and problems of overheating in the East, particularly in and around Edinburgh. While the 2001 Census indicates that there have been some changes in patterns of inequality and deprivation, and there are clear signs of an economic upturn in parts of the Glasgow Conurbation, the difference between the West and East remains.

To address some of the above patterns, Scottish Enterprise and the Scottish Executive have identified nine economic development zones as the principal foci for the development of key industries and knowledge economy clusters (Figure 6.1). The National Planning Framework stresses the importance of ensuring that these zones have good links to the rest of Scotland and the wider world, and that the strategic business locations which they contain are well connected with each other and readily accessible from residential areas.

Figure 6.1   Scotland's economic development zones

Source: Scottish Enterprise and Highlands and Islands Enterprise
The map clearly illustrates the series of economic development zones located in Scotland's central belt, along with those identified in Aberdeen and Inverness. The illustration also identifies the areas associated with the range of economic development zones.

In addition to these social problems, Scotland's industrial past has left a range of environmental problems too, with significant areas of under-used and neglected land, some of it contaminated. Over 100km² is classed as vacant or derelict, 34 per cent of which is in Glasgow and the Clyde Valley. Much progress has already been made in addressing this issue. Major land reclamation in former mining areas and projects such as the creation of a Central Scotland Forest have improved the environment and opened up new opportunities for economic development and recreation. However, more requires to be done to ensure that the communities of the Central Belt are attractive places to live and work, enjoying the quality of environment and infrastructure which allows them to contribute to Scotland's success as a competitive place.

Scotland's Cities as 'Drivers of the Economy'

Scotland's distinctive settlement pattern and the distribution of its largest cities, and the key role these are seen as playing in its spatial strategy, have been referred to already. In 2002 the Scottish Executive undertook a *Review of Scotland's Cities* which examined the condition of the cities and their potential contribution to the country's future. It highlighted the distinctive characters of Edinburgh, Glasgow, Aberdeen, Dundee and Inverness and their important strategic role as drivers of economic activity. To address the role of Scotland's capital first, Edinburgh's current economic success is based on financial and business services, public administration, culture and tourism, and a large university sector with strengths in computer science, informatics and the life sciences. Incomes are high, unemployment is low and the city is ranked very highly in quality of life indices. Both population and the number of households are projected to grow substantially. However, the city is coming up against constraints to future growth in the form of traffic congestion, difficulties in filling job vacancies, steeply rising land values (residential land values have risen by more than 200 per cent in six years), house price inflation, high commercial rents, and a shortage of development land. There is also concern that high prices are squeezing essential workers on lower incomes out of the housing market. The key challenge for Edinburgh is therefore the management of growth.

Glasgow – Scotland's largest city – has undergone a period of major economic restructuring. As a result of the decline of its traditional industries, its population fell by a third between 1961 and 1981, amongst the most severe experiences of city decline in Europe. The city, fortunately, is now showing very positive signs of recovery. It has outperformed the other Scottish cities in employment growth in recent years, with significant increases in the knowledge economy and the service sector. Glasgow is ranked as the second most successful retail centre in the United Kingdom (behind London's West End) and the city is attracting increasing numbers of tourists. However, the new prosperity co-exists with significant areas of poverty and dereliction and economic activity rates remain among the lowest in the UK. There are substantial areas of deeply-rooted social exclusion which remain poorly connected to growth areas in the city and surrounding region.

The city of Aberdeen has established itself as the oil capital of Europe and has a GDP 30 per cent above the Scottish average. Full employment, high incomes and good urban and rural environments combine to provide a good quality of life for much of the population in the city and surrounding region. However, traditional sectors of the economy such as fish processing and food are under pressure, parts of the city require restructuring and small but persistent pockets of deprivation remain. There is also a danger that today's success may inhibit future performance. High house prices, traffic congestion and problems in delivering land for development could discourage the establishment of new businesses. Aberdeen's fortunes contrast markedly with those of Dundee. In Dundee, many traditional industries have had difficulties in adapting to new technologies and markets. This has led to a fall in population, high unemployment, social deprivation, and significant areas of vacant and derelict land. However, a major improvement in external image has been achieved through revitalisation of the city centre, with long-term investment in retail and cultural facilities and the public realm. On the west of the city, a new economy is emerging in the form of clusters at the leading edge of biotechnology, medical science and multi-media software development. Finally, Inverness is the main administrative, medical, retail and leisure centre for the Highlands. It has grown a lot in recent years, its population increasing by a third since the 1970s. The environmental and cultural resources of the Highlands support a substantial tourism industry and mean that the city is able to offer a high quality of life. Sectors such as retailing, public administration and business services have expanded significantly. However, the city's economic base remains relatively narrow and there is a need to diversify and attract a wider range of high quality jobs.

While the cities are key drivers of the economy, many Scots live in large, medium and small towns. Some of these have suffered a loss of vitality in recent times as a result of the decline of traditional industries, changing patterns of retailing and the centralisation of public administration and other services. Areas which have been reliant on a narrow range of business and industry have found themselves vulnerable to economic change. Examples include the former mining towns of West Central Scotland, the textile mill towns of the Borders and the fishing ports of the North East. In areas to the South and West of Glasgow the decline in manufacturing has not been compensated by new employment in the service sectors (Ayrshire Economic Forum 2003).

Infrastructure: The Challenge of Improving Connectivity

The National Planning Framework focuses strongly on the infrastructure required to ensure that places can compete both domestically and internationally. There is evidence that investment in physical infrastructure has been declining in Scotland and is lower than in its European neighbours. Yet improving and investing in transport infrastructure is recognised as being of crucial importance to Scotland's future development and the Framework highlights the need to develop external links, improve internal connectivity and promote more sustainable patterns of transport and land use. It reflects the Executive's commitment to investing in public transport and moving a higher proportion of freight by rail and water. The Scottish Executive is strongly committed to investing in sustainable transport. By 2006 expenditure on transport will have reached £1 billion, 70 per cent of which will be on public transport. There are also important implications for the movement of goods, with the emphasis on moving a higher proportion of freight by rail and water.

Given Scotland's geographical position and the effects of peripherality, good external links are critical. The Framework stresses the importance of good air links and improved port facilities, as well as the need to strengthen euro-routes to continental Europe and Ireland, and the potential of deep water harbours as European transhipment facilities (Figure 6.2). Passenger numbers through Scottish airports almost doubled in the ten years to 2002, to reach 9.8 million per annum. The expansion of the services offered by the low-cost airlines has made a major contribution to this growth. A Route Development Fund has been established to promote improvements in Scotland's international connections through new direct air services which benefit business and tourism. There has also been progress in developing the role of gateway ports, as is also emphasised in the Framework. In 2002, a new daily ferry service between Rosyth and Zeebrugge in Belgium was established. The Scottish Executive is committed to improving Scotland's ferry links to mainland Europe and identifying opportunities for transporting a higher proportion of goods by sea. These actions not only help to deliver the objectives of the National Planning Framework, but also support wider, European spatial planning objectives. The ESDP, for example, explicitly recognises the importance of strengthening West-East links in Northern Europe. Recent accession of the new European countries also opens up opportunities, with the National Planning Framework indicating that strengthening the historic links with the growing economies of the Baltic Region offers considerable potential. The emphasis here on improving external connections is clear, yet internal connectivity is also recognised as important in supporting the Framework's objectives. If the cities are to be the key drivers of the economy, then there is a need to focus on reducing journey times between them. There is a need to link areas to the South and West of Glasgow more closely to the main population centres of the Central Belt. There is also a need to reduce journey times to and from the North.

The National Planning Framework also addresses a series of other infrastructure issues besides transport infrastructure. Among these other issues is the supply of water and drainage. A lot of existing water and drainage infrastructure is ageing and in need of replacement or repair. Lack of capacity in water and drainage systems is beginning to constrain development in some parts of the country. Major investment is required and the role of the National Planning Framework is to set national priorities. Another important infrastructure-related issue is renewable energy. At present, electricity is generated by nuclear, coal and oil-fired power stations, hydroelectric schemes and wind farms. More than 50 per cent of the supply is generated by three nuclear power stations, all of which are expected to close over the next 25 years. Scotland's climate provides a great deal of potential for deriving energy from renewable sources such as wind, wave, tide and water. In 2003, the Scottish Executive set a target of deriving

Figure 6.2   Scotland's freight transport plan

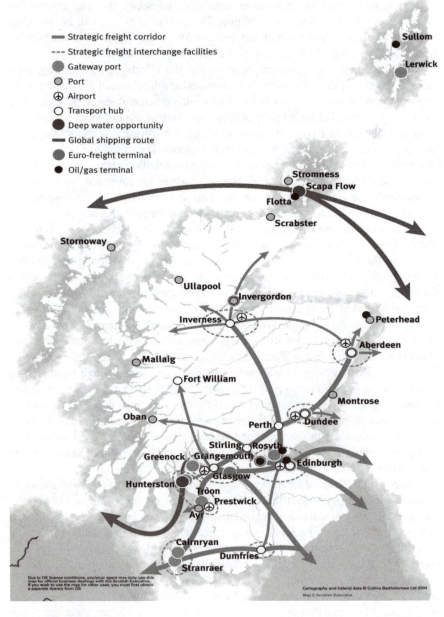

Source: Scottish Executive
The map identifies strategic freight corridors cutting across Scotland, a series of strategic freight interchange facilities and ports, gateways and hubs. Global shipping routes are also identified.

40 per cent of the electricity generated in Scotland from renewable sources by 2020. The National Planning Framework highlights the improvements to the electricity transmission network which are required to realise the potential of Scotland's renewable energy resources. The Framework also addresses the question of access to broadband internet services. Lack of broadband coverage has been identified as an impediment to economic development, particularly in rural areas. Last year the Executive made a commitment to extending broadband services to 70 per cent of households by 2004. There are a wide range of projects underway to stimulate demand in rural areas and explore the use of innovative delivery technologies (2002c). Some 90 per cent of Scottish households now have access to broadband services. Finally, infrastructure capacity to better manage waste is also addressed by the Framework. Scotland's waste recycling record has been poor by Western European standards and a network of new waste management facilities is required to meet the targets set in the National Waste Plan published in 2003 (see also Slater and Gemmell, 1999). There will be a need for local authorities to work closely together over the delivery of these facilities in order to avoid duplication and achieve economies of scale, particularly in the Central Belt. The National Planning Framework highlights the scale of change required and encourages the identification of sustainable locations for new facilities.

Spatial Perspectives

The National Planning Framework identifies priorities and opportunities for different parts of the country in a series of spatial perspectives. These are presented for the Central Belt, the East Coast, Ayrshire and the South West and Rural Scotland. These spatial perspectives address spatial planning issues of national importance which cut across city-region and local government boundaries, to provide a context for planning by local authorities:

- For the Central Belt, the Framework highlights the need for close collaboration between Edinburgh and Glasgow to promote Central Scotland as a destination for business investment of European significance. It emphasises the importance of creating high quality living environments and providing fast and efficient transport links between the cities. It identifies West Edinburgh, the Clyde Waterfront and the Clyde Gateway as areas where major change is already occurring and the scale and complexity of the issues is such that co-ordinated action is needed in the national interest. It draws attention to the need to ensure that the towns of the Central Belt have good public transport links to Edinburgh and Glasgow to provide access to jobs and city facilities and to make them attractive locations for new business investment.
- West Edinburgh is the gateway to the Capital and a West Edinburgh Planning Framework (2003) has been prepared to promote its potential for high quality economic development. Investments in improvements to public transport are committed and land has been safeguarded for a second runway at Edinburgh Airport.

- The Clyde Corridor is the primary focus for strategic economic development in the West of Scotland. On the Clyde Waterfront development is already underway. In the Clyde Gateway area, the construction of an extension to the motorway network will improve the accessibility of large areas, providing major opportunities for urban regeneration and new development. Scottish Enterprise is currently leading the development of a long-term strategy for the Clyde Gateway.
- Scotland's East Coast corridor is identified as having strategic development potential based on the knowledge economy expertise associated with centres such as Aberdeen, Dundee, St. Andrews, Edinburgh and Newcastle. Investment in transport infrastructure to reduce journey times between these centres can help to unlock that potential.
- The Framework recognises the important gateway roles of Prestwick Airport and the South-West ports and highlights the need to tie areas to the South and West of Glasgow more closely to the major urban centres of the Central Belt. It points out that Ayrshire's good international links provide opportunities for cultural, business and activity-based tourism and identifies the need to strengthen environmental quality in former coal mining areas.
- For rural Scotland, the Framework places emphasis on economic diversification allied to a strong commitment to environmental stewardship. It stresses the importance of higher education, cultural assets, telecommunications infrastructure and renewable energy resources as drivers of economic and community renewal. The Framework identifies the need to address the particular challenges facing the Western Isles within the context of the wider programme for fragile areas which has been developed by Highlands and Islands Enterprise.

Strategic Environmental Assessment: A New Challenge for Strategic Spatial Planning

The National Planning Framework for Scotland was prepared before the provisions of EU Directive 2001/42/EC on the assessment of the effects of certain plans and programmes on the environment came into effect (see Fischer and Seaton, 2002, and Therivel, 2004). The Directive will have implications for public bodies across Europe, including for those charged with the preparation of spatial strategies or regional development strategies. It will impact in particular on the processes by which such strategies are prepared. The Scottish Executive nevertheless took the decision that all plans and strategies prepared by public bodies should be subject to Strategic Environmental Assessment, even in advance of the Directive taking effect. Consultants were therefore engaged to advise on a method of assessment appropriate to spatial planning at the national level. There are, of course, some shared concerns over the application of the Strategic Environmental Assessment Directive to national spatial planning, and some have suggested that territorial impact assessment would be more appropriate at the national scale. The development of practical and proportionate approaches to assessing the environmental and territorial effects of spatial strategies may be one area in which the Celtic and Baltic countries can make a valuable contribution to European practice.

One of the outcomes of securing advice on applying the Directive to the National Planning Framework was the establishment of a working group comprising representatives of public agencies and non-governmental organisations to provide expert advice on potential environmental effects. The approach adopted drew on a report which the Scottish Executive had previously commissioned on the environmental assessment of development plans (2003c). The Environmental Report prepared for the National Planning Framework (2004d) was one of the first attempts to apply Strategic Environmental Assessment to a national spatial strategy. While the experience was valuable in helping the Executive to develop a method of assessment applicable at the national level, the assessment did not comply with the terms of the EU Directive in every respect. There was, for example, no explicit consideration of alternative strategies and no consultative draft. In order to comply with the regulations introduced to implement the Directive in Scotland it will be necessary to issue a consultative draft and this has significant implications for the preparation timetable. The first National Planning Framework took 18 months to prepare. With a consultative draft factored in, the process of preparing future Frameworks is likely to take at least two years. One of the substantive issues highlighted by the Strategic Environmental Assessment was the emphasis which the National Planning Framework places on expanding direct air links to improve connectivity. There is evidence that efforts in this area are having a positive economic impact. The latest International Passenger Survey indicates that the number of tourists visiting Scotland in 2004 was up 13 per cent on the previous year. The Irish Republic has been pursuing a similar strategy, establishing direct flights between Dublin and the capitals of the 10 new EU states. However, given the need to address the climate change agenda, environmentalists are questioning whether such an approach is sustainable in the long-term. If it is not, Europe's peripheral territories will face the challenge of finding alternative ways of improving their connectivity.

Conclusions

Learning the Lessons

The National Planning Framework has been very well received. It has been welcomed by local authorities, the business community and the planning profession. It has also won recognition as an example of good practice in spatial planning throughout the United Kingdom and internationally. It has raised the profile of spatial issues and stimulated debate about Scotland's long-term territorial development. The strategic role of the Framework has been generally accepted and the development priorities it identifies are being reflected in emerging structure plans. This does not mean that some constructive criticism has not been made of the Framework. A number of organisations and individuals have offered comments on the content, status and role of the Framework and the process by which it was produced. Several local authorities considered that the Framework needed to say more about implementation and delivery and that a more systematic approach to decision-making on strategic infrastructure provision was required. Some called for stronger links with the investment plans of public agencies and infrastructure providers and argued that the Framework would benefit from having an Action Plan. A number of commentators considered that the National Planning Framework would carry greater weight if it were presented to the Scottish Parliament. Some stressed that clear political leadership would be required if the Executive's strategic development objectives were to be achieved (Lloyd & Peel, 2004). Others considered that the relationship between the Framework and development plans needed to be more clearly articulated. The Royal Town Planning Institute (RTPI) in Scotland called for the identification of appropriate indicators for the economy, the environment, communities and sustainability and the further development of procedures for consultation and review. The revision of the Framework will provide a valuable opportunity to address some of these comments (see below). However, progress is already being made on monitoring and implementation as the focus for some of the above criticisms. The consensus emerging in the UK and Ireland is that monitoring of spatial strategies should be reported on a biannual basis. The Scottish Executive intends to produce a monitoring report for the first National Planning Framework in Spring 2006. Monitoring will draw upon the indicators of territorial development being developed by the European Spatial Planning Observation Network (ESPON) (2004) as well as experience in other parts of Britain and Ireland. It will also make reference to the *Indicators of Sustainable Development for Scotland* which the Executive has developed as a basis for assessing progress towards sustainable development (2003d).

An especially positive outcome from the preparation of the Framework has been the development of closer links between different arms and agencies of government, and with policy-makers in the fields of planning, economic development and transport. These agencies and organisations are now working to a common spatial agenda. There has been very positive buy-in from the enterprise network which is giving renewed emphasis to the importance of place and actively espousing the city-region concept (see Peel and Lloyd, 2005). The Framework has also had a direct influence on other strategic documents and contributed to a renewed interest in long-term strategic thinking generally. The revised *Framework for Economic Development in Scotland* and the Scottish Executive's strategic guidance to the enterprise network (2004c) have been given an explicit spatial dimension. The Executive is currently preparing a National Transport Strategy which will be followed in 2007 by a review of major transport infrastructure projects (the Strategic Projects Review). The Presiding Officer of the Scottish Parliament has established a Futures Group and consideration is being given to the future of small towns. The Framework has, therefore, had a very valuable influence on a range of different policy areas, from promoting policy integration to enhancing spatial considerations in individual policy fields.

The Scottish Executive is taking forward the cities agenda through the *Building Better Cities* initiative (2002d). City Visions have been prepared for the 6 Scottish cities and a Cities Growth Fund (£173 million between 2003 and 2008) has been established for investment in improved urban infrastructure. The EU's *Interim Territorial Cohesion Report* identifies Edinburgh and Glasgow as Metropolitan European Growth Areas (MEGAs) with potential for further development (2004). Research on the geography of the knowledge economy indicates that Edinburgh and Glasgow are strong knowledge economy centres in UK and European terms (Hepworth & Pickavance 2004). Scotland is unusual outside the core area of the European Pentagon in having two such growth centres so close together and that is an attribute on which the Executive is keen to build. Working closely with the enterprise network, Edinburgh and Glasgow city councils have formally agreed a common agenda for strategic collaboration in areas such as transport, economic development, education and training, tourism promotion and international events.

Looking to the Future

In June 2005, the Scottish Executive published the White Paper, *Modernising the Planning System*, which sets out its agenda for planning reform (2005). The White Paper states the Executive's intention to build on the success of the National Planning Framework by making it a more powerful instrument for securing the delivery of national policies and programmes. The Executive is committed to reviewing the National Planning Framework every four years. The second Framework (NPF2) will be published in 2008, providing a strategy for sustainable spatial development in the period to 2028. It is intended that NPF2 should set out the Executive's strategic development priorities more precisely than its predecessor. It will play a key role in ensuring the sustained co-ordination of policies with a spatial dimension, integrating and aligning strategic investment priorities and indicating where inter-regional choices need to be made. It will place more emphasis on implementation than its predecessor, identifying responsibilities and outputs for services and facilities in key policy areas such as health, education and affordable housing. There will be close links to the Executive's Infrastructure Investment Plan (2005b) and the investment programmes of public agencies and infrastructure providers. Like the first Framework, NPF2 will have to focus strongly on priorities for the improvement of infrastructure to support Scotland's long-term development. For transport infrastructure, it will need to look beyond the current delivery programme, drawing upon the National Transport Strategy and the outcome of the Strategic Projects Review. It will set out strategic priorities for investment in water and drainage capacity and waste management facilities, and consider the requirements of the next generation of high bandwidth communications technology. It will reflect the Executive's policy commitments on climate change, sustainability and regeneration and the outcome of consultations on marine spatial issues.

The Planning Bill which the Scottish Executive will introduce before the end of 2005 will make provision for the National Planning Framework to be used to identify projects of national strategic importance. Major transport, water and drainage, electricity supply and waste management projects and major areas of urban regeneration or expansion may fall within this category of development. The Executive intends that identification in the Framework should be the mechanism for establishing the need for such developments and the new legislation will require their incorporation into development plans. However, the proposal has provoked opposition. Environmental organisations have expressed concern that it could result in large and controversial developments being promoted without sufficient scrutiny. This raises the related question of wider stakeholder engagement in preparation of the Framework and ensuring opportunities to challenge the policies and proposals in it. The level of engagement achieved by initiatives to publicise the preparation of the first National Planning Framework was disappointingly low, perhaps because stakeholders remained uncertain about the nature of the document. However, the White Paper has clearly signalled that the Framework is to play a key role in setting strategic priorities and stakeholders now have a much clearer idea of what to expect. Given the higher status envisaged for the second Framework and the controversy over its role in promoting national developments, the Executive anticipates a much higher level of stakeholder interest in NPF2.

As a 'bridge to Europe', the National Planning Framework is helping to inform engagement with the European Union's competitiveness, cohesion and environmental agendas. It provides the starting point for collaboration with other parts of the UK on spatial planning matters of common interest and for Scotland's participation in wider European spatial planning initiatives. Scotland has participated in the preparation and updating of Norvision, the strategy for Europe's North Sea Region (2000), and the National Planning Framework has contributed to the strategy being prepared for the Atlantic Arc. Scotland's Chief Planner served on the Steering Group for Ireland's National Spatial Strategy (2002) and Five Administrations meetings provide a useful mechanism for sharing experience between England, Scotland, Wales, Northern Ireland and the Republic of Ireland. Discussions have been held with Government Offices and local authorities in the North of England with a view to making the necessary connections between the National Planning Framework and the Northern Way. An ESPON seminar in Belfast in February 2005 recognised the need for the Celtic countries and the North of England to strengthen links and work together in the context of North-West Europe. The GRIDS project and the publication of this book demonstrate that the Celtic and Baltic countries face similar challenges and have much to gain from collaboration and the sharing of experience. Looking beyond the EU, Scotland also has important links with Norway, Iceland and the Faroe Islands. A submarine power line between Iceland and Scotland has been mooted and Aberdeen is looking to develop shipping links to the North Atlantic. Scotland's early experience of national spatial planning has therefore been very positive, but the work is just beginning and many exciting challenges lie ahead.

References

Allmendinger, P. (2001), 'The Head or the Heart? The Limits of a Distinctive Planning System in Scotland', *International Planning Studies*, vol. 6, no. 1, pp. 33–54.

Allmendinger, P. (2002), 'Planning under a Scottish Parliament: A Missed Opportunity?', *European Planning Studies*, vol. 10, no. 6, pp. 793–798.

Ayrshire Economic Forum (2003), *Ayrshire – Scotland's Western Gateway*, Ayr, March 2003.

Bailey, N. and Turok, I. (2001), 'Central Scotland as a Polycentric Urban Region: Useful Planning Concept of Chimera?', *Urban Studies*, vol. 38, no. 4, pp. 697–715.

Commission of the European Communities (1999), *European Spatial Development Perspective: Towards Balanced and Sustainable Development of the Territory of the European Union*, Luxembourg, May 1999.

Cooke, P. and Clifton, N. 2005, 'Visionary, Precautionary and Constrained "Varieties of Evolution" in the Economic Governance of the Devolved UK Territories', *Regional Studies*, vol. 39. no. 4, pp. 437–457.

Department of the Environment and Local Government (2002), *The National Spatial Strategy for Ireland 2002–2020: People, Places and Potential*, Irish Government Publications, Dublin, Ireland.

Estonian Ministry of Environment (2001), *Estonia 2010 – National Spatial Plan*, Tallinn, Estonia.

European Communities (2004) *Interim Territorial Cohesion Report: (Preliminary Results of ESPON and EU Commission Studies)*, Luxembourg.

EU Council Directive No. 2001/42/EC on *The Assessment of the Effects of Certain Plans and Programmes on the Environment* (the SEA Directive).

Fischer, T.B. and Seaton, K. (2002), 'Strategic Environmental Assessment: Effective Planning Instrument or Lost Concept?', *Planning Practice and Research*, vol. 17, no.1, pp. 31–44.

Glasgow and the Clyde Valley Structure Plan Joint Committee (1999), 'A Common Economic Development Perspective for Glasgow and the Clyde Valley Metropolitan Area, Glasgow', Scotland, August 1999.

Goodstadt, V. (2001), 'The need for Effective Strategic Planning: The Experience of Glasgow and the Clyde Valley', *Planning Theory and Practice*, vol. 2 (2), pp. 215–221.

Goodwin, M., Jones, M., Jones, R., Pett, K. and Simpson, G. (2002), 'Devolution and Economic Governance in the UK: Uneven Geographies, Uneven Capacities? *Local Economy*, vol. 17, no. 3, pp. 200–215.

Hayton, K. (1996), Planning Policy in Scotland, in: Tewdwr-Jones, M. (ed.) *British Planning Policy in Transition*, Planning in the 1990s, London: UCL Press, pp. 78–97.

Hepworth, M. and Pickavance, L. (2004), *The Geography of the Scottish Knowledge Economy*, A Report prepared by Local Futures for Scottish Enterprise, June 2004.

Kumar, A. and Paddison, I. (2000), 'Trust and Collaborative Planning Theory: The Case of the Scottish Planning System', *International Planning Studies*, vol. 5, no. 2, pp. 205–203.

Lloyd, G. (1997), 'Structure and Culture: Regional Planning and Institutional Innovation in Scotland', in Macdonald, R. and Thomas, H. (eds) (1997), *Nationality and Planning in Scotland and Wales*, University of Wales Press, Cardiff, pp. 113–132.

Lloyd, G. (1999), 'The Scottish Parliament and the Planning System: Addressing the Strategic Deficit Through Spatial Planning', in McCarthy J. and Newlands, D. (eds) (1999), *Governing Scotland: Problems and Prospects*, Ashgate, Aldershot, England, pp. 121–133.

Lloyd, G. and Peel, D. (2004), 'Spatial Capacity Building?', *Town and Country Planning*, June 2004.

Lloyd, G., Roberts, P.W., Illsley, B., Chapman, M., Hayton, K., Slipper, R., Walker, L., Tewdwr-Jones, M., Colwell, A., and Lyddon, D. (2000), *Towards a National Planning Framework for Scotland*, Royal Town Planning Institute in Scotland, Edinburgh, July 2000.

Northern Way Steering Group (2005), *Moving Forward: The Northern Way*, Action Plan – Progress Report, England, January 2005.

Norvision Working Group (2000), *Norvision: A Spatial Perspective for the North Sea Region*, May 2000, Essen, Germany.

Pacione, M. (2004), 'Household Growth, Housing Demand and New Settlements in Scotland', *European Planning Studies*, vol. 12, no. 4, pp. 517–535.

Peel, D. and Lloyd, G. (2005), 'City-Visions: Visioning and Delivering Scotland's Economic Future', *Local Economy*, vol. 20, no. 1, pp. 40–52.

Purves, G. (1988), *The Life and Work of Sir Frank Mears*, PhD thesis, Heriot-Watt University, Edinburgh, Scotland.

Purves, G. (2002), *National Planning Framework*, Scottish Executive Planning Bulletin, Edinburgh, Scotland, December 2002, pp. 4–5.

Rowan-Robinson, J. (1997), 'The Organisation and Effectiveness of the Scottish Planning System', in Macdonald, R. and Thomas, H. (eds) (1997), *Nationality and Planning in Scotland and Wales*, University of Wales Press, Cardiff, pp. 32–53.

Scottish Executive (2002a), 'Review of Strategic Planning: Conclusions and Next Steps, Edinburgh', Scotland, June 2002.

Scottish Executive (2002b), 'Review of Scotland's Cities', Edinburgh, Scotland, December 2002.

Scottish Executive (2002c), *Connecting Scotland – Our Broadband Future*, Edinburgh, Scotland, October 2002.

Scottish Executive (2002d), *Building Better Cities*, *Edinburgh*, Scotland, December 2002.

Scottish Executive (2003a), *Securing a Renewable Future: Scotland's Renewable Energy*, Edinburgh, Scotland, March 2003.

Scottish Executive (2003b), *West Edinburgh Planning Framework*, Edinburgh, Scotland.

Scottish Executive (2003c), *Environmental Assessment of Development Plans*, a Report by David Tyldesley and Associates for the Scottish Executive Development Department, Edinburgh, Scotland, August 2003.

Scottish Executive (2003d), *Indicators of Sustainable Development for Scotland*, Edinburgh, Scotland, February 2003.

Scottish Executive (2004a), *National Planning Framework for Scotland*, Edinburgh, Scotland, April 2004.

Scottish Executive (2004b), *Framework for Economic Development in Scotland*, Edinburgh, Scotland, September 2004.

Scottish Executive (2004c), *A Smart, Successful Scotland: Strategic Direction to the Enterprise Networks and an Enterprise Strategy for Scotland*, Edinburgh, Scotland, November 2004.

Scottish Executive (2004d), *National Planning Framework – Environmental Assessment Report*, Edinburgh, Scotland, April 2004.

Scottish Executive (2005a), *Modernising the Planning System*, Edinburgh, Scotland, June 2005.

Scottish Executive (2005b), *Building a Better Scotland – Infrastructure Investment Plan: Investing in the Future of Scotland*, Edinburgh, Scotland, March 2005.

Scottish Executive/Scottish Environmental Protection Agency (2003), *The National Waste Plan 2003*, Edinburgh, Scotland.

Scottish Office (1963), *Central Scotland: A Programme for Development and Growth*, HMSO, Cmnd. 2188, Edinburgh, Scotland.

Scottish Office (1966), *The Scottish Economy 1965–1970: A Plan for Expansion*, HMSO, Cmnd. 2864, Edinburgh, Scotland.

Slater, A.M. and Gemmell, A. (1999), 'Land Use Planning and Waste Management in Scotland', *Journal of Environmental Planning and Management*, vol. 42, no. 6, pp. 861–874.

Tewdwr-Jones, M. (2001), 'Grasping the Thistle: The Search for Distinctiveness in the Devolved Scottish Planning System, *International Planning Studies*, vol. 6 no. 2, pp. 199–213.

Tewdwr-Jones, M. (2002), *The Planning Polity: Planning, Government and the Policy Process*, London: Routledge.

Therivel, R. (2004), *Strategic Environmental Assessment in Action*, London: Earthscan.

Turok, I. and Bailey, N. (2002), 'A Development Strategy for Central Scotland?', *Scottish Affairs*, vol. 39, pp. 71–95.

Wannop, U. (1986), 'Regional Fulfilment: Planning into Administration in the Clyde Valley: 1944–1984', *Planning Perspectives*, vol. 1, no. 3, September 1986, p. 207.

Chapter 7

Balanced Regional Development and the National Spatial Strategy: Addressing the Challenges of Economic Growth and Spatial Change in Ireland

Finian Matthews and Jeremy Alden

Introduction

Ireland was the poorest of the member countries of the European Community when it joined in 1973. Its Gross Domestic Product (GDP) per capita was just under 60 per cent of the average for the European Community. Yet by 1999, some twenty-five or so years later, Ireland had caught up with the European average. This period has been one in which Ireland has experienced 'incredibly rapid integration into the world economy' driven to a large extent by export-oriented industrialisation (Boyle, 2002, p. 173). This apparent transformation in Ireland's economic position continued and in 2002 Ireland's GDP stood at 120 per cent of the EU average, second only to Luxembourg. Mullally (2004, p. 25) describes this emergence of the 'Celtic Tiger' as 'a story of re-invention, self-confidence and unprecedented growth'. The question of how Ireland, as a country of around 3 million inhabitants in 1973, achieved these remarkable results has attracted a great deal of attention by both academics and policy-makers. The fact that the country is now populated by just over 4 million people and has recorded the highest OECD growth rate in recent years (8.1 per cent between 1998 and 2002) has served to only reinforce interest in Ireland as a case study. In many cases, others have looked to the country's economic success hoping to replicate Ireland's impressive growth trajectory. It has become 'the envy of other small countries' (O'Leary, 2003a, p. 1), including countries within the United Kingdom and the countries that acceded to the European Union in 2004. Both Kirby (2004), approaching Ireland's economic success from a development studies perspective, and Walsh (2000) explain the wider significance of Ireland's example:

> the Irish case is particularly significant since it has been claimed to be a model of how a small, peripheral and relatively underdeveloped country can achieve developmental success under the conditions of actually existing globalisation.
>
> (Kirby, 2004, p. 302)

The experience of dynamic economic adjustment in Ireland over the past decade shows that a weak, underdeveloped and very open region in the European periphery can undergo a rapid transformation that will reduce the economic differentials between it and the core regions of the EU.

(Walsh, 2000, p. 134).

The effective targeting and careful use of European Structural and Cohesion Funds played an important role, with Ireland being the recipient of significant Structural Funds from the European Union over successive programming periods (see, for example, Mullally, 2004). Yet other important factors also contributed to achieving these unprecedented growth rates, such as high birth rates resulting in a young population and increasing workforce with appropriate skills, thanks to investment in education and training. Pro-active policies in attracting Foreign Direct Investment were also important (see White, 2005). Development strategies strongly focused on innovation constitute a unifying policy factor that has propelled Ireland from a strongly rural economy into a predominantly service economy. However, one of the unintended consequences of these developments has been a tendency for economic growth to concentrate in those parts of the country that are already economically buoyant, with the lion's share of economic activity concentrating in the Greater Dublin Area. A small number of other areas, particularly in the south, west and mid-west have also played some part in driving the country's economic success. The National Spatial Strategy (NSS), adopted by the Irish Government in 2002, aims to correct these imbalances, while continuing to recognise the role of Dublin as a national growth engine.

This Chapter firstly provides an introduction to the institutional context for regional development and spatial planning in Ireland, including the relatively recent establishment of regional assemblies as well as the prevailing local government context. It then provides a portrait of Ireland, focusing in particular on exploring some of the dimensions of the 'Celtic Tiger' phenomenon of the 1990s and the various explanations for Ireland's profound economic changes over the past decade. The account then sets out the various policies which have been put in place in Ireland to achieve more balanced regional development, focusing in particular on the National Spatial Strategy (NSS) (Department of Environment, Heritage and Local Government, 2002). It assesses how successful these policies have been and looks at how the challenges facing the successful implementation of these policies can be overcome into the future.

The Institutional Context for Regional Development and Spatial Planning

Ireland is a parliamentary democracy and the powers of its government and related bodies are derived from a formal constitution established in 1937. Ireland's national parliament consists of two separate houses (the House of Representatives and the Senate), whose powers are defined in the constitution, and also includes a President who effectively acts as a guardian of the constitution. The Irish Government itself is headed by the Taoiseach (Prime Minister), formally appointed by the President on the nomination of the House of Representatives. The Government's functions are organised into fifteen Departments of State, including separate Departments for: Environment, Heritage and Local Government; Enterprise, Trade and Employment; and Transport. There is also a separate Department of the Taoiseach which has certain roles in integrating different policy areas, as well as dealing with European Union affairs.

In relation to regional planning activity, Ireland is divided into two NUTS II level regions, the Border, Midlands and West Region on one hand and the South and East Region on the other. The establishment of Regional Assemblies in 1999 for these two regions represented a new approach in regional policy and in the administration of Structural Funds in Ireland. The Assemblies comprise of nominated elected representatives of the regional authorities at the NUTS III level within each region. The Southern and East Regional Assembly accounts for three-quarters of the State's population and includes thirteen counties stretching from Dublin to Waterford and across to Kerry and Clare. Four of the five existing 'gateway cities' in Ireland are in the Southern and East Region. The Border, Midlands and West Region also covers thirteen counties, but is sparsely populated and is largely rural in character. The region covers almost half of the State's land mass but contains just over one quarter of the population. Only one-third of its population lives in urban areas compared with the national average of 60 per cent. The two regions are therefore very different in character and reflect the two sides to Ireland characterised by Horner (2000, p. 144, cited in Mullally, 2004, p. 29) as 'city-region Ireland' and 'rural and small town Ireland'. The main responsibilities of the two Regional Assemblies are to manage regional operational programmes under the Irish National Development Plan, monitor the general impact of all European Union programmes in both regions, and promote the co-ordination of public services in their regions. In addition, the Assemblies also have a responsibility to highlight issues of regional concern and ensure that national policies take the regional dimension into account.

At the NUTS III level Ireland is divided into seven regions: the Border Region, Dublin and Mid East Region, Midlands Region, Mid West Region, South East Region, South West Region and West Region. The regional authorities for each of these regions have functions that mirror somewhat those of the regional assemblies. In addition to that, the NUTS III regional authorities co-ordinate the development of economic, social and cultural strategies for their regions and also have functions relating to physical planning. These authorities have been given a key role in the 'roll-out' of the Irish National Spatial Strategy at the regional level through the preparation and implementation of statutory regional planning guidelines. These guidelines are designed to provide a strategic spatial framework for local authority development plans.

The Irish local government system consists of a number of municipalities within a complex arrangement of county, city, town and borough councils. There are 29 County Councils (Tipperary has 2 local government counties and Dublin now has 3 local government counties), 5 City Councils (Dublin, Cork, Limerick, Galway, Waterford), 75 Town Councils and 5 Borough Councils. Members are elected to local authorities through the proportional representation system of voting and exercise what are called 'reserved' functions. These are functions that are defined in law as being a matter for the members. A City or County Manager manages the executive functions for each city or county council as well as any other borough corporation, urban district council, board of town commissioners and every body whose functional area falls within that county. Local authority services fall under the following main areas: housing and building, road transportation and safety, water supply and sewerage, development incentives and controls, environmental protection, recreation and amenities. Local authority spending is about €2,000 million per annum, corresponding to approximately 5.5 per cent of GNP. Local authority expenditure is divided into current expenditure and capital expenditure. Most of the capital expenditure is financed by State grants while current expenditure, which is almost twice capital expenditure, is funded through rents, charges, fees, levies, commercial rates, charges for services provided, as well as State grants.

Economy, Society and Environment: A Portrait of the Region

For most of the 1990s the Irish economy expanded at three times the EU average, with the late 1990s usually acknowledged as one of the most successful and remarkable periods in Ireland's process of economic transformation (Boyle, 2002, p. 176; Walsh, 2000, p. 117). Various authors have commented upon Ireland's 'impressive record of export-led and job-rich growth in the late 1990s' (Kirby, 2004, p. 307). The pattern of growth has since been curtailed by the slowdown in the global economy, although the deceleration has been gradual, with the economy still growing at a faster rate than its European Union neighbours and with no significant weakening across a range of economic variables. The gains made by the Irish economy over the last decade are reflected in the increase in national GDP, estimated to have reached €125 billion by the end of 2002. On a per capita basis this is equivalent to €31,900 per person, which is approximately 120 per cent of the EU average, the second highest in the EU after Luxembourg, with larger states such as Britain and Germany standing at approximately 103 per cent of the EU average. Ireland's overall rate of economic growth is still well above that in most OECD economies, with prospects remaining favourable for 2006 and beyond. Like everywhere else, Ireland faces the challenges of high crude oil prices, flat European markets and intense competition from the developing economies in Asia. These risks are manifesting themselves in recent increase in inflation, job losses in manufacturing industry and weak exports. However, the domestic part of the economy is still performing extremely well. Consumer spending is strong and investment demand is buoyant. High employment growth continues. While inflation has risen somewhat, it is likely to remain at around 2.5 per cent in 2006. In overall terms GDP growth rate in 2005 will be about 5 per cent. This is likely to accelerate in 2006 and 2007 moving towards at least 5.5 per cent per annum.

A wide range of different factors help to explain Ireland's transformation, with various studies exploring which of the factors best explains the country's obvious economic success. The studies explore some of the more obvious issues, such as favourable macro-economic policies and the availability of an expanding, well-educated workforce (see Breathnach, 1998; Walsh, 2000), through to particular aspects of Ireland's governance arrangements (House and McGrath, 2004). It is widely agreed that key factors in Ireland's economic achievements in the 1990s included a young population meaning a rapidly growing labour supply, large flows of inward investment, strategic deployment of European Union Structural and Cohesion Funds, pragmatic and innovative government policies, a social partnership approach to economic and social development, openness to international trade and, lastly, an emphasis on education and technological innovation.

Ireland's demographic history provides interesting and important insights into Ireland's recent economic success. As a country with a long-established tradition of emigration, it has managed to reverse its population decline and this has been an important factor in its recent economic success. Ireland has also been undergoing what Walsh (2000, p. 132) describes as 'a delayed demographic transition' (see also Kirby, 2004). In contrast to most of Western Europe, Ireland has a strongly expanding labour supply resulting from a combination of factors including a baby boom in the 1970s, increased participation by females in the labour force and in-migration. Between 1993 and 2001, Ireland managed to expand its labour force five times faster than the rest of the EU. During the 1990s its ratio of annual school leavers to people already at work was about two thirds higher than the rest of the EU. Declining post-1980 birth rates, a slow-down in the rate of returning emigrants and reducing female participation levels are now beginning to slow the growth in the labour force, but its anticipated continuing growth, at least until 2010, will be sufficient to support the targeted economic growth rates over that period.

These general population changes are underpinned by a distinctive pattern of population distribution across Ireland. Out of a total Irish population of 3,917,336, the Greater Dublin Area constitutes just under 40 per cent (1.5 million). Dublin city itself has a population of 1 million which is over 5 times the size of the next biggest city, Cork, with a population of 180,000. Limerick has 79,000, Galway 57,000 and Waterford 44,000. This pattern of urban settlements is usually identified as one of the distinctive spatial characteristics of Ireland's urban system:

> Two features of the urban system should be noted. These are the dominance which a small number of relatively large size places holds in the overall distribution of population within the state, and the very large number of small settlements that exist.
>
> (Cawley, 1996, p. 86; see especially Table 1).

Gross Value Added for the goods and services produced in the Greater Dublin Area in 1999 amounted to 48 per cent of the national total, underlining imbalances in economic activity but also highlighting the fact that the economic performance of this area is pivotal to the overall economic performance of Ireland. Results from the Census of Population over the last 20 to 30 years confirm that the proportion of Ireland's population living in or near the Greater Dublin Area has been steadily increasing (Central Statistics Office, 2002). There have also been some strong points of growth in other regions most notably associated with the main cities. The proportion of persons living in rural areas continues to fall generally, particularly in the case of remoter areas and in areas with few towns. Demographic change and redistribution of the population along these lines have prompted calls over the past decade for some form of national planning strategy (see Cawley, 1996, p. 89), being a necessary intervention to prevent increasing disparities. These trends have also confirmed the view of spatial planners that areas will only sustain strong economic and population growth if they have a dynamic urban structure, or are closely associated with one. Within this perspective, towns with a population of 5,000 or more are seen as having a particularly important role in their ability to retain populations and show significant growth.

Because of favourable demographic factors, Ireland's dependency ratio (of those aged under 15 and over 65) is the lowest in Europe. Within the EU Ireland has the highest proportion of its population within the most economically active age group of 16 to 64. The significant expansion in the numbers of people at work has seen employment levels increasing by around two thirds over the past decade, with unemployment levels falling by over two thirds since 1993. Out of its population of just under 4 million at the end of February 2003, 1.77 million people were in employment in Ireland. Of these, 114, 000 (6 per cent) are employed in the primary sectors of agriculture, forestry, mining and fishing, 506,000 (28 per cent) are employed in the secondary sector, including production industries and construction and the balance, 1.19 million (66 per cent), are employed in tertiary or service sector. The latter sector includes wholesale and retail trade, hotels and restaurants, transport logistics, financial and business services, public administration, defence, education, health and other services. The most dramatic changes in employment in Ireland started in 1993. Employment then was only 130,000 higher than it had been in 1961. However, between 1993 and 2000 over 450,000 net new jobs were created mainly in the services sector, transforming the economic and physical landscape of Ireland in less than a decade. The IT sector (computer manufacturing by foreign firms, software development, call centres) accounted for a sizeable share of job creation, with Ireland now dubbed the 'Silicon Isle'. One very striking feature of the composition of employment in Ireland, illustrated by the above figures, is the relatively small size to which the agricultural sector has shrunk. For example, there are now more people employed in education and health or financial and business services or the wholesale and retail trade than in agriculture. Reflecting the importance of the tourism sector, more people will soon be employed in hotels and restaurants than in the entire agricultural sector. The services sector is now over three times the size of the manufacturing sector. Growth is concentrated in the wholesale and retail trade, hotels and restaurants, transport, financial and other business services.

Key Challenges for Regional Development and Spatial Planning

As is the case elsewhere, much of the type and location of business activity happening in Ireland today is, and will in the future, be strongly influenced by the global economy. The country's open economy must be responsive to what is occurring internationally. Generating the local business activity and attracting investment from abroad necessary to drive regional development will depend on assembling, at nationally strategic places, critical success factors. These are a business-friendly and efficient operating environment, a capacity to innovate through educational opportunity based on life-long learning, excellent physical and social infrastructure, a quality natural and urban environment and also participation of a private sector formulating its own investment proposals. Regional policies and regional development activities will have an important role to play in bringing about or sustaining these conditions and fostering the critical success factors. Yet Ireland has experienced a varied history of regional policy making. Cawley's (1996) account of the history of regional policy measures in Ireland suggests that an approach in the 1960s and 1970s based on the identification of selected growth centres to counteract the dominance of Dublin subsequently faded during the 1980s. More general forms of regional policy are therefore cited as 'a relatively recent phenomenon' in Ireland, introduced in the late 1980s as a consequence of reform of the Structural Funds, and designed to provide a more effective regional framework for implementation of funded projects (Mullally, 2004, p. 26). The Irish Government's decision to progress a National Spatial Strategy marked an important development from preceding regional policies and signified a return to a stronger form of strategic planning at the national level, designed to promote more balanced regional development and support the conditions for continuing economic success. The Strategy therefore represented a positive response by the Government to calls for a more integrated approach to regional policies, addressing economic, social and environmental change in a coherent manner (Walsh, 2000, p. 134). The following sections outline the process of making the National Spatial Strategy and its principal aims and objectives.

'People, Places and Potential: The National Spatial Strategy for Ireland 2002–2020'

Introduction

The National Spatial Strategy, '*People, Places and Potential*', was published in 2002 following the decision some three years previously by the Irish Government to design a policy instrument that specifically addressed the challenges of promoting more balanced regional development across Ireland. The following sections identify some of the important process involved in making the strategy, including the building of wide ownership and consensus as well as later addressing the important issue of implementation. In addition, the overall aims and objectives of the NSS are outlined, focusing in particular on the identification of particular geographic areas – referred to as Gateways – where the assembly of critical success factors is key to the success of the Strategy as a whole. The section also briefly addresses the ongoing programme of Government decentralisation of some of its own activities from Dublin to other parts of Ireland, looking at this in the context of the NSS, and also looks at cross-border collaboration on spatial planning issues with Northern Ireland.

The Strategy-making Process

Once the Irish Government decided in November 1999 to prepare a National Spatial Strategy, the approach taken to that task was aimed at building ownership and wide consensus. The significance of developing a broad consensus was also reinforced in commentary on the proposed strategy-making process (Walsh, 2002). In particular, emphasis was put on promoting a high level of public awareness and consensus, building support for mutually beneficial policies across levels of government and basing the new spatial direction for Ireland on a strong and rigorous programme of consultation. In response to this, the defining features in the process of preparing the NSS were: (a) consultative, across a wide spectrum involving social partners, local and regional authorities and different interest groups as well as cross-departmental; and (b) analytical, in terms of understanding why Ireland is developing in the way it is, drawing on a range of national and international research and expertise. There were a number of steps involved in the consultation process including an initial consultation phase on what the NSS should address, presentations of key research findings and discussion of strategic issues at national/regional events and interaction with government departments and agencies, as well as key social and economic interests. The consultation process culminated in the publication in September 2001 of the NSS Public Consultation Paper, entitled 'Indications for the Way Ahead'. In that document the broad elements of a suggested new spatial framework for Ireland were set out. A wide range of submissions was received from social partners, local and regional authorities, infrastructure providers, various interest groups and the general public. In overall terms, while many different issues were raised, most responses supported the broad elements of the emerging NSS framework. Many of the detailed suggestions were incorporated in the Strategy adopted by the government, published in November 2002. The strategy making-process in Ireland and the time taken to deliver the Strategy compare well with other, similar attempts at strategy-making in parts of the United Kingdom and in other parts of Europe. So, while some commentators might have wished to see earlier publication of the Strategy (O'Leary, 2003b, p. 25), it has been progressed in a timely and consultative fashion. Its relatively early publication has also resulted in significant interest in Ireland's experience from countries subsequently preparing their own spatial strategies (see Chapters 5 and 6).

The Scope and Content of the National Spatial Strategy

The Irish National Spatial Strategy (NSS) is based on tackling many of the challenges identified in the preceding sections and trying to bring these together to help to build the *critical mass* of population needed to foster and attract large scale enterprise and investment and energise the *potential* of the broader areas to which strengthening urban centres relate. This will provide attractive employment for both the local population and people moving into an area. The National Spatial Strategy (NSS) is the spatial framework for Ireland through which government departments, their agencies as well as the wider public and private sectors, can co-ordinate their plans, programmes and activities in bringing about the Irish government's objective for more balanced regional development. Studies of the concept of balanced regional development within the context of the Irish National Spatial Strategy point to how the concept has been interpreted in a way that focuses on a region's potential rather than attempts at redistribution of activities (Walsh, 2002). Such an approach does not take equitable distributions as its policy objective (in terms of ensuring an even (re)distribution of activity), but instead aims to foster and support the potential of different regions. Walsh (2002) explains how a 'functional areas' approach emerged during the strategy-making process in Ireland, with an attempt made to identify geographic areas that shared common characteristics and faced similar issues. This approach adopted in the NSS has also been influential in other approaches adopted, for example, by the Welsh Assembly Government and the Scottish Executive.

The National Spatial Strategy is focused primarily on addressing key spatial planning issues occurring within Ireland, with an emphasis on promoting balanced regional development. However, the Strategy also has a role to play in relation to reflecting and promoting wider European policy agendas. For example, territorial cohesion, as understood in a European context, and balanced regional development, as defined in the NSS, are very similar concepts. There is a high degree of consistency therefore between the aims of EU policy in relation to Territorial Cohesion and the NSS. There are also strong links between the aims of the NSS and those of the EU Lisbon (competitiveness) and Gothenburg (sustainable development) agendas. This is because the NSS fundamentally recognises that the balanced territorial development of Ireland will depend on developing regional potential through improving the competitiveness of the different parts of Ireland and tackling the causes of less sustainable development patterns. Additionally, by strengthening the international competitiveness of Ireland through a coherent national territorial policy framework, Ireland can make a strong contribution to the positioning of the EU territory as the world's most dynamic and sustainable economic space in the longer term.

The National Spatial Strategy is, like many similar spatial plans and strategies, a document that addresses a wide range of different policy issues and elaborates on a number of different spatial planning issues. However, the NSS in particular calls for:

1. Focusing of investment and growth potential around a network of competitive, innovative and attractive national-level urban centres or gateways supported by a range of other urban areas, such as hubs and county towns, in order to drive the development of the surrounding, mainly rural hinterlands.
2. Supporting improved territorial competitiveness across Ireland through better spatial planning, targeted infrastructural investment and development of new and expanded economic sectors that draw upon the distinct development potential of different parts of Ireland.
3. Addressing emerging trends of unbalanced and unsustainable development such as long-distance commuting and urban sprawl through better national regional and local spatial planning integration, targeted investment in public transport and other infrastructure to encourage more sustainable development patterns such as more compact urban form and greater use of public over private transport.

The Irish National Spatial Strategy sets out the way in which spatial development will be structured, co-ordinated, linked and organised to achieve more balanced development between regions and within regions. The Strategy has four complementary elements that work together. These are:

- A competitive Dublin continuing to play a key role at the national and international levels;
- Strategically located, large urban centres, performing at the national and international levels;
- A strong structure of towns and villages supporting regional and local economic and social activity;
- Vibrant and diversified rural areas that play to their strengths through harnessing their resources.

The NSS sees smaller towns, villages and rural areas working in partnership with cities and larger towns to form a strong structure supporting regional economic and social development. This is an important element in strengthening Ireland's urban system and addressing some of its historical weaknesses (see Walsh, 2000, p. 133). The NSS approach for each region has since expanded through more detailed planning guidelines and strategies at regional and county/city levels, taking into account the uniqueness of different areas. The NSS provides a planning framework for developing the potential of all parts of the country. As this happens, the rate at which Dublin is increasing its national share of population is intended to level off. Other regions' share will start to increase. This will not mean moving large numbers of people, investment and jobs away from Dublin. The drawing power provided through the spatial strategy is intended to attract investment and jobs to all regions. This will allow both Dublin and the rest of the country to develop and grow more evenly. The strategy elaborates a place-hierarchy of sorts, reflecting both the existing pattern of settlements and how these are planned to evolve during the implementation of the strategy. This place-hierarchy comprises a series of different components, including:

*   Gateways, including defined 'Atlantic Gateways';
*   Hubs;
*   Other urban centres; and
*   Rural areas.

Each of these components is briefly described hereafter.

Figure 7.1   Gateways and Hubs identified in the national spatial strategy

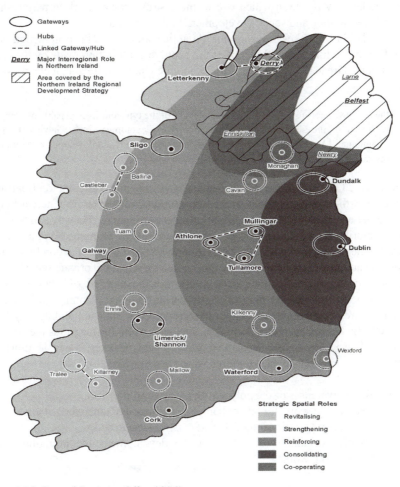

Source: Irish Central Statistics Office (CSO)

a. GATEWAYS: Taking the five existing gateways identified in the National Development Plan, the NSS recognises Dublin's pivotal role in national economic success. It is essential for balanced regional development that the performance of the Dublin area be built upon and consolidated. In relation to the other existing Gateways, the NSS concludes that the emerging critical mass of Cork, Limerick/ Shannon, Galway and Waterford needs to be strengthened, to complement Dublin's successful national spatial role. Building on the growing strength of these cities offers immediate prospects of establishing more balanced patterns of development over the next few years. Four new national level Gateways are to be developed. These will require a high standard of infrastructure and services to fulfil their national-level role. The new Gateways include Dundalk and Sligo. In addition to that, Letterkenny/ (Derry), and Athlone/Tullamore/Mullingar, will act as 'linked centre' Gateways, in the same way that Limerick/Shannon is a linked centre Gateway at present. A linked centre Gateway is one in which two or more strong towns work in partnership to promote economic and social development in their region.

The NSS also makes provision for 'Atlantic Gateways'. This is in recognition of the fact that, while the NSS identifies the positive contribution made by the critical mass of the Greater Dublin Area to the economic vitality of Ireland, it clearly signals that:

> the best prospects for establishing critical mass of the type and scale capable of competing with that of the Greater Dublin Area, points to developing Cork, Galway, Limerick/ Shannon and Waterford as an increasingly inter-connected and developed network of co-operating and complementary cities.

An Atlantic Gateways Project has been undertaken in a first attempt to visualise and develop further what this aspect of the NSS might involve in terms of networking the key larger cities outside Dublin i.e. Cork, Limerick/Shannon, Galway and Waterford and exploring the potential for joint approaches to their promotion and accelerated development. Much of what is contained in the NSS is a call to action by local and regional authorities, community and business leaders and the private sector to better co-ordinate their activities and objectives towards the objective of balanced regional development. Building on progress in preparing regional planning guidelines and the measures being taken to embed the NSS at Governmental and agency levels, the Atlantic Gateways study attempts to make more real the measures the NSS calls for to achieve more balanced regional development. The key issues, learning from international experience, being addressed in the project are to:

- Build awareness of the polycentric message of the NSS;
- Explore the scope for and potential contribution of a network of cities;
- Examine international models and experiences; and
- Identify workable objectives for the development and promotion of the Gateway network.

With the support of the Department of the Environment, Heritage and Local Government, the project is being developed by Shannon Development, the development authority for the Mid West region in Ireland, in collaboration with the Regional Authorities of The West, Mid West, South West and South East Regions. A national steering group for the project has been established. The steering group is chaired by the Department of the Environment, Heritage and Local Government.

b. HUBS: The NSS identifies a national-level role for eight, strategically located, medium sized 'Hubs'. These will support and be supported by the Gateways and will link out to wider rural areas. The Development Hubs identified include Ennis, Kilkenny, Mallow, Monaghan and Wexford. In a similar way to the linked-centre Gateways the NSS also proposes that Ballina and Castlebar and Tralee and Killarney act as linked development hubs working together to promote regional development in their areas.

c. OTHER URBAN CENTRES: There are many other county or medium-sized towns in Ireland, which provide a wide range of services. The NSS recognises that these towns are critical elements in the structure for realising balanced regional development, acting as a focus for strengthening their own areas. The roles that they will play in the future, which will differ from area to area depending on the particular conditions and circumstances, are summarised in the NSS and will be spelled out in more detail in the regional and county strategies and plans that will build upon the Strategy.

d. RURAL AREAS: Rural areas in Ireland are undergoing a profound process of change because of the changing nature of agriculture, diversification in the rural economy and the influence of nearby urban areas. Employment on the land is falling. Establishing an alternative basis for vitality in rural areas, with a particular emphasis on rural towns and villages becoming a focus for local investment, economic activity and housing development will therefore be of increasing importance in supporting the development of rural areas. The NSS outlines measures through which rural potential can be developed, building upon local strengths in tourism, agriculture, local enterprise, land- and marine-based natural resources.

Making progress towards the spatial structure outlined by the various gateways, hubs and other urban centres will depend in large part on improvement in infrastructure within Ireland. The function of the NSS in relation to infrastructure is to establish a broad spatial framework for the co-ordination of investment and to support that framework. It will play a key role in supporting actions designed to address a series of recognised capacity constraints and priorities for infrastructure investment (O'Leary, 2003, p. 6, Reynolds-Feighan, 2003). Concerning transportation, the NSS states that the national spatial structure needs to be supported by a national transport framework providing for an improved network of roads and public transport services, enhancing access and connections throughout the country. This framework will be internationally connected through key points such as airports and ports with links to Northern Ireland, the United Kingdom, the remainder of the European Union and the broader global economy. In relation to communications, energy and social infrastructure, such as third level education facilities, the NSS proposes that the Gateways and Development Hubs be a particular focus for the public and private investment needed to give these centres the capacity to drive national and regional development.

Figure 7.2   The national transport framework identified in the national spatial strategy

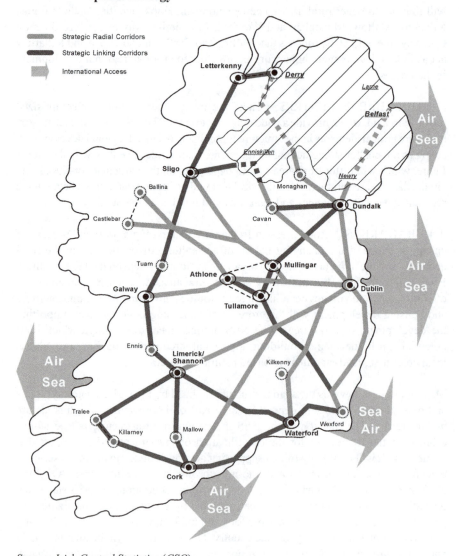

Source: Irish Central Statistics (CSO)

Public Reaction to the National Spatial Strategy

The preparation of the NSS was supported, over the three years of the process, by a well-resourced and carefully planned communications campaign, assisted by external communications consultants. This paid off in terms of a fairly widespread welcome for the Strategy. Acceptance of the NSS approach was assisted hugely by the fact that people could see that issues and concerns they had raised during the consultation process had been taken on board in the final published document. The main criticism of the Strategy in the media centred on a contention that too many gateways and hubs had been designated, and that considerably fewer should have been selected to concentrate resources more effectively. On the other hand, there was criticism from local interests in some towns who felt that they had been excluded from the Strategy. O'Leary (2003a, p. 4) remarks that protest from towns not defined in the Strategy as either gateways or hubs was only to be expected as they tried to position themselves within the overall strategy. These opposing criticisms suggest that the balance in selecting gateways and hubs under the NSS was probably just about right!

Progress to Date in NSS Implementation

In adopting the National Spatial Strategy the Irish Government decided that all relevant public sector policies and programmes must be consistent with the NSS. To support this decision, structures and mechanisms to implement the National Spatial Strategy at Government, departmental, state agency, regional and local levels have been put in place. These arrangements are intended to ensure that the Strategy becomes embedded in public sector planning, policies and programmes, including future decisions on investment priorities. So, while some commentators have argued that the implementation aspects of the NSS needed improvement (O'Leary, 2003b, p. 26), all Government Departments and relevant agencies have been involved in a process of examining their policies and activities from the point of view of their relevance to the NSS. This has involved evaluating their contribution to its implementation, considering whether it can be enhanced, identifying how capital investment strategies can support the NSS spatial framework, and defining the specific measures the Department/agency proposes to facilitate implementation and monitoring of the NSS. The introduction of Regional Planning Guidelines has also been an important element in developing and refining the implementation aspects of the NSS.

The Minister for the Environment and Local Government is leading the Strategy's implementation and reports on a regular basis to a Cabinet Sub-Committee. The support of regional and local authorities has been engaged through the preparation and adoption of statutory regional planning guidelines. These will create a crucial link between the national level NSS and local authority development plans at the municipal level. Integrated planning frameworks are also being put in place to set the foundations for the process of strengthening, consolidating and developing new and existing Gateways and Hubs. The overall approach to the Strategy's implementation is intended to be as inclusive as possible of all of the different State, regional and local bodies, interests and groups having a stake in regional development.

The initial phases of NSS implementation focused on embedding the policies contained in the NSS within key Government Departments, their agencies and in regional and local authorities. One example of this has been the Department of Finance's requirement that agreements between it and other relevant Departments on multi-annual capital spending envelopes demonstrate how their investment programs take account of the NSS. Other significant milestones in implementation include:

- Further articulation of the NSS at regional level through the adoption of Regional Planning Guidelines (RPG's) by the NUTS III Regional Authorities setting the strategic policy agenda for local authority development plans at city and county levels;
- Ongoing public investment in essential infrastructure such as key road and rail links under the National Development Plan investment programmes to interlink key locations domestically and internationally;
- A 10 year plan for transport – Transport 21 – that takes account of the National Spatial Strategy;
- Adoption of local strategic spatial plans for the gateways of Cork, Galway, Limerick, Waterford and Sligo, with work on similar frameworks advancing in other gateways, as well as public investment to underpin key elements of such spatial plans such as the proposals announced for substantial investment in new suburban rail services in Cork city.

Ongoing priorities in implementing the NSS include:

- Establishing a monitoring framework to report on progress in implementing the NSS, with a special emphasis on identifying and agreeing on a number of key indicators;
- Co-ordination of investment in the areas of housing, environmental and water services infrastructure provision and local roads programs within the Department of the Environment, Heritage and Local Government;
- Better co-ordination between government Departments and agencies in order to effectively link their strategic and longer term planning of investment to the priorities identified in the NSS and in Regional Planning Guidelines;
- Vetting of County and City Development Plans and Local Area Plans to ensure they are consistent with the objectives of the NSS;
- Supporting effective co-ordination between the NSS and its equivalent – the Regional Development Strategy – in Northern Ireland in ensuring that an all island spatial development perspective is informing matters such as strategic infrastructure investment and regional and local planning.

One of the earliest 'tests' of the effectiveness of the National Spatial Strategy, particularly in its ability to influence the decisions and investment programmes of Government itself, is the decision to decentralise a significant level of civil service posts and functions from Dublin to other parts of Ireland. In his Budget Statement of December 2003 the Irish Minister for Finance announced a programme to relocate 10,000 civil and public servants from the Dublin City area to 53 different locations throughout Ireland. In some cases entire Departments of government and other public bodies are to be relocated, while in other cases various offices within Departments are being moved. In adopting and publishing the Strategy the Government had stated that it would take full account of the NSS in moving forward the progressive decentralisation of Government offices and agencies. When the details of the decentralisation programme were announced there was widespread comment to the effect that the NSS had been ignored in the development of the decentralisation proposals. In overall terms, however, the decentralisation programme takes account of the NSS, but the Government also had to take account of a wide range of other factors in selecting suitable locations for the new decentralisation programme announced in the Budget. These other factors included:

- the core business and nature of the relevant Department or Agency;
- the location of their customer base;
- the location of existing decentralised offices;
- the desirability of clustering a Department's decentralised units within a region;
- the importance of respecting the scale and character of locations in terms of their capacity to absorb the new jobs involved;
- the existence of good transport links and the general infrastructure capacity in the locations selected.

In addition to gateways and hubs the NSS identified the need to strengthen the county town and large town structure and the need for a renewed emphasis on the potential of small towns, villages and rural areas. The Strategy envisages that county towns and other medium-sized towns would continue to play important roles as 'local capitals', developing their enterprise and service functions and continuing to provide opportunities for employment both in the towns themselves, and in related smaller towns, villages and rural areas. The relocation of public service employment to many of these towns will help to underpin the important role which many of them must continue to play into the future.

Collaboration on Spatial Strategies on the Island of Ireland

Since work started on developing the National Spatial Strategy, there has been liaison with relevant authorities and agencies in Northern Ireland on an informal basis (see Department of Regional Development, 2001; Neill and Gordon, 2001; Healey, 2004, pp. 54–58). This has been important both practically, in terms of addressing strategic planning issues that impact on both territories, and also politically, given the past history shared by the two countries. The Department of Regional Development in Northern Ireland was, for example, represented through its Chief Planning Officer on an Expert Advisory Group of national and international experts established to assist and support the development of the NSS. Representatives from relevant authorities in the North also attended various consultative forums, particularly those held in the Border region. The Public Consultation Paper on the National Spatial Strategy, *Indications for the Way Ahead*, published in Autumn 2001, signalled the need to consider the role played by the North South Ministerial Council in Ireland in supporting co-ordination of strategies between the two jurisdictions.

There is considerable potential for synergy between the National Spatial Strategy and the Regional Development Strategy for Northern Ireland, *Shaping our Future*, adopted by the Northern Ireland Assembly. For example:

- The Dublin – Belfast Economic Corridor has a combined population of 2.5 million (in the 2 city regions), enhancing its critical mass and allowing for more effective competition in European and world markets, through joint co-operation;
- Letterkenny – Derry has been recognised in the NSS as a linked Gateway, suggesting the need to build on existing links in a complementary and mutually supporting way. This development corridor has the potential to provide a strong joint regional capital for energising the whole North West of the Island;
- Dundalk (within the Dublin-Belfast Corridor) as a gateway will help areas on both sides of border, enhanced through increased linkages with Newry;
- Transportation corridor development will improve and extend options for external/international access points for both North and South, including the improvement of such access to/from the North West.

While some co-operative arrangements to promote cross border economic and social development are already in place, for example between Donegal and adjacent areas in Northern Ireland, these efforts could be intensified in the context of the two Strategies and supported through measures such as joint promotion of shared strategic sites for employment uses, measures to facilitate labour mobility, the promotion of regional accessibility and regional third level education provision.

In the course of on-going contact between Departments in the South and North of Ireland it has been agreed that a joint framework is required to support co-ordinated cross border implementation of spatial policy. This framework will elaborate on the approach of the RDS and the NSS, as they relate to cross-border co-ordination of development and planning issues and investment prioritisation. It is envisaged that the core elements of the framework will include:

- Arrangements for information, data gathering and sharing to support the development of policy;

- identification of 'demonstration projects' to establish information needs and collaborative mechanisms for taking forward features the two strategies in the North and South have in common e.g. the Letterkenny-Derry corridor; and
- setting out a process for taking forward other collaborative policy development aspects of the implementation of the two strategies.

The proposed joint framework will not be an all-island spatial strategy as such. The two separate spatial strategies for both parts of the island will remain intact. The joint framework is about how to collaborate on a cross-border basis in taking the two strategies forward. The collaborative process was given a significant boost in the joint communiqué issued following the summit meeting of the British-Irish Intergovernmental Conference on 27 June 2005 attended by the Irish Taoiseach (Prime Minister) and the British Prime Minister. The communiqué included a statement endorsing the significant potential for effective cooperation for mutual benefit on strategic issues such as infrastructure development and spatial planning. It was agreed that the modalities of taking forward such co-operation would be explored with a view to a further discussion at a future meeting of the Conference.

Conclusions

Learning the Lessons

Which lessons can be learned from Ireland for other economies, such as those in the Baltic States, which must deal simultaneously with the legacies of their past and the processes of globalisation? The first lesson suggested is that, given proper use of Structural Funds, an economy can, under certain conditions, undergo profound changes and dramatically increase its GDP. Yet the effective and proper use of Structural Funds itself relies on having in place effective institutions, policies, delivery mechanisms and procedures. Forward-looking and long-term strategies sustained by and aiming at innovative sectors (ICT), combined with adequate infrastructure and human capital to attract foreign direct investment have been and continue to be at the forefront. In addition, Ireland's position as a 'gateway to Europe' (Kirby, 2004, p. 307) for United States investment will continue to be important and emphasises the importance of the so-called 'strategic positioning' of a territory, an activity that spatial planning can usefully contribute towards. Recognising that foreign direct investment can also benefit small to medium-sized enterprises and that the domestic sector needs to be strong, because the level of foreign is often dependent on external factors such as the global economy, is also important. A further key factor, but an understated one, has been the governance arrangements in Ireland over the past two decades. This has taken the form of 'a unique set of institutional innovations for creative, dynamic, and self-reflexive governance for social and economic development' centred on a social partnership model of governance (House and McGrath, 2004, p. 30).

Lastly, since sustained high growth levels can often lead to increased regional disparities, as well as increased environmental concerns, it is advisable to anticipate and plan to respond to these trends. Corrective measures through regional policy, giving a fair chance to each region in developing its assets, must integrate the need for adequate and well-distributed human capital, a mobile work force and appropriate transportation and other infrastructure. There are important commitments on sustainable development in the strategy, and in other documents, and the National Spatial Strategy has an important role to play in promoting sustainable development. Others too have welcomed the introduction of regional spatial planning as 'a significant boost to planning for sustainable development' (Mullally, 2004, p. 29). In many ways, the NSS is a positive and significant response to the variety of calls for a national framework that have been made over the past decade.

Facing the Future

In overall terms substantial progress has been made in implementing the Irish National Spatial Strategy. The challenges now are to build on the successes achieved to date so that the Strategy continues to be a key influence on Ireland's economic, social and, indeed, environmental development in the coming years. The future competitiveness and dynamism of the gateways in particular, and also their wider regional economies, is of critical and central importance to the success of the NSS, both in terms of maintaining national growth and promoting more balanced regional development. Recent population forecasts suggest that on a non spatial policy intervention basis, some of the gateway regions may grow only modestly compared to strong growth of the Greater Dublin Area and a small number of other regions (Central Statistics Office, 2005). Bolstering the competitive economic offer of all of the gateway regions though co-ordinated actions in areas such as spatial planning, transport, innovation and enterprise and social and cultural development will be key areas through which the development of the gateways and their regions can be spurred on.

The Department of the Environment, Heritage and Local Government, in conjunction with Forfas, the Irish development agency has recently issued research on key development issues and investment priorities within the gateways. The critical issues for the gateways emerging from the report on this research include:

1. The need to enhance the innovation capacities of the regions and specifically regional centres of learning and third level education such as those in gateway locations especially though linkages to the enterprise sector and inter-firm linkages so that the regions improve their capacities to attract and generate investment and business development opportunities.
2. The need to counteract extensive urban sprawl associated with the gateways through a co-ordinated effort to both open up areas with significant development potential closer to the gateways and support a transition towards greater usage of sustainable transport modes such as local bus networks, walking, cycling

linked to efficient inter-gateway transport networks to be developed under Transport 21.

3. The need to strengthen secondary accessibility between the gateways and their wider regions so that regions surrounding the gateways can both contribute to and benefit from enhanced regional competitiveness by investment in regional road networks and under utilised rail routes, airports and ports.

Following the publication of the recent report of the Enterprise Strategy Group (2004) 'Ahead of the Curve' and considering the conclusions of the NSS Gateways Investment Priorities research, bolstering regional innovation and innovation transfer capacity will be the key issue underpinning regional competitiveness into the future. At the national level, initiatives through Science Foundation Ireland are playing a key role in strengthening Ireland's international innovation capacity. However, enhancing innovation within the regions and between regions is also vital. Regional innovation can be promoted by sponsoring the development of regional centres or alliances of excellence, inter-firm and inter-firm third-level institution linkages.

Many of the gateway locations have put in place ambitious development frameworks to cater for substantial economic development and growth and within a consolidated physical fabric. Attention is turning to the potential for brownfield development and the re-use of underutilised and strategically located urban areas. Many of the gateway development strategies have highlighted the development potential of sites such as former docklands and industrial areas. There is considerable potential for parts of such areas to contain contaminated sites and land that can be prohibitively expensive to develop. Measures to stimulate investment in the rehabilitation of such sites would contribute greatly to their redevelopment, to the achievement of NSS objectives and the enhanced development of the gateways as drivers of regional growth. Another aspect of making gateways more attractive to investment is in the area of sustainable urban public transport. Outside of the five main cities of Dublin, Cork, Galway, Limerick and Waterford, urban public transport systems are limited and outside of Dublin and Cork, integrated urban public transport systems are still being developed. Internal transport is becoming a key competitiveness issue for the gateways and will become a more pressing one after national level investment that will improve travel times between many of the gateways. A mechanism to provide incentives for local authorities to make the necessary alterations to local urban transport networks, such as bus prioritisation and green routes for walkers and cyclists, would make a positive contribution to the competitiveness and sustainability of the gateways.

Ensuring that the gateways are successful is an important element in making the strategy work, yet the future challenges facing the NSS do not stop there. It will also be vitally important that wider rural areas surrounding the gateways, including smaller urban areas and remoter countryside areas, can both contribute to and benefit from improved regional competitiveness. Rural areas contain many important natural and fragile assets such as a high quality natural environment, distinctive natural and cultural heritage and capabilities for development in relation to natural resources, local enterprise and tourism. Accessibility to gateways and wider markets is very important in this regard. A further important aspect of the NSS is that balanced regional development is about achieving balance between and *within* regions. Making sure that the more outlying parts of regions can both participate in, and contribute to, the development of the region as a whole is an important strategic objective of the NSS. The balance between larger towns and smaller settlements has been an important aspect of Irish industrial and regional policy over several decades (see Cawley, 1996), and looks set to continue within the context of the National Spatial Strategy. Regional ports and airports, as well as national hubs on the rail network are important nodes that more outlying parts of regions need to access easily and reliably so that both the attractiveness of such parts to new economic activity such as tourism and the contribution of such parts to a regions labour pools and skills is maximised. Having regard to the foregoing, investment in improved connectivity to national/international transport nodes and corridors through investment in regional road networks, community railway initiatives linking intercity rail services with local feeder rail services has potential for development and is called for in the Regional Planning Guidelines.

References

Boyle, M. (2002), 'Cleaning up After the Celtic Tiger: Scalar 'Fixes' in the Political Ecology of Tiger Economies', *Transactions of the Institute of British Geographers*, vol. 27, no. 20, pp. 172–194.

Breathnach, P. (1998), 'Exploring the 'Celtic Tiger' Phenomenon: Causes and Consequences of Ireland's Economic Miracle', *European Urban and Regional Studies*, vol. 5, pp. 305–326.

Cawley, M. (1996), 'Town Population Change in the Republic of Ireland: The Need for an Urban Policy Review', *Regional Studies*, vol. 30, no. 1, pp. 85–89.

Central Statistics Office (2002), *Census of Population*, Dublin: Stationery Office.

Central Statistics Office (2005), *Regional Population Forecasts to 2031*, Dublin: Stationery Office.

Commission of the European Communities (2005), *Working Together for Growth and Jobs, a New Start for the Lisbon Strategy, Communication to the Spring European Council*, COM (2005) 24.

Department of Environment, Heritage and Local Government (2002), *The National Spatial Strategy: 2002–2020, People, Places, Potential*, Dublin: Stationery Office.

Department of Regional Development (2001), *Shaping Our Future, Regional Development Strategy, 2025*, Belfast: Corporate Document Services.

Enterprise Strategy Group (2004), *Ahead of the Curve – Ireland's Place in the Global Economy*, Dublin: Forfas.

Healey, P. (2004), 'The Treatment of Space and Place in the New Strategic Planning in Europe', *International Journal of Urban and Regional Research*, vol. 28, no. 1, pp. 45–67.

House, J.D. and McGrath, K. (2004), 'Innovative Governance and Development in the New Ireland: Social Partnership and the Integrated Approach', *Governance*, vol. 17, no. 1, pp. 29–58.

Kirby, P. (2004), 'Development Theory and the Celtic Tiger', *The European Journal of Development Research*, vol. 16, no. 2, pp. 301–328.

Mullally, G. (2004), 'Shakespeare, the Structural Funds and Sustainable Development, reflections on the Irish experience, *Innovation*, vol. 17, no. 1, pp. 25–41.

Neill, W.J.V. and Gordon, M. (2001), 'Shaping our Future? The Regional Strategic Framework for Northern Ireland', *Planning Theory and Practice*, vol. 2, no. 1, pp. 31–52.

O'Leary, E. (2003a), 'Introduction', in O'Leary, E. (ed.), *Irish Regional Development: A New Agenda*, Dublin: The Liffey Press Limited, pp. 1–12.

O'Leary, E. (2003b), 'A Critical Evaluation of Irish Regional Policy', in O'Leary, E. (ed.), *Irish Regional Development: A New Agenda*, Dublin: The Liffey Press Limited, pp. 15–37.

Reynolds-Feighan, A. (2003), 'Accessibility, Transportation, Infrastructure Planning and Irish Regional Policy: Issues and Dilemmas', in O'Leary, E. (ed.), *Irish Regional Development: A New Agenda*, Dublin: The Liffey Press Limited, pp. 163–179.

Walsh, J. (2000), 'Dynamic Regional Development in the EU Periphery: Ireland in the 1990s', in: Shaw, D., Roberts, P and Walsh, J. (eds), *Regional Planning and Development in Europe*, Aldershot: Ashgate, pp. 117–137.

Walsh, J. (2002), 'The National Spatial Strategy as a Framework for Achieving Balanced Regional Development', in: McDonagh, J. (ed.), *Economy, Society and Peripherality: Experiences from the West of Ireland*, Galway: Arlen House, pp. 55–79.

White, M.C. (2005), 'Assessing the Role of the International Financial Services Centre in Irish Regional Development', *European Planning Studies*, vol. 13, no. 3, pp. 387–405.

PART IV

Regional Development and Spatial Planning in the Baltics

Chapter 8

National Spatial Strategies in the Baltic States

Neil Adams

Introduction

As with other parts of the former Soviet Union that acceded to the EU in May 2004, the Baltic States of Estonia, Latvia and Lithuania have undergone enormous structural changes since independence. These changes provide a complex background within which planners and others have had to work in all three countries. Before examining the various approaches to regional development, the context will be set by taking a brief look at the countries' location and history, the socio-economic conditions and some of the institutional structures. This will be followed by a brief description of some of the spatial characteristics of each country, providing those that are not familiar with this part of Northern Europe with an insight into these beautiful, complex and rapidly changing countries. The second part of the chapter will focus in more detail on the various approaches that each country has adopted to regional development in general and spatial planning in particular and try to assess what lessons can be learnt for the future. The importance of joined-up government, a strategic, inclusive and transparent approach and the problems of interpreting concepts that mean different things to different people clearly need to be addressed by policy makers and planners in the Baltic States as they do in other countries throughout the EU and beyond. In a situation where current EU policy is paradoxically helping to increase regional disparities within each Baltic State, it is clear that the regional level in each country does not yet possess the tools, capacity and resources to redress this balance. This issue will need to be addressed if more balanced patterns of development are to be achieved at the national level.

Context

Location

Estonia, Latvia and Lithuania are located in the Northeast of the European Union, sandwiched between the Nordic countries, Russia, and Central and Western Europe (see Figure 8.1). Estonia is the most northerly of the three with Latvia situated in the middle and Lithuania to the south. The Baltic Sea forms the western boundary of all 3 states, Russia and Belarus the eastern boundary, whilst Poland and the isolated Kalinigrad Region of Russia form Lithuania's southern border. The collapse of the Soviet Union and accession to the EU has had a significant impact on the macro-geographic position of the Baltic States and this is discussed in more detail in Paalzow's Chapter 9.

Figure 8.1   Location of the Baltic states

Source: Cartography by Jan Edwards, Cardiff University

A Shared History?

Anyone who knows the Baltic States well will tell you that whilst there are similarities between the countries there are also significant differences in terms of outlook and culture. Estonians seem to look towards Finland and other Nordic countries for inspiration whilst Lithuanians possibly feel closer to Poland and Central Europe, and Latvians find themselves between the two. There is little doubt however that the history of all three since the end of the first World War has dictated that their collective memories and experiences have converged to a large degree. After almost 50 years of Soviet rule and sovietisation (Mertelsmann, 2003) since the end of World War II, the Supreme Council of Lithuania proclaimed the restitution of Lithuanian independence in March 1990, becoming the first of the Soviet republics to do so (Lieven 1994). Estonia and Latvia soon followed suit and independence was declared in both in mid-1991. Dramatic political and economic transition followed in the early 1990s culminating in accession to the EU in May 2004. The transition process for the former members of the Soviet Union is highly complex (Thomas, 1998) and it is clear that during the transition period the Baltic States were and continue to be confronted with a situation of trying to look to the future whilst still dealing with the legacy of the past. The scale of the changes that have occurred and indeed are ongoing is something that is difficult for people in the remainder of Europe to comprehend.

Socio-economic Context

Upon accession to the EU, the Baltic States were amongst the poorest in the new EU-25 according to GDP per capita in purchasing power standards. Estonia was rated the fourth poorest with 46 per cent of the average for the EU25, Lithuania second poorest with 42 per cent and Latvia the poorest with 39 per cent (European Commission 2005). On the other hand in terms of economic growth, GDP in the Baltic States is growing faster than anywhere else in the EU25 with Estonia (7.2 per cent) leading the way in 2004 followed by Lithuania (6.8 per cent) in second and Latvia (6.4 per cent) in third (European Commission 2005). Such high rates of growth have lead in some quarters to talk of the Baltic Tigers, although such levels will need to be sustained over a number of years before real comparisons can be made with the Irish economic miracle. The transformation of Ireland from an economic backwater to one of richest members of the EU has often been held up as a source of inspiration to the Baltic States and other transition countries. Recent forecasts by Eurostat predict that annual growth rates in the Baltic States are likely to remain between 6 per cent and 10 per cent in the short to medium term. In each case, in a process mirroring the dominant role of Dublin in the economic growth in Ireland in the 1990's (O'Leary 2003), these high levels of growth have been driven primarily by the capital cities and a limited number of other large centres, whilst the rural areas and smaller centres have been developing at a much slower rate, if at all.

In terms of the distribution of population and economic activities the Baltic States share many common characteristics with the Celtic countries. A significant proportion of the national populations are concentrated in the capital cities of Tallinn (30 per cent in the City and 40 per cent in the capital region), Riga (32 per cent and 47 per cent in the capital region) and Vilnius (15 per cent and 25 per cent in the capital region). The concentration of economic activity in the capital regions is even more marked, fuelling increasing disparities within each country. The Riga region in Latvia accounts for 70 per cent of the national GDP, more than 60 per cent of industrial output and between 80–90 per cent of financial and other services (Latvian

State Regional Development Agency 2004). Figures for Estonia show 60 per cent of GDP and 80 per cent of foreign investments being concentrated in and around Tallinn (Estonian Ministry of Finance 2004). Similar concentrations are to be found in Vilnius and the surrounding area and evidence suggests that these disparities are increasing (Lithuanian Ministry of Interior 2005). Maandi (2001) comments that in many ways Tallinn is too small for Europe and too large for Estonia and this statement is equally applicable to the capitals of Latvia and Lithuania. Such concentrations of population, finance and activities coupled with ever growing internal regional disparities have important implications for planners and policy makers. In Lithuania, for example, the difference in GDP per capita between the richest (Vilnius) and poorest (Taurage) counties in the country increased by more than 4 times between 1997–2003, whilst four counties had GDP per capita below 75 per cent of the national average in 2003 compared to one in 1997. Such rapidly increasing disparities illustrate the inherent contradictions of pursuing balanced and polycentric development simultaneously at both the EU and national levels.

The complexity of the situation facing policy makers in the Baltic States is exacerbated by a highly fluid and worryingly negative demographic situation. Ireland again serves as inspiration with Eurostat predicting that, after decades of population decline, Ireland's population will increase by almost 36 per cent to 5.3 million by 2050 (European Commission 2005). The situation is not currently looking so rosy in the Baltics however. Between 1997–2004 the population declined by 6 per cent in both Estonia and Latvia and by 4.6 per cent in Lithuania (European Commision 2005). The indications are that this process is likely to continue. Eurostat population projections for the period between 2005 and 2050 predict a decline of between 14 and 15 per cent in each country. Pessimism among sections of the population and an increased awareness of internal and external disparities feed a desire to immediately acquire the perceived higher standards of living and personal wealth being enjoyed by the citizens of Western Europe. The combination of these circumstances provides an ideal breeding ground for out-migration and a negative natural balance in terms of population. The loss of young, dynamic and often highly-skilled human resources is a serious threat to the future ability of each Baltic State to be competitive on the EU stage. At the national level the loss of this critical mass from the rural areas and smaller centres is creating a human resources deficit in these areas that in turn adds further fuel to the ever-growing disparities. Such processes have important implications for the spatial distribution of activities and services, both in terms of maintaining existing services and providing new ones in the future.

Institutional and Legislative Context

The collapse of the Soviet Union required the construction of an entirely new institutional, economic and political system, which as Downes (1996) pointed out had never been undertaken at such a scale previously. Indeed, the scale of the institutional changes in various EU countries as discussed in Albrechts, Alden, and

Pires (2001) pale into insignificance compared to the scale of changes experienced in the Baltic States and other former Soviet republics. Currently the need to absorb the EU's Structural Funds is a dominant force in the institutional landscape. The current institutional organisation of each country is illustrated in Figure 8.2. It should be stressed that only the national and local levels in each country are directly elected with the intermediate levels being appointed by central government. The incentive provided by the availability of the Structural Funds has driven a determined effort to increase capacity at all levels and there is little doubt that significant strides forward have been made. The EU however gave a clear indication that they felt that the sub-national levels lacked sufficient capacity to manage and implement the Structural Funds when they decided that each individual Baltic State would be considered as a single region. As a result, Structural Funds are allocated nationally leaving the national governments to reallocate them to the regions. Kratke (2002) predicted that this decision would allow the national level to allocate funds to the stronger regions in order to drive national development, and on the basis of the evidence so far this prediction seems to be coming true (see Chapter 9 and Chapter 10 of this volume by Paalzow and by Adams *et al.*). It is fair to say that in general terms these intermediary levels tend to lack extensive powers and often also lack the capacity in terms of human, financial and physical resources to be able drive a strong regional agenda at this time. The formal hierarchical structure, the limited resources and capacities and the long-term process required to foster effective vertical and horizontal co-operation provide a difficult context within which to address the considerable challenges being faced in the Baltic States in the field of regional development.

Figure 8.2   Regional and local government in the Baltic states

	Estonia	Latvia	Lithuania
Regional level	15 county administrations	5 planning regions	10 county administrations
Sub-regional level		26 districts	
Local level	+/- 250 urban and rural municipalities	7 city administrations and 530 municipalities	56 city and district municipalities

Source: Neil Adams (2006)

The institutional structures in each country have developed rapidly and are still in a process of evolution. In Estonia, further reorganisation of ministerial responsibilities took place in 2004 with the regional development and spatial planning functions being transferred from the Ministry of the Environment to the Ministry of the Interior despite the fact that these functions would appear to have more in common with environmental issues than the other responsibilities of the Ministry of the Interior, such as police and national security. Discussions regarding institutional reform are ongoing in Latvia where the Law on Regional Development in 2002 facilitated the formation of five planning regions with responsibilities in the field of regional development and spatial planning. As discussed in Chapter 9, in effect the legislation legitimised the existing situation as the regions had already been established before the legislative framework was in place. The aim of the ongoing reform is to make administrations and service delivery more effective by reducing the number of municipalities from well over five hundred to approximately one hundred and sixty by 2009 and to amalgamate the functions of the districts and the planning regions to create five regional administrations. Continual changes to the institutional framework do not provide the stability necessary for strategic, long-term planning and are likely to continue to hamper efforts in this field until some degree of stability can be achieved. Such stability however is likely to be a long way off yet for countries in transition and is only likely to be achieved in the longer term in the Baltic context. In the meantime, planners are likely to have to deal with various changes of direction as their political masters continue to change.

During the early 1990s the need to develop a framework for spatial development became apparent and policy makers and planners sought inspiration from abroad under various bilateral agreements and various EU-sponsored initiatives. One such initiative was the Vision and Strategies Around the Baltic Sea (VASAB) initiative sponsored by the Interreg programme. The VASAB initiative bought planners from the countries of the Baltic Sea Region together and was particularly influential, providing an opportunity for Baltic planners to share experiences with colleagues in Germany, Poland and the Nordic countries (Maandi 2001). This helped to facilitate a process whereby planners and policy makers in the Baltic States started to develop a tailor-made system to suit their own needs, to a certain extent through a process of trial and error. Through legislation dating from the mid-nineties (revised in Estonia and Latvia in 2002) each Baltic State introduced a formal hierarchy of statutory planning documents to be prepared by the national, regional and local levels in a system with similarities to the comprehensive integrated approach favoured in Flanders, the Netherlands and parts of Scandinavia. The legislation prescribes the responsibilities at the national and also the lower levels of government in each country in a highly formalised way.

Spatial Context and Territorial Capital

The development perspectives of any region are to some extent determined by the specific and unique spatial characteristics that form the territorial capital of that region. The Baltic States have numerous spatial qualities with many well-defined, compact cities with good public transport systems, vibrant centres and beautiful public parks coupled with vast rural areas with exceptional natural qualities. Ironically, the rapid transition and economic growth forms a serious threat to some of these qualities as pressure for development, sub-urbanisation and growth increase. The traditional, dispersed settlement structure that characterised this part of Northern Europe was heavily influenced during the Soviet period by policies of heavy industrialisation in certain centres and the policy of collective farming in the rural areas. Transport infrastructure focussed on linking the major Baltic cities with Moscow rather than with each other. As stated in the Estonian National Spatial Plan (NSP),[1] 'Tallinn was not developed as the capital city of Estonia, but rather as one of the industrial centres in the north-western part of the Soviet Union' (Estonian MoE 2002, Chapter 1). Lithuania arguably has the strongest urban structure with five cities of over 100,000 population spread relatively evenly around the country. The population density in Lithuania is over 50 people per km², significantly higher than both Estonia (31/km²) and Latvia (36/km²), and similar to Scotland (65/km²), although still extremely low compared to many parts of Western Europe such as Belgium (339/km²) and even Wales (142/km²). In Estonia three of the five largest centres (population over 40,000) are concentrated in the north of the country. Fourteen centres had a population over 10,000 in 2004. Latvia is characterised by a weak urban structure due to the high concentration of population in Riga and the vast distance between the next two largest cities, Daugavpils (113,000 in 2003) in the east and Liepaja (87,500 in 2003) in the west. There were twenty-two centres with a population of over 10,000 in Latvia in 2003 with the majority between 10,000–20,000. The vast rural areas in each country are characterised by large areas of forests, lakes and wetlands with high natural values as well as extensive, but relatively unstructured, agricultural areas.

Improvements to the transport infrastructure in order to improve internal and external accessibility are high on the agenda. International seaports in Tallinn, Riga, Ventspils (Latvia), Liepaja (Latvia) and Klaipeda (Lithuania) are competing for a share of the increasing east-west transport flows. Port infrastructure and the rail infrastructure linking the ports to their hinterlands and eastern markets are undergoing modernisation although this is likely to be a long process. However, despite all of the rhetoric at the EU level regarding sustainable transport and rail being a priority, evidence suggests that in reality the EU spending on roads is being prioritised (as discussed in Peters, 2003 and in Chapter 10 of this volume by Adams et al). Whilst high profile EU infrastructure projects – such as the planned high speed rail link between the Baltic States and Western Europe via Warsaw and Berlin and the high investment in international road connections – will undoubtedly increase the external accessibility of the Baltic States, it is highly questionable whether they will ultimately deliver the levels of economic benefits that some claim and many hope for.

Approaches to Regional Development and Spatial Planning in the Baltic States

The Europeanisation of spatial planning and the increasing importance of the territorial context within EU regional policy has been well documented (Faludi, 2004, Bynens and Van der Lecq, 2005) and this new form of planning has been embraced in the Baltic States. The complex historical, socio-economic and institutional contexts of

---

[1]   For the sake of clarity the national spatial planning documents of each Baltic State will be referred to as NSP's.

the Baltic States meant that the elaboration of NSPs was never going to be easy, although in many ways such complexity provides a context within which spatial planning can be a valuable instrument. Estonia and Lithuania have succeeded in preparing and adopting their national strategies. Estonia 2010: the National Spatial Plan and the Comprehensive Plan of the Territory of the Republic of Lithuania were adopted in 2001 and 2002 respectively and are in the process of being implemented. Internal tensions and institutional reform in Latvia, however, have prevented the successful preparation and adoption of the NSP although the process now appears to be on course for a successful conclusion in 2007. The responsibility for the preparation of the NSPs currently rests with the Ministry of the Environment in Lithuania, the Ministry of Interior in Estonia and the Ministry of Regional Development and Local Government in Latvia. The respective ministries in Estonia and Latvia are responsible for both regional policy and spatial planning whilst in Lithuania these responsibilities are split between the Ministry of the Environment (spatial planning) and the Ministry of the Interior (regional policy). Up until May 2004 both regional development and spatial planning in Estonia were also the responsibility of the Ministry of the Environment and there is considerable debate throughout the EU as to the most effective division of tasks and responsibilities between these various related fields. At the EU level, there appears to be an increasing recognition that regional policy and spatial planning are inextricably linked and there can be little doubt that regional policy is a policy area that has a significant spatial dimension, although the same could be said of transport and environmental policy.

The issue of joined-up government is undoubtedly one of the hot issues and main challenges facing policy makers and planners today. The perceived division of the regional policy and spatial planning functions leads to many disputes in countries throughout the EU about where and how policies should be targeted. Whereas in principle one could argue that it is likely to be more effective to pursue increased joined-upedness across ministerial boundaries, in practice the integration of regional and spatial policy may be easier if both functions are housed within the same ministry. Evidence from the Baltics in relation to this issue would appear to support this view although it is not entirely conclusive. A comparison of the Regional Development Strategy of Estonia and the Estonian NSP reveal that the objectives of the two documents, prepared under one ministerial umbrella, are similar and appear to be well integrated. In Lithuania however, where separate ministries prepared the respective policies, the integration is less apparent. The recently approved Lithuanian Regional Policy Strategy until 2013 prepared by the Ministry of the Interior identifies five regional growth centres and a number of social development territories where actions should be targeted in the period until 2013 in an attempt to reduce regional disparities (see Dagiliene, Chapter 11). The selected centres and the adopted approach, however, differ from the approach adopted in the Lithuanian Comprehensive Plan (the NSP), and although these two documents currently form the cornerstone of Lithuanian regional policy and both contain a strong commitment to balanced regional development, integration between them is not always apparent.

The Challenges and Focus of the NSPs

All three NSPs are statutory documents. Not only is preparation of the NSPs required but the relevant legislation, especially in Latvia and Lithuania, is relatively detailed in relation to the form and content of the documents and process. The Estonian document has a relatively short time horizon up until 2010. The Lithuanian and Latvian (once finalised) documents look further ahead to 2020 and 2025 respectively. Within the context of transition countries, the adoption of a longer time horizon would appear to be more challenging and ambitious. The Latvian and Lithuanian legislation also identify a number of general and relatively abstract principles that should be adhered to in all spatial planning documents. The purpose of spatial planning and of the NSPs is prescribed in each case in the relevant legislation and the theme of stimulating or facilitating balanced development features strongly, although as with concepts such as polycentricity, the term balanced development is not specifically defined and tends to mean different things to different people (Shaw and Sykes 2004). As Maandi (2001) recognised in the case of Estonia, the relatively small and declining populations, the dispersed settlement structure, with a high concentration of population in a small number of centres, means that the pursuit of balanced development in the Baltics will be particularly challenging. The magnitude of this challenge is emphasised by recent research undertaken as part of the ESPON initiative (ESPON 2004). The research examined three dimensions of polycentricity: the size and importance of the cities, their spatial distribution and the connections between them, and concluded that the Baltic States and Hungary are the least polycentric of all of the new member states. The legislation in each country has a commitment to balanced development at its core, a concept that was established at the EU level via the European Spatial Development Perspective (European Commission 1999). Clearly, the incentive of accessing the Structural Funds places the EU in a strong position in terms of influencing the adoption of EU principles and concepts, at least in principle, in many of the new member states. The apparent dominance, however, of the efficiency over the equity approach to resource allocation (as discussed in Chapters 9 and 10 of this volume by Paalzow and Adams et al and see also Petrakos, 2001) suggests that the goal of balanced development is as yet not being pursued with any vigour in practice, at least at the national and sub-national level.

The apparent national commitment to balanced development in Latvia is illustrated by the fact that it is the only Baltic State where the concept of territorial cohesion features strongly in the Single Programming Document (SPD, Latvian Government 2003), which details the strategy and measures for accessing the EU objective 1 funds for the period 2004–2006. The promotion of territorial cohesion is identified as one of the five national priorities in the SPD. Partly due to pressure from the EU, territorial cohesion is also likely to be identified as an objective in other key programming and planning documents currently under preparation in Lithuania (see Dagiliene Chapter 11 of this book) and Estonia. There is a tendency, however, for transition governments to pursue the efficiency rather than the equity approach to regional development, concentrating resources in order to gain maximum impact in the shortest possible time. In these circumstances it is unclear whether the objective to pursue balanced development will be translated into action via a more equitable, gradual and ultimately more sustainable approach to growth and resource allocation, as advocated by Ovin (2001). The pursuit of polycentric regional development at the EU level (where each individual Baltic State is classified as one region) via its regional policy and the natural tendency for private investment to be concentrated in the capital cities complicates the pursuit of similar objectives at the national level still further. As a result there is a feeling that regional disparities are actually likely to increase within each individual Baltic State for the foreseeable future.

The emphasis in the Estonian NSP apparently changed during the preparation process. In the political foreword to the document, then Secretary General for the Ministry of the Environment, Sulev Vare, states that the initial priority of economic success was replaced by a broader human needs based approach (Estonian Ministry of the Environment 2001). The Estonian NSP focuses very firmly on the promotion of a balanced settlement structure and promoting spatial equity, whereas the role of the Latvian NSP, as identified by Upmace (2001), focuses more on protecting the interests of the State, providing a framework for the lower levels of government and facilitating co-ordination between various levels and sectors. In Lithuania, the Law on the Planning of the Territories (1995) also identifies other objectives relating to the formulation of development policies in various spheres, the rational use of land, the conservation of natural environments and balancing the interests of numerous stakeholders. The emphasis is on the provision of a framework for spatial co-ordination rather than the proactive stimulation of development. Given the economic context, it is perhaps surprising that generating prosperity does not feature high on the list of objectives for any of the spatial planning systems or the relevant national spatial planning approaches in the Baltic States. Rather, the pursuance of balanced development is very much the dominant theme. Whether the powerful line ministries responsible for other key policy areas and spending programmes, and whether elected national politicians in often fragile coalitions, are as yet in accordance with this approach is doubtful. The possibility of accessing EU Structural Funds provides a strong incentive to adopt the EU objectives and concepts, although the allocation of the funds at the national rather than the regional level makes the actual pursuance of this objective in practice unlikely and this provides a challenging context for any NSP.

Stakeholder Engagement and Transparency: A New Phenomena?

Whilst there are many similarities in the approaches to spatial planning in the Baltic States, there are also some significant differences. The recent history of the countries and the characteristics of the centrally-planned economy meant that there was no culture of stakeholder engagement and consultation prior to independence. This culture therefore had to be created, which is no easy task and, whilst a certain level of consultation has been achieved, much work remains before it can be claimed that all relevant stakeholders are being truly engaged in planning processes. The challenge of engaging stakeholders is not exclusive to the Baltic States and is ongoing in countries with much more mature democracies. Throughout the EU, stakeholder engagement in the preparation of regional development strategies has become increasingly important in recent years. An open and inclusive process is generally considered to being critical to increasing the ownership of such strategies and thus ultimately to their chances of success. There are three possibilities. Stakeholder involvement can be organised in a highly formalised and structured way where the plan maker has a statutory duty to consult various bodies at specified moments during the process. The other extreme is to organise everything on an informal basis relying on informal contacts and the readiness of stakeholders to participate in the process. The third possibility, and the one that is adopted in most cases, is to use a combination of the two.

A more informal approach can facilitate the involvement of a wider group of stakeholders, some of whom may be wary of becoming involved in a highly formalised statutory process. The reverse side of that coin, however, is that unless powerful line ministries, for example, are compelled to participate in the process there is a danger that they will fail to see the relevance or added value of their participation and will continue to pursue their own sectoral approach. Estonia opted to pursue a more informal approach than the one adopted in Lithuania and the one prescribed by legislation in Latvia. Significantly, and in contrast to their Baltic neighbours, there is no statutory requirement for the Estonian NSP to be subjected to public consultation, display or discussion. The general principles of the plan, however, are required to be published in the national media and the plan also has to be drawn up in co-operation with the county administrations, line ministries and county associations of local governments. Despite an apparently less formal approach, the process in Estonia still took six years (1995–2001) before the NSP and associated Action Plan was approved. A similar amount of time was required in Lithuania, with the process being started in 1996 and the Comprehensive Plan being approved in 2002, although the associated implementation plan was not approved until the following year. As mentioned previously, the NSP is yet to be finalised and adopted in Latvia despite the process being initially started in 1998. Such long preparation times are perhaps not surprising given the context and the fact that that it is the first time that each country had prepared such a document, especially when one considers the fact that excessive preparation times remain an issue in plan processes in many other countries. There is a danger, however, that such documents are out of date before they are approved (Petkevicius 2001) and the Lithuanian MoE was swift to recognise this, introducing amendments to simplify procedures and speed up the plan preparation process (VASAB 2000). Achieving a shorter preparation period however, although recognised as being desirable, is not going to be an easy task given the necessity of increasing stakeholder engagement and the rapidly evolving institutional landscape.

There is little doubt that each country has taken significant strides forward in recent years in relation to the transparency of public administration. However, none of the NSP documents or processes were subject to any form of independent appraisal. The instability of national governments in these young democracies, where fragile coalitions have fallen regularly since independence, means that true transparency can be dangerous, and this is yet another consequence of dealing with the legacy of the past. The pursuit of transparency will take time, although the credibility and quality of both process and plan would be enhanced greatly if a more transparent process can be achieved in the revisions of the existing documents.

Formality and Informality

In the years after independence Estonian planners sought inspiration from a number of countries but primarily from Finland, especially in relation to the concept of strategic planning and this had a significant influence on both the planning legislation and the NSP. The Estonian Planning Act of 2002 strengthened the emphasis on the need for the NSP to be strategic after the Ministry of the Environment concluded that some elements of Estonia 2010 were too detailed for a national strategy (VASAB 2000). A working group comprising academics and government officials was established in 1995 by the Ministry of the Environment and given the task of leading the process to draw up the NSP under the banner Estonia 2010. One of the key aims of the working group was to make the plan process as open and inclusive as possible. The process ultimately consisted of four basic stages. The first stage involved looking at experiences and examples of other countries, investigating public opinion in relation to visions for the future and posing the question of what the world could look like in 2010. The relatively short time horizon reflects the highly fluid and rapidly changing context in transition countries. The second stage involved analysing key themes of future development and considering what the role of Estonia could be in these possible new worlds (Estonian Ministry of the Environment, 1996). In the third stage two working groups including prominent academics and policy makers from the various sectors and levels of government were established to develop four alternative scenarios for the future development of the country. The four scenarios were variants around two key factors that would influence the future development of the country: the type and extent of geopolitical and geo-economical integration in global markets, structures and processes and the country's success, or otherwise, in rising to the challenge of IT evolution and creating the pre-conditions for a successful knowledge based economy (Loogma, 1997). This approach aimed to generate knowledge and encourage thinking and learning and it was never the intention to adopt one of the four scenarios as the basis for the NSP (Raagma and Sotarauta 1997). The knowledge generated within this scenario process, however, did form the basis for the document. Such an approach, whereby knowledge is generated in order to shape minds, has similarities with the ESDP approach as discussed in Faludi (2001).

The process in Latvia and Lithuania was (and is being in the case of Latvia) organised in a more formal way in accordance with the statutory requirements of the relevant legislation. In Latvia, the NSP will consist of four parts: a report on the existing situation, the development perspectives containing the vision and strategy until 2025, the binding regulations and finally the national planning guidelines. Each part is subject to rigorous rounds of consultation and approval. Up until the start of 2005, only the report on the existing situation had been approved, although the delays that have occurred have ensured that even this part is now out of date. Whilst the delays in Latvia have undoubtedly caused difficulties (see Paalzow, Chapter 9), the expertise that has been developed in the meantime within the regional development agencies can be put to good use and it is important that the Latvian Ministry of Regional Development and Local Government allow them to play a positive and proactive role in the process of national policy formulation. The improved co-operation between the Ministry and the regions that has developed in recent years means that a genuine two way process is now possible, something that would not have been so just a few years ago. The Latvian Ministry recognises that the delays could ultimately work to their advantage, allowing them to learn more from the experiences of others. In these circumstances they would be well advised to try to strengthen the informal networking in relation to the plan process to supplement the highly formalised structure prescribed in the legislation. A similar but ultimately more successful path (the Comprehensive Plan has been approved) was followed in Lithuania. The report on the evaluation of existing situation was prepared in 1996. The draft preliminary solutions were approved in 1999 after public consultation and evaluation of national sectoral programmes and the Comprehensive Plan was approved in 2002.

Who is the NSP for?

An important consideration in determining the type of approach to be adopted is the identification of the primary and secondary audience for the NSP. Clearly, it is important to both organise the process and to write the document in a style that is accessible and appealing to the intended audience. Invariably, NSPs are intended to act as a framework for the actions and decisions of a wide range of public sector organisations, although a wider group is often intended as secondary audience (Adams and Harris 2005). The issue of language is important in relation to the accessibility of a NSP. Social exclusion in relation to the Russian speaking population is a hot issue in the Baltic States especially in Estonia (26 per cent of total population ethnic Russians in 2004)[2] and Latvia (29 per cent of total population ethnic Russians in 2004)[3] where the proportion of the population that is ethnic Russian is significantly higher than in Lithuania. The high national proportions hide even greater concentrations particularly in the east of the countries, with Ida-Viru County in North-East Estonia having 71 per cent ethnic Russians and parts of the Latgale Region of Eastern Latvia over 50 per cent. The Russian language issue appears to have been given little attention at the institutional level during the preparation process. Occasionally during the process, workshops or seminars in relation to national planning issues have unofficially taken

---

[2]   Statistics Office of Estonia http://pub.stat.ee/px-web.2001/dialog/saveshow.asp.
[3]   Latvia Statistics www.csb.lv/EN/database/annualstatistics.

place in Russian when they have taken place in areas with high concentrations of Russian speakers. Understandably, given the historical context and the ongoing tensions between the Baltic States and their large eastern neighbour, this is an extremely complex and difficult issue. However, it is clear that further consideration will be required in the preparation/revision of future documents if the issue of social inclusion is to be seen as an objective.

In relation to the accessibility of the document, the provision of a summary in English and/or other relevant major languages is especially relevant in small countries with distinct languages. This can be useful in terms of spreading good practice and generating debate, as well as raising the profile of the area and possibly helping to attract foreign investment. In short, it helps to make the region more accessible to outsiders. Primarily due to the necessity of translating documents for consumption in Brussels, Baltic ministries have become more and more accustomed to translating documents into English. Ministries in Estonia seem to have adopted this practice early and detailed English summaries of a wide variety of documents, including the NSP and the Estonian Regional Development Strategy (Estonian Government 1999), are available. The Estonian NSP has a 40 page English summary, in a highly attractive layout with all the key elements of the document and supporting schematic diagrams. There is also an overview of the Action Plan attached. In contrast, the Lithuanian Comprehensive Plan contains a three page English summary of the process and the applied methodology. Regardless of the qualities of the respective documents, the international impact of the Estonian document is likely to be greater due to the availability of a qualitative detailed English summary. The priority given to the provision of a detailed English language summary in Estonia reflects a more open and internationally-orientated approach being adopted compared to the Lithuanian approach and has, for example, led to increased contacts and co-operation between Estonian and Scottish planners. Often the lower levels have taken the lead here and a number of the Lithuanian counties and Latvian regions have published English summaries of their regional development plans and strategies. The Latvian Ministry of Regional Development and Local Government have also become increasingly active in recent years in promoting exchange of good practice in the international arena and it is likely that a qualitative English summary of the final version of the NSP will be published once the document has been finalised.

A final aspect in relation to accessibility is the writing style and structure of the document and the use of graphics, layout and literary devices. It is clear from looking at the documents that significant attention has been paid to providing an attractive and appealing layout in both the Estonian and Lithuanian NSPs, as well as in the Latvian report on the existing situation. Each of the documents is printed in colour on high quality paper with generous use of photographs and other images. The structure, use of language and chosen methodology in Lithuania, however, create the feel of a more scientific and therefore less accessible document. Elements of the Lithuanian and Latvian methodology are similar to the structure planning approach adopted in Flanders with detailed categorisation of the various elements of the spatial structure. Such an approach requires detailed technical justification and can lead to endless disputes that are ultimately irrelevant to the achievement of the overall strategy. The categorisation of the various structures is far less detailed in the Estonian NSP and consequently the text and supporting illustrations appear less technical and therefore more accessible to a non-specialist audience. The differences in the approaches are reflected in the differences between the form of the illustrative material used in the documents as can be seen by comparing the examples in Figures 8.3 and 8.4.

Figure 8.3   Estonian settlement structure

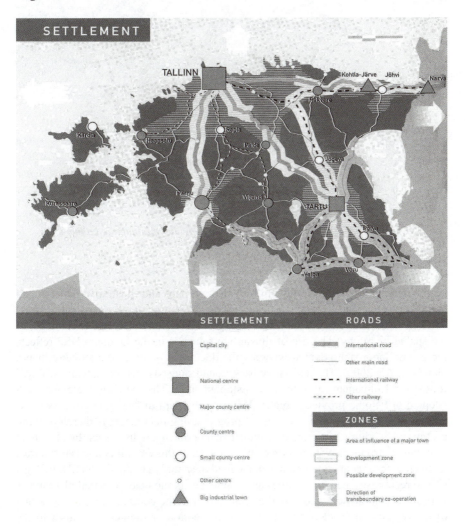

Source: Estonia 2010 National Spatial Plan, Estonian Ministry of the Environment (2001)

Figure 8.4   Lithuanian urban structure

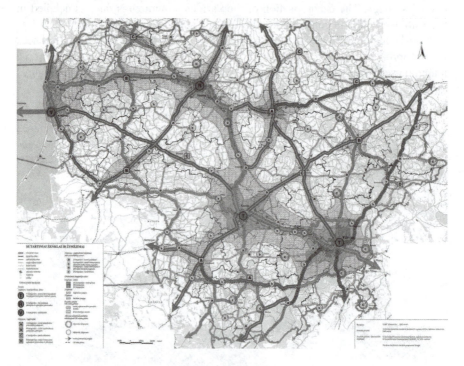

Source: Comprehensive Plan of the Territory of the Republic of Lithuania, Lithuanian Ministry of the Environment (2002)

This difference in the level of detail provided on maps and illustrative material can be clearly seen. The Lithuanian Comprehensive Plan contains nine such detailed plans of the whole country on a GIS background to illustrate various elements of the spatial hierarchy. The use of illustrative schemes in the Estonian NSP reflects the general approach adopted whereby the document is more of a strategy than a plan (VASAB 2000). The legislative background suggests that the Latvian NSP will follow the Lithuanian more than the Estonian style. The more strategic approach adopted in Estonia provides greater flexibility to adapt to changing circumstances and the link with the relevant national programming documents is therefore more abstract. The more prescriptive Lithuanian approach on the other hand, whilst providing a stronger link to resource allocation, lacks this flexibility and is in contrast to much of the recent good practice in the field of spatial planning in the EU. Pallagst (2006) recognises the complexities and challenges in the field of spatial planning as a result of enlargement and it will be interesting in the coming years to see which of the two scenarios identified by Pallagst, retention or merger, are closer to the truth. The retention scenario sees eastern Europe developing its own spatial planning approaches whereas the merger scenario would see convergence between eastern and western European approaches with the ingredients being made up of elements of each. Undoubtedly the EU would prefer the latter as the former scenario would also require a serious rethink of EU resource allocation and regional policy.

Implementation, Monitoring and Evaluation

Implementation, monitoring and evaluation often seem to receive relatively little attention during the preparation of the strategy itself. Spatial planning implementation, especially at the strategic level, is a fluid concept that is consequently not easy to measure in purely quantitative terms. NSPs usually provide a framework of values and objectives to work towards rather than to achieve and planners are having to develop an increasing diversity of soft instruments, such as workshops and visioning, to achieve consensus and work towards these objectives. Implementation, monitoring and evaluation are therefore difficult issues that are challenging the minds of planners not only in the Baltics, but throughout the EU and elsewhere. In the Baltic States, as in many countries, the bodies responsible for spatial planning do not possess the extensive financial budgets, capacity or powers required to implement the NSP and therefore have to rely on influencing the budgets of other ministries and administrations as well as accessing the EU Structural Funds. This increases the necessity for collaborative working and having these other stakeholders on board in the process.

Another tendency throughout the EU is for the sub-national levels increasingly to be in possession of the diversity of instruments necessary to implement national policies. Morgan (2004) argued that whilst the national (and supra-national) level may retain the power to decide in terms of priorities and policies, it is increasingly the sub-national level that has the power to deliver in the forms of instruments and funding. The fact that the EU classifies each individual Baltic State as a single NUTS II level region for allocation of the Structural Funds means that the national levels currently retain a large proportion of the power to deliver in the Baltic States. In order for this to change in the future the sub-national levels will need to be strengthened in terms of capacity and resources, a process that would be made easier if EU regional policy becomes more targeted in the next programming period from 2007–2013. Clearly, strong regionalism will need to be nurtured and will require time to develop in the Baltic context. As mentioned previously it is ironic that the current policy vacuum at the national level in Latvia is ultimately likely to have some benefits. In the absence of a NSP, the regions have had the freedom to search for their own innovative solutions. The knowledge generated in this bottom-up process is likely to be beneficial in the finalisation of the NSP, not least because the regions are now in a stronger position to play a positive and proactive role in the process due to the experience they have gained. The delay has also given the Latvian Ministry the opportunity to examine good practice from other countries in more detail and they have been doing so actively in recent years. The implementation of the NSPs in both Estonia and Lithuania is detailed in a dedicated action plan. The action plans of both documents identify short-term actions to contribute towards the achievement of the long-term strategy, although the Lithuanian Action Plan also identifies longer-term actions. Both are monitored annually, building flexibility into the process and providing the opportunity to react to changing circumstances and take advantage of windows of opportunity. Successful implementation of the NSPs is crucial if spatial planning in general and the NSPs in particular are to retain credibility. Failure and disappointment could be fatal, increasing the importance of implementation being realistic and focussed. There are some significant differences between the two approaches.

The Estonian Action Plan was approved and adopted alongside the NSP. The political foreward in the NSP states that 'plans tend to remain purely an academic exercise, unless accompanied by an outline of concrete steps for implementation ... An action plan also clarifies the message of the spatial plan, turning the plan into a living, continuously evolving and functioning document' (Estonian MoE 2001). The Estonian Action Plan identified thirteen high level strategic and primarily soft actions, the necessary tasks, the deadline and the responsible body. These soft actions include the preparation of various feasibility studies or pilot projects to investigate or stimulate specific actions or encourage stakeholders to assess the spatial implications of their policies. Others are aimed at fostering and stimulating increased horizontal and vertical national and international co-operation. The main focus is on assessing ways of supporting the dispersed settlement structure through measures to support the economy, transport or services in order to maintain the viability of different centres. A second focus is on increasing international connections. The Action Plan focussed on short-term strategic actions that could lead to longer term actions and had a time horizon of three years, although ultimately the implementation of these measures took four and a half years. The delays were due to a variety of factors including a lack of enthusiasm amongst some ministries that seemed determined to maintain a sectoral approach and could not be convinced of the added value of their participation in the process or the need to consider the spatial implications of their spending programmes. This situation highlights the difficulties of achieving 'the consensus needed for co-operation between different ministries within colourful coalitions' within a transition context (Ovin, 2001, p. 144). Other external factors such as delays in relation to various trans-national projects also slowed progress. In common with the Lithuanian implementation process, collaboration and consensus are the primary delivery mechanisms. The lack of financial, human and physical resources and powers to implement the NSP and the necessity therefore to influence the spending budgets of other ministries dictates that this is inevitable. In Estonia, there are currently no regular inter-ministerial meetings about the implementation process in general although they do happen on an action per action basis. The small size of the country means that regular contacts often occur anyway on an informal basis although recent decentralisation of some ministerial departments to other cities has reduced these possibilities to a degree. The Estonian Ministry of Interior started work in the autumn of 2005 on the new Action Plan, and once that has been implemented the NSP will be revised.

The Lithuanian Action Plan was prepared and approved in 2003, a year after the approval of the Comprehensive Plan itself. The Action Plan is much more long-term and detailed than its Estonian equivalent. A total of 119 actions are identified and split into three main sections corresponding to the themes/topics identified in the plan (common territorial structures, specialised territorial structures and spatial integration). Each action is explained, the responsible body and expected results identified and, where at least some of the funding is to come from the EU, this is also specified. The Action Plan is more detailed in everyway than the Estonian version and as a result the actions are often more concrete and tangible. This attention to detail is a common feature of the Lithuanian approach. The specialised territorial structures include actions in relation to the rural economy, the development of recreation territories and technical infrastructure and other functional territories. There is a strong focus on measures to stimulate the development of what the plan calls the technical infrastructure territories with almost half of the 119 actions aimed at supporting this priority. Technical infrastructure primarily covers transport infrastructure but includes elements of energy, logistics and economic infrastructure. Whilst investment in transport infrastructure is relatively easy and will undoubtedly have benefits, especially with increasing east-west transport flows, the dangers of an over-reliance on such investment is well documented (Peters, 2003). Some of the large-scale actions are broken down into detailed smaller actions with a date given for the implementation of each phase. The section on common territorial structures covers actions aimed at supporting the urban system and protecting the natural and rural structure and these provide another important focus in the Action Plan. The Ministry of the Environment is responsible for the monitoring and evaluation of the Action Plan and is required to report progress annually to the Government. The structure of the Action Plan, the inclusion of expected results and the tangibility of many of the actions identified mean that in some ways the monitoring of the implementation process may be easier than in Estonia. The number of actions and the level of detail however mean that monitoring is a time consuming and complex process. In addition the fact that well over half of the identified actions rely on accessing the Structural Funds increases the complexity and level of uncertainty in relation to the implementation process.

Despite the differences in approach there are numerous similarities that are currently hampering the implementation process in both Estonia and Lithuania and are likely to do the same in Latvia. The lack of qualified planners, especially in small municipalities and rural areas, is one such example. As in Flanders in the nineties, the sudden increase in demand for planners caught the education system unaware and universities and colleges are likely to take a number of years before they are in a position to meet this demand. Another challenge common to each Baltic state is the need to strengthen the credibility of spatial planning amongst stakeholders. Some sceptical line ministries remain unconvinced that spatial planning can be a positive and proactive instrument that can help achieve strategic cross-sector goals. The difficulties of achieving inter-ministerial consensus and joined up government in the context of transition countries should not be underestimated and has been documented by Ovin (2001) amongst others. The necessary resources and consensus amongst ministries to implement the action plans is not always evident in the Baltic States although this lack of joined up-edness is common in many countries including many established EU member states.

Conclusions and Lessons for the Future

Each of the Baltic States appears to have embraced EU regional policy principles and themes such as balanced and polycentric development. Despite the similar backgrounds, principles and audiences, the approaches and methodologies adopted in each country are different. The characteristics and demographic tendencies of the Baltic States and the ever-increasing regional disparities within each country mean that achieving any form of balanced development will be extremely difficult, especially when there appears to be no general consensus about what balanced development actually means and what its implications are at the various spatial levels. The impact of the current round of Structural Funds and the tendency for private investment to go to the capital regions further exacerbate the problem and this is something that the respective Baltic governments will be hoping can be addressed in the next round of Structural Funds from 2007–2013. It is clear, however, that a sustained long-term commitment by successive governments will be required if any sort of balanced development is to be achieved, although such long-term commitment is unlikely to occur within a context of fragile, unstable and short-lived coalitions. Such long-term commitment does not sit easily with election timetables or the drive to maximise economic growth and reduce the disparities between national level and the EU average, and in such circumstances transition governments tend to pursue the short rather than the long-term perspective (Ovin 2001). Regional policy and spatial planning will always be complex issues politically. Any policy that directs development to one place at the perceived expense of another will, by definition, be politically contentious. In order for more balanced development within each country to be achieved it is likely that the county and regional levels are going to have an increasingly important role to play in delivering EU and national policies. This will require the significant strengthening of these levels in terms of capacity and physical, financial and human resources to provide them with the necessary tools to deliver. Whilst vertical and horizontal co-operation is improving there is still some way to go. Joined up government is only likely to be achieved via a strong commitment to cross-sector consensus building over a number of years. Both the Estonian and the Lithuanian NSPs provide a road map for the future development of their national space. The Lithuanian Comprehensive Plan is a traditional style plan whilst the Estonian NSP is more of a strategy. The structure and nature of the action plans also reflect this difference. The Lithuanians have adopted a more concrete, project-led approach that is more closely linked to the Structural Funds than is the case in Estonia. Whilst the Latvian NSP is still in the process of preparation it would appear from the legislative framework that they aim to pursue a similar course to the

Lithuanians. The Latvians, however, have the distinct advantage of having been able to look and learn from the experiences of their Baltic neighbours and, if they can use this knowledge to feed into their own process, they have an opportunity to adopt good elements from each and adapt them to their own situation.

Figure 8.5   Key lessons for the future

1. Joined up government, an open and inclusive process and an accessible document are key to successful NSP implementation;
2. Spatial planning is a dynamic and ongoing learning process that should encourage innovative local solutions and involves a wide diversity of stakeholders;
3. General consensus amongst stakeholders over the meaning and implications of concepts such as balanced development at various levels is required if such concepts are to be meaningful;
4. More balanced development is only likely to be achieved through a long-term across the board commitment by successive governments;
5. A more equitable approach to the allocation of EU funds would support more balanced patterns of development at the national level;
6. The global/regional context and specific territorial capital of the subject area are the starting points for the preparation of the strategy;
7. A combination of top-down and bottom-up approaches and formal and informal contacts is desirable;
8. The capacity and accountability of the sub-national levels require significant strengthening over time if they are to play an increasingly important role in delivering EU and national policies;
9. A strategic mix of hard and soft instruments in a flexible implementation process will allow the implementing agency to react to changing circumstances and take advantage of windows of opportunity;
10. Strategic documents should be strategic and not be overly prescriptive.

Source: Adapted from Adams and Harris (2005)

The Estonian NSP adopts a far less prescriptive and detailed approach and aims to integrate the actions of numerous government bodies and sectors in pursuance of high-level strategic goals and, in this sense, is close to the approach adopted in the Celtic countries and adopts the ESDP philosophy of shaping minds (Faludi 2004 and Shaw and Sykes 2004), relying on reaching a high level of consensus and on the goodwill of a wide variety of stakeholders. Whilst this approach is challenging in a young democracy still dealing with the legacy of its past, it does have the advantage of having a higher level of flexibility built in, which is appropriate in a highly fluid and rapidly changing context. Considering the histories of each country and the lack of a culture of stakeholder engagement, all three countries are making strenuous efforts to facilitate open and inclusive plan processes. By combining the more informal Estonian approach with the more formal Lithuanian approach, the Latvians may reap the benefits of both. Shorter preparation times will also be something that planners and policy makers in each country will be striving for in the future as they try to build on the experience gained so far.

The importance of accessibility in both the process and the plan seems to have been recognised judging by the level of attention given to aspects such as writing style and layout. Spatial policies are no longer written and implemented by planners but require a diverse mosaic of stakeholders from different fields to buy into the process. Whilst recognising the political sensitivity, if such documents are to be widely considered as socially inclusive in the future then further attention is likely to be required for Russian language issues. On the basis of the experiences so far in the field of national spatial policy in the Baltic States a number of key lessons for the future can be identified and these are summarised in Figure 8.5.

External global and continental forces obviously play an increasingly important part in the destiny and development direction of small nations, and in the case of the Baltic States the influence of EU regional policy is particularly strong. The increasing regional disparities within the Baltic States support the view of Pallgast (2006) that ultimately EU enlargement will require more than simply an eastwards extension of existing EU policies. In light of the strength of these forces that are currently driving potentially disastrous demographic tendencies in the Baltics it is uncertain how successful even the best NSP could be in the pursuance of balanced development at the national level. What is clear however is that each country is learning fast and that some of the work being done in the field of regional development and spatial planning in the Baltic States is at the cutting edge of the discipline today. If the future challenges are to be met then it is crucial that the responsible bodies continue to foster an open, inclusive and collaborative culture in both the national and international contexts. The Estonian NSP is a strategic document and in that sense is closer to some of the recent good practice that has emerged in the field of spatial planning in the Celtic periphery. The more comprehensive and structured approach adopted in Lithuania more closely reflects the national programming documents in relation to the allocation of EU funding. The Latvian approach is likely to be somewhere in between and it remains to be seen which of the approaches will ultimately achieve most success. Given the context and certainly given the current methods of allocation of the EU monies it is clear that spatial planning in each country faces considerable challenges if any form of balanced development is to be achieved, and it is possible that these challenges may prove too difficult to overcome. Therefore, whilst the quality of some of the work that has taken place gives some cause for optimism, it is clear that a long and difficult journey lies ahead.

References

Adams, N., Ezmale S. and Paalzow, A. (2006), 'Towards Balanced Development in Latvia: The Experience of the Latgale Region', in Adams, N., Alden, J. and Harris, N. (eds), *Regional Development and Spatial Planning in an Enlarged European Union*, Chapter 10, Ashgate.

Adams, N. and Harris, N. (2005), *Best Practice Guidelines for Regional Development Strategies*, Cardiff University.

Albrechts, L., Alden, J. and Pires, A. da Rosa (2001), *The Changing Institutional Landscape of Planning*, Ashgate, Aldershot.

Bynens, J. and Van der Lecq, R. (2005), *Connecting Europe to its Regions: Territorial Cohesion as a Toolkit for an interwoven Spatial Development Approach*, Paper for AESOP Conference, Vienna, Austria, June 2005.

Dagiliene, G. (2006), The Response to Regional Disparities in Lithuania, in Adams, N., Alden, J. and Harris, N. (eds), *Regional Development and Spatial Planning in an Enlarged European Union*, Chapter 11, Ashgate.

Downes, R. (1996) 'Regional Policy Development in Central and Eastern Europe', in Alden, J.D. and Boland, P. (eds), *Regional Development Strategies, a European Perspective*, Regional Studies Association, pp. 256–272.

ESPON (2004), *Particular effects of enlargement of the EU and beyond on the polycentric spatial tissue with special attention on discontinuities and barriers*, Third Interim Report.

Estonian Government (1999), *Regional Development Strategy of Estonia*, Tallinn.

Estonian Government (2002), *Planning Act*, Tallinn.

Estonian Ministry of the Environment (1996), *The World and Estonia*, Future Trends, Tallinn.

Estonian Ministry of the Environment (2001), *Estonia 2010 National Spatial Plan*, Tallinn.

Estonian Ministry of Finance (2004), *National Development Plan for the Implementation of the EU Structural Funds: Single Programming Document 2004–2006*.

European Commission (1999), *European Spatial Development Perspective, Towards Balanced and Sustainable Development of the European Territory*, CEC: Luxembourg.

European Commission (2004), *Third Report on Economic and Social Cohesion*.

European Commission (2005), Eurostat general and regional statistics http://epp.eurostat.cec.eu.int/portal/page?_pageid=0,1136162,0_45572073&_dad=portal&_schema=portal accessed December 2005.

Faludi, A. (2001), 'The Application of the European Spatial Development Perspective: Evidence from the North-West Metropolitan Area', *European Planning Studies*, vol. 9, no. 5, pp. 663–675.

Faludi, A. (2004), Spatial planning traditions in Europe: Their role in the ESDP process, *International Planning Studies*, vol. 9, no. 2–3, May–August 2004, pp. 155–172.

Kratke, S. (2002), 'The Regional Impact of EU Eastern Enlargement: A View from Germany', *European Planning Studies*, vol. 10, no. 5, pp. 651–664.

Latvian Government (2002), *Law on Spatial Planning* (unofficial translation), Riga.

Latvian Government (2002a), *Law on Regional Development* (unofficial translation), Riga.

Latvian Government (2003), 'Single Programming Document', *Objective 1 Programme 2004–2006*, approved by European Commission, 18 December 2003.

Latvian Government (2004), 'Regional Policy Guidelines', Riga.

Latvian Ministry of Environmental Protection and Regional Development (2001), *Report on the Use of the Territory of the State*, Riga.

Latvian State Regional Development Agency (2004), *Development of Regions in Latvia*, Riga Regionu attistiba Latvija.

Lieven, A. (1994), The Baltic Revolution: Estonia, Latvia and Lithuania and the path to independence, London, Yale University Press.

Lithuanian Ministry of the Environment (2002), Comprehensive Plan of the Territory of the Republic of Lithuania, Vilnius.

Lithuanian Ministry of Finance (2003), *Single Programming Document 2004–2006*, Vilnius.

Lithuanian Ministry of Interior (2005), *Regional Policy Strategy until 2013*, Vilnius.

Loogma, K. (1997), *Estonia future scenarios for year 2010* paper World Futures Studies Association XVth World Conference Brisbane, Australia 28 September–3rd October 1997 www.wfsf.org/pub/publications/Brisbane_97/LOOGMA.pdf accessed 1 August 2005.

Maandi, J. (2001), 'Estonia and European Spatial Development Perspectives in Spatial Planning', in Hansen, M. and Bohme K. (eds), *Baltic Sea Region: Implications of European Spatial Development Perspectives*, pp. 20–24.

Mertelsmann, O. (2003), *The Sovietisation of the Baltic States 1940–1956*, Tartu, Kleio.

Morgan, K. (2004) 'Sustainable Regions: Governance, Innovation and Scale', *European Planning Studies*, vol. 12, no. 6, September 2004.

O'Leary, E. (2003), 'A Critical Evaluation of Irish Regional Policy', in O'Leary (ed.), *Irish Regional Development: A New Agenda*, Chapter 2, Liffey Press, Dublin.

Ovin, R. (2001), 'The Nature of Institutional Change in Transition', *Post Communist Economies*, vol. 13, no. 2, pp. 133–146.

Paalzow, A. (2006), 'Barriers to Regional Development in the New Member States: the Latvian Experience', in Adams, N., Alden, J. and Harris, N. (eds), *Regional Development and Spatial Planning in an Enlarged European Union*, Chapter 9, Ashgate.

Pallagst, K. (2006), 'European Spatial Planning Reloaded: Considering EU Enlargement in Theory and Practice', *European Planning Studies*, vol. 14, no. 2, pp. 253–268.

Peters, D. (2003), 'Cohesion, Polycentricity, Missing Links and Bottle Necks: Conflicting Spatial Storylines for Pan-European Transport Investments', *European Planning Studies*, vol. 11, no. 3, pp. 317–339.

Petkevicius, A. (2001), *Regional Policy in Lithuania on the Eve of the Structural Funds*, Local Government and Public Service Reform Institute, Open Society Institute.

Petrakos, G. (2001), Patterns of Regional Inequality in Transition Economies, *European Planning Studies*, vol. 9, no. 3, pp. 359–383.

Raagma, G. and Sotarauta, M. (1997), *Estonian Futures: Scenarios and Strategic Issues of a Small Country in Transition*, paper presented to European Regional Science Association, 37th European Congress, 26–29 August 1997, in Rome, Italy.

Shaw, D. and Sykes, O. (2004), 'The Concept of Polycentricity in European Spatial Planning: Reflections on its Interpretation and Application in the Practice of Spatial Planning', *International Planning Studies*, vol. 9, no. 4, pp. 283–306.

Thomas, M.J. (1998), 'Thinking about Planning in the Transitional Countries of Central and Eastern Europe', *International Planning Studies*, vol. 3, no. 3, pp. 321–334.

Upmace, D. (2001), 'Latvia and European Spatial Development Perspectives in Spatial Planning', in Hansen, M. and Bohme, K. (eds), *Baltic Sea Region: Implications of European Spatial Development Perspectives*, pp. 24–31.

VASAB 2010 Secretariat (1994), *Vision and Strategies around the Baltic Sea 2010*, VASAB, Tallinn, December 1994.

VASAB 2010 Secretariat (1998), *Spatial Planning for Sustainable Development in the Baltic Sea Region*, VASAB, Gdansk, April 1998.

VASAB 2010 Secretariat (2000), *Compendium of Spatial Planning Systems in the Baltic Sea Region Countries*, VASAB, Gdansk, May 2000.

Chapter 9

Barriers to Regional Development in the New Member States: The Latvian Experience

Anders Paalzow

Introduction and Context

Introduction

Latvia is a rather atypical country of the European Union seen from a territorial or spatial planning perspective. The constraints and challenges that she faces in relation to regional development and spatial planning stemming from its peripheral location in the north-eastern part of the EU are exacerbated by the legacy of having to address close to 50 years of Soviet rule. Like all other post-communist transition countries, Latvia was not a *tabula rasa* when it regained independence in 1991. The legacy of the old regime was and is still there and will continue to loom large over Latvia and the other transition countries, having a significant impact on the transition process for years to come. As discussed in Crawford and Lijphart (1995) and more recently in Hughes *et al.* (2005), one of the most underestimated aspects of the post-communist transition is how this legacy influences the transition process. Furthermore, as argued in Downes (1996) and Petrakos (2001), spatial planning and regional development play an important role in the post-communist transition process.

In a spatial planning context, the importance of institutions has become more evident during recent years. As Alden *et al.* (2001) argue: 'Planning is embedded in social relations and is therefore heavily dependent upon a mix of cognitive, cultural, social and political institutions'. Hence, to understand spatial planning and its prospects in a transition country like Latvia, it is not sufficient to focus on the physical heritage from the old regime such as the infrastructure. The institutional heritage has to be taken into account as well. This chapter adopts this approach and analyses the barriers to spatial planning and regional development along these lines.

The background to Latvia's geography, history and planning framework is covered briefly below and followed by four sections each covering a separate theme pin-pointing the spatial planning and regional development challenges the country is facing. The first theme considered is the change in Latvia's macro-geographical position that resulted from the break up of the Soviet Union and Latvia's entry into the European Union. This change resulted in Latvia moving from close to the Soviet gravity centre to the geographical periphery of the European Union. Secondly, internal asymmetries and regional disparities are discussed, a theme that is increasingly occupying policy makers not only in Latvia but also in many of the other new Member States. The third theme covers the development of spatial planning and regional development in Latvia with particular emphasis on the institutional framework and the bottom-up approach to planning that, for various reasons, has been prominent up until now. The respective consequences of this will also be examined. The final theme relates to the role of civil society in this new participatory approach to planning where stakeholder participation and engagement are a high priority. The concluding section discusses the lessons learnt from the Latvian case study and the future challenges facing Latvian spatial planning and regional development. Although the case of Latvia is discussed in this chapter, many of the findings may well be relevant to the other post-communist transition countries which have joined, or are about to join, the European Union.

The Latvian Context

Geographic and Demographic Context
The Republic of Latvia is situated in the North-East of Europe, on the shores of the Baltic Sea. Latvia's only distinct border is the Baltic Sea coast, which extends for 531 kilometres. In the north Latvia borders with Estonia (267 kilometres common border), in the south with Lithuania (453 kilometres), in the east with Russia (217 kilometres), and in the south east with Belarus (141 kilometres), the latter two being EU external borders. The territory of Latvia is 64,589 square kilometres, a size surpassing that of Belgium, Denmark, the Netherlands, and Switzerland. About 40 per cent of the country is covered by forests.

The population of Latvia in 2005 is approximately 2.31 million (Latvian Statistical Bureau, 2005) of which close to 60 per cent are ethnic Latvians. The proportion of ethnic Latvians has actually increased since independence although the absolute number is falling. Nationally, close to 30 per cent of the population are ethnic Russians with much higher concentrations in certain parts. In general terms, the proportion of ethnic Russians increases towards the east and the Russian border. The remaining 10 per cent is to a large extent comprised of ethnic Belorussians, Ukrainians, Poles and Lithuanians. Approximately 20 per cent of the population (mainly ethnic Russians) have the unenviable status of non-citizens, many of them not speaking Latvian which has been reinstated as the official language since independence. A non-citizen is ineligible to vote in both parliamentary and local elections and is excluded from many positions of employment in the public sector. Issues in relation to the Russian minorities have contributed to the often-strained relations between Latvia and her much larger eastern neighbour in recent years.

Historical Context

Before Latvia declared its independence in 1918, the area which today constitutes Latvia was ruled over for several centuries by German bishops and princes, Polish and Swedish kings, and Russian czars. However, throughout the centuries Baltic German feudal lords and merchants along with Russian governors, bureaucrats and traders had a significant influence on the region. It was not until the emancipation of the serfs and the early industrialisation in the late nineteenth century that ethnic Latvians were allowed to take an active role in administration and policy formulation as discussed in King *et al.* (2004), Pabriks and Purs (2002) and Plakans (1995). The first period of Latvian independence between 1918 and 1940 ended when the Soviet Union occupied Latvia as a consequence of the 1939 Molotov-Ribbentrop Pact, which in effect assigned Latvia to the Soviet Union. The first Soviet occupation lasted until 1941 and was followed by more than three years of German occupation. After the German occupation, Soviet rule as well as the sovietisation of Latvia and the other Baltic States resumed in 1945 and lasted until 1991 when independence was restored. From an early stage of transition from the planned to the market economy, the idea of Latvia joining the European Union was seen as the goal (Ancans *et al.*, 2000). Nissinen (1999) recognised this process stating that 'Latvia has pursued consequent reform polices since regaining independence in order to accelerate its transition to a fully fledged market economy'. Equally important to many Latvians, bearing in mind recent history, was the issue of national security and sovereignty and Latvia therefore pursued membership of NATO with equal enthusiasm. The strategy paid off and Latvia achieved both of these goals in 2004, joining the EU on 1 May.

Planning Context

In Latvia, like in many other post-communist countries, one of the first democratising reforms after the fall of communism was the re-introduction of the local and municipal self-government and the structure that prevailed in 1939 was to a large extent re-introduced. Despite the reintroduction of local government, the euphoria of independence and the huge challenges and reforms that this stimulated meant that the first years of independence were characterised by little, if any, regional development or spatial planning. As in other former Soviet states, the concept of planning was also associated with the central planning of the former system and this was another reason why it received little priority or attention. There are now four planning levels in Latvia: national, regional, district, and local. According to the Law on Territorial Planning from 2002, territorial plans are required for each level at an appropriate scale. Only the lowest level plans are binding on the citizen, although all other levels of plans are binding on the lower levels of government.

At the national level the Ministry of Regional Development and Local Government (which was formed in 2003) is responsible for i.a. spatial planning, regional policy, local government and local government reform. Unlike its Baltic neighbours, Estonia and Lithuania, Latvia has been unsuccessful until now in preparing and adopting either a National Development Plan (NDP) or a National Spatial Plan (NSP). The responsibility for developing these documents lies with this relatively new Ministry with both documents due to be completed during 2006 and 2007.

The purpose of the NDP is to determine the national interests and requirements for the use and development of the whole territory of the country. According to the Law on Regional Development, the NDP is a medium-term strategic development document with a time horizon of seven years (tied to the period of EU programming periods). National priorities are identified in the NDP and the document serves as a coordination framework for public investment as well as EU and private financing. The NDP is also required to address the social, economic and environmental situation. The NSP will provide an analysis of the current situation and a perspective for the future development, settlement structure, infrastructure, open space etc. It will also provide binding regulations for the lower levels and guidelines for territorial development. The process in relation to the preparation of the Latvia NSP is discussed in more detail by Adams in Chapter 8.

The 2002 regional development legislation legitimised the establishment of five planning regions with responsibilities in the field of regional development and spatial or territorial planning. The five planning regions are Kurzeme in the west, Latgale in the east, Vidzeme in the north, Zemgale in the south and the Riga capital region in the centre. The first four are the historical regions of Latvia, although their boundaries as defined by the Cabinet of Ministers do not coincide exactly with those of the historical regions. During the period 1999–2003, all five regions were classed as NUTS III level regions but in response to concerns regarding the institutional and administrative capacities of the regional structures Latvia is now classed as a single NUTS II level region. Each region has its own regional development agency (RDA) and there are regular meetings with the Ministry of Regional Development and Local Government. Each region is required to prepare development programmes and territorial plans that will determine development opportunities, trends and restrictions in relation to the regional territory. Work is ongoing on these territorial plans and to a certain extent the regions have had to wait for the relevant Ministry to provide the necessary framework, which in relation to the Regional Territorial Plans has only been in place since early 2005.

Latvia has two tiers of local government, whose activities and functions are defined in the 'Law on Local Government'. The higher tier of local government comprises 26 districts (rajons). The districts mainly have a coordinating role and have few independent functions of their own. During Soviet rule, the districts (and the seven Republican cities discussed below) served as second-level territorial institutions. They provided structures and services to support military, political and economic activities and as a result they lost much of their community character and became mere extensions of Soviet power (King *et al.*, 2004).

The lower tier of local governments is known as towns (pilseta), villages/parishes (pagasts), and novads. The latter comprise an amalgamation of several smaller municipalities (towns and villages/parishes). In addition, Latvia's seven republican cities have the rights and responsibilities of local governments. In total, there are 530 local governments in the lower tier (53 towns, 444 villages/parishes, 26 novads, and seven republican cities). The republican cities are (ranked according to population): Riga, Daugavpils, Liepaja, Jelgava, Jurmala, Ventspils and Rezekne. The lower tier of local governments are directly elected whereas the district level is appointed and therefore an extension of the state. The large number and, consequently, the small size of many of these local administrations mean that financial, human and physical resources, as well as the administrative capacity of many of them, are extremely limited. According to Vanags (2005), the average population of the rural municipalities is approximately 1,500 and more than 70 per cent of them have a population of less than 2,000. The reasons for this plethora of local administrations in the first tier are primarily historical and can be explained by the fact that when Latvia regained independence in 1991, the initial wave of reforms was composed of *ad hoc* measures to re-instate many of the pre-war institutions of independent Latvia, which to a large extent were based on the constitution of 1922. Zacesta and Pucis (2005) stated that the need for regional reform was recognised by the Cabinet of Ministers as early as 1993 and was legitimised through legislation in 1998.

The legislation facilitated the amalgamation of town and village administrations to form a new structure called novads and it was hoped at the time that this would lead to a reduction in the number of administrations to 102. However progress has been much slower than anticipated and so far only 26 novads have been created, thus reducing the number of the lowest tier local governments to the current figure of 530. The reason for the slow amalgamation process, according to Zacesta and Pucis (2005), is that there is no conviction among the general public that such a regional reform is necessary. However, the Ministry of Regional Development and Local Government is currently making a renewed effort to bring about such reform which, if successful, could see the formation of regional municipalities through the reorganisation of the planning regions and the districts and a drastic reduction in the number of local municipalities. With the Latvian public clearly not convinced of the need for such reform, it remains to be seen if the Ministry will be successful.

Both the district and the local levels are required to adopt territorial plans identifying development opportunities, trends and restrictions as well as defining the permitted land use at their respective levels. They are also required to translate the requirements laid down in higher levels plans to the local level. The legislation therefore provides a framework for a hierarchical top down structure of plans, although the reality is somewhat different as will be discussed in more detail later. Having gained an insight into the complex array of circumstances that have combined to form the modern context within which regional development in Latvia operates, consideration will now be given to four specific challenges that have emerged.

Barriers to Regional Development

Latvia's Changed Macro-Geographical Position

The transition of the former socialist countries poses a major challenge for regional policy and spatial planning, not only because central control mechanisms have been abandoned in favour of market mechanisms, but also because the countries' macro-geographical position has changed. Research by Sachs (1997) and Gallup *et al.* (1999) emphasises the role of geography in economic transition and economic integration. Along the same lines are the findings in Petrakos (2000), showing that the integration of the former socialist countries into the economy of the European Union has a macro-geographical dimension which is related to the proximity of each of the countries to the Union's development centres. Hence, to understand the challenges facing Latvia in terms of spatial planning, the country's macro-geographical position has to be considered.

Latvia's macro-geographical position changed drastically with the fall of the Soviet Union. Its strategic position within the Soviet Union was very strong given its proximity to the Soviet gravity centre formed by the triangle Moscow-Leningrad (now Saint Petersburg)-Minsk. Hence, part of Latvia's Soviet legacy is an infrastructure system built to serve the gravity centre of the former Soviet Union. The legacy is illustrated for example by the fact that many of the infrastructure networks still reflect the needs of the centrally planned economy and old political borders, resulting in a need to restructure the national transportation system in order to fit the new geopolitical and economic realities.

After the fall of the Soviet Union, Latvia moved from occupying a strategic geographical location within the hierarchy of the Soviet economic space, to occupy a peripheral location in the hierarchy of the European Union economic space. The country has swapped its position of relative power to become a peripheral country in a peripheral region of the European Union. As discussed in Petrakos (2000) and Coccossis *et al.* (2005), countries that occupy a geographically peripheral location are likely to be integrated more slowly and selectively than countries located close to the core, as the countries located near the core will experience the benefits of an eastward-directed dispersion of development more rapidly. With the elimination of the administrative barriers within the European Union, geographical factors such as distance, accessibility and centrality emerge as important factors in the spatial organisation of activities. Whilst there is no unanimous agreement over the exact gravity centre or core of the EU, and this has been discussed and debated by many including Faludi (2001), it is clear that Latvia is far from any such gravity centre. The location in relation to the pentagon (one of the areas put forward as the EU core) formed by London, Paris, Milan, Munich and Hamburg emphasises this point. As a result, it is likely that it will be extremely difficult for Latvia to attract higher order economic functions and to develop multiple strategic cities or regions that will be placed in the upper part of the European hierarchy. The only exception, when it comes to experiencing a positive net effect from increased openness, is the Riga metropolitan area, possibly together with the western port cities of Ventspils and Liepaja.

On the other hand, the eastern parts of Latvia are more likely to experience unfavourable consequences of openness which will further intensify their problems and make restructuring more difficult. Eastern parts of Latvia in particular (which were the ones closest to the Soviet gravity centre) have experienced a considerable change in their relative macro-geographical position with the fall of the Soviet Union resulting in a collapse of the economic base in Daugavpils, as well as in Latgale in general. However, if the Russian-Latvian relations improve and if Russia opens up to the European Union, then its strategic position will once again change considerably and Latvia will be able to fully exploit the comparative advantage that stems from its geographical location on the shores of the Baltic Sea in close proximity to important development centres of the Baltic Sea Region and Russia. In other words, Latvia would be in a position to fully capitalise on its location by becoming the main strategic crossroads of important communication routes between Western Europe and Russia. Indeed, Latvia has previously enjoyed such status and before the First World War, for example, about 25 per cent of Russia's total imports and exports were conveyed through the Latvian ports of Riga, Liepaja and Ventspils. This has played a significant role in the development of the territory that now constitutes Latvia. Crohn-Wolfgang (1923) argues that the advantages of Riga and Latvia:[1]

> ... were a product of nature which could not be changed by political events and will never be changed by these ... Irrespective of the political changes in the east, one thing is certain, namely that the geographic area constituting European Russia even in the future will continue to use Riga as its main gateway; and here all human reason suggest that Riga's future as port is determined, as is that of Latvia as a transit region. Specifically, the country will continue to be the coastal transit zone for Russia and the bridge between Western Europe and Russia.

However, even if Russia opens up, Latvia will remain far from the EU gravity centre and one legitimate question to ask is then whether the European Spatial Development Perspective (ESDP) will be of any help when addressing the issues related to Latvia's changed macro-geographical position. Although the ESDP to some extent discusses the problems and challenges facing the (at the time) EU-Accession countries, the issue of change in the macro-geographical position of the Baltic States is not addressed. It therefore remains an open issue whether, and if so to what extent, the ideas, principles and perspectives outlined in the ESDP will assist the Latvian planners and policy makers in addressing the planning and development challenges stemming from the country's new macro-geographical position. However, there is reason to believe that the ESDP's potential relevance for Latvia with respect to the macro-geographical challenges will be rather limited. It is therefore likely that, to a large extent, the Latvian planners and policy-makers will have to rely on their own

---

[1]   Translated from German by the author of this chapter.

ideas and visions, maybe supplemented by EU cross-border funds and initiatives, when it comes to dealing with these challenges.

Internal Asymmetries and Regional Disparities

Latvia has one of the most concentrated demographic structures in the European Union, as the metropolitan area of Riga with close to 900,000 inhabitants comprises almost 40 per cent of the national population. As discussed in Coccossis *et al.* (2005), only Greece has possibly a higher concentration of the national population living in the capital Athens. Statistics from the Latvian Statistical Bureau (2005) show Daugavpils as the second largest Latvian city with approximately 150,000 inhabitants in the metropolitan area.[2] The port city of Liepaja and the city of Jelgava are third fourth with 130,000 and 100,000 inhabitants in the respective metropolitan areas. The rest of the urban system is comprised of medium sized and smaller cities/ towns with a population between 1,300 and 55,000.

Compared to the relatively balanced pre-1991 situation, regional disparities within Latvia have increased considerably. At the regional and local levels GDP/capita figures show large and increasing regional disparities. According to the figures from the Latvian Statistical Bureau (2004) quoting figures from 2002, the Riga Region is by far the richest region within Latvia, its GDP per capita is 182 per cent of the Latvian average, while the other four regions are all below the average. The poorest region of Latvia is the eastern region of Latgale with a GDP per capita of just 48 per cent of the national average. The levels of unemployment provide a mirror image of the GDP figures – in the Riga region the level of unemployment is less than 5 per cent, whereas it is higher than 20 per cent in a number of rural districts.

In comparison to the other new member states, Latvia has a GDP per capita of 76 per cent of the average. Only the Riga Region exceeds the average per capita income of the new member states with 138 per cent of the average whereas the figure for Latgale is only 37 per cent. At a lower level the port city of Ventspils has a GDP per capita that is more than three times higher than the national average, although this is the result of the main source of income in the port city coming from the transit industry, in particular the export of Russian oil products through the port. On the other hand, there are parts of the Latgale region where GDP per capita is just one-third of the national average. As discussed in Krisjane (2005), this is partly due to the low level of economic activity in the rural areas of Latgale, partly due to the structural problems in the region, and partly due to the lack of promotion and support of business activity in rural as well as smaller and medium-sized urban areas. Furthermore, the east-west split when it comes to economic development is further reinforced by the above discussed shift in Latvia's macro-geographical position where the country's eastern parts were the ones that suffered the most.

---

[2]   The metropolitan area in this context is defined as the administrative areas of the respective city and surrounding district.

Recent development trends in Latvia would seem to confirm the findings of Downes (1996) and Petrakos (2001) that economic transition is likely to increase regional disparities in the short to medium term at least. Metropolitan areas and the more western regions, i.e. Riga and Kurzeme (including the Baltic ports of Ventspils and Liepaja), would appear to be in a better position to adapt to the transition process than the more rural and more eastern regions. The increase in these core-periphery disparities have been exacerbated due to the Riga metropolitan area attracting the lion's share of foreign capital, joint ventures, new enterprises and so on and the Kurzeme ports of Liepaja and Ventspils have also been able to benefit to a lesser degree from the new trade opportunities. In addition, regional disparities are further strengthened by the fact that the Soviet planning system allowed very few functional relationships between urban areas and/or regions. As discussed in Nijkamp (1995) and Coccossis *et al.* (2005), these functional relationships form the basis for clusters, corridors and networks and help to foster economic integration between urban centres and regions, promoting economic growth and development, and hence reducing regional disparities.

The basic objectives of the ESDP (in particular the development of a polycentric and balanced urban system and the strengthening of the partnerships between urban and rural areas) seem to be highly relevant to the current Latvian situation since many of the asymmetries Latvia is facing are to a large extent generic. However, even though the asymmetries can be labelled as generic in a European context, Latvia's internal conditions differ considerably. As discussed above, in addition to having a highly concentrated urban structure, there are very few functional relationships between the urban centres within Latvia as well as between Latvia's urban centres and those of the neighbouring countries. Consequently, the objective of developing a polycentric system within Latvia, as well as between Latvia and the neighbouring EU countries, will be extremely challenging and the development of European-level clusters and networks will be further hampered by the lack of functional relationships. The specific Latvian response in terms of regional development and spatial planning will be examined further in the next section.

The Development of Regional Development and Spatial Planning in Latvia[3]

Regional planning in Latvia has undergone a transition of its own in parallel with the economic and institutional transition since the early 1990s. When Latvia regained independence in 1991 it faced a planning legacy that went back to the end of the Second World War when the Soviets introduced a new territorial organisation that neither observed the existing Latvian territorial organisation nor the local or regional identities. The new territorial organisation was based on two main pieces of logic.

---

[3]   Sources: Much of the material in this section comes from presentations by and discussions with various Latvian Stakeholders at the Conference 'National Planning and Regional Development' in Kurzeme, November/December 2004 as well as the Interreg IIIc GRIDS workshop in Latgale, April 2005.

First, what Hughes *et al.* (2005) label a power logic; the state should be organised in a way that secured the power and control of the communist party. Second, the functional logic was that the state organisation was configured to maximise the expected efficiency from the centrally-planned economy. Hence, the role of regional and local government was to maintain political control by the Communist Party and to manage the centrally-planned economic system. Although local and regional governments were re-introduced soon after independence, the early years were characterised by little if any regional development or spatial planning. After close to half a century of central planning, planning was not in *fashion*. There were also more pressing issues such as the restitution of property and organising a land book. Furthermore, relevant legislation was to a large extent absent, hence most of the 1990s can be characterised as a period of 'laissez faire' from a planning perspective.

Towards the end of the 1990s, however, interest in relation to regional development and spatial planning among the Latvian regions grew. Regional Development Agencies (RDAs) were formed by the municipalities in the respective regions. It should come as no surprise that the first region to form a RDA was the region facing the biggest challenges, namely Latgale. The Latgale Regional Development Agency was founded in 1999 and soon after the other four regions followed Latgale's example. All of the regional bodies were set up voluntarily. Four of them are non-governmental organisations (NGOs), whereas one (Zemgale RDA) has the status of a public body. The legal basis for each RDA is formed by the agreements between the respective region's two levels of local government, the districts and the municipalities with the signing parties contributing financially to the running of the RDA. Around 10 per cent of each RDA's budget comes from local funding and approximately 20–25 per cent from central government. The remaining part has to be self-generated from different projects and programmes. As a result of this, numbers of permanent staff at the RDAs are kept to a minimum and much of the work has to be outsourced to consultants once funding is secured for a particular project. The low level of core funding has so far to a large extent prevented the RDAs from acting as developers. In addition, the large proportion of self generated project and programme financing forces the agencies to be innovative in generating new projects. In turn, this means that the agenda of the individual RDAs is to a large extent determined and governed by the available funding opportunities making it difficult for them to plan too far ahead.

There were several driving forces behind the regional initiatives to set up RDAs. The growing disparities between Riga, on the one hand, and the regions on the other, more or less forced the regions to take some action and they also found support with the increasing importance given to the regional agenda by the EU. The real catalyst for the increased interest in regional development and spatial planning, however, was the incentive of funds being available from the EU pre-accession funds and other funds available from certain established EU member states under various bilateral agreements. These projects provided the regions with the financial means to involve international partners in the development of spatial plans and regional development strategies. Flemish partners were active in the Baltic States, for example, and worked together with the development agencies in Kurzeme, Latgale and Vidzeme on various capacity building projects in the planning field. The influence of Flemish concepts and methodology can still be seen in many regional planning and development documents as well as in the legislation.

Up until now, Latvian regional development and spatial planning has, for a variety of reasons, been primarily a bottom-up process led by the regions and the RDAs. The initiatives at the regional level have had a spill-over effect on the lower levels in the sense that not only the regions but also the districts and municipalities are developing their own plans. Despite the lack of a guiding framework at the national level, 14 out of the 26 districts have approved territorial plans. Furthermore, out of the 530 local governments in the first tier, only five have not yet started developing their own plans. Hence, all four levels are working on planning documents simultaneously and in the absence of a guiding framework. It is possible that this may result in severe problems once the national framework is in place, since the lower level plans have to take the higher level plans into account and are not allowed to be in conflict with them.

Although a bottom-up approach has several advantages, there are disadvantages as well, in particular in a country like Latvia with limited experience of spatial planning and regional development and an institutional framework that is still in its infancy. To a large extent, the work at the regional level has been done in an institutional vacuum with the Latvian Law on Territorial Planning coming into effect 2002 and the Ministry of Regional Development and Local Government only being established in 2003. The formation of the new Ministry brought together the regional development and spatial planning functions, which had previously been split between various ministries, under one umbrella. In addition, the fact that the regions took the lead, combined with the political instability at the central government level (since independence in 1991 the average Latvian government has not lasted more than a year), resulted in a situation where the central government is *lagging behind*. This is somewhat of a paradox in a system where the legislation has a strong top-down focus and most of the power in relation to regional development and its funding is retained by central government.

With the guiding framework at the national level to a large extent missing, there is a risk that central government policy decisions may reverse some of the developments at the regional and local levels. The absence of both the NDP and the NSP has created a vacuum in which the lower levels have had to work. The long-awaited regulations governing the territorial plans have only been in place since early 2005 and work is ongoing to see just how much of the considerable amount of work undertaken previously at the regional level is in line with the new regulations. It is to be hoped that the work already undertaken at the regional level can serve as a basis for the preparation of the statutory documents now that the regulations have been approved and once the NDP and the NSP have been adopted. Many working at the regional and local levels have been highly critical of this situation, recognising that work that they have done previously could become invalid once the national framework is in place.

In addition to creating a vacuum, the slow progress made by central government in relation to the national framework has led to a sort of rivalry in certain areas between central government and the lower levels. One of the issues discussed has been the administrative borders of the regions as, in certain cases, there has been some debate as to which town or city belonged to which region. Jekabpils is one such example, having historically been part of the Latgale region but now belonging to the Zemgale administrative region. The town of Tukums in the west is another example, having historically belonged to the Kurzeme region but now being included within the Riga administrative region. Such debates tend to be inevitable when discussing administrative boundaries and despite the debate, it should be recognised that it is impossible to please everybody in such cases.

In this environment, the ESDP has to some extent served as a substitute for the national guiding framework. Many of the concepts developed in the ESDP, such as the development of a polycentric urban system, the development of transportation corridors and the development and conservation of the natural and cultural heritage, have been embraced and can be found in numerous documents in Latvia. One characteristic of these Latvian documents is the prominence of aspects in relation to cultural heritage and social inclusion. The emphasis on how to preserve and further develop the (Latvian) cultural heritage is not surprising when viewed in the context of close to fifty years of *sovietisation* of the Latvian culture and the need to integrate the large number of Russians living in Latvia into Latvian society. The decline and removal of many of the social safety nets available under the Soviet system has also led to increasing concern for issues such as unemployment, ethnic integration and alcohol abuse, and these are often aspects explicitly addressed in the documents.

Throughout the post-communist transition the division of labour between the central and local levels has changed radically from the centralized point of departure in the beginning of the 1990s to the current situation where the lower tiers have often been the driving force for regional development. It remains to be seen, however, if this situation will prevail or if there will be a swing back towards the central government when the national framework is in place. Whilst the bottom-up approach to regional development and spatial planning has achieved some degree of success, and the administrative capacity at the sub-national level has undoubtedly been strengthened, there still remain many challenges. Financial, human and physical resources remain scarce and it is likely that the current unbalanced patterns of development may reinforce the existing inequalities between the rich and the poor regions. The former may well find themselves in a position to implement most or all of their strategies, whilst the latter struggle to attract a fraction of the funding for which they are potentially eligible. The current fragmented administrative structure in Latvia, with numerous small and relatively weak administrative units, poses an additional threat to the future development. Without effective administrative reform the lack of adequate resources in administrative units in the lower tier may jeopardise the entire bottom-up approach. As always, discussions regarding administrative reform are delicate and sensitive and they continue to be so in Latvia. The outcome of the current ongoing debate about administrative reform will be an important factor in the success or otherwise of regional development in this particular Baltic State.

In conclusion, the bottom-up approach has had a number of benefits so far. The approach does, however, face many challenges and even if these challenges are met it remains to be seen if the bottom-up approach will continue to be a success in the Latvian context. As argued by Lorentzen (1996) and Petrakos (2000), the sustained success of the bottom-up approach is likely to be more difficult for transition countries, such as those of the former Soviet block, than it would be in established EU-member states with a strong history and culture of stakeholder participation and private sector initiative. These aspects will be looked at in more detail in the next section.

The Formation of Partnerships and the Role of the Civil Society

The increased interest in spatial planning and regional development, in particular at the regional and local levels, has highlighted the need to involve various stakeholders in the planning processes, i.e. what Pires *et al.* (2001) call participatory planning. Alden (2001) argues, when discussing the new planning agenda, that there is a need for a partnership between all stakeholders and discusses a concordat between the local government, business and the voluntary sector. Although the ESDP does not explicitly address the issue of partnerships and local initiatives, the absence in the ESDP of policy maps can, as argued by Faludi (2001), be interpreted as an emphasis on an endogenous policy agenda relying on local initiatives and networking. These findings are in line with those of Logan and Molotch (1987) who claimed that growth coalitions, involving and cooperating with local politicians, media, public leaders and semi-public institutions (such as development agencies, chambers of commerce, employers' federations and trade unions) with a view towards generating a coherent vision and strategy, are crucial when it comes to the economic development of a city (and by extension a region). Furthermore, the success of a growth coalition, and hence of a city's or region's economic development, is dependent on and related to the nature and structure of its political and, in particular, economic elites. Swyngedouw (2000) further discusses the role and importance of involving civil society in the process. Failure to bring broad layers of the civil society in line with the growth coalition's vision might result in conflicts that have the potential to erode the base on which successful development rests.

Taken together, the above suggests that for the sustainability of participatory planning as well as the sustainability of the Latvian bottom-up approach to planning, it will be important for the planners to involve civil society in planning processes at the local and regional levels. In this respect, Latvia faces a major challenge, not only because of the large minority of non-citizens, but again because of the Soviet legacy. In looking at the latter, North (1990) argued that the actions and behaviour of individuals, as well as the functioning of institutions are path-dependent. Applied to Latvia, this means that its Soviet past might still play an important role when trying to understand individual behaviour and actions. According to Schrader (2004), post-socialist societies face a situation where the social capital of the entire society is weak compared to the social capital based on personal networks. This in turn has a negative impact on the emergence of a dynamic and well-functioning civil society.

In relation to Latvian planning, this means that Latvian planners work in an environment characterised by a much weaker civil society in comparison with their Western European counterparts. As a result, they therefore face specific challenges in trying to adopt the *Western European model* or Western European approaches whereby active stakeholders participate in and contribute to the planning process as well as developing private-public partnerships. Failure to meet the challenge will result in a situation where planning is merely an exercise for planners. The evidence so far, however, is not very promising. With the exception of Riga, the extent of stakeholder participation in planning processes has been limited. In order to implement the new planning agenda Latvian planners, in particular the RDAs, face the task of raising the profile and credibility of planning through educational effort aimed at the general public. People need to be convinced of the added value of planning without having their expectations raised unrealistically. Another aspect is the need to raise the capacity of stakeholders and local communities so that they can play a full and active role in the planning process. This would be a challenging task in any society, but even more so in the Latvian context as it continues to struggle with the legacy of the past.

Conclusions and Lessons for the Future

We have seen that for a variety of reasons the Latvian approach to regional development and spatial planning has up until now been primarily a bottom-up approach. Stimulated to a large degree by the possibility of EU and other sources of funding, the Latvian regions took the lead vis-à-vis the central government in the field of regional development and spatial planning in the late 1990s. At the same time, the political instability whereby the government has changed frequently since independence has hampered central government in the provision of the necessary institutional framework. Whilst leaving the regions to a large extent in a policy vacuum, it has provided them with the opportunity to set the rules of the game to a large degree, hence leaving central government trying to catch up. It should also be said that the situation has resulted in some innovative approaches within the various regions and this has provided the Ministry with the opportunity to examine these approaches as well as good practice from elsewhere, an opportunity that they may not otherwise have had. Although the Latvian example has shown a number of positive elements to the bottom-up approach, successful planning processes also obviously require the participation, involvement and agreement of central government at some stage. This is particularly the case when it comes to providing the institutional framework in terms of legislation and administrative reform. There are also potential conflicts that may arise when the central government eventually catches the lower tiers up and the national framework is in place. It is therefore important to close the gap between central government and the regions and to divide the necessary tasks between the various levels in order to create a stable planning framework that can meet the many long term challenges facing the country. To create an effective planning structure, it is therefore necessary to combine the bottom-up approach pursued by the RDAs with a more top-down approach as manifested in the legislative framework. Another crucial factor in order for this approach to be successful will be the implementation of effective administrative reform that will see the number of administrations at the first tier of local government considerably reduced and a considerable strengthening of the regional level.

The Latvian case illustrates the effects of the dramatic shift in terms of macro-geographical position that all three Baltic States have experienced since the collapse of the Soviet Union and the restoration of independence and subsequent membership of the EU. The move from close to the Soviet geographic and economic core to the outer periphery of the EU has had a dramatic impact. The relative success of the Riga capital region and, to a lesser degree, the more western parts, especially the port cities, has increased regional disparities within the country. Consequently, the challenge facing regional development and spatial planning in the country is a double one of trying to simultaneously deal with this drastic change in position whilst at the same time addressing growing internal disparities.

We have also seen that the Soviet legacy is not only limited to the infrastructure system but also reflected in society in general. Current good practice in planning has participation and stakeholder engagement at its heart and much work remains to be done in Latvia, by all concerned, in order to convince and enable people to play a full and active part in the planning process. The culture of participation and stakeholder engagement will take time and considerable effort to become established and effective, a situation that Latvia shares with many other post-communist societies. This is something that will not only hamper the planning process, but will also limit opportunities when it comes to developing private-public partnerships.

In conclusion, the Soviet heritage in Latvia and other post-communist transition countries adds additional restrictions to spatial planning and regional development in a number of ways making the transition process on the one hand and the integration (with the EU) on the other extremely complex. This in turn means that many ideas and structures developed in Western Europe cannot simply be transferred and used as a blueprint to address many of the challenges facing such countries in transition. Latvian policy makers and planners cannot therefore afford to simply rely on the EU's regional policy agenda as manifested in the ESDP and via the Structural Funds to secure the future development of the country. It is crucial that the Latvians take their future into their own hands and develop their own visions and ideas when addressing the unique challenges they are facing. Much innovative work has already been done, the challenge is now to see whether the progress so far can be sustained long into the future.

References

Adams, N., Paalzow, A and Ezmale, S. (2006), 'Towards Balanced Development in Latvia: a look at the Latgale Region', *Regional Development and Spatial Planning in and Enlarged EU*, Ashgate, Aldershot.

Alden J. (2001), 'Planning at National Scale: A New Planning Framework for the UK', in Albrechts, L., Alden, J. and Pires, A. da Rosa (eds), *The Changing Institutional Landscape of Planning*, Ashgate, Aldershot.

Alden J., Albrechts, L. and Pires, A. da Rosa (2001), 'In Search of New Approaches for Planning', in Albrechts, L., Alden, J. and Pires, A. da Rosa (eds), *The Changing Institutional Landscape of Planning*, Ashgate, Aldershot.

Ancans, H., Pocs, R. and Steinbuka, I. (2000), 'Economic Development (1992–1999)', in Steinbuka, I. (ed.), *Latvia Entering the XXIst Century*, Nacionalais Medicinas Apgads, Riga.

Coccossis, H., Economou, D. and Petrakos, G. (2005), 'The ESDP Relevance to a Distant Partner: Greece', *European Planning Studies*, vol. 13, no. 2, pp. 253–64.

Crohn-Wolfgang, H.F. (1922), Die Republik Lettland und ihre wirtschaftliche Zukunft, *Jahrbücher für Nationalökonomie und Statistik*, pp. 420–432.

Crawford, B. and Lijphart, A. (1995), 'Explaining Political and Economic Change in Post Communist Eastern Europe: Old Legacies, New Institutions, Hegemonic Norms and International Pressures', *Comparative Political Studies*, vol. 28, no. 2, pp. 171–99.

Crohn-Wolfgang, H.F. (1923), *Lettlands Bedeutung für die östliche Frage*, Walter de Gruyter & Co., Berlin and Leipzig.

Downes, R. (1996), 'Economic Transformation in Central and Eastern Europe: The Role of Regional Development', *European Planning Studies*, vol. 4, no. 2, pp. 217–24.

EU Employment Observatory (2004), *Monthly Labour Market Update for Latvia*, European Commission, November 2004.

Faludi, A. (2001), 'The European Spatial Development Perspective and the Changing Institutional Landscape of Planning', in Albrechts, L., Alden. J. and Pires, A. da Rosa (eds), *The Changing Institutional Landscape of Planning*, Ashgate, Aldershot.

Gallup, J., Sachs, J. and Mellinger, A. (1999), *Geography and Economic Development*, Working Paper, Center for International Development, Harvard University, Cambridge, MA.

Hughes, J., Gwendolyn, S., and Gordon, C. (2005), *Europeanization and Regionalization in the EU's Enlargement to Central and Eastern Europe: The Myth of Conditionally*, Palgrave Macmillan, Basingstoke.

King, G.J., Vanags, E., Vilka, I., and McNabb, D.E. (2004), 'Local Government Reforms in Latvia', 1990–2003: Transition to a Democratic Society, *Public Administration*, vol. 82, no. 4, pp. 931–50.

Krisjane, Z. (2005), *Regional Disparities and Development Trends in Latvia*, Mimeo, Department of Human Geography, University of Latvia, Riga.

Latvian Statistical Bureau of Latvia (2005), *Demography 2005*, Riga.

Logan, J., and Molotch, H. (1987), *Urban Fortunes: The Political Economy of Place*, University of California Press, Berkeley, CA.

Lorentzen, A. (1996), 'Regional Development and Institutions in Hungary: Past, Present and Future Development', *European Planning* Studies, vol. 4, no. 3, pp. 259–77.

Nijkamp, P. (1995), 'Borders and Barriers in the New Europe: Impediments and Potential of New Network Configurations', in Coccossis, H. and Nijkamp, P. (eds), *Overcoming Isolation: Information and Transportation Networks in Development Strategies for Peripheral Areas*, Springer, Heidelberg.

Nissinen, M. (1999), *Latvia's Transition to a Market Economy: Political Determinants of Economic Reform Policy*, Macmillan, Basingstoke.

North, D.C. (1990), *Institutions Institutional Change and Economic Performance*, Cambridge University Press, Cambridge.

Pabriks, A. and Purs, A. (2002), 'Latvia the Challenges of Change', in Smith, D.J., Pabriks, A., Purs, A. and Lane, T. *The Baltic States: Estonia, Latvia and Lithuania*, Routledge, London.

Petrakos, G. (2000), 'The Spatial Impact of East-West Integration in Europe', in Petrakos, G., Gaier. G. and Gorzelak, G. (eds), *Integration and Transition in Europe: The Economic Geography of Interaction*, Routledge, London.

Petrakos, G. (2001), 'Patterns of Regional Inequality in Transition Economies', *European Planning Studies*, vol. 9, no. 3, pp. 359–83.

Pires, A., Albrechts, L. and Alden, J. (2001), 'Conclusions: Driving Process for Institutional Change', in Albrechts, L., Alden, J. and Pires, A. da Rosa (eds), *The Changing Institutional Landscape of Planning*, Ashgate, Aldershot.

Plakans A. (1995), *The Latvians: A Short History*, Hoover Institution Press, Stanford.

Sachs, J. (1997), *Geography and Economic Transition*, Working Paper, Center for International Development, Harvard University, Cambridge, MA.

Schrader, H. (2004), 'Social Capital and Social Transformation in Russia', *Journal for East European Management Studies*, vol. 9, no. 4, pp. 391–410.

Swyngedouw, E. (2000) Elite Power, 'Global Forces and the Political Economy of 'Glocal' Development', in Clark, G.L., Feldman, M.P. and Gertler, M.S., *The Oxford Handbook of Economic Geography*, Oxford University Press, Oxford.

Vanags, A. (2005), *The Governance of Employment and Economic Development in the Baltic States*, paper presented at the conference: Employment, Economic Development and Local Governance in Latvia, organized in Riga in January 2005 by OECD and the LEED Programme.

Zacesta and Pucis (2005), *The Possibility to Create Large-Scale Regional Governments in Latvia*, Paper presented at the conference: Employment, Economic Development and Local Governance in Latvia, organized in Riga in January 2005 by OECD and the LEED Programme.

Chapter 10

Towards Balanced Development in Latvia: The Experience of the Latgale Region

Neil Adams, Sandra Ezmale and Anders Paalzow

Introduction

In Latvia, as in most EU countries, there is a pervasive struggle between the richest and poorest regions in the country. For Latvia, being the poorest country in the EU with a GDP per capita just above 40 per cent of the EU average, this poses a major challenge in terms of regional development policy. Furthermore, according to the European Commission (2004), the variation within Latvia between the highest and lowest income per capita region in 2002 was 3.8:1, considerably higher than the figures for her Baltic neighbours Estonia (2.6:1) and Lithuania (2.5:1). Regional disparities within the three Baltic States are discussed in detail in Fokins *et al.* (2005). According to GDP per capita, Riga Region is by far the richest in Latvia with 76 per cent of the EU average, while Latgale is the poorest, with 20 per cent. Hence, the capital region is by far the richest Latvian region, and this difference, as discussed in Fokins *et al.* (2005), has increased further over the last decade during a period of rapid economic growth. The Latvian population is also strongly concentrated in Riga where the city has one third of the national population, seven times more than the country's second largest city, the Latgalian city of Daugavpils.

Fokins et al (2005) argue that the less significant disparities in Lithuania and Estonia probably reflect the smaller relative size of the respective capital cities to the rest of the country. The pattern of the capital city region becoming relatively richer leaving the other regions further behind however can also be seen clearly in Estonia and Lithuania. The similarities to the patterns of development observed in Ireland in the 1990s are apparent. As discussed in Barry (2003) and O'Leary (2003), Dublin being the most prosperous region exhibited considerably higher growth rates than the rest of the country, resulting in a situation where the prosperity generated by the *Celtic Tiger's* growth miracle was far from being evenly distributed throughout the country. The subsequent widening of the prosperity gap between Ireland's rich and poor regions led to claims of unfair treatment of the less developed regions and, not surprisingly, such claims have also been heard in Latvia spurring a debate on regional development and the major challenges facing the Central as well as local governments.

The discussion in this chapter will focus on Latgale. The Latgale Region is of particular interest, not only because it is the poorest region in Latvia, but also because, and maybe as a consequence of being the poorest region, it was the first Latvian region to work actively with regional policy after harnessing EU pre-accession funds. Using Latgale as a case study, the chapter will analyse the regional policy context and the Structural Funds interventions in Latvia and provide an outline of the basic principles and instruments of Latvian regional development policy with a special focus on Latgale Regional Development Agency (RDA). The chapter will also include a discussion on how the strategic partnership approach has been used in Latgale as well as a discussion of the policies and strategies aimed at reducing the prosperity gap between Latgale and the rest of the country.

The Institutional Context

The Ministry of Regional Development and Local Government, established in 2003, is the main institution responsible for the preparation and implementation of national regional policy. Before the establishment of this Ministry, the responsibilities were split between a number of governmental institutions. The Ministry is also responsible for the co-ordination and allocation of state assistance within its field of competence. Latvian planning can basically be divided into two groups of activities, development planning and spatial planning. Both aspects are governed by legislation dating from 2002 in the form of the Regional Development Law and the Spatial Planning Law (Priede and Strazda, 2003). The aim of Latvian development planning is to determine the development goals, strategies and the measures necessary to achieve these goals. The relevant legislation defines the general system for regional policy including the hierarchy of planning documents, the institutional competence, financing and the provisions for identifying assisted areas. As discussed in Priede and Strazda (2003) the legislation was forward-looking in the sense that it defines several provisions linked to the planning and co-ordination of EU Structural Funds as well as formalising the necessary institutional structures of the five planning regions. The latter is particularly relevant in that the RDAs, and hence the associated planning regions, were actually operational for about four years before the institutional framework was established giving rise to a feeling in the regions that they were always waiting for Central Government to catch up. Both pieces of legislation are similar in that they are relatively formal, certainly in comparison to the more informal approaches adopted in the Celtic countries, and both identify a number of principles to be observed at every level in the fields of regional development and spatial planning. The institutional structure for regional development and spatial planning is illustrated in Figure 10.1.

Being the poorest of the Latvian regions, it could be argued that Latgale had most to gain from a proactive regional policy and strong regional institutional structures. This is reflected in the fact that Latgale RDA was the first to be founded in Latvia in 1999. At that time an amendment to the Law on Local Government permitted local governments to from regional structures to deal with regional issues.

Figure 10.1 Institutional structure of the planning system in Latvia

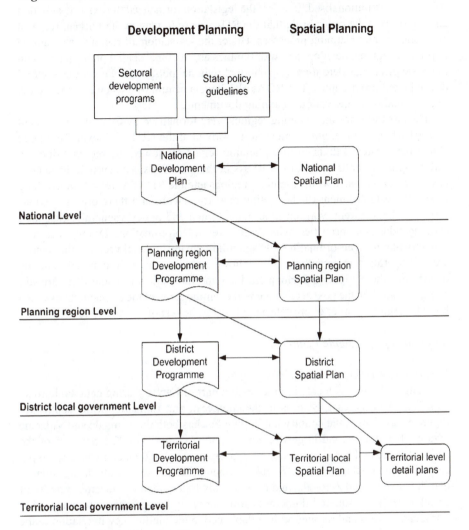

Source: Latgale Spatial Structure Plan

The establishment of similar structures in the other Latvian regions, Kurzeme, Riga, Vidzeme and Zemgale, soon followed the formation of Latgale RDA. The legislation at the time did not address the issue of planning at the regional level and neither were the exact territories of the regions formally defined. As a result a bottom-up process whereby the regions set the agenda as well as the rules of the game to a large extent drove the formation of the regions. It was not until 2002, when the new legislation on regional development and spatial planning came into effect, that planning at the regional level was regulated and that the role of the RDAs was institutionalised. In effect the legislation formalised the existing situation and legitimised the central role that the RDAs were to play in the Latvian regional development and planning processes. Under the legislation all regions are required to prepare regional development programmes and regional spatial plans in line with the basic principles determined by national regional policy and the various sectoral development programmes. The RDAs also have a central role when it comes to the implementation of the various planning documents.

The territories for the planning regions were formalised by Central Government in 2003 when five planning regions were formed at the NUTS III level. To a large extent the territorial division into planning regions followed the regional division following the establishment of the RDAs in the late 1990s. The current difficulties have been exacerbated as the planning regions and the RDAs were operational long before the establishment of the institutional framework and therefore the regions were to a large extent working in an institutional and policy vacuum setting their own agendas and priorities with little overall co-ordination. Despite the new Ministry playing a co-ordinating role and filling the institutional vacuum, the regions are still operating in something of a policy vacuum as the main national planning documents, the National Development Plan and the National Spatial Plan, are still being prepared. In the next section we will examine some of the characteristics of the Latgale Region in order to provide a context for the rest of the discussion.

A Portrait of the Latgale Region

Population, Administration and Geography

The Latgale Region is located in the eastern part of Latvia sharing national borders with Russia in the east, Belarus in the southeast, and Lithuania in the south (see Figure 10.2). Within the country the Region borders both the Zemgale and Vidzeme regions. It is the second largest region in Latvia comprising 22.5 per cent of the national space and has a population of approximately 370,000, equivalent to 16 per cent of the national population. Whilst the population density of Latgale is similar to that in Kurzeme and Zemgale, and considerably higher than in Vidzeme, a figure of 25 inhabitants per square kilometre is still extremely low compared to many other European regions and implies an inevitable economic inefficiency in relation to the provision of services.

The scale of the actual and predicted decline in population, not only in Latgale but throughout the Baltic States, between the end of the Soviet period and 2050 is staggering. Current predictions by EUROSTAT specify in the worst case scenario a decline of up to 19 per cent in the Latvian population between 2004–2050 (EUROSTAT, 2005) and this clearly provides an extremely challenging context for regional development. Given the geographic and economic peripherality of the Latgale Region, even within the Latvian context, it is likely that the Region will find it even more difficult than other Latvian regions to retain population, especially the more economically active and well-educated sections of the population.

The total population in Latgale has fallen by 5.14 per cent since 1999, over one and a half times the national average, and fell by almost three times the national average between 2003–2004. At district level, four of the five districts with the highest negative demographic change since 1999 in the entire country are located in Latgale. The decline is considerably higher than any other Latvian region and is fuelled by both out-migration and a negative natural balance. Two of Latvia's seven Republican cities are located in Latgale with the largest, Daugavpils, having a population of 111,000 whilst Rezekne has approximately 37,000 inhabitants, although the population in both continues to fall. Administratively, apart from the two Republican cities, the Region is divided into 6 administrative districts (rajons) – Balvi, Rezekne, Ludza, Preli, Daugavpils and Kraslava and 138 urban and rural municipalities at the local level. However, the small size and limited capacity of many of these administrations severely restrict their opportunities and potential in implementing strategic projects and absorbing the Structural Funds and, without institutional reform, it is likely that the financial, human and administrative resources and capacity of these administrations will decline further as discussed in the case of Estonia by Jauhiainen (2006).

Figure 10.2   Location of the Latgale region

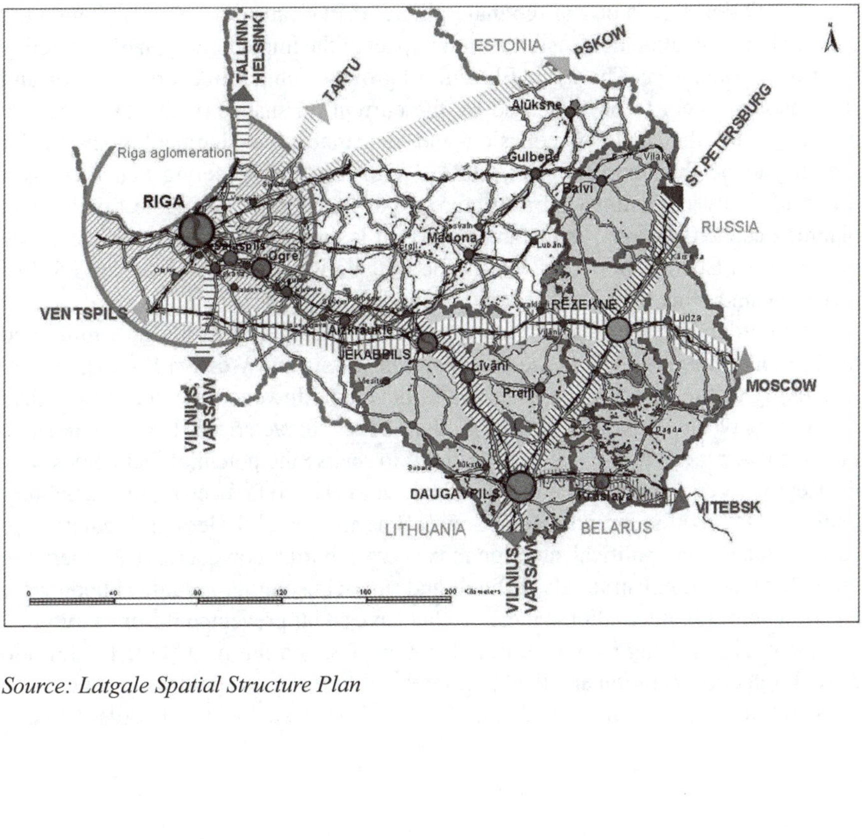

Source: Latgale Spatial Structure Plan

A specific challenge in Latvia in general, and in Latgale in particular, is the high proportion of ethnic Russians living in the Region. Ethnic Russians accounted for over 40 per cent of the population in Latgale in 2003 (Latvian Central Statistics Bureau 2004), with higher concentrations in the larger urban centres (50 per cent in Rezekne and 55 per cent in Daugavpils) and some rural areas. These proportions are the highest in Latvia and considerably higher than the national average (29 per cent). The integration of this large Russian minority, many of whom do not speak the Latvian language, has been a source of tension between Latvia and Russia since independence. A significant proportion of this group has the status of non-citizens meaning, amongst other things, that they are not allowed to vote in national or municipal elections and are barred from many jobs in the public sector. Whilst they have been given the opportunity to return to Russia, it is thought that most will remain due to higher standards of living and quality of life within the EU than in many parts of Russia.

In terms of territorial capital, the Latgale Region is characterised by important transport infrastructure, numerous lakes and a high quality landscape. Several international rail lines connecting Russia with Western Europe pass through the Region. Lines connecting Moscow with the Baltic ports and connecting Saint Petersburg with Warsaw cross at the important junction at Rezekne. A number of international road corridors also run through Latgale, primarily running parallel to the rail lines. A number of these connections are included in the Trans-European Network (TEN) that is one of the main pillars of EU transport policy, although the debate about the rationale, feasibility and impact of the implementation of this policy is far from conclusive. The stated EU aims of growth, competitiveness, cohesion and sustainability seem to be ill-served by the current pursuance of the TEN priority projects, with the goals of cohesion and sustainable development in particular seeming to be threatened (Peters, 2003). With a growing feeling that there is a mismatch between planned infrastructure expansion and the available funding and planning capacity, as well as the actual need, it is far from certain that the presence of numerous EU transport corridors in the Latgale Region will deliver the level of economic and other benefits that some would have us believe.

The border location has a strong influence on Latgale's territorial capital and the Region promotes itself as the link between Russia and Western Europe, as well as looking to the east for opportunities to develop. However, the current political tensions between Russia and Latvia that have characterised the period since independence mean that it has been difficult to realise the potential that comes with the Region's geographical location, and the location has so far been more of a liability than an asset. Whilst the relationship with Belarus is slightly less problematic, the current Belarussian political situation makes cross-border contacts and co-operation unpredictable, administratively difficult and time-consuming. Latgale is hoping for an easing of these international tensions that have so far prevented it from exploiting the potential stemming from its border location. The commitment at the EU level to cross-border co-operation and the likelihood that funds in this field will be increased in the future provide some hope that the potential associated with the border location will increase. The impact of the collapse of the Soviet Union and accession to the EU on Latgale's macro-geographic position is discussed in Chapter 9 (Paalzow, 2006). It would appear, however, that spatial adjustments in transition countries will tend to favour metropolitan and western regions (Petrakos, 2001), being the regions closest to the main drivers of development in the EU, further emphasising the challenges facing Latgale.

The presence of over one thousand lakes in the Region offers potential to develop a high quality natural identity and tourism product and the Region is often referred to as the Land of Blue Lakes. The high quality natural structure is further strengthened by the presence of Latvia's largest river, the Daugava, which flows through the Region on its way to the Bay of Riga and the extensive forests that cover approximately 35 per cent of the territory. The diversity provided by the mosaic of lakes, hills, forests and lowlands form a typical Latgalian landscape. The quality of the natural structure is reflected in over seventy protected nature areas. Given these characteristics it is not surprising that the RDA is working hard to develop concepts such as the Land of Lakes and the diverse cultural heritage into sustainable tourism products. A number of cross-border initiatives in the field of tourism have already been initiated involving eastern Lithuania and Belarus, although their long-term impact is as yet unclear due to the large number of external factors such as international relations that will primarily determine the future in this respect.

Socio-economic Factors

A quick analysis of recent EUROSTAT data makes bleak reading for Latgale. The Region has the dubious distinction of being not only the poorest Region in Latvia, but also the poorest of over 1,200 NUTS III level regions in the EU according to GDP at market prices with only 9.6 per cent of the EU average (EUROSTAT 2006). Neighbouring Latvian regions Zemgale and Vidzeme, with 11 and 11.4 per cent of the EU average respectively, closely follow Latgale. The rate for Riga is between three and four times greater than these figures, making it clear that Latvian, and more specifically Latgalian regional development and spatial planning are facing significant challenges in order to reduce relative poverty and large income inequalities between Riga and the rest. Despite containing some 16 per cent of the national population, Latgale only contributes 8 per cent to the national GDP and this figure is still falling due mainly to the considerably higher rates of growth in Riga. At the national scale the Ministry of Regional Development and Local Government administers a Regional Fund to specially assisted areas defined at the level of local municipalities on the basis of poor performance against a number of socio-economic indicators. A review of the assisted areas reveals that virtually the whole of Latgale is eligible for such assistance and since the Fund was established in 1998 over 700 projects have been submitted from Latgale, more than the total for all other Latvian regions put together (State RDA, 2004).

Such regional imbalances are not unique to either Latvia or Latgale (Fokins 2005), although there have been a variety of reasons contributing to the decline. One of the main reasons was the decline of Daugavpils, which was an important industrial city in the Soviet Union, but saw its economic base collapse after independence. The orientation towards the nearby Eastern markets put Daugavpils at a severe disadvantage in terms of industrial relations and, coupled with the inefficient industrial base, this meant that a drastic process of restructuring was inevitable. The two main branches of the economy, manufacturing and transport, collapsed with gross added value falling by almost 60 per cent in each sector between 1996 and 2000. Figures for gross industrial output during the same period reveal the extent of the collapse. Whilst Daugavpils was second behind Riga in terms of gross industrial output in 1996, the figure for the western port city of Liepaja was twice as high as that for Daugavpils by 2000. Other economic indicators reveal stubborn structural problems for the Region. Unemployment, at approximately 16 per cent, remains significantly higher than the national average of approximately 11 per cent. Latgale has also failed to attract significant levels of investment and investment per capita is around one third of that in Riga. Accordingly, the number of active enterprises per 1,000 inhabitants, which was around nine in 2003, is low and close to half of the national average. Latgale does however have a relatively high number of higher and further education institutions. There are a number of higher education institutions including Daugavpils University, Rezekne University College, local branches of the University of Latvia, Riga Technical University and branches of the Baltic Russian Institute. In addition, there are twenty-three institutions of further and professional education. In total this amounts to over 11,000 students. These institutions are perceived to be an important regional asset and could have a crucial role to play in the long-term development of the Region as experience from other European regions that have used education as a vehicle to drive regional development shows. An important issue in this context is the question of whether Latgale will be able to retain the qualified human resources generated by these institutions. Although there is a lack of statistical data to analyse this, there is a feeling that retention will be extremely difficult as graduates are attracted by the opportunities offered by Riga and elsewhere. It is clear from this brief portrait of Latgale that the Region possesses certain characteristics typical in the two forms of problem region identified by Barjak (2001). First, it is primarily a rural region and peripheral to the main agglomerations of Latvia and the EU; and second, in the city of Daugavpils there are obvious similarities to conditions found in declining industrial regions. These factors, combined with the Soviet legacy (see Paalzow, Chapter 9), provide an indication of the magnitude of the problems facing the Region.

The EU Regional Policy Context and Structural Funds

The whole of Latvia is designated as an Objective 1 region at the NUTS II level meaning that the entire country is eligible for the full range of Structural Funds. Not surprisingly, the expectations in relation to the impact of the Structural Funds in all of the new member states are high and there is a tendency in some quarters to think that the Funds will cure all ills. The reality, however, is likely to be quite different.

There is an increasing body of thought that the economic forces driving an increasing divergence between regions are simply too strong for regional policies, such as the Structural Funds, to counteract (Peters, 2003). There is also an increasing literature attempting to assess the effectiveness of EU regional policy in actually reducing regional disparities. Sosvilla-Rivero *et al.* (2006) have assessed the effectiveness of regional policy, and more precisely the Structural Funds, on the basis of a Spanish Objective 1 region. The methodology involved an assessment of progress in the region according to various indicators with and without the EU financial support. The research concluded that there was a slight convergence towards the EU average in terms of per capita income with the EU support and that there is likely to have been a slight divergence without this support, although the difference is not as dramatic as one might anticipate. Importantly, it was felt that an over-estimation of the benefits of the Structural Funds could be dangerous and it is essential to pursue other innovations simultaneously in order to achieve a sustainable convergence, and this would appear to be an important lesson for Latvia and Latgale. The situation however differs with Spain in that the EU decided to treat Latvia as a single region, meaning that funds are allocated nationally rather than regionally. This provides the opportunity for Central Government to allocate a higher proportion of the funds to the stronger regions in the hope that this will drive national development towards convergence at a faster rate. Indeed, some have argued that the decision by the EU to allocate funds nationally goes against the principles of EU structural policy 'which primarily strived for a balanced regional structure within the member states' (Kratke, 2002 p. 656). It is, however, recognised that the Latvian regions do not yet possess the necessary capacity to manage and implement the Structural Funds individually and this was clearly the worry and the motivation behind the decision of the EU. Kratke also argues that increased regional disparities at the pan-European scale were an inevitable consequence of enlargement as the main winners, at least in the short to medium term, were always going to be the structurally strong regions in both Eastern and Western Europe.

Whilst EU Structural Policy now aims to promote income convergence at the EU level, it is felt that the policy is increasing regional disparities at lower levels and this is considered the responsibility of the individual member states. The presence of large regional disparities within Latvia means, therefore, that the distribution of Structural Funds poses additional challenges. The Latvian priorities in relation to the Structural Funds are set out in the Single Programming Document (SPD) covering the period 2004–2006. The priorities of the SPD are to achieve sustainable, competitive and knowledge-based economic development with a focus on competitiveness, human resources and infrastructure. Territorial cohesion is an additional objective, although it is unclear exactly what this means and how it will be achieved. The responsibility for the administration of the Structural Funds is shared among several institutions making management and co-ordination a complex process and the promotion of regional development in general more difficult. These co-ordination difficulties are evident in relation to the various national and EU development support mechanisms and instruments. In many cases regional disparities are addressed on a rather *ad hoc* basis with insufficient co-ordination between different programmes, and these shortcomings are particularly felt at the regional level. The feeling that the regional dimension is neglected in the national programming documents is strong in Latgale and the other provincial regions.

There is a general dissatisfaction outside Riga with the way the Structural Funds have been managed until now. As can be seen in Figure 10.3, the vast majority of the Structural Funds so far have been allocated within the Riga Region. The other four regions are therefore advocating a more equitable approach with increased emphasis on the reduction of regional disparities. The plea for an equity-based approach appears to be in sharp contrast to the current efficiency-based approach whereby funds appear to be being allocated using a cost benefit approach at the national level. Despite territorial cohesion and balanced development being identified as a priority in some national documents, the equity approach has not been effectively operationalised by any policy documents leading to a growing resentment in the regions. Supporters of the efficiency-approach argue that concentrated economic growth at the national level will trickle down to the other regions in time, although the actual extent of this process is far from proven. There does however appear to be an inherent contradiction between the mid-term objectives and priorities identified in the SPD, which to a large extent focus on the equity approach, and the actual management of the Structural Funds. Peters (2003), amongst others, has acknowledged the likelihood that in order to obtain a more equitable allocation of EU funds there would need to be a reduction in overall prosperity and competitiveness targets. As in many other countries, the debate about generating or redistributing prosperity and the apparent conflict between the pursuance of the dual goals of competitiveness and cohesion is highly relevant in the Latvian context.

The perceived inequitable allocation of the Structural Funds is supported by recent research by Vanags and Pobyarzina (2005) who have examined preliminary data for the implementation of Structural Fund projects in the current programming period. The research reveals that out of one hundred and seventy eight approved projects, ninety-nine of them, totalling EUR 24 million, are in Riga. In comparison, only seven projects totalling EUR 2 million had been approved in Latgale. A contributory factor to this inequitable allocation has been the fact that the RDAs, local municipalities and local businesses responsible for preparing and submitting applications in the weaker regions often lack the necessary human resources, financial and institutional capacity making it more difficult to prepare and co-finance projects. Currently, there are approximately 350 rural municipalities in Latvia with a population of less than 2,000. Latgale has the highest number of local municipalities of all five planning regions and 25 per cent of the total number in Latvia. The proportion of municipalities with less than 2,000 population is also considerably higher in Latgale than the national average, standing at approximately 85 per cent in 2003. It is hardly surprising that such small administrations lack the institutional capacity to prepare projects, let alone the necessary funds to co-finance them, and it is important that this problem is addressed. Vanags and Pobyarzina (2005) conclude that the regional dimension appears to have been added as something of an afterthought into the current programming documents and there is very little current evidence to contradict this view. Given the distribution of approved projects so far, it seems reasonable to assume that they have contributed to increasing the regional disparities within Latvia rather than reducing them. However, it is important to bear in mind that, as discussed in the Irish context by Barry (2000), the equity approach does not necessarily guarantee income convergence.

Figure 10.3 Approximate distribution of the structural funds between the Latvian regions 2004–2005

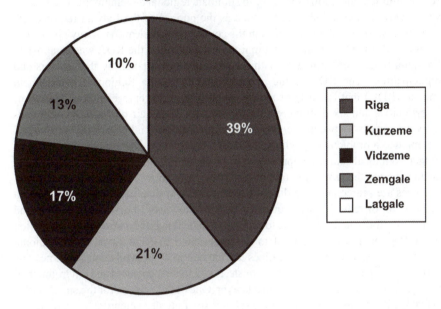

Source: Latgale Regional Development Agency calculus

As stated previously, Latvia is currently designated as an Objective 1 area, since its GDP per capita is less than 75 per cent of the EU average. Although GDP per capita is the lowest in Europe, the country is also experiencing one of the highest growth rates in the EU with real GDP increasing by more than 60 per cent since 1996. With strong economic growth and low incomes, and poorer countries like Bulgaria and Romania waiting to join the EU, Latvia may run the risk of achieving the 75 per cent threshold, albeit unevenly distributed throughout the country. This would mirror the situation in Ireland in the mid 1990s where the success of the Irish economy meant that the country as a whole no longer qualified for maximum EU structural funding (O'Leary 2003). The Irish solution was therefore to sub-divide the country regionally in order to maintain Structural Funds support outside the Dublin capital region. It is possible that at some point in the future a similar solution may be necessary for Latvia, although such a scenario is still some time away. In the meantime, Latgale will be watching closely to see if the means of allocating funding during the next programming period from 2007–2013 will be on a more equitable basis and pay greater attention to the regional dimension.

The Role of the RDA and the Rise in Regionalism

Latgale RDA, the first RDA in Latvia, was established in September 1999, initially with only two staff and a mission to capitalise on the opportunities offered by the EU commitment to regions and to try to stimulate regional development. The Region was already well-established at the time as the poorest of the Latvian regions and, given its eastern peripheral location in the country, it was clear that many challenges lay ahead. As mentioned at the beginning of the Chapter, the RDA was established through a bottom-up approach, with the initiative being taken by the districts and municipalities. The RDA is the executive body for the Regional Development Council (RDC) that consists of sixteen politicians, two representatives of each of the two cities and six districts within the Region. The chair of the RDC alternates every six months between the various administrations. Right from the early days, funding was a problem and today the RDA receives approximately 10 per cent of its budget from local sources, approximately 25 per cent from Central Government and has to generate the remaining 65 per cent itself through project income. As a result, resources are scarce and it is difficult for the RDA to plan too far ahead or to be a major driver of regional development. The RDA now has 10 permanent staff spread over three offices and was quick to recognise that, alongside a strong representation in the Region, it was important to be represented in Riga close to the national administrations. The two local offices are located in Daugavpils and Rezekne. The staff is made up of a mixture of economists, geographers, business and environmental management experts, engineers and a lawyer. One of the reasons for the small staff is so that the RDA can offer competitive salaries (by Latgale standards) in the hope that staff can be retained and this strategy seems to be reasonably successful with almost half the staff being employed by the RDA for four years or more.

The RDA is required to prepare development programmes and a regional spatial plan and we will examine the various regional planning documents in the next section. A large portion of staff time is spent co-ordinating activities, fostering regional partnerships and preparing projects to be submitted for the Structural Funds. Due to the limited human and financial resources, Latgale RDA cannot be compared to RDAs in England or the Welsh Development Agency for example, although it has undoubtedly had a significant impact as a focus for regional issues. In the ever-changing world of regionalism there is a feeling that RDAs need to move beyond the primarily economic remit that most seem to follow, to pursue a broader agenda linked to quality of life (Morgan, 2004). With the prospect of administrative reform in Latvia, and with talk of the amalgamation of the districts and the planning regions to form regional administrations, the future for the RDA is as uncertain as ever.

However, there is a strong feeling within Latgale and the other provincial regions that the regional level will have a key role to play in the future development of Latvia. Latgale has the advantage of having a strong regional identity based on cultural, linguistic, historical and religious traditions. It has been argued by Paasi (in Knap *et al.* 2004) and others that regions are continually reproduced and transformed by a complex variety of processes at various spatial levels in what Paasi refers to as the 'socio-spatial process of the institutionalisation of regions' (Knap *et al.* 2004 page 328). The process according to Paasi consists of four stages: territorial shape (localisation of social practices and power relations that give the region its boundaries), conceptual shape (the attachment of particular symbols to the region to facilitate the formation of regional images and consciousness), institutional shape (establishment of a sphere of formal organisations and informal institutionalised conventions and customs) and established role (maintenance and continued reproduction of the region as a social entity). It can be argued that Latgale is in at least the third stage of this process, although the institutional shape is still evolving and the individual stages are not entirely distinguishable from one another. In this sense Latgale at least possesses some of the characteristics that a region requires to function effectively. Whilst other factors are undoubtedly also important, Raagma (2002) amongst others has also identified the importance of regional identity in the organisation of economic, social and cultural activities.

The strong regional identity coincides with a strong commitment to regions at the EU level and a growing body of literature on regionalism that emphasises the importance of the sub-national level as the level to which the supra-national and national levels increasingly have to look to implement policies. As stated by Morgan (2004), whilst the supra-national and national levels in the EU invariably retain the power to decide, it is increasingly the sub-national level that has the power to deliver. In time, it is hoped that the inter-dependence of the different levels on each other will facilitate increased co-operation and allow the Latvian regions to have a real say in their own destiny. In order to do this effectively, the regional level must ensure that it has sufficient capacity to fulfil this role whilst the national and EU levels must ensure that they possess the necessary tools. Clearly, this transformation will need to take place over time and Latgale RDA has long since tried to embrace all opportunities to strengthen capacity amongst regional stakeholders, and ongoing institutional reform will be important in this respect.

Planning Documents of the Latgale Planning Region

The Latgale Region considers itself in many ways as being a pioneer in regional development and planning in Latvia. As mentioned previously, Latgale was the first Latvian region to establish a RDA and was also first to harness international funds aimed at strengthening administrative capacity. As a result, the RDA has acquired considerable experience in the field of regional development. In this section of the chapter a number of policy documents prepared in Latgale will be examined. The documents include:

- Latgale Regional Development Plan/Latgale Development Strategy (2000);
- Latgale Urban Development Strategy (2001);
- Latgale Spatial Structure Plan (2003);
- Latgale Partnership Strategy (2003);
- Latgale Regional Development Programme (to be approved 2006).

Any discussion in relation to these documents needs to be placed within the context of the policy vacuum at the national level mentioned earlier. As a result, a number of the documents listed above, although approved by the RDC, do not have a recognised status. The value of the processes involved in the preparation of these plans and documents however cannot be underestimated and the capacity within the Region has undoubtedly increased dramatically as a result.

Prior to joining the EU, Latvia, like the other candidate countries, had access to pre-accession funds. Arguably the most important of these for the field of regional development was the PHARE programme that was devoted to strengthening economic and social cohesion. In Latgale's case, this resulted in the Integrated Development Programme for Latgale, which was a part of the PHARE National Programme 1997. The EU was quick to recognise that local government in Latvia, as in other former members of the communist bloc, was ill-equipped to develop the new type of plans needed in the post-communist environment. The general objectives of the Integrated Development Programme were to prepare a Regional Development Plan (RDP) and to increase regional capacity in effectively accessing and managing national and international assistance programmes. The development of the RDP was also a driving force in the establishment of the RDA. A key aspect of the project was to strengthen capacity in the use of regional planning data and planning techniques, including the provision of guidelines as well as providing practical experience and training in regional development and planning. An interesting parallel can be drawn to what happened in Portugal after the fall of the dictatorship in 1974, when Portuguese local authorities faced similar problems to the local authorities in the post-communist countries when adapting to the new institutional environment. As discussed in Pires (2001), the EU influence on the approach to development policy was considerable and in many cases reflected the need to facilitate, access and manage the EU Structural Funds.

The RDP was prepared with support from an international team and there are many elements of international good practice. There are, however, some distinctive features reflecting the particular challenges facing Latgale Region, such as the issue of ethnic participation and integration of the large Russian minority. On a basic level, the cultural differences and the fact that a high proportion of this group only speak Russian are the most obvious challenges and these issues are discussed in Metuzale-Kangere and Ozolins (2005). In addition, the RDP devotes attention to measures aimed at strengthening the Latgalian culture and identity, including the use of the Latgalian language. The RDP also has a strong emphasis on social problems, where special attention is paid to reduction of poverty and the problems associated with widespread alcoholism. In addition to the establishment of the RDA and the preparation of the RDP in Latgale, over two hundred people throughout the country received training and this intangible element is likely to have been the most important output and most lasting legacy of the Programme. The Pilot RDP was approved by the RDC in 2000 as the Latgale Development Strategy. The Development Strategy is based on three pillars, the development of the productive sectors, the development of infrastructure, and the development of human resources. It would appear that Latgale has adopted a combination of the Greek-Portuguese model, focussing on support for business and infrastructure, and the Irish model, devoting substantial resources to the development of human resources (Alasejeva 2003). The early commitment to the development of human resources is important and the large number of educational institutions located in the Region support this process, although it is far from certain that graduates from these institutions are being retained in the Region. Vanags and Pobyarzina (2005) suggest that the Latgalian choice reflects the overall Latvian position in relation to the use of the EU Structural Funds, a position in between the Greek-Portuguese and the Irish models.

Building on this experience, the Latgale Urban Development Strategy (UDS) was prepared and approved by the RDC in 2001. In recognition of a part of the Soviet legacy, whereby there were few if any functional relationships between urban centres, the UDS aimed to create a functional urban network at the regional level. The concept of polycentric development at the regional level formed the basis, complemented by a division of roles and tasks among urban areas. The division was based on the specific characteristics of each centre as well as its position in the urban hierarchy in order to capitalise on the respective strength and potential of each centre in a complementary and mutually reinforcing way. Furthermore, the strategy focussed on the creation of an effective communication network for facilitating flows of people, goods, services and information between the urban areas. The UDS identified familiar themes and priorities such as the promotion of entrepreneurship and business development, the importance of social integration and the renovation of urban environments. The UDS, together with the RDP, provided the basis for spatial planning at the regional level and served as a starting point for the preparation of the Latgale Spatial Structure Plan approved in 2003 with the aim of providing spatial expression to the other strategies and programmes. Flemish partners were involved in this process and the Flemish influence is extremely strong both in terms of the form and the content of the plan, with various Flemish spatial concepts forming the basis of the Plan. The Structure Plan was the first spatial plan to be developed in Latvia at the regional level and was considered as something of a pilot project for the rest of the country. As mentioned previously, the bottom up approach, whereby the regions were actually ahead of the national level, meant that the Plan was approved two years before the regulations for such regional plans were in place in early 2005. Work is ongoing to harmonize the Structure Plan with the requirements of Central Government legislation and regulations and it remains to be seen how much of the work undertaken will ultimately be able to be used in the statutory document. This uncertainty has also been a source of much tension between Central and regional bodies.

The importance of partnership between regional stakeholders was becoming increasingly apparent during the various planning processes and therefore the next logical step was the preparation of the Latgale Partnership Strategy, which was approved by the RDC in 2003. The objectives of this strategy were to facilitate effective participation between various stakeholders in the Region in order to increase capacity in the absorption of the EU Structural Funds. The mobilisation of existing capacity and the creation of a simple and efficient regional co-operation system were important sub-objectives. Significant progress has been made in the development of effective partnerships and networks, although most stakeholders recognise that much remains to be done. Such processes require considerable time to become embedded and this will be discussed more in the following section. Under the provisions of the Regional Development legislation of 2002, the planning regions were required to elaborate Regional Development Programmes and this process started in Latgale in 2003 and should be completed by the end of 2006. The Programme will to a large extent build on the knowledge, concepts and priorities developed in the previous documents and processes. The Programme will provide an integrated vision and strategy for the whole Region as well as providing a mechanism to prioritise projects to be submitted for Structural Funds assistance for the EU programming period 2007–2013. The Programme will also feed into the preparation of the national planning documents. In the following section the approach to developing strategic partnerships in Latgale will be examined in more detail.

The Strategic Partnership Approach

Local and regional partnerships have emerged as an effective instrument of regional development in many EU countries since the early 1990s. The partnership approach has gradually established itself as one of the main pillars of EU regional and cohesion policy and effective partnerships are often a prerequisite of receiving EU financial support for regional development activities (Boland, 1996). Each member state is required to establish effective cross-sector partnerships between various parts of the public, private and voluntary/NGO sectors at various spatial levels. The number of projects relying on the partnership approach has grown rapidly in Latvia during recent years and this development can be attributed to a large extent to the EU pre-accession funds. In Latgale, as well as in the other Latvian planning regions, the establishment and the work of the RDAs is in itself one of the most significant examples of co-operation and partnership between municipalities within each of the regions. The financial, human and physical resources available for development in the Latgale Region are extremely limited and as a result there are few organisations with the resources and capacity necessary to prepare and implement large-scale regional projects. The partnership approach can therefore be seen as an effective way of stimulating and facilitating the preparation and implementation of such projects. The need to develop the partnership approach in Latgale gave rise to a capacity-building project with the PHARE programme in 2002–2003. The project resulted in the Latgale Regional Partnership Strategy (LRPS), which contains a number of recommendations for the formation of regional partnerships although only a few have been implemented so far. The underlying theme of the LRPS is that the involvement of various partners in regional development not only contributes to the pooling of resources, but also to ensuring that the development embraces different institutions, interests and activities. In addition, it is hoped that it will help to avoid duplication of tasks and hence facilitate better usage of the limited resources available as well as improving the integration and co-ordination of activities and policies at the regional level.

The LRPS proposes a three-tier structure with political, managerial and practical tiers being assigned different responsibilities. At the political level the Latgale Regional Partnership Forum (consisting of the RDC and social partners) is responsible for implementing the LRPS, securing sustainable development objectives and pursuing regional priorities. This task is to be undertaken in co-operation with the government institutions concerned with decision making in issues related to the EU Structural Funds. An annual Partnership Forum is to be organised and an annual Goodwill Agreement on the development objectives based on the Latgale Development Programme will be worked out and signed by the main partners. At the managerial level the RDA, in co-operation with an Advisory Board comprising representatives from the second level municipalities, the public and private sectors as well as NGOs, will implement the partnerships. The objective of the partnerships at the managerial level is to ensure involvement of both public and private sector resources in order to achieve the objectives outlined in the Agreement. At the practical level, the partnership will be implemented by Project Groups, which will comprise four to eight specialists in particular fields and who will work on the projects selected by the Advisory Board. The RDA will be responsible for the co-ordination as well as for the actual work on these projects. The three tier system, together with other recent developments in Latgale, suggests that the RDA is assuming a role of a catalyst in terms of initiating and coordinating different projects. This development is similar to that in the EU in the early 1990s when many RDAs evolved into co-ordinators and catalysts of economic development, while to a large extent leaving their traditional roles of being exclusive, direct deliverers of policies and strategies behind (Halkier, Danson and Damborg, 1998 and Cameron, Danson and Halkier, 2000).

Conclusions and Lessons for the Future

During the course of this chapter we have presented a case study of Latgale, the poorest region in the poorest country of the EU. We feel, however, that the lessons learnt could well be of relevance not only in Latgale and Latvia but also in other current and future regions of the EU with similar characteristics. Latgale possesses many of the characteristics of a geographically and economically peripheral area (DETR 2000). The challenges posed by the ongoing effects of transition and the Soviet legacy and the impact of both private and EU investment combine to form significant constraints to future development. The sheer weight of external and even internal factors constraining the future development of the Region is overwhelming and it is clear that the RDA cannot solve these problems alone, and even with outside help it is likely to take a considerable amount of time to address them effectively. In the meantime, the inevitable process out-migration of will further diminish the social and economic capital of the Region. A difficult dilemma arises in such circumstances as to whether resources should be invested to try and avert the inevitable or whether these resources should be diverted to a more long-term, gradualist and more realistic approach to sustainable development. In a theoretical world it is easy to opt for the latter but that ignores the political reality. It is, however, crucial to be realistic and to invest according to a long-term strategy. Clearly, an integrated response from regional, national and EU levels is required to tackle problems of such magnitude. One of the strengths of the EU is that it provides an opportunity to learn from the experiences of others and this lesson has been, and will continue to be, embraced in Latgale.

At the regional level it is important that ongoing initiatives to strengthen the capacity of regional stakeholders continue and facilitate both vertical (between levels) and horizontal (between sectors and areas) co-operation. Experience shows that more can be achieved in such circumstances through co-operation and consensus rather than isolation and conflict. Latgale RDA has established a strong tradition of taking the intiative, being proactive and learning by doing and the importance of this should not be underestimated. Another important lesson for Latgale is to build on your strengths. The sheer weight of factors mentioned in the opening of this final section mean that it is unlikely and unrealistic to expect Latgale to be able to compete in the long-term with the economic core of the nation (Riga) and of the EU for higher order economic functions. Kunzmann (2005) used the Ruhrgebiet in Germany as an example of how to turn problems into potentials in regional planning and much has been written (see Danielzyk and Wood 2004) about the success achieved in transforming the declining old industrial areas of Germany. Whilst it is clear that the Ruhrgebiet has significant advantages over Latgale in terms of location and the availability of critical mass, important lessons can never the less be learnt. Learning to know the region is a crucial first step and, whilst extensive knowledge has already been built up during the course of the various planning processes, it is crucial that this learning process continues. Such knowledge generated through the involvement of a variety of stakeholders is crucial if the available territorial capital is to be mobilised (Kunzmann 2005) and regional identity is to be strengthened and utilised. The involvement of civic society in every step of the process will help to create networks and success stories and these success stories can then be used as a stepping-stone to further success. Appropriate historical, cultural and political occasions can be used to get decisions and using the media as partners can enhance this process. Experience from other regions shows that it is important that peripheral regions exploit their assets to achieve long-term sustainable development. The example of the Ruhrgebiet also shows that such regional knowledge and the knowledge of how to transform regions can become a regional asset and product to be marketed and sold (Kunzmann 2005).

The national level also clearly has a key role to play in the development of the regions and the choice between pursuing either the efficiency or the equity approach will have a strong impact on the future development of Latgale. The ongoing discussions in relation to institutional reform in Latvia need to deliver strong regions and it is important that Latgale RDA and other regional stakeholders play a positive and proactive role in this process. Institutional reform is a thorny issue and it is important that Latvia gets it right. It is the responsibility of the national level to ensure that an institutional framework is in place where the first and second tier administrations possess sufficient capacity to absorb the Structural Funds. If this is not the case, as at present in Latvia, the inevitable conclusion is that the prosperity gap between the strong and the weak regions will widen further. The bottom-up approach clearly had significant advantages in Latvia but the Latvian experience illustrates that there are also significant disadvantages of working in a non-existent or incomplete institutional and policy framework. This experience is also likely to be important for future candidate countries such as Romania and Bulgaria.

The decision of the EU to allocate Structural Funds at the national level in Latvia has certainly had an impact, although the decision is understandable due to the limited administrative capacity of the Latvian regions at the time. However the EU clearly has a key role to play and the enlargement process was always going to 'require more than just an eastward extension of EU's existing policies' (Pallagast 2006 p. 269). If the current system of Structural Funds allocation continues into the next programming period it is highly likely that the pressure on the national government will ensure that they continue to pursue an efficiency-based rather than an equity-based approach to the allocation of resources.

We feel that the main conclusion of this Chapter is that whilst EU policies offer significant opportunities for the development of a region like Latgale, they are not sufficient in isolation to close the prosperity gap, and indeed as we have seen are likely to increase disparities under certain conditions. Despite this, stakeholders at the regional level in Latgale need to continue to seek innovative solutions to the challenges that they are facing and to work in partnership and learn from shared experiences. A wide diversity of external factors will have a strong influence on the future development of Latgale, and whilst the Region can take some steps to influence these factors, it should focus most attention on areas that it can exert a strong influence over. Parity with average EU levels of prosperity remains a distant – and, possibly, ultimately elusive – dream for Latgale. However, by harnessing the region's human resources, building on its assets and pursuing a long-term view of sustainable development, the goal of an improved quality of life may just be achievable.

References

Alasejeva, J. (2003), 'Īrijas skola – kā vislabāk izmantot ES naudu?', http://www. politika.lv/index.php?id=106534&lang=lv accessed December 2005.

Barjak, F. (2001), 'Regional Disparities in Transition Economies: A Typology for East Germany and Poland', *Post-Communist Economies*, vol. 13, no. 3, pp. 289– 311.

Barry, F. (2000), 'Convergence is not Automatic: Lessons from Ireland for Central and Eastern Europe', *World Economy*, November 2000, pp. 1379–94.

Barry, F. (2003), 'European Union Regional Aid and Irish Economic Development', in B. Funck and L. Piazatti (eds), *European Integration, Regional Policy and Growth, the World Bank*, Washington DC.

Boland, P. (1996), 'Regional Development Strategies in Europe: A Summary of the Key Issues', in Alden, J. and Boland, P. (eds), *Regional Development Strategies: A European Perspective*, Jessica Kingsley, London.

Cameron, G., Danson, M. and Halkier, H. (2000), 'Institutional Change, Governance and Regional Development: Problems and Perspectives', in Danson, M., Halkier, H. and. Cameron, G. (eds), *Governance, Institutional Change and Regional Development*, Ashgate, Aldershot.

Danielzyk, R. and Wood, G. (2004), 'Innovative Strategies of Political Regionalisation: The Case of North Rhine-Westphalia', *European Planning Studies*, vol. 12, no. 2, pp. 191–207.

DETR (2000), *Peripherality and Spatial Planning*, DETR, Rotherham, July 2000.

EUROSTAT (2006), GDP market prices at NUTS III level viewed at http://epp. eurostat.cec.eu.int/portal/page?_pageid=1996,45323734&_dad=portal&_schema =PORTAL&screen=welcomeref&open=/general/regio/econ-r/gdp95&language=e n&product=EU_MAIN_TREE&root=EU_MAIN_TREE&scrollto=736 accessed March 2006.

Fokins, V., Hansen, M., Sidorovs, R. and Umpirovica, N. (2005), 'Economic Inequality in the Baltics: Regional Disparities', *Baltic Economic Trends*, no. 2, pp. 25–36.

Jauhiainen, J. (2006), 'Demographic, Employment and Administrative Challenges for Urban Policies in Estonia', *European Planning Studies*, vol. 14, no. 2, pp. 273–283.

Halkier, M., Danson, M., and Damborg, C. (1998), 'Regional Development Agencies in Europe – an Introduction and Framework for Analysis', pp. 13–25, in Halkier, H., Danson, M. and Damborg, C. (eds), *Regional Development Agencies in Europe*, Jessica Kingsley, London.

Knapp, W., Kunzmann, K. and Schmidt, P. (2004), 'A Co-operative Spatial Future for Rhein-Ruhr', *European Planning Studies*, vol. 12, no. 3, pp. 323–349.

Kratke, S. (2002), 'The Regional Impact of EU Eastern Enlargement: A View from Germany', *European Planning Studies*, vol. 10, no. 5, pp. 651–664.

Kunzmann, K. (2005), *How to Turn Problems into Potentials in Territorial Development*, unpublished paper presented at Interreg IIIc GRIDS conference, Cardiff, Wales 17 November 2005.

Latgale Regional Development Agency (2000), Pilot Regional Development Plan for the Latgale Region (Phare National Programme 1997).

Latgale Regional Development Agency (2001), Latgale Urban Development Strategy (Special Preparatory Programme for Structural Funds, Latvia).

Latgale Regional Development Agency (2003), Latgale Region Partnership Strategy.

Latgale Regional Development Agency (2005), Latgale Draft Region Development Programme.

Latgale Regional Development Agency/WES (2003), Latgale Spatial Structure Plan.

Latvian Central Statistical Bureau of Latvia (2004), Latvia's regions in figure/ collection of statistical data, Riga.

Latvian Government (2003), Single Programming Document, Objective 1 Programme 2004–2006, approved by European Commission, 18 December 2003.

Latvian Government (2002), Regional Development Law.

Latvian Government (2002), Spatial Planning Law.

Latvian Ministry of Finance and UNDP (2005), EU Structural Funds and Development Territories in Latvia, Research Report Assistance to Implementation of EU Structural Funds: Strengthening of Communication, 2005.

Latvian Ministry of Regional Development and Local Government (2004), RDA Handbook, Regional Planning Manual (EuropeAid funded project 'Development of Business Environment in Latvia').

Latvian State Regional Development Agency (2003), Development of the regions in Latvia, Riga.

Latvian State Regional Development Agency (2004), Development of Regions in Latvia, Riga.

Metuzale-Kangere, B. and Ozolins, U. (2005), 'The Language Situation in Latvia 1850–2004', *Journal of Baltic Studies*, vol. XXXVI, no. 3, pp. 317–44.

Morgan, K. (2004), 'Sustainable Regions: Governance, Innovation and Scale', *European Planning Studies*, vol. 12, no. 6, pp. 871–889.

O'Leary, E. (2003), 'A Critical Evaluation of Irish Regional Policy', Chapter 2, pp. 15–39 in O'Leary. E. (ed.), *Irish Regional Development: A New Agenda*, The Liffey Press, Dublin.

Pallagst, K. (2006), 'European Spatial Planning Reloaded: Considering EU Enlargement in Theory and Practice', *European Planning Studies* vol. 14, no. 2, pp. 253–272.

Peters, D. (2003), 'Cohesion, Polycentricity, Missing Links and Bottlenecks: Conflicting Spatial Storylines for Pan-European Transport Investments', *European Planning Studies*, vol. 11, no. 3, pp. 317–339.

Petrakos, G. (2001), 'Patterns of Regional Inequality in Transition Economies', *European Planning Studies*, vol. 9, no. 3, pp. 359–383.

Priede M. and Strazda, A. (2003), 'Capital Investment Funding in Latvia', pp. 63–84, in Davey, K. (ed.), *Investing in Regional Development, Policies and Practices in EU Candidate Countries*, LGI Books, Open Society Institute, Budapest.

Sosvillo-Rivero, Bajo-Rubio and Diaz-Roldan (2006), 'Assessing the Effectiveness of the EU's Regional Policies on Real Convergence: An Analysis Based on the HERMIN Model', *European Planning Studies*, vol. 14, no. 3, pp. 383–396.

Vanags, A. and Pobyarzina, J. (2005), 'Latvia and Cohesion Policy', in Eriksson, J., Karlsson, B.O. and Tarschys, D. (eds), *From Policy Takers to Policy Makers, Adapting EU Cohesion Policy to the Needs of the New Member States*, SIEPS 2005:5, Swedish Institute for European Policy Studies, Stockholm.

Chapter 11

The Response to Regional Disparities in Lithuania

Gaile Dagiliene

Introduction

The phrase *Lithuania needs more efficient regional development policy* has once again become a popular slogan, becoming louder and stronger before each election. It can be heard from the President, Members of Parliament, in the Government, from the scientists and policy analysts as well as members of the general public. At first glance it appears that everybody is referring to the same issue. With closer scrutiny however, it becomes apparent that the phrase means different things to different people and this situation is exacerbated by an inflation of terminology. The difference between terms such as *regional development*, *spatial development*, *urban development* and *territorial cohesion* is often subtle and difficult to define. This is also true in relation to concepts such as *regional policy*, *structural policy* and *cohesion policy*, which are often used interchangeably in the EU context. What is clear is that EU regional policy is facing a challenging future in the light of enlargement and there are questions as to whether current regional policy will lead to a convergence or divergence in regional disparities and what the policy impact of this will be at different spatial levels.

This chapter will examine some of these issues in relation to Lithuania, although it does not claim to provide any clear-cut answers to these questions. In reality, it is highly unlikely that a definitive and clear-cut answer exists, although practical reasons would suggest that a solution has to be found. Soon after the reclamation of Independence in 1990, when Lithuania stepped on the path towards a market economy, regional disparities emerged and have been constantly growing ever since. The ongoing rapid growth of the capital Vilnius means that, to all intents and purposes, Lithuania can currently be divided into the capital and the rest. Not surprisingly, this is a cause of great concern and unrest for the population in the provinces and has been seized upon eagerly by the mass media. The nicknames the *elite* and the *beetroots* are frequently used and there is an increasing realisation that this situation cannot be allowed to continue unchecked if any form of political stability is to be achieved. The question is, can regional policy provide an answer to these problems?

In seeking to answer this difficult question, this chapter aims to provide an insight into Lithuania's attempts to overcome both internal and external (in the context of the

European Union) regional disparities via its regional policy. The chapter is organised in three main sections. First, the scene will be set by looking briefly at the historical and institutional context for regional policy in Lithuania and at some of the socio-economic characteristics of the country. This will involve looking at the nature of some of the internal regional disparities. Second, the chapter will examine the dual nature of regional policy at the moment in Lithuania and how changes in the position of the national Government and, to a certain extent, the European Commission have affected the situation. The various interpretations of regional policy and its link with spatial planning and EU structural policy and implementation mechanisms are discussed. In the final part of the chapter conclusions will be drawn from Lithuania's experience in dealing with these regional disparities to see what lessons can be learned for the future.

Setting the Scene

In order to set the context for the chapter it is important to briefly consider the location and the history of the country. Contrary to popular belief, Lithuania is a Central rather than an Eastern European country and is situated at one of the largest crossroads of the European continent. Lithuania shares borders with fellow Baltic State Latvia to the north, Belarus to the southeast, Poland to the south and the Kaliningrad region of Russia to the southwest. The western border is formed by approximately 100 kilometres of sandy coastline in the form of the Baltic Sea. It is the largest of the three Baltic States, both in terms of territory and in terms of population (territory – 65,200 sq. km, population – 3.4 million). 83.5 per cent of the Lithuanian population are ethnic Lithuanians who speak the Lithuanian language (one of two surviving members of the Baltic language group), which was reinstated as the official language after Independence. Several sizable minorities exist, such as Poles (7 per cent), Russians (5 per cent), and Belarusians (1.5 per cent) although generally speaking the proportion of indigenous nationals in Lithuania is higher than the respective proportion of Latvian and Estonian nationals in the other two Baltic States where the proportion of ethnic Russians are considerably higher at between 25–30 per cent of the total population (see Chapter 8).

In 2009 Lithuania will celebrate its millennium (since its first mention in Quedlinburg annals in 1009). However, most Lithuanians would claim that the golden age of the country was during the rule of Grand Duke Vytautas in the fourteenth and fifteenth centuries at which time the Great Duchy of Lithuania stretched from the Baltic Sea to the Black Sea and was one of the largest feudal states in Europe. Two other important dates in Lithuanian history are 16 February 1918, when Lithuania proclaimed the Act of Independence and Restoration of Statehood, and 11 March 1990, when Lithuania freed herself from the Soviet regime. The end of one journey was the start of another that ultimately led to Lithuania joining both NATO and the EU in the spring of 2004.

The Background and Origin of Regional Policy in Lithuania

Soviet Times

In order to understand the present situation it is important to consider the legacy of the past. During the Soviet years, Lithuania had a policy which can be regarded as the forerunner of the present national regional policy. In 1962–1964 the General Regional Planning Scheme (the first Master Plan) was drafted. The scheme had a significant impact on the development of Lithuania up until 1980 and provided a framework for the settlement structure consisting of 10 regional, 26 district and 174 local service centres. The development of Vilnius and Kaunas was to be restricted and 5 new regional centres, Alytus, Jurbarkas, Marijampolė, Plungė and Utena, were earmarked for development with a target population of between 50–80,000. In most cases, these target populations represented a significant increase. In addition, rapid development of 6 new small industrial centres, Mažeikiai, Ukmergė, Jonava, Kėdainiai, Rokiškis, Švenčionėliai, was also foreseen. The implementation of the scheme provided a framework for the development of industry, the balancing of the labour force, the formation of regional growth centres and the development of small towns (Tiskus 2001).

The majority of the industry was to be concentrated in the second and fourth largest cities of Kaunas and Šiauliai. The third largest, the port city of Klaipėda, was earmarked as the transport centre whilst other centres were primarily agricultural. After World War II, industry became the main engine of regional development and industrial growth was planned taking account of geographical aspects, accessibility and the characteristics of the labour force. As a result, virtually all branches of industry were present in the biggest cities, whereas other regions and centres became more specialised. Druskininkai and Birštonas were resort towns, Akmenė became the centre for construction materials, Kėdainiai and Jonava became centres for the chemical industry, Radviliškis became a major railway junction and Ignalina became the energy centre.

Reclamation of Independence in 1990

After independence in 1990, the economic, social and institutional landscape changed dramatically. Major restructuring of the established economic system began while resources and traditional markets disappeared. The changes led to the modernisation of industry and technology, the emergence of small and medium sized enterprises, an extensive search for new niche markets and increased partnership with foreign countries. The combined effect of these processes had a significant impact on the balance of the established system of urban centres. There is a feeling that insufficient attention was given to the controversial issue of territorial reform during these early years. During the transition period, problem regions emerged where there was an over-reliance on declining industry and long-term structural economic and social problems became apparent. As many authors, such as Thomas (1998), have observed, the spatial development of the city is often anarchic during transitional and early post-communist periods, particularly where city and district administrations are reliant on land sales or development taxes to finance their expenditure and compete to attract development. The consequences of this spatial anarchy are becoming apparent and it is likely that Lithuania will have to deal for many years to come with the problems associated with the rapid sub-urbanisation and some of the other ill-conceived development processes that took place in the early years after independence.

New Impetus for the Formation of National Regional Policy Since 1997

From 1997 onwards, regional policy started to receive more attention in Lithuania. An Annual Report by the European Commission (EC 1997) noted that Lithuania was facing serious regional development problems and that the response from the Lithuanian Government was not dealing with the issue effectively. With accession to the EU the top priority at the time, such statements carried substantial weight and instigated a number of important changes in the legal system and steps to strengthen institutional and administrative capacity. The formation of coherent regional policy started in 1998 with the adoption of the Lithuanian Regional Policy Guidelines (Ministry of Finance, Republic of Lithuania, 2003). National regional policy, as a coordinating policy, had to be integrated into all national sectoral programs which was obviously an enormous task, especially where sectoral line ministries were enjoying their new-found freedom and were understandably determined to stamp their authority on the future development of the country. The leading institution in the process was the Ministry of Public Administration Reforms and Local Authorities. In 1999, the National Regional Development Committee was formed although this *ad-hoc* structure was replaced by the institutions established by the Law on Regional Development in 2000.

The Lithuanian approach towards regional policy formation was designed with the help of the European Commission DG Enlargement and the EC were obviously in a strong position to influence proceedings due to the availability of the pre-accession and, later, the Structural Funds. The prevailing policy line was to build regional policy by supporting lagging regions in strengthening capacity in preparation for accession. Three target regions were identified for the first period: Klaipeda-Taurage, Utena and Marijampole. They were to be followed by the remaining regions in later years. The main programming document, the National Development Plan, was approved and the three target regions started administering PHARE Economic and Social Cohesion (ESC) programme assistance. This pre-accession assistance focused on two main aspects, strengthening institutional structures and administrative capacity and implementing pilot projects for the regions corresponding to the Objective 1 programs (Ministry of Finance, Republic of Lithuania, 2003).

The Law on Regional Development, adopted in 2000, formalised and legitimised the existing legal and institutional basis. The current institutional system consists of two levels of directly elected government, the national level and 60 local municipalities. There is no directly-elected regional government in Lithuania; the

10 county administrations are appointed by the Government and led by Government representatives in the form of the county governors. Each of the 10 counties are named after their principal city and have responsibilities in the field of regional development and territorial planning and their role will be discussed in more detail later. Internal regional disparities between the counties continued to grow worryingly in the period between 1998–2001. The disparities were the result of a complex, ongoing process of economic restructuring. The less investment-friendly regions, those focussed primarily on eastern markets and those with a limited economic base, suffered most. Not surprisingly, the private sector was slow to invest in the peripheral areas and the service sector remained relatively static. Border regions suffered due to the concentration of economic activities in a limited number of large centres and the restrictions due to the new political map whereby former internal borders were now external borders. New investments in infrastructure were also concentrated in the larger centres and this produced little benefit, if any, to the lagging regions and a worrying picture began to emerge.

The Policy Shift in 2000

The new millennium was marked by a considerable policy shift, primarily on the basis of recommendations made by the European Commission DG Regional Policy. There remained concern that the administrative capacity at the county and local levels was still inadequate to administer the EU Structural Funds. DG Regio therefore proposed the development of a centralised EU Structural Funds management system to replace the existing decentralised one. The main programming document, the National Development Plan, was also identified as not being in line with Community regulations underlying the principles of Structural Funds management. In 2000, the functions of regional policy formation and implementation were transferred to the Ministry of the Interior, while the Ministry of Finance assumed responsibility for preparations for the management of Structural Funds in 2000. The discussions relating to the management of the Structural Funds are still the source of considerable political and public debate in the country today.

Socio-economic Context: The Need for National Regional Policy

Having looked at the history of regional policy in Lithuania up until recent times, it is important to examine the current challenges that Lithuanian regional policy is trying to address before looking at current policy in more detail in the next part of the chapter. At the time when negotiations for accession began in 1999, Lithuanian GDP per capita was only 37 per cent of the average for the EU25 including other accession countries. This figure is currently approximately 51 per cent, similar to some other new member states such as Latvia (46.4 per cent), Estonia (55.1 per cent) and Poland (50 per cent), but still significantly lower than others such as the Czech Republic (72.7 per cent), Slovenia (81.2 per cent), and Cyprus (84.5 per cent) (Eurostat 2005). Lithuania, along with the other Baltic States and Poland, remains one of the poorest EU Member States. In addition to this unenviable status, the prosperity gap within the country continues to grow. An examination of Gross Domestic Product (GDP) per capita over recent years (see Figure 11.1) illustrates the growing internal economic disparities within the country as the gap between Vilnius County and the rest continues to increase.

Figure 11.1   GDP per capita in the counties (per cent of country average)

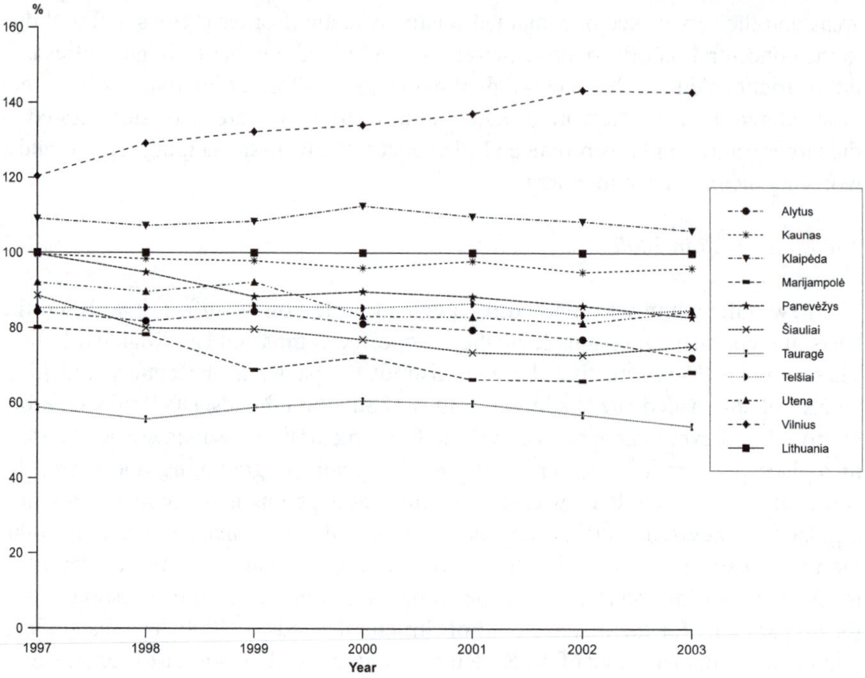

Source: Lithuanian Department of Statistics, year 2005

Official statistics reveal that GDP per capita by purchasing power standards in Lithuania reached 5983 Euro in 2005 (Lithuanian Department of Statistics, 2006), equivalent to 50.9 per cent of the EU average (Eurostat 2006). Recent growth rates have been dramatic with GDP per capita in Lithuania increasing by 10.5 per cent in 2003 and approximately 7 per cent in 2004 and 2005 (Eurostat 2006). Such high growth rates make it one of the fastest growing economies not only in the EU, but in the world, and similar levels of growth in the two other Baltic States have led to talk of the Baltic Tigers. Only time will tell if these growth rates can be sustained long enough to warrant real comparisons with the growth of Ireland, the Celtic Tiger, since the start of the 1990s.

As can be seen clearly in 11.1, the highest level of GDP per capita in Lithuania is unsurprisingly in Vilnius County at over 7,500 Euro with the lowest level in Tauragė County on the border with the Kalinigrad Region of Russia where the figure was 2.6 times less than that of the capital region at only 2,900 Euro per capita. Between 1997–2004, the gap between the richest and poorest counties increased by an alarming 250 per cent. Only two of the counties, Vilnius and Klaipeda, have a GDP higher than the national average meaning that the remaining 8 counties can be classed as lagging. The natural market tendencies for private investment to concentrate in the strongest counties combined with a tendency for a high proportion of the EU funds to also be concentrated in these areas, decreases the likelihood of closing this gap and it is predicted by many that the current trends will continue for the foreseeable future leading to a further increase in regional disparities.

An examination of other macro-economic indicators tell a similar story. If anything, the figures for foreign direct investment make even more dramatic reading as illustrated in Figure 11.2.

Figure 11.2   Foreign direct investment in the counties (per cent of the country average)

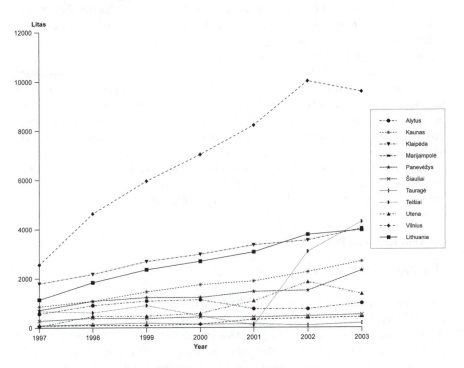

Source: Department of Statistics of Lithuania, year 2005

It is clear from Figure 11.2 that the lagging regions lack the levels of investment necessary to foster economic growth. At the end of 2004, average Foreign Direct Investment (FDI) per capita in the country was 1,369 Euro. Traditionally, by far the highest proportion of FDI has been concentrated in Vilnius County and, at the end of 2004, FDI in Vilnius County had reached 3,395 Euro per capita, well over twice the national average (although the size of this gap had been slightly reduced compared to the figures for the end of 2002). The lowest level of FDI again was in Tauragė County, which at 47 Euro per capita was an alarming 29.1 times less than the national average and 60.2 times less than in the capital region.

As can be seen in Figure 11.2, FDI in Klaipėda County was also close to the national average. The relative wealth of Klaipėda can be explained partly due to the economic activity and investment in relation to Klaipėda Seaport. FDI per capita in neighbouring Telšiai County is also higher than the national average due to international investments in the Mažeikiai oil refinery. The presence of the oil refinery tends to distort the figures and the relatively low population in Telšiai County make these investments even more visible in the statistics. Apart from Vilnius, Telšiai and Klaipeda counties, all of the other seven counties were below the national average and three of them (Tauragė, Šiauliai and Marijampolė) were below 15 per cent the average. The privatisation of state-owned enterprises and associated investment was another major influence on the de-facto levels of FDI. The counties where large scale privatisation did not take place had to rely purely on entirely new investment, the levels of which were always likely to be insufficient to have a significant impact given that these were generally the lagging and geographically more peripheral counties.

As time progressed, the performance of the larger centres with a population over 100,000 (Vilnius, Kaunas, Klaipėda, Šiauliai and Panevėžys) improved as new activities and services continued to develop leaving the five smallest and more peripheral counties, such as Taurage, further behind. The interaction between various processes combine to form a vicious circle of decline where personal development opportunities (economic and social) become more and more limited, leading to further out-migration and a further weakening of the social and economic capital in the smaller centres. In the next section of the chapter the current regional policy response to these problems will be examined in more detail.

Current Regional Policy in Lithuania

Dual Regional Policy in Lithuania

The changes in 2000 and the increasing internal disparities led to a division between national regional policy and EU regional (structural) policy. There was a policy shift from a regional policy as a set of vertical interventionist measures to a dual policy at the national and EU levels. From this point, the attention of the national Government focussed on the preparations necessary to absorb the EU Structural Funds and concern was expressed as to the danger of pursuing two separate regional policy mechanisms. This concern proved to be unfounded, however, and no separation of the two policies occurred. In many ways, the two aspects sit side by side, substituting and complementing each other. The national Government views regional policy from two perspectives – national regional policy on the one hand, and regional policy in the context of integration to the EU on the other. In this second part of the chapter, EU regional policy will be discussed before looking in more detail at policy in the field at the national and sub-national level.

EU Regional (structural) Policy in Lithuania

EU regional policy is primarily formulated in Brussels and deals mainly with the effective administration and management of the Structural Funds. The main aim of this structural policy is to reduce socio-economic disparities at the EU level. The term *social and economic cohesion* forms the cornerstone of this policy, having also been joined more recently by the term *territorial cohesion* (EC 2004). Territorial cohesion is defined as the balanced distribution of human activities across the Union and is complementary to economic and social cohesion. Hence, it translates the goal of sustainable and balanced development assigned to the European Union into territorial terms (EC 2004). In the context of the EU Structural Funds, Lithuania is regarded as one single Objective 1 region at the NUTS II level. There is evidence to suggest that this classification of the national space into one region is contributing to increasing internal disparities in Lithuania and the other Baltic States, as the majority of funds have tended to go to the capital regions for a variety of reasons. The stronger administrative capacities in Vilnius and other big cities, the availability of more funds for co-financing, the presence of a more attractive investment environment with the associated infrastructure and the availability of a qualified workforce all tend to reinforce this process. Therefore, whilst EU regional policy is addressing regional disparities at the EU level, it appears to be actually fuelling increasing disparities within the country.

From the point of view of implementing EU regional policy in Lithuania, the process of administering and managing both the Structural Funds and the Cohesion Fund is both complex and challenging and the threat of Lithuania not being able to absorb the level of funds to which it is entitled is very real. Between 2004 and 2006, Lithuania is entitled to receive a total of 895.2 million Euro from the Structural Funds, which is approximately 2 per cent of the national GDP. In order to access and absorb these funds the Ministry of Finance, together with other ministries, prepared the Single Programming Document (SPD), which is an integrated document planning EU investments in the country in the current programming period (until end of 2006). Virtually all national budget lines and funds are being used to co-finance these allocations. The SPD is based on a thorough analysis of the state sectors. It sets the goals for the programming period and the strategy to achieve these goals, as well as specifying investment priorities and eligibility criteria.

In contrast to EU regional policy that classes Lithuania as one single region, national regional policy regards the country as consisting of 10 different regions (counties). As in all rapidly developing transition countries, it is crucial to stimulate rapid development of the national economy and to increase international competitiveness. Public investments are often therefore distributed to achieve greatest economic growth in the shortest possible period of time. National public investments and market forces cause unbalanced territorial development, and, as a consequence, uneven standards of living and quality of life. The gap between the stronger and the lagging regions continues to grow with marked disparities in terms of social and economic development.

Present Priority – Territorial and Social Cohesion

Various recent studies analysing the period between 1997–2003 seem to confirm the presence of these social and economic disparities and their tendency to increase. The so-called Cohesion Index[1] in Lithuania currently stands at -1.7 (average of the years 1997–2003) compared to an average of -1.2 in the years 1993–2003 and clearly any further delay in taking interventionist measures will result in further increases. If a reduction in such disparities is to be achieved, then a co-ordinated and targeted national regional policy, with financial allocations both from national budget and EU Structural Funds, is urgently required. Importantly, the national Government recently identified balanced territorial and social cohesion as one of the strategic priorities for the development of the country. In addition, the same priority is identified in the National Regional Policy Strategy until 2013 implying that the Government is determined to pursue the balanced economic, social and territorial development of the country and in so doing to reduce regional disparities. The cohesion issue remains high on the political agenda and was once again discussed recently in bilateral negotiations between Lithuania and the European Commission. On 4 March 2005 the European Commission recommended that social and territorial cohesion should be identified as one of the priorities in the next programming period 2007–2013. There is an apparent convergence of objectives at the EU and Lithuanian level in relation to economic, social and territorial cohesion, although it is as yet unclear how – and even if – this dual pursuance of similar goals at different spatial levels can be achieved in practice. In addition, rhetoric is easy but evidence from other transition countries shows that transition governments often tend to opt for short-term rather than long-term goals (Ovin, 2001).

The Basis for National Regional Policy

National regional policy is defined in the appropriate legislation as 'targeted activity of state institutions to influence, by legal, economic and administrative measures, the social and economic development of the regions, aiming at reducing regional socio-economic disparities and sectoral disproportions within the regions

---

[1] $\sum_{i=(1...n)} | x_{(avg)} - x_i | / n$ where n is the number of the regions, x is GDP per capita in the region, $x_{(avg)}$ is countries average.

themselves, as well as to promote sustainable development throughout the whole territory of the State' (The Law on Regional Development of the Republic of Lithuania, 2000). The clear aim of the policy is the reduction of socio-economic disparities within the country, in other words, disparities between the statistical (in most cases administrative) units of the country. The legislation requires that national regional policy must be implemented in all 10 Lithuanian counties. Current national regional policy in Lithuania is translated into a diverse raft of legislation and official documents: the Law on Regional Development, the Law on County Management, the Long-term National Development Strategy, the National Regional Policy Strategy until 2013, the Comprehensive Plan of the Territory of Lithuania (the national spatial plan), the Long-term Economic Development Strategy until 2015 and the National Sustainable Development Strategy. Importantly, there is a division between regional policy, which is covered in the National Regional Policy Strategy until 2013 prepared by the Ministry of the Interior, and regional development which is covered by the Comprehensive Territorial Plan prepared by the Ministry of the Environment. The perceived division between the two disciplines and the need for joined up government has received much coverage by academics and others throughout the EU (Adams and Harris, 2005).

A highly-centralised model provides the institutional set-up for the national regional policy, with the national Government and its subordinate bodies having a dominant role. The Government defines measures for the implementation of national regional policy whilst the Ministry of the Interior is authorised to act as co-ordinator of sectoral policies. The National Regional Development Council provides a forum for representatives of local authorities whilst Regional Development Councils (the representative regional bodies) and social and economic partners are also involved. The county governors' administrations are responsible for the preparation and implementation of regional development plans (Astrauskas, 2004). The regional development plans (RDPs) of the counties have a socio-economic focus, rather than a spatial focus although elements of the strategy and the associated development programme obviously have a significant spatial impact. There are various sources of funding available for national regional policy measures, including the EU Structural Funds, national budget allocations (co-financing), the State Investment Program and a variety of other programmes financed by budget allocations and credits as well as guarantees (in case of emergencies, to be covered by the state budget). One of the most useful regional policy financial instruments has been the PHARE Cross–border Co-operation programme and European Community Initiatives programme INTERREG IIIA, IIIB and IIIC, which have been enthusiastically embraced by numerous administrations throughout the country.

Another important financial instrument is the Regional Development Programme from which resources are used to finance specific measures such as: the drafting of the county regional development plans; drafting regional and municipal project applications for EU Structural Funds support; payment of membership fees of the regions in associate structures such as the Assembly of the European Region, Council of Peripheral and Maritime regions; and the Association of Border regions. Whilst relatively small in terms of the absolute levels of funding available, these funds are nevertheless crucial in supporting activities that help to strengthen the capacity within county and local administrations.

Planning at Sub-national Level

In the period immediately after independence, planning in Lithuania was regarded as a Soviet relic associated with the old centrally-planned economic system with all associated negative connotations. However, when various foreign partners and consultants started to provide technical assistance, and more importantly when the EU started to emphasise the importance of planning in modern democratic states, the new form of planning and programming was quickly embraced in Lithuania. It was quickly understood that that such skills would be crucial if Lithuania was to be able to absorb a significant amount of the pre-accession funds (PHARE, ISPA, SAPARD) and, ultimately, the Structural Funds.

Until 2000 neither counties nor municipalities have had their own strategic development plans apart from a limited number of territorial or spatial planning documents. In order to facilitate the preparation of such documents some Lithuanian municipalities and counties sought foreign assistance using EU funds such as SIDA and PHARE as well as other international agreements. A bilateral agreement with the Flemish Government, for example, meant that Flemish companies were active and worked with a number of Lithuanian counties supporting the preparation of planning and development documents. The diversity of strategic planning experiences exerting influence in Lithuania meant that there was no common planning methodology adapted to Lithuanian conditions. The Ministry of the Interior therefore initiated a process to prepare RDPs at the county level according to a uniform methodology. The Ministry also provided support to the counties by consulting them in the process and undertaking evaluation of the documents and by 2003 all ten counties had adopted their RDPs.

As noted earlier, the majority of local politicians, specialists and community representatives were initially sceptical about planning due to the negative connotations left over from the Soviet period and this proved to be a major problem that needed to be overcome. There is little doubt that, ultimately, the necessity of having such documents in order to be able to access EU funds provided the incentive for these administrations to embrace the new form of planning and to prepare the necessary documents. The Regional Policy Department of the Ministry of the Interior undertook extensive work building capacity in relation to regional projects and the eligibility criteria determined in the SPD. Whilst the quality of the first round of RDPs was variable, the fact that all 10 counties prepared and adopted the documents within a relatively short space of time can be considered a success in itself.

Establishing Partnerships and Engagement at the Sub-national Level

RDPs that had been drafted by consultants were discussed, analysed and elaborated by special working groups established in the 10 counties. Gradually, a broad circle of community members joined the process. In a country with no culture of stakeholder participation, engaging stakeholders was always going to be a challenge and in reality there were varying levels of success. Approximately 170 stakeholders participated in the process to elaborate the Kaunas Regional Development Plan and approximately 80 in Vilnius County. In the smaller counties, such as Telšiai and Tauragė, participation was more limited with approximately 20–30 people taking an active part in the process. At the local level, participation was often higher with over 200 people participating actively in the planning process in Vilnius City Council. As the local level is the closest level to the people, and therefore the easiest for people to relate to, this is not surprising. Additional comments were also sought via other means such as the Internet. Considering that public participation and community engagement is still in its infancy in Lithuania, the levels of participation achieved in this first round of planning processes can be considered a success, although clearly a quantitative analysis of numbers cannot be considered as a reliable indicator for genuine stakeholder engagement. Many civil servants however have stressed the positive contribution that this stakeholder engagement made to the quality of the process and ultimately the documents. The engagement also generated numerous common projects in the public sector as well as in the fields of business and science, some of which have already been successfully implemented. Possibly the most positive aspect, however, is that a consensus seems to have been created that partnership and working together is the key to accessing resources and therefore increasing the possibility of becoming a winning rather than a losing region. The importance of reaching this consensus in a country where knowledge and experiences have tended to be protected rather than shared should not be underestimated.

During the evaluation process the county governors identified the art of prioritising projects as being the most difficult task. When all project ideas were put together initially, it quickly became clear that the Christmas wish-list that resulted was completely unrealistic in terms of the available budget and the capacity of the administrations to absorb such levels of funding. It was estimated that the initial proposals would require each county receiving approximately double the national budget in order for all projects to be implemented. Therefore, only priority projects with a possible major effect on the development of the region were selected with projects identified in the relevant RDP receiving priority. Therefore initial resistance to the concept of planning and the preparation of these documents was swept away.

National Regional Policy Strategy until 2013

The National Regional Policy Strategy until 2013 (Lithuanian Ministry of Interior, 2005) is a new programming document prepared by the Ministry of the Interior. It binds the measures of national regional policy to the main spatial planning document, the Lithuanian Comprehensive Territorial Plan prepared by the Ministry of the Environment (Lithuanian Ministry of the Environment, 2002). The Comprehensive Plan provides the long-term spatial vision for the country and identifies a hierarchy of urban centres and other elements of the spatial structure. The National Regional Policy Strategy until 2013 identifies 5 regional centres surrounded by territories where living standards are relatively low but which, due to their economic potential and infrastructure, can perform the functions of regional growth centres. The centres identified in Figure 11.3, Alytus, Marijampolė, Utena, Tauragė and Telšiai (with dipoles Telšiai-Mažeikiai and Utena-Visaginas), were selected on the basis of a limited number of socio-economic indicators. In the context of limited financial resources the Strategy is based on the concept of concentrating resources in a limited number of selected centres in order to maximise their impact. The selection of the centres is shown in Figure 11.3.

Figure 11.3   Growth centres defined in national regional policy strategy

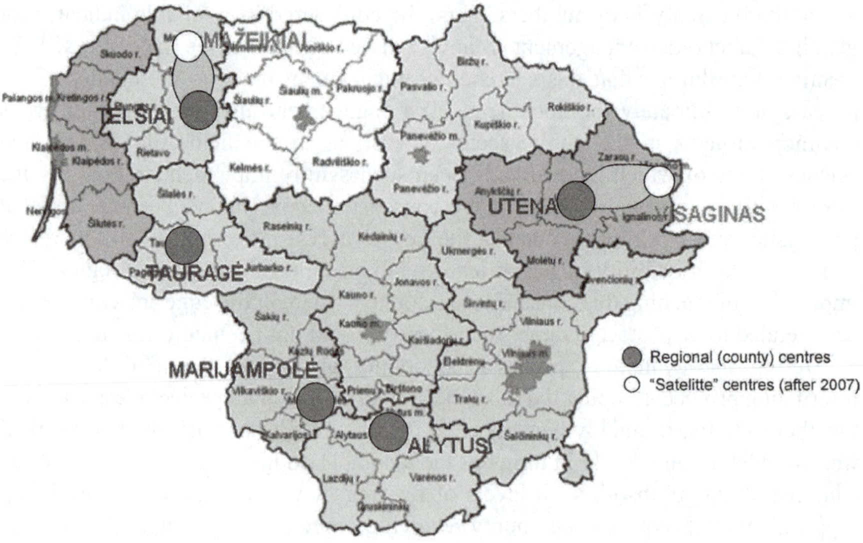

Source: MoI Lithuania, Regional Policy Department, 2005

Interestingly, the methodology and selection employed in the preparation of the Comprehensive Territorial Plan differs from that adopted in the preparation of the National Regional Development Strategy and, as a result, there is a discrepancy between the hierarchy of the centres in each case. The apparent conflict between these two documents reflects a lack of joined-upness that is common in numerous countries throughout the EU (Adams and Harris, 2005). Despite the fact that these two documents form the backbone of policy in relation to regional development in Lithuania, and despite the fact that both documents have the pursuance of balanced regional development at their heart, the level of integration between the two is clearly limited. Shaw and Sykes (2005), amongst others, have identified this tendency for concepts such as polycentric development and balanced development to mean different things to different people and this would certainly seem to apply in the fields of regional policy and regional development in Lithuania.

Figure 11.4   Growth centres and social development territories

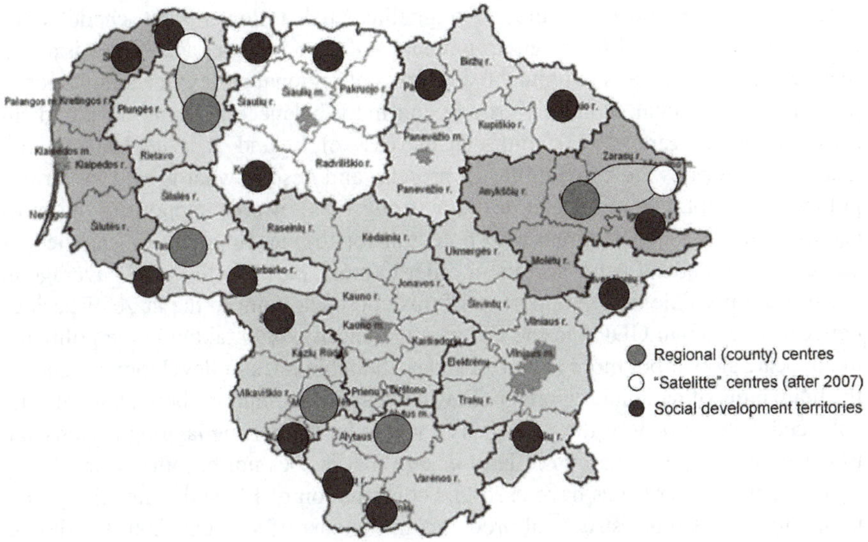

Source: *MoI Lithuania, Regional Policy Department, 2005*

The pursuance of social cohesion means that it is important to strive for uniform levels in terms of quality of life throughout the country. It is therefore a priority to target funds at places of high unemployment, extensive social problems and high levels of deprivation. In order to facilitate this approach the Government adopted a number of criteria for identifying the social development territories (see Figure 11.4) in January 2006 and these territories are eligible for additional incentives and financial allocations in order to raise living standards and improve quality of life indicators.

Conclusion

Lessons Learned from the First Programming Period

A number of lessons can be drawn from the experience of Lithuania so far and it is crucial for the future of the country that they are learnt and learnt fast. Although the current SPD is widely considered to have been a reasonably successful first attempt, a number of shortcomings have been identified. There is a feeling that the regional specific needs and disparities receive insufficient attention in the document. The regional dimension in the analysis is limited to general information about the regions with little or no attention to disparities and problems. The only exception is in relation to the proposed closure of the Ignalina Nuclear Power Plant scheduled for 2009 and the associated social, environmental and economic impacts. There is also a feeling that the SPD fails to unite the dual aims of regional policy: the simultaneous pursuance of national economic growth and more balanced regional development although, as O'Leary (2003) argues in the case of Ireland, it is unclear whether these two priorities are compatible. At present, and despite what is said in various policy documents, there appears to be a strong bias towards supporting the most economically dynamic regions with potential for the development of knowledge-based and high added value sectors in order to reach parity with the EU average in the shortest possible time. Supporters of this approach point to the large disparities between Lithuanian GDP and the EU average and it would take a brave politician to advocate slower but more balanced and sustainable rates of development. One of the main aims of national regional policy, however, is to support the sustainable and balanced development of the country as a whole by supporting lagging regions and to close the prosperity gap, or at least ensure that it does not become wider. Many established member states have used this combination of EU and national regional policy to solve similar structural problems in the past (Grumadas, 2005), although such attempts have by no means always been successful. It is anticipated that these provisions will be amended in the next programming document in order to find a better balance between national, regional and local development and to be more responsive to specific regional characteristics and challenges.

There has also been criticism that, despite considerable efforts to engage social and economic partners in the drafting process, this was not entirely successful and contributed to the perceived lack of a regional dimension. Whereas it is possible that this could have been achieved through a bottom up approach, in practice the approach was clearly top down in nature due to realities such as tight deadlines and inadequate administrative capacities in many counties and municipalities. Neither municipalities nor counties had prepared their development plans and strategies at the time the SPD was being drafted and as a result the drafting process was heavily centralised. The SPD still provides the development framework for the counties and municipalities during this programming period, even though the sub-national levels perceive that their needs are not fully reflected in the document. Work is ongoing to address these issues. In the meantime, local and regional actors are involved to a much greater extent in the preparations for the new programming period of 2007-2013. Importantly, all 10 counties and the majority of the 60 municipalities have now prepared and adopted their strategic development plans and the priorities they have identified can therefore be fed into the preparation process for the new programming documents. A decision has also been made to try to integrate EU and national regional policy. Therefore, territorial and social cohesion will be identified as one of the strategic priorities for future national development and will be distinguished as a separate priority measure for social cohesion in the Operational Programme for the local and regional problems (Grumadas 2005). The inherent contradictions in pursuing this dual goal at different spatial levels, whereby EU structural policy is perceived to actually increase regional disparities within the national space, mean that whilst the objective has been identified, it is likely to be extremely difficult to achieve.

One of the most important lessons so far is the importance of working together at all levels and there are signs that both horizontal and vertical co-operation is improving. The concepts of joined-up government and joined-up governance, as discussed by authors such as Evans *et al.* (2005), whereby all parts and levels of government and society as a whole work together towards a common goal, need to be embraced quickly in Lithuania. While substantial progress has been made in this field, the apparent contradictions between the two key national regional policy/regional development strategies prepared by the ministries of Interior and Environment discussed earlier illustrate that there is still some way to go. There does however appear to be an increasing willingness to work together and this is vital if real progress is to be made.

Facing the Future

It is clear that the issue of regional policy and regional development in Lithuania, as elsewhere, is extremely complex. The initial scepticism in relation to planning in the period after independence is understandable given the historical context of the Soviet legacy. Planning had to reinvent itself and establish its credibility at a time when the system was trying to adapt itself to the rigours of the free market economy. Whereas territorial planning initially dominated the field of regional development in Lithuania, building on the basis of former Soviet territorial planning, it was felt in some quarters that this approach was not meeting the needs and challenges of the new Lithuania. The introduction of EU regional policy and the need to prepare for EU Structural Funds provided additional challenges making the search for an appropriate regional policy response far from easy. The relationship between spatial, regional and structural policies, as well as their different traditions and interpretations, complicates matters further. In the search for a policy response appropriate to Lithuania's needs, different models have been tried, many at the suggestion of the European Commission, although ultimately Lithuania must develop a specific approach suitable to local needs.

The chapter illustrates clearly that regional disparities within the country and between the regions are significant and cannot be ignored. At the beginning of the process of regional policy formulation only external disparities in comparison to the EU average were taken into account. In order to close the gap with the EU average, economic growth and competitiveness were identified as the main national priorities. It was only later that the increasing regional disparities were acknowledged as requiring attention, leading to social and territorial cohesion being adopted as national priorities. Despite the problems of adapting from the Soviet system to embrace the new market based system, Lithuania has made progress towards an integrated regional policy capable of dealing with these regional disparities. In summary, regional policy in Lithuania will be implemented through the strategies and programmes of various branches or sectors of the economy. In order to do this a regional dimension (horizontal dimension) will be required to tackle specific regional problems (vertical dimension). The availability of the Structural Funds provides a golden opportunity that is not to be missed and the way in which these funds are allocated in the next programming period 2007–2013 and beyond will have a major impact in the pursuance of cohesion and more balanced development at both the EU and the national levels.

Preparations for the next programming period 2007–2013 are already well advanced. A new form of programming document, a Strategic Reference Framework, has been drafted with widespread consultation. The three priorities that have been identified relate to the pursuance of a knowledge-based society, a competitive economy and social cohesion. These priorities will be implemented within three Operational Programmes (OPs). The Social Cohesion OP will have a separate Priority Measure, which will be directly linked with the implementation of the National Regional Policy Strategy until 2013. Targeted assistance will be allocated to the economic growth centres specified in the strategy. In order to improve quality of life, assistance will be targeted at the 16 social development territories. The Social Cohesion OP will deal with local and regional infrastructure and will provide a much stronger regional dimension for EU support. Local and regional infrastructure covers a wide variety of potential fields including local transport infrastructure, traffic safety, education, health care, social, community and cultural facilities, sport, leisure and recreation amongst others. The aim of this OP is to provide counties with the opportunity and means to strengthen regional competitiveness and improve the quality of life.

There is little doubt that capacity in planning at the central and, more importantly, also at the regional and local levels has increased dramatically in recent years, although the retention of high quality staff remains a problem due to the substantially higher wages available in the private sector. The counties have already started revising the first round of RDPs and are currently identifying priorities for the 2007–2013 programming period. It is likely that the process of preparation necessary to absorb the EU Structural support as well as for the measures financed by State will be simplified in the hope of making them more effective. The integrated priorities of municipalities and counties will be fed into national documents, strategies and programmes. This planning process will be simpler, not only because almost all municipalities now have their strategic development plans, but also due to the established planning system and accepted common methodology.

In conclusion, the key document that defines the general provisions on the Structural Funds, Council regulation No. 1260/1999, states that 'in order to ensure integrated approach into development, it is essential, considering specific features of a concrete region, to make compatible activities of different Funds with policies, implemented by the Community, also to pursue compatibility between the labour, economic and social policies of member states and strategies of national regional policy of member states'. As stated in the first sentence of this chapter, it is widely accepted that Lithuania needs more effective regional policy and although there is still some way to go, the author believes that Lithuania is on the right track.

References

Adams, N. and Harris, N. (2005), 'Best Practice Guidelines for Instruments of Regional Development and Spatial Planning in an Enlarged EU', Cardiff, Cardiff University.

Astrauskas, A. (2004), 'Proposals on the Territorial-Administrative Division of the Republic of Lithuania, with the Evaluation of the Aims and Objectives of the EU Structural and National Regional Policies', Ministry of the Interior, Vilnius.

Bagdzevičienė, R. (2002), 'The Plan of Measures for Economic and Social Restructuring of Ignalina NP Region', presentation for the Parliament. http://www.lrti.lt/veikla/RB_Ignalinos.doc (accessed August 2005).

Bagdzevičienė, R., Rimas, J. and Venckus, A. (2002), 'Strategy for the Economic Development of the Regions', Kaunas University of Technology, Lithuanian Institute for Regional Research, Presentation for the conference, 'Regional development 2002', 3–4 October 2002.

European Commission (1997), 'Agenda 2000: Commission Opinion on Lithuania's Application for Membership of the European Union', DOC/97/15, Brussels, 15 July 1997.

European Commission (2004), Interim Territorial Cohesion Report, Preliminary results of ESPON and EU studies – DG Regional Policy, Luxembourg: Office for Official Publications of the European Communities available at http://europa. eu.int/comm/regional_policy/sources/docoffic/official/reports/coheter/coheter_ en.pdf (accessed December 2005).

European Commission (2004a), *A New Partnership for Cohesion: Convergence, Competitiveness and Co-operation*, Third Report on Economic and Social Cohesion, EC Belgium 2004.

Eurostat (2005), GDP in PPS, Eurostat, 2006, forecast available at http://epp. eurostat.cec.eu.int/portal/page?_pageid=1996,39140985&_dad=portal&_schem a=PORTAL&screen=detailref&language=en&product=EU_strind&root=EU_ strind/strind/ecobac/eb011 (accessed December 2005).

Eurostat (2006), Real GDP Growth Rate, available at http://epp.eurostat.cec.eu.int/portal/page?_pageid=1996,39140985&_dad=portal&_schema=PORTAL&scr een=detailref&language=en&product=STRIND_ECOBAC&root=STRIND_ECOBAC/ecobac/eb012 (accessed January 2006).

Evans, B., Joas, M., Sundback, S. and Theobold, K. (2005), 'Governing Sustainable Cities', Earthscan, London.

Graužinis, A. (2001), 'Regional Structure of Lithuania in the Context of the European Union', unpublished paper from Regional Development Conference 2001, Kaunas, available at http://www.nrda.lt/news6.htm (accessed August 2005).

Grumadas, A. (2005), 'Harmonizing of National Regional and EU Structural Policies in the New Member States, The Perspectives of Implementing the Lithuanian National Regional Policy in the Years 2007–2013 (Study)', MoI RPD, Vilnius, 2005.

Lithuanian Department of Statistics databases (1997–2005), available at www.std.lt (accessed December 2005).

Lithuanian Department of Statistics (2004), Statistical Yearbook of Lithuania (2004), Department of Statistics, Vilnius.

Lithuanian Department of Statistics (2006) Preliminary GDP per capita, available at http://www.std.lt/uploads/docs/BVP_vie_gyv_05_%20IV.doc (accessed January 2006).

Lithuanian Government Regulation on Social Development Territories No. 96, 31.01.2006 (amending the Regulation No. 428).

Lithuanian Ministry of the Environment (2002), Comprehensive Plan of the Territory of the Republic of Lithuania, Vilnius.

Lithuanian Ministry of Environment (2002a), Rulebook, adopted by the Regulation of the Government No. 1138, 22.09.1998, New redaction No. 260, 20.02.2002, available at http://www.am.lt/VI/rubric.php3?rubric_id=115 (accessed August 2005).

Lithuanian Ministry of Finance of the Republic of Lithuania (2003) Economic and Social Cohesion Report available at http://www.finmin.lt/finmin/selectpage.do?doclocator=%2Fweb%2Fstotis_inf.nsf%2F0%2F4B8473220DED4845C1256D1B00352F54%3FopenDocument&pathid=6EE16121B3BB55DCC2256F2400310656 (accessed January 2006).

Lithuanian Ministry of Finance (2003), Lithuanian Regional Policy Guidelines, adopted by the Regulation of the Government 21.07.1998 No. 902, available at http://www3.lrs.lt/pls/inter2/dokpaieska.showdoc_l?p_id=60217&p_query= (accessed January 2006).

Lithuanian Ministry of Finance (2004), Single Programming Document for the years 2004–2006, adopted by the Regulation of the Government No. 935, 22 August 2004.

Lithuanian Ministry of the Interior (2004), Regional Policy of Lithuania and the Optimising of the Territorial Setup, Vilnius.

Lithuanian Ministry of the Interior (2005), Lithuanian Regional Policy Strategy until the Year 2013, Vilnius, adopted by the Regulation of the Government of the

Republic of Lithuania No. 575, 23 May 2005.

Nakrošis, V. (2003), *Regional Policy of the European Union and the Management of the Structural Funds*, Vilnius, Eugrimas.

O'Leary, E. (2003), *Irish Regional Development: A New Agenda*, Liffey Press, Dublin.

Ovin, R. (2001), The Nature of Institutional Change in Transition, Post-Communist Economies, vol. 13.

Shaw, D. and Sykes, O. (2004), The Concept of Polycentricity in European Spatial Planning: Reflections on its Interpretation and Application in the Practice of Spatial Planning, *International Planning Studies*, vol. 9 nr. 4, pp. 283–306.

Thomas, M.J. (1998), Thinking about Planning in the Transitional Countries of Central and Eastern Europe, *International Planning Studies*, vol. 3 no. 3, pp. 321–334.

Tiskus, G. (2001), Planning processes in Lithuania: Comprehensive Plan of the Republic of Lithuania, National Development Plan and their Impact on the Regional Development in the Country, unpublished paper from the Strategic Planning of the Cities conference 28–29 June 2001, Centre of the Economic Research, Vilnius.

Vilkas, E. (2000), National Review Lithuania, p. 143–153, in Bachter, J. and Downes, R., Gorzelak, G. (eds), Transition, Cohesion and Regional Policy in Central and Eastern Europe, Ashgate, Aldershot.

Wikipedia, Demographics of Lithuania, http://en.wikipedia.org/wiki/Lithuania#Demographics (accessed December 2005).

PART V

Key Challenges for the Future

Chapter 12

Sustainable Development: Reality or Myth?

Lowie Steenwegen

Introduction

Spatial planners have increasingly come to regard the discipline as a comprehensive instrument to balance cross-sector development goals, measure impacts and allocate resources. These activities are translated in strategic spatial visions that have become increasingly popular throughout the EU. The concepts of sustainability and sustainable development have become one of the main pillars of these visions as well as being an important objective. This chapter seeks to provide an overview of ways in which these concepts are being translated in such strategies and examines the relationship between spatial planning and sustainability in regional development strategies.

The use of the concepts of sustainability and sustainable development became extensive after the publication of the Report 'Our Common Future' (World Commission on Environment and Development, 1987). In this report sustainable development was defined as a means '... to ensure the needs of the present without compromising the ability of future generations to meet their own needs. The concept of sustainable development does imply limits, not absolute limits, but limitations imposed by the present state of technology and social organisation on environmental resources and by the ability of the biosphere to absorb the effects of human activities' (Our Common Future, 1987, p. 43). Soon after this declaration, the concepts were adopted in numerous planning documents. The UN Rio Conference on Environment and Development in 1992 predicted that the continual pursuance of existing development practices would lead to severe impacts on environment, health and social coexistence. By giving meaning to the concepts, regional planning became a more integrated and complementary activity (Roberts and Lloyd, 1999) whereby the impact of sectoral decisions had to be assessed. A framework for sustainable decision-making was required and planning processes became more important in the preparation of policy documents. Although the main focus on of the Rio Conference was the preservation of environmental values, the declaration in general and Agenda 21 in particular identified many aspects of sustainable development, which are closely linked to the activities of spatial planners. The new approach required integration between ecological, economic and social aspects such as human settlements, environmental protection and migration flows and this increased the importance of planning processes, the involvement of stakeholders and raising public awareness.

The Johannesburg Conference on Sustainable Development in 1998, the Johannesburg Plan of Implementation and the UN Commission on Sustainable Development all identified the strong relationship between sustainable development issues and the daily practice of spatial planners. The common goals became more visible and activities such as conferences and workshops with a sustainability theme became more popular. The first cycle of activities organised by the UN Commission on Sustainable Development focussed on water, sanitation and human settlements. The Millennium Declaration (United Nations, 2000) stressed once again the relationship between ecological, economic and social aspects of development processes and regional planning. In the following sections the changing attitudes towards sustainable development are examined and the role of planners in the pursuit of sustainability goals. This is followed by a discussion about various planning instruments illustrated by some examples of good practice whereby spatial planning has helped to facilitate sustainable development. Finally conclusions on the current and potential relationship between spatial planning and sustainable development will be drawn.

A New Zietgeist

During the nineties sustainability became fashionable to such an extent that the meaning almost became lost. This process occurred simultaneously with a general revival of interest in the field of spatial planning in Europe. The elaboration and adoption of the European Spatial Development Perspective (EC 1999) was a defining moment in this process and by specifying the need for more balanced patterns of development and underlining the spatial dimension of sectoral planning and the role of the public, the ESDP clearly indicated the need and opportunity to work towards a more sustainable Europe. Use of the concept of sustainable development was not limited to planning documents however as private investors and even marketing consultants introduced sustainability into their documents and reports as a means of justifying their proposed strategies. Many feel that the concepts became a victim of their own success and by becoming popular, sustainability lost a part of its content and meaning. Organisations, institutions, stakeholders and planners tried to anticipate the general use of sustainability. Indicators were developed and in several countries sustainability institutions were established. These institutions (public as well as non-governmental) started to develop research to assess the sustainability of proposed strategies and decisions at different spatial scales as a means of producing specific advice as well as to measure the effects of implementation. Whilst on the one hand the concept lost part of its meaning, on the other hand the importance of the sustainable approach was also brought into question. In a struggling and declining economy the impact of planning documents in general and sustainability in particular became less accepted. The new economic context meant that spatial planning was often seen as a bureaucratic instrument hindering private initiatives and economic development (Theil, 2005).

Planning and sustainability were no longer universally accepted as they were perceived to stand in the way of economic growth. The 'Zeitgeist' or 'spirit of time' turned because of the economic stagnation and the debate shifted in many Western-European countries from environmental and sustainability aspects to the hard issues such as jobs, money and welfare (Neumann and Petersen, 2001). The Bush administration was the main advocate of this line of thought. By resisting the acceptance of the Kyoto protocol, the administration publicly questioned the need for a sustainable policy. Also in many other countries the previously indicated programmes and actions were increasingly questioned and restricted. As Kunzmann identifies in Chapter 3 of this book, the influence of spatial planning was shrinking due to the increasing economic and welfare crisis. So despite the increased attention to spatial planning at the European level, the commitment to planning and sustainability in many Western European countries such as Belgium, Germany and the Netherlands was already under severe pressure at the start of the new millennium (Faludi 2002). Planners and stakeholders have had to adapt to this new situation in various countries. The period where (sustainable) spatial planning documents were more easily accepted was over (D'hondt 2006) and had been replaced by calls for less planning, less market intervention and less regulation.

Key Challenges for Spatial Planners

The processes outlined above provided an increasingly difficult dilemma for planners: how to cope with the fact that on the one hand planning is more necessary (due to the environmental problems and the need for social economic and territorial cohesion in an enlarged EU) but on the other hand planning is less accepted due to the economic stagnation and new deregulation tendencies. The common view remains that regional development and economic growth should not conflict with environmental protection but in practice, sustainable aspects are often pushed aside and traded off for economic gains. Nevertheless the main environmental threats are increasing. The German ecology-economist Richard Tol for example supported the need for planning as a means of dealing with climate change and rising sea levels (Tol, 2002) and concluded that important decisions and large-scale investments were required. Important environmental problems have however returned to the discussion table of main policy players and global warming was a key issue at the G8 summit at Gleneagles in Scotland in 2005. EU enlargement has increased the need for cohesion within the Community and failure could easily lead to an unstable situation between East and West and drastically increased levels of economic and social migration. Whilst the goals of cohesion appear to be clearly identified the means of achieving cohesion is far less apparent and is threatened by a lack of capacity and experience at all levels. The question remains as to whether planning can play an important role in strategy formulation and implementation to address these challenges, and if so what initiatives are necessary to make planning a more attractive and acceptable means of guiding development processes in a sustainable way?

Non Planners Views about Sustainable Development and Spatial Planning

Sustainable development is regarded as 'a dynamic process which enables all people to realise their potential and improve their quality of life in ways which simultaneously protect and enhance the Earth's life support systems' (Regional Futures, 2004, p. 4). In addition it can be argued that the pursuit of sustainable development is a long term process that will ultimately provide benefits for all and prove to be a good investment. It is interesting that it is not only planners who are appealing for more planning intervention but that an increasing number of non-planners are also stressing the relationship between planning and sustainable development. This relationship and the necessity of planning is recognised and acknowledged by a wide diversity of stakeholders.

1.1   Dynamic Developments in Creative Centres

Richard Florida argued that geography is not dead (Florida, 2002). Internet and modern telecommunication, including modern transport systems are not likely to remove the importance of place as argued by Kelly (1998). Rather 'People remain highly concentrated and the high-tech, knowledge based and creative-content industries that drive so much the economic growth continues to concentrate in specific places' ... 'Place and community are more critical factors than ever before' (Florida, 2002, p. 219). The value of human capital is also recognised by Patricia Beeson, Professor of Economics at the University of Pittsburgh and Associate Editor of the International Regional Science Review. Beeson explored how investments in various sorts of infrastructure have affected city and regional growth. She argues that investments in higher education infrastructure generate growth far better than investments in physical infrastructure like canals, railroads or highways (Florida, 2004, p. 222). Florida states that regional economic growth is driven by the location choices of creative people and that aspects such as a buoyant labour market with diverse job opportunities, a vibrant lifestyle, social interaction, diversity, authenticity and identity are the crucial factors influencing choice of location. Florida binds all these elements together into one term, the quality of space (Florida, 2002, p. 232). It would appear to be no coincidence that Florida stresses the spatial dimension by using this term and that spatial characteristics and spatial policies are crucial to attract people and stimulate development. The quality of space is determined by what is there (spatial characteristics), who is there (community) and what is going on (vibrancy of life) (Florida, 2002, p. 232).

Florida's hypothesis is interesting because it is a view of a non-planner that spatial planning can have a significant impact on the regional economic development by working on places and with people. By indicating that there is an important relationship between spatial planning and regional development, his views strengthened the idea that urban and regional planning and the creation of vibrant spaces and places is central to retain and attract vibrant and creative people and stimulate initiatives and investments. Numerous cities and towns have recognised the strong relationship between spatial planning and regional development. Other more traditional needs such as the renewal of economically and socially deprived areas have been seen in a wider perspective and the importance of space and place has risen up the planning agenda. The static view of traditional land-use planning has changed towards an attitude that urban settlements on different scales are competing to retain and attract dynamic people and investments and city marketing has increased dramatically. One of the best known examples where spatial planning and urban renewal are closely linked with regional development goals and the city marketing remains Barcelona which is discussed in detail in Marshall (2004). In a period of twenty years, Barcelona transformed itself and became a main driver of the Spanish economy. The City developed from an introvert place to an open community for people with different cultural backgrounds and is now attracting visitors from all over the world. In a time where companies and people are becoming footloose it is important to retain an open mind and focus on good relations between government, citizens and stakeholders. Barcelona is now widely recognised as one of the most successful cities in the world, internationally acclaimed for its innovative urban planning. It has survived the economic, environmental and social changes of the last decades through focusing upon the provision of knowledge-based and information services to place itself at the forefront of a new urban wave, in which city planning provides high-quality opportunities for people to live and work. The transformation of Barcelona was given focus with the preparations for the 1992 Olympic Games. Faced with serious problems of urban decay in both inner-city and peripheral areas, planners took a holistic approach and used the Games as a vehicle for city-wide reforms. Olympic facilities were spread through neglected urban areas and the city turned its face towards the sea. Barcelona undertook a third wave of transformation with a high technology zone (22@), hyper-community (Diagonal Mar), the Universal Forum of Cultures 2004 and a new container port and logistics park. Barcelona is often used as an example where economic, social and environmental sustainability issues were combined in a balanced way and where the integrated communicative approach of planners was a productive tool to guide decision and implementation in regional development processes.

The practice of using mega-events to increase international recognition has been adopted by many other cities although not all have been as successful as Barcelona, and even Barcelona as the most expensive Olympic Games ever held, has its critics. The fact that the use of mega-events as a vehicle for regeneration is extremely complex and a high-risk strategy and the economic benefits are questionable is well documented (Gratton *et al.* 2005, Thornley 2002). However it appears that some such events chose to completely ignore the possibilities, the EURO 2000 football championship is one such example. Despite being the biggest sporting event ever organised in the Netherlands and Belgium the focus was primarily on law an order issues with little or no attention for regeneration. As a result no planning, regeneration or city marketing initiatives were undertaken and whilst there was initially some talk of building a new stadium in Belgium's second largest city, Antwerp, ultimately a lack of agreement meant that no stadium was built and Antwerp did not even host a match, leaving some lamenting the lost opportunity. The organisers of EURO 2004 in Portugal on the other hand also sought wider benefits from the event in terms of urban regeneration. Investments were not limited to the construction of the new football stadiums as new access roads and infrastructure were constructed, private investments were stimulated and real estate projects were developed as part of the implementation of a wider spatial vision.

Working Towards Sustainable Development

Harcourt (2004) argues that quantified strategic goals in many programmes (like the UN Millennium Goals) will only have a successful outcome if there is a strong co-operation between public institutions and stakeholders. Such large-scale challenges can not be addressed by a simplified technocratic approach as the world has become too complex for such an approach. Harcourt argues that it is only through extensive capacity building, strong co-operation and sharing responsibilities that the planned goals might be achieved. The use of quantitative targets, especially when used in addition to qualitative targets, offer a valuable framework for planning and monitoring and also for development and implementation. The real challenge however is not to find a consensus over the goals but to develop strategies and attitudes for co-operation and implementation at different scales and between different stakeholders. This challenge can be tackled by stimulating bottom-up cooperation. The facilitation of the bottom-up approach does not require new campaigns but rather improved co-ordination of existing activities to formulate a shared vision that can be used as a framework. 'Sustainable development is a process with economic, ecological and social dimensions. The interrelationship between these dimensions is essential' (Harcourt, 2005, p. 45). Integrated planning processes are important instruments and if done well, planning can operate as an instrument for implementation, co-operation and monitoring.

The Structure Plan of Flanders (Ministry of the Flemish Community, 1997), adopted by the Flemish Parliament in 1997, is a good example of the danger of good intentions getting stuck during the implementation process and where the monitoring system did not work as anticipated. At the time the Structure Plan was at the cutting edge of good practice in spatial planning in terms of content, approach and process (Albrechts 2001). After a long preparation process the Plan was ultimately accepted by most stakeholders. The Structure Plan provided a frame of reference with a strategic spatial vision and a number of associated actions. However the quantitative approach adopted in terms of indicators meant that it was soon seen as a bureaucratic instrument that hampered economic initiatives. As a result the Structure Plan failed in many ways to work as anticipated and failed to achieve specific initiatives that could have served as demonstration projects. The faltering Flemish economy led to increasing pressure on the objectives and the vision of the Plan. Despite the efforts of Flemish spatial planners they were often unable to stand in the way of many unsustainable sectoral demands at the implementation stage and at lower levels. There are numerous examples where the main vision and concepts of the Structure Plan are neglected or withdrawn. An example of this is that in order to protect what little open space remains in an intensively sub-urbanised region, a minimum of 60 per cent of new homes were to be built in urban areas. This part of the vision had many sustainable principles in the field of development and mobility at its core. However powerful interests managed to achieve a reduction in the target so that the objective could not be achieved. The lack of criteria to measure the sustainable impact became clear and the exercise only served to portray a negative image of planning as being a means of reducing personal choice.

Energy for Sustainable Development (NRG4SD)

Representatives of Regional Governments gathered in Johannesburg during the World Summit on Sustainable Development and established a network called 'Energy for sustainable development' (NGG4SD). The network agreed to be a voice for regional governments at the global level, promoting sustainable development and partnerships at the regional level around the world. In their declaration they stipulated that regional governments are, because of proximity, efficiency and spatial dimension, strategically of crucial importance for the development of policy and implementation in relation to sustainable development. The Gauteng Declaration (2002) stresses the need for an integrated approach wherein economic, social and environmental objectives are balanced in order to create the best possible conditions for human development now and in the future. The document specifies that the pursuance of sustainable development needs a strategic framework for all governments. 'Regional Governments need sustainable development strategies as central frameworks for linking all their other strategies, ensuring that each is sustainable and that they are mutually supportive of each other ... Such strategies need to be developed in cooperation with the broadest possible array of relevant stakeholders and partners, and there should be opportunities for active participation and engagement by stakeholders in their implementation' (Gauteng Declaration, 2002, p. 2). The network strives to develop regional sustainable development strategies that provide a vision and a framework for sustainable development within the region and promote best practice in the development of these strategies. The declarations stress the need to engage all actors in civil society in the development and implementation of these strategies, a view that is supported by an increasing body of literature (Evans *et al.* 2005). The current activities however are thematically clustered in a sectoral approach: energy, industrial development, air pollution, climate change, ... and this is reflected in the activities and policy papers. A sustainable development strategy should provide a common framework for action, mainstream sustainable development decisions, provide consistency of definition and appraisal, explain opportunities, strengths and concerns for the region and provide common indicators and measures. Principles for use in these strategies include the integration of economic, social and environmental objectives, intergenerational equity, promoting sense of place and identity, meeting basics needs, tackling poverty and promoting equity, good governance and participation.

Summary: An Appeal for an Integrated Approach to Sustainable Development

Contrary to the popular view that the changing Zeitgeist reduces the need for planning, an increasing number of stakeholders and institutions seem to be indicating that an integrated approach is necessary to achieve sustainable development. The characteristics of spatial planning lend themselves to an integrated approach, a long-term vision, the spatial dimension and stakeholder engagement. Apart from the general spirit of time and the limited impact of spatial planning, nature and environmental planning still receive much attention, resources and support. A stronger combination of sustainability and regional development issues could lead to more integrated strategies, with increased stakeholder ownership and a stronger contribution of planning towards sustainable regional development.

Despite the close relationship between spatial planning and sustainability there is a significant difference in the interaction between the two at different spatial scales. At a more strategic regional level, it is more difficult to assess the sustainability of the actions and this becomes more apparent at the project level. This is illustrated by the fact that the environmental impact assessment of projects has become common practice throughout the EU whilst the implementation of the EU Strategic Environmental Assessment Directive that requires assessment of the environmental impacts of programmes, policies and plans may well be more difficult to implement. In many countries spatial planning is still seen as a purely passive regulatory instrument indicating where building initiatives can be permitted. However effective spatial planning is orientated more towards a dynamic vision and strategy including the indication and implementation of sustainable aspects in a diversity of projects. The next section looks at some of the instruments available to spatial planners to make projects more sustainable.

Planning Initiatives in Pursuit of Sustainable Development

1.1   Development of New Planning Instruments

Many newly developed land use plans and spatial regulations are elaborated within a sustainable vision and contain obligations and restrictions to guide initiatives towards more sustainable practices. The main focus points range from thematic ones such as the sustainable use of space, water management and the stimulation of alternatives for car transport to more specific measures such as the assurance of a minimum standard of insulation in new buildings. Many of these documents are seen as part of a local agenda 21 wherein different sectoral approaches are integrated into one planning initiative. The efforts to integrate elements of sustainability into planning instruments vary strongly from region to region and situation to situation and in many regions there is no obligation to implement the sustainability goals. Even when such goals are included in documents, the implementation is not always assured due to a difference between intention and obligation and the often insufficient control mechanisms. In Flanders there is no general obligation to implement elements of sustainability into planning instruments and sustainability is often no more than a starting point for many planning documents. Specific obligations are rare, the use of indicators exceptional and control mechanisms often fail. Sustainability aspects that are included at the beginning of the planning process are often traded off during the process because of the intervention of stakeholders. Generally only the issue of water management has become embedded in the planning process in Flanders. General regulations on the Flemish level (the highest institutional level in the field of spatial planning in Flanders) have been elaborated to ensure the installation of a rain water tank in every new house, the separation of the rain water drain and sewage pipe system and the prohibition of new building initiatives in wetlands.

The Euronet European research and exchange network consisting of research institutes and consultancy organisations have a group on the Urban Environment who stated that, 'in the main, local authorities are more successful in their attempts at sustainability with a short-term policy. Concrete and implementation-orientated projects also produce better results than policy pre-occupation. Local Agenda 21 and waste policy, for instance, are proving to be important mechanisms for local authorities to start developing a bottom-up consultative policy for sustainability. Spatial development and mobility are policy fields which are more complex, have huge short and long-term impacts, a wide range of repercussions and also require regional and national interventions. Local authorities do not succeed, in general, in tackling this kind of problem' (EURONET, 2000). The Government of the Netherlands also require municipalities to play an important role in the pursuance of sustainable development. An integrated approach requires more than calculating the effects from one sector to another. The best results tend to be obtained from processes with an open attitude towards the involvement of stakeholders from an early stage of the development process. In existing settlements this is even a condition for success (Duurzaam Gelderland, 2005). Euronet specified that the role of tools and statutory provisions should not be overestimated. 'Tools and instruments are only means. They can provide an insight into certain considerations but decision-making depends upon the perception of the various actors' (EURONET, 2000, p. 9).

1.2   Planning Implementation

In a more active planning approach planners are actively involved in developing new (sustainable) initiatives for housing areas and industrial zones. Some of these developments are identified as best practice, many performing a demonstration role for other initiatives. Housing projects in Germany and the Netherlands in particular have shown that the early intervention of planners can guide the projects towards sustainable solutions. Well known examples in the Netherlands of new sustainable housing are Ecolonia (Alphen aan den Rijn), Ecodus (Delft) and Vondelpark en Westerpark (Amsterdam). In Germany hundreds of sustainable housing areas of different kinds, size and themes are developed among them ecological settlements, car free areas and zero emission settlements. The diversity of these projects indicate that sustainability is indeed a broad issue covering numerous themes. The involvement of the inhabitants however is always a major concern in the planning processes. There are also numerous initiatives in the development of sustainable business and industrial parks focussing on qualitative architecture, a high proportion of green spaces and park management. Integrated industrial parks where the waste products of one activity are used by another however are as yet few and far between and often do not get further than the planning stage. These projects often have a demonstration role to illustrate the possibilities for sustainable practices. Such examples show that the vision can be realised and that these projects do not only have environmental but also economic and social benefits. In addition there is an extensive literature and numerous advice organisations dedicated to the pursuance of sustainable development.

1.3   Sustainability Indicators

Numerous initiatives have been undertaken to develop sustainability indicators to measure the impact of decisions and to compare different options. Figures are used as an instrument to control the impact of a process and to guide new initiatives in a certain direction to achieve the goals. Many institutions and local and regional authorities are developing these indicators to evaluate the impacts of their policies. The evaluation is based on putting sustainable principles into practice where principles reflect fundamental goals and practices. A number of these principles of sustainability are shown in Figure 12.1.

On the basis of these principles a variety of indicators can be developed and applied to evaluate sustainability in regional development strategies. These include specific, measurable indicators that reflect progress towards community development objectives. The Practical guide for sustainable planning of the European Council of Town Planners (ECTP, 2003) is a step towards the creation of precise indicators. Due to the fact that sustainable development requires different approaches depending on who is involved, the stage of the planning process and the local or regional planning context, the guide does not indicate precise indicators but rather offers guidelines for a sustainable approach and stresses the relationship and cooperation between spatial planning and sustainable development.

The Welsh Assembly Government has consciously decided that sustainable development should be at the heart of all its policies and it is a requirement that this is built into all its policies and strategies. The Wales Spatial Plan 'People, Places and Futures' (2004) therefore was critically examined to improve the contribution of the plan to sustainable development. The independent appraisal resulted in recommendations on the context, objectives and delivery as well on area-based initiatives.

Figure 12.1   Sustainability principles

Comprehensive Analysis	Sustainability requires planning that considers economic, social and environmental impacts, including those that are indirect, long-term and non-market. This requires adequate information and evaluation tools that allow stakeholders and decision-makers to understand the effects of their decisions.
Integrated and Strategic Planning	Sustainability planning requires that individual decisions support a community's long-term strategic objectives. For example, transport planning decisions should be subordinate to strategic economic, social and land use plans.
Focusing on Goals, Performance and Outcomes	Sustainability requires that planning be based on goals and outcomes, such as improved social welfare and equity, ecological health and access. It does not limit analysis to financial impacts and market activities.
Consideration of Equity	Sustainability emphasises that equity impacts should be considered in decision-making, including those that are indirect and long-term (imposed on future generations).
Market Principles	Market principles include consumer-choice, full-cost pricing and economic neutrality can support sustainable outcomes. This requires market reforms that eliminate incentives to over-use natural resources and to degrade the environment.
Precautionary Principle	Sustainability supports the Precautionary Principle, which emphasises the importance of incorporating risks in decision-making and favouring policies that minimise such risks when possible. It values resilience.
Conservation Ethic	Sustainability favours solutions that increase efficiency and reduce resource consumption, due to uncertainties about future market conditions and environmental impacts.
Transparency, Accountability and Public Involvement	Sustainability requires a clearly defined, transparent planning process, adequate opportunities for stakeholder to become informed about issues and be involved in decision-making, and good communication between professionals and the general public.

Source: Victoria Transport Policy Institute (2005)

These recommendations are about the spatial policy itself: building sustainable communities, providing greater focus on tackling health inequalities, strengthening the opportunities linked to cultural diversity and sport, the role of the Plan in delivering community safety and so on. The independent sustainability appraisal also provides recommendations on the area appraisals. These recommendations do not deal with the question of the implementation of the Plan nor the way sustainability can be balanced and assured when making certain choices. For this purpose a Welsh Assembly Government integration tool was elaborated. The tool is meant to help to stimulate dialogue, generate new ideas and encourage 'joined-up' thinking. The tool is an instrument to help stakeholders and policy makers to evaluate projects by comparing the answers of key questions with the (effects) of proposed objectives. The integration tool seems to be an effective way to measure, compare and discuss the proposed actions and initiatives. Even though the tool could be used as an evaluation tool at different levels and points in time, the tool does not focus on the implementation of the Plan and the proposed actions. An important step has been taken but without clear indicators and monitoring during implementation, the results should not be taken for granted.

Developing Spatial Strategies

Sustainable planning issues are not limited to concrete planning implementation at the lower administrative levels. Sustainable planning at a regional scale deals with issues such as unbalanced development, mobility generation, deterioration of the quality of life and destruction of the environment. These environmental and sustainability issues are often linked to each other and have to be incorporated in regional development strategies. Closer cooperation between sustainable planning initiatives and regional planning could lead to faster results and an easier implementation of the proposed goals. The link between more integrated and dynamic regional planning and sustainable regional development strategies however is weak especially where spatial planning is still seen as a purely passive instrument. There have however, been a number of examples of good practice.

The widely acclaimed IBA Emsher Park initiative in the Ruhrgebiet of Germany (see Shaw, 2002) is perhaps one of the best known success stories of a successful combination of the indication of general development perspectives and the goal of improving the environmental conditions in an area. Spatial planning successfully combined regional development goals and environmental issues and the implementation of both issues supported the whole project to the desired transformation of the region. Whilst it was never going to be possible in the short or medium term to replace the huge job losses in the iron, steel and coal industries in the region, the region transformed its image and turned outward migration into a new immigration on the basis of new knowledge-based economic activities. The region has retained important elements of its heritage in the form of landmarks and through old buildings receiving new uses as well as the retention of the link to energy. Whereas the old regional identity was based on coal energy the brave new region profiles itself as a region of environmental industry and renewable energy. The success story of the Emsher Park is acknowledged by the State Government of Nordrhein-Westfalen who developed an instrument to stimulate the elaboration of comprehensive development plans with an important spatial planning aspect in different parts of the region to reduce the prosperity gaps within the region. The 'Regionale' are integrated planning and implementation processes organised in different parts of the Federal State. The Regionale support initiatives in parts of the region in the fields of tourism, recreation, culture and economic development. The initiatives are required to be sustainable and much attention is given to the environmental issues. The results of these initiatives are shown to the public in a special in field exhibition. The process has to lead to visible results within a strict time schedule.

The Euregio Maas-Rhein on the borders of Belgium, Germany and the Netherlands has been identified as the Regionale 2008 in an attempt to stimulate cross border contacts and economic development. The idea is to increase these contacts through a common theme. The theme is the black land, the mining area which crossed the borders of all three countries. The three central themes are:

- Stadtfinden (to find place, to find an urban environment);
- Fremdgehen (going abroad);
- Grenzwissen (know about borders).

There is a strong focus on sustainability in the proposed strategy and initiatives are set up to improve living conditions through new housing projects, the creation of recreational areas and sustainable economic redevelopment by strengthening cross border relationships and partnerships. Environmental issues include the preparation of brownfield sites for redevelopment, the renewal of river valleys, the development of ecological parks and upgrading the quality of residential areas by linking these to parks and cycling routes. The projects are being elaborated by diverse stakeholders and the implementation of approved projects is supported by subsidies and logistical help. All the project ideas are linked to the central themes and sustainability is guaranteed by the central coordination and the support for a limited number of demonstration projects. Due to the co-operation and collaboration between all stakeholders the selected projects are implemented and operate as demonstration projects which will act as an example towards new processes outside the Euregionale Programme.

The initiative of the Regionale illustrates that sustainable projects can be developed within a clear programme and with the availability of subsidies. All different programmes are discussed in a broad forum and the results are shown and discussed with the public. As the direct impact of the programme is limited and the exhibition approach is employed the sustainable aspect is easy to control. The organisation of the Landesgartenschaus (Garden Exhibition) in Germany often used a similar approach. There are examples from other regions where such events are used as a motor to stimulate regional development with an important spatial element. The strategy of the Rhine-Scheldt estuary is another example of integrated planning with concrete and positive results. The deepening of the Scheldt River is accepted by offering more space to the river, creating valuable natural areas, helping to prevent flooding by supplying polder areas by high water and developing initiatives for tourism and recreation. The organisation of big events is often closely linked with spatial planning initiatives and attempts to reinvent the image of an area.

This combination should not be taken for granted. In Lithuania for example the Comprehensive Plan of the Territory of the Republic of Lithuania (Lithuanian Ministry of Environment 2002) was approved on in 2002. The Plan is the main spatial planning document, guiding long-term spatial development of the state. In accordance with the ESDP the Plan focuses on polycentric and balanced development. As in many other documents the Plan stresses that it is based on the principles of sustainable development, specified in general terms such as avoiding damage to the natural and cultural environment, safeguarding the interests of contemporary and future generations and co-ordinating the use of protected territories. However the Plan remains vague as to how sustainability will be operationalised making it difficult to see how this will happen in practice. The relationship with the Lithuanian National Strategy for Sustainable Development (Lithuanian Ministry of Environment 2003), is quite weak. The vagueness inherent in the Comprehensive Plan in relation to sustainability issues mean that the sustainability benefits of the Plan are likely to be limited. On the other hand, the sustainable development strategy indicates clear goals, which are not limited to environmental issues. The regional development chapter however is limited and the spatial impact is not examined in detail. A closer co-operation in the elaboration of such documents could have lead to clearer and more strategic products. The lack of policy integration in Lithuania is common in many other countries. Depending on place and time there can be successful links between spatial planning and regional development as the examples from Barcelona and the IBA Emscher Park illustrate. When space is a central focus in the formulation of the vision it appears likely that the chances of sustainable solutions are increased.

1.4   A New Debate on Sustainable Development

The EU enlargement policy illustrates the need for a closer relationship between sustainability principles and practice. The enlargement policy illustrates the EU commitment towards its sustainable development principles. Under communist rule sustainable and environmental issues were neglected due to the strong relation between economic and political leaders, the priority given to production quotas rather than on meeting environmental standards and the limited power of non-governmental organisations (Baker, 2006). The EU is assisting the new member states by offering funding and assistance in the improvement of environmental management, promoting ecological modernisation and stimulating democratic participation. However the integration process is already showing signs that the new countries are making similar mistakes as the established member states did in periods of fast economic growth leading to environmentally degraded regions.

The new pressure on the environment in the eastern countries is not just caused by the growing consumer society and consumer waste, a growing need in energy and the rise of road transport and the use of private cars. Baker (2006) argues that EU regulations, such as the Common Agricultural Policy (CAP) and the Trans European Networks (TEN), are also responsible for a decline of the environmental qualities. The introduction of the CAP is exerting strong negative pressure on the environment and leading to a loss of bio-diversity, erosion and water pollution. The EU seems unable to adapt the needs in the west caused by an over intensive agriculture into a new approach for the east. By implementing the CAP in the east the intensification policy will lead to more pollution problems and limit the habitats in the traditional agriculture areas characterised by a strong cooperation between agriculture, nature and landscape. Also in transport programmes the EU policy is supporting massive expansion of road infrastructure programmes which in the long-term will lead to similar problems as in the west: increasing road transport and congestion, stimulating private car use and increasing pollution. The EU appears unable or unwilling to transfer a traditional road infrastructure orientation towards more sustainable rail investments despite rhetoric to the contrary. The sustainability mandate has not helped much to bring about the much talked about modal shift towards more environmentally friendly systems of transport (Peters, 2003). The principles of sustainable development are often not or only partially implemented in practice. EU enlargement offers the opportunity to indicate, reflect and discuss the implementation of regional development implementation and its sustainability content but unfortunately this opportunity appears to be going to waste. The debate on sustainable development is shifting from more practical and low scale initiatives to high scale investments and initiatives. The results however are less obvious and less visible than on lower scale initiatives.

Conclusion: A New Challenge for Spatial Planners

In recent decades planning has changed dramatically due to increased awareness of environmental dangers and qualities. On the one hand sustainability issues are still hot issues discussed on the highest international forum (UN, G8, EU). On the other hand however, there is a movement towards less rules, less legal and administrative limitations and less planning. During the course of this chapter it has been argued that the conviction that environmental pressure will lead to increasing negative impacts on the environment, social structures and economic functioning formed the basis for the sustainable development mission and approach. Gradually more and more plans are seeking to follow sustainable themes and principles although the extent to which the concept of sustainable development is actually being made operational is extremely variable, with the better results often at lower spatial scales. Whilst there is awareness about sustainable development amongst various planning and policy levels, the translation of this awareness into practice is proving to be extremely difficult.

Spatial planners can play an important linking role and include sustainable development principles into implementation programmes at different spatial scales. The spatial planning approach is so closely linked with the sustainable development principles that stronger co-operation will increase benefits for both disciplines (Gibbs, 1998, p. 365). Spatial planners can play a key role in combining aspects of sustainable development as part of corporate governance. By offering a frame for integrated regional strategy objectives, elements and goals of sectoral plans can be integrated into a global package for implementation. Planning can play a more active role in supplying the negotiation process, help to clarify issues, build understanding and consensus and identify compensation issues.

Spatial planning is a useful instrument in the pursuance of sustainable development at all spatial scales. As indicated above, the lower the level, the more concrete the issue, the easier it is to achieve sustainability in practice. Spatial planners can indicate that a sustainable development is closely related to good governance but it needs a model of partnership and collaboration and cannot easily be imposed from above (Roberts 2002). Planners are able to engage stakeholders and to give them a stake in the outcomes. Politicians and sectoral stakeholders however will often shift towards their own short-term targets and will often neglect long term goals. With a stronger orientation on the sustainable aspects of planning, opportunities will grow to achieve more sustainable development in practice. By focussing on both top-down and bottom up approaches planning can facilitate and strengthen the sustainability agenda. The involvement of the international community ensures that sustainable development remains on the political agenda. Without these international, national and regional driving forces the ambition for practical implementation will be tempered.

Planners however have to indicate how sustainable development can be implemented without adding extra layers of administration or bureaucracy and how a spatial vision on the regional level can offer a vehicle for planning and sustainable development (Roberts 2002). The use of sustainability indicators can help to guide the discussion and decision making but planners have to be aware that a rigid use of the tool might lead to a more technocratic approach making planning less dynamic. Planners need to develop dynamic planning, convincing, guiding and retaining actors in the process as well as engaging and convincing stakeholders and policymakers. An overly technocratic approach to the indicators might break these processes. Therefore the indicators should be used as an instrument to discuss options and rationalise decisions. A more direct orientation on sustainable development can function as a motor to steer many planning and implementation processes. Planners should indicate that sustainability can also have visible positive effects in the short-term. This will strengthen the involvement and create more support to achieve the implementation of sustainable ideas in practice. The objectives and actions of a plan or strategy should be developed from objective towards action, implementation and evaluation. This means that (some) proposed actions should be followed by a time schedule, a budget, the setting-up of evaluation indicators, and an evaluation moment. Without an implementation programme some players will only pay lip service to the goals and objectives whilst pursuing separate objectives through independent expenditure processes (Roberts, 2002, p. 152).

When spatial planners can prove that they can make a significant contribution to achieving sustainable development principles, this would strengthen the credibility and profile of spatial planning amongst policy makers and the public. As success breeds success this will lead to increased support and the current negative attitude to planning in some countries could be changed in the near future providing a new impetus and new challenges for spatial planners. In order to achieve this however planners must first prove to a sometimes sceptical world that they can deliver concrete and tangible results in the pursuance of a more sustainable future.

References

Albrechts, L., Alden, J. and da Rosa Pires, A. (eds) (2001), *The Changing Institutional Landscape of Planning*, Ashgate, Aldershot, 2001.

Baker, S. (2006), *Sustainable Development*, Routledge, London.

D'hondt, (2006), 'Europese Planning in Vlaanderen, Of hoe ver Brussel kan zijn van de Eigen Hoofdstad', in Janssen-Jansen, Leonie and Waterhout, Bas (eds), *Grenzeloze Ruimte, Regionale Gebiedsgerichte Ontwikkelingsplanologie in Europees Perspectief*, Reeks Planologie, Sdu Uitgevers.

Duurzaam Gelderland (2005), Referentiekader stedelijke ontwikkeling, available at: http://www.gelderland.nl/referentiekader_dso/DSOWEB/Start.htm accessed February 2006.

EURONET (2000), 'Expert group on the Urban Environment', *Governance & Management or Sustainability in Cities and Towns in Europe*, executive summary, Utrecht.

European Commission (1999), *European Spatial Development Perspective*.

European Council of Town Planners (2003), 'Try It This Way' – Checklist on Sustainable Urban Development, *Good Practice Guide on Planning for Sustainable Development*, http://www.ceu-ectp.org.

Evans, Joas, Sundback and Theobold (2005), *Governing Sustainable Cities*, London, Earthscan.

Faludi, A. (2002), *The making of the European Spatial Development Perspective: No Masterplan*, Routledge, London.

Florida, R. (2002), *The Rise of the Creative Class*, Basic Books, New York.

Gauteng Declaration (2002), www.nrg4sd.net.

Gibbs, D. (1998), 'Regional Development Agencies and Sustainable Development', *Regional Studies*, vol. 32, pp. 365–368.

Gratton, C., Shibli, S. and Coleman, R. (2005), 'Sport and Economic Regeneration in Cities', *Urban Studies*, vol. 42, no. 5–6, pp. 985–999, May 2005, Routledge.

Harcourt, W. (2005), *The road to the Millennium Development Goals*, NCDO, available at: www.ncdo.nl/index.php/filemanager/ download/128/Harcourt.pdf, accessed February 2006.

Kelly, K. (1998), *New Rules for the New Economy*, pp. 94–95, Penguin.

Lithuanian Ministry of the Environment (2002), *Comprehensive Plan of the Territory of the Republic of Lithuania.*

Lithuanian Ministry of the Environment (2003), *Lithuanian National Strategy for Sustainable Development*, available at: http://www.am.lt/files/cd_en.pdf, accessed February 2006.

Marshall, T., Glasson, J. and Headicar. P. (eds) (2002), Regional Planning and the Environmental Dimension of Sustainable Development, *Contemporary Issues in Regional Planning*, p. 145, Ashgate, Aldershot.

Marshall, T. (2004), *Transforming Barcelona*, Routledge, London.

Neumann, E.N. and Petersen, T. (2001), Zeitenwende der Wertewandel, 30 Jahre später, *Aus Politik und Zeitgeschichte*, vol. 29.

Peters, D. (2003), Cohesion, Polycentricity, Missing Links and Bottle Necks: Conflicting Spatial Storylines for Pan-European Transport Investments, *European Planning Studies*, vol. 11, no. 3, pp 317–339, Carfax Publishing.

Regional Futures (2004), Spatial Planning in the Regions, Research Report, October 2004, available at: http://www.regionalfutures.org.uk/newsdigest/SPintheregions_page1953.aspx, accessed February 2006.

Robert, P. and Lloyd, G. (1999), Institutional aspects of regional planning, management and development: Lessons from the English experience', *Environment and Planning B*, vol. 26, pp. 517–531.

Shaw, R. (2002), The International Building Initiative (IBA) Emscher Park, Germany: A Model for Sustainable Restructuring? *European Planning Studies*, vol. 10, no. 1, 2002, Carfax Publishing.

Theil, S. (2005), The greens are wilting, *Newsweek International*, edition, 18 July 2005.

Thornley, A. (2002), Urban Regeneration and Sports Stadia, *European Planning Studies*, vol. 10, no. 7, 2002, Carfax Publishing.

Tol, R., (2002). New estimates of the damage costs of climate change, part 1, benchmark estimates, *Environmental and Resource Economics*, vol. 21, no. 1, pp. 47–73.

Tol, R, Fankhauser, S. Richels, R. and Smith J. 2000, How much damage will climate change do?, Recent estimates, World Economics, 1 (4), 179–206.

United Nations Millennium Declaration 2000, Resolution adopted by the General Assembly, 55/2, 8th plenary meeting, 8 September 2000.

Victoria Transport Policy Institute (2005), TDM Encyclopaedia, Sustainable Transportation and TDM, Planning That Balances Economic, Social and Ecological Objectives available at http://www.vtpi.org/tdm/tdm67.htm, accessed February 2006.

Welsh Assembly Government, (2004), The Wales Spatial Plan, 'People, Places and Futures', Cardiff.

World Commission on Environment and Development (1987), Our Common Future, Oxford Paperbacks.

Chapter 13

Reviewing Experience of Regional Development and Spatial Planning in Europe

Neil Adams, Jeremy Alden and Neil Harris

Introduction

The various examples of regional development and spatial planning activity in the preceding chapters illustrate how some of the smaller and more recent regions and member states of the European Union are responding to changed economic, social and governmental contexts. In some cases, the activity of strategic spatial planning at the 'regional' scale has emerged with some clarity over the past half-decade. Spatial planning has been embraced in countries such as Ireland, Scotland and Wales where spatial plans or strategies have been published. Experience in Estonia, Latvia and Lithuania is varied. In some cases, spatial planning has also been defined with some clarity, while in others it remains an emerging activity. The processes of restructuring that have been in place since independence in the early 1990s are ongoing, and their many and varied effects provide a challenging context for spatial planning practice. It is perhaps too easy to regard transition as already having taken place, yet the reality is that certain parts of these territories are still undergoing significant structural change. There are some other examples – the case of the Flanders Spatial Structure Plan included in this volume is one – of mature spatial planning systems that can provide lessons for others where it has yet to fully develop. Yet many questions remain. These include some significant and far-reaching questions, including how to understand the relationship between regional development and spatial planning, what impact can spatial planning have on achieving more balanced forms of regional development, and questions on the capacity for implementation in spatial planning and its effectiveness as an instrument with which to effect spatial change over the longer term? These and other questions form the basis for some of our concluding comments, but also serve as a framework for further evaluation of spatial planning practice as it deals more fully with aspects of implementation, monitoring and review.

Europeanisation, Regional Development and Spatial Planning

The European Union and its various policy initiatives and agendas inevitably feature in the various case studies in this volume. This is perhaps most clearly seen in how regional development and spatial planning activities have been impacted on by the securing and distribution of Structural Funds. The case studies drawing on experience in the Baltic States demonstrate how regional development activity has been driven to a large extent by developing capacity for absorption of Structural Funds. In certain cases, the accounts provided in the preceding chapters could be read in a way that suggests this concern to be able to absorb European monies has been too great an influence on the design and management of regional development systems. A number of the contributors also raise concerns that the manner in which such funding has been secured and managed has led to exacerbation of certain regional development problems. Even in the cases where capacity for absorbing EU Structural Funds has not necessarily acquired the profile that it has in the Baltic States, such as in Ireland and Scotland, it has clearly been a significant background issue.

The influence of the European Union can also be identified in other ways apart from the more obvious impacts of funding programmes. The influence can be found in how national and regional spatial strategies reflect the various discourses of European development policy (see Shaw and Sykes, 2005 and Dabinett and Richardson, 2005). Some of the accounts, including those on Scotland and Ireland in particular, demonstrate that spatial planning initiatives have provided an opportunity to think about 'positioning' a territory within a changing European space. In most explicit terms, this has manifested itself in thinking about the enlargement of the European Union that has since taken place. Strategies in the Celtic periphery may therefore anticipate that enlargement potentially increases their actual and perceived peripherality as the centre of gravity of the European Union shifts eastwards. For the new member states of the European Union, including the Baltic States, spatial planning exercises can be used to reposition themselves, working through new orientations and devising new roles and relationships in European and transnational spaces (see Pallagst, 2006). Perhaps most interestingly, this demonstrates a recognition among spatial planners that spatial strategies can be important instruments in linking a territory to other networks and structures and finding a new 'position' within them. To the extent that national and regional spatial strategies make some form of connection to European spatial development and related agendas, they provide an interesting insight into how such wider, European issues are dealt with simultaneously with internal, domestic regional development and spatial planning issues. The latter of these are arguably of greater focus and interest in the various strategies studied by the contributors to this volume. So, while domestic spatial development issues still predominate, they are increasingly understood within or influenced by European development matters. The European Commission's emphasis on the reduction of disparities and the promotion of greater economic, social and territorial cohesion will ensure that European policy issues continue to feature in regional planning and spatial development practices. Various policies of the European Union and its

Member States – including the European Spatial Development Perspective published in 1999 and the European Union's Cohesion Report published in 2004 – attempt to combine aspects of both cooperation and competition between the regions of Europe. Some of the chapters provided in this volume demonstrate that pursuing these multiple agendas is carried out with varying degrees of success. Some of the perceived tensions and contradictions in European Union policies will be most readily apparent as these are played out in different national and regional contexts.

Comparing and Contrasting the Approaches

In our conclusions in this section, we first try and characterise the particular 'styles' of regional development strategies and spatial plans that have emerged in our two geographic areas of particular focus. The differences across each of the cases are evident, yet we suggest that spatial planning and regional development activity can be characterised as of two types. A more formal approach to these activities is evident in the Baltic States, while less formal approaches have emerged in the Celtic periphery. However, we identify some trends and developments that suggest that even the less formal approaches that have emerged in the Celtic countries examined here will become increasingly formalised as they progress. There is, for example, already evidence that spatial planning is becoming embedded in statute and related statutory processes. This ability to review experience of preparing regional development strategies and spatial plans across the case studies allows a simple classification of two different approaches. The first is a highly formalised strategy in which the contents of the strategy and its principal objectives may be prescribed in legislation. Legislation may also prescribe some of the procedural requirements for plan preparation, such as the key stages in the process, opportunities for consultation and the requirement to engage particular actors or stakeholders. Due to this formalised, legislative context, emphasis is also placed on the conformity of plans within a hierarchy, ensuring that plans at successive tiers elaborate a series of common principles or objectives. This more formal type of strategy is usually based on extensive data collection and analysis, much of it of a spatial character, and illustrated to a large extent in the strategy itself through maps and GIS-based diagrams. In some cases, the strategy becomes a compendium of spatial data and information rendered in quantitative form. This more formal type of strategy is capable of expressing detailed actions and programmes for implementation in quite specific and concrete form. Consequently, implementation, monitoring and review may also be well-developed as part of the strategy. In contrast, approaches at the other end of the spectrum are less formal in terms of content and process and, in some ways, reflect the kind of approach adopted in development of the European Spatial Development Perspective. Informal approaches to preparing a strategy are usually undertaken without any basis in legislation. Neither the objectives of the strategy nor the process by which it is prepared are defined in legislation. Stakeholders and other public agencies will have opportunity to become involved in the process of preparing the strategy, yet these are not clearly defined and are typically offered in terms of general consultation on policy development. Opportunities for involvement are not defined as 'rights' to be consulted or to participate. Nevertheless, there may be multiple and often quite significant opportunities available to stakeholders to influence the direction and contents of the strategy. This informal type of regional development or spatial strategy is likely to occupy a position within a much wider field of policies and related documents, and will have important relationships with other strategies at national, regional and local levels. These relationships are important and will usually be a key aspect of the strategy's implementation. Yet these relationships are negotiated and in flux, rather then prescribed or clearly defined. Certainly, its relationship with other strategies and documents will not be framed in terms of conformity. Indeed, the aims and objectives stated in the document may not readily be translated into specific actions without further elaboration in related documents and other strategies. Such a strategy may be best conceived of as a platform or framework for further policy development and action by others. As a direct consequence of this, matters of implementation, monitoring and review are underdeveloped or simply not considered relevant or appropriate to a strategy of its kind. This very simple and crude characterisation – between more and less formal types of strategy – is one that has emerged from the sharing of experience within the project that has inspired this collection of case studies. The case study chapters themselves flesh out the details and identify where different components or aspects of the strategy may in fact be more or less formal. However, the categorisation aligns in broad terms with the less formal approaches emerging in the Celtic periphery and the more formal approaches based in continental Europe and the Baltic States.

The activity of spatial planning has quite rapidly become embedded in the institutional and policy landscape in the three cases drawn from the 'Celtic periphery'. Of the examples included in this volume covering experience in Ireland, Scotland and Wales, it is the National Spatial Strategy for Ireland that has generated most interest as the earliest of the documents to be prepared. Published in 2002, it has acted as an early approach to national spatial planning that has inspired similar or related approaches elsewhere. In the case of both the Scottish Executive and the Welsh Assembly Government, the Irish Government's progress on its strategy has provided a learning process that the others have been able to draw upon. In many ways, the Irish Spatial Strategy has emerged as one of the more robust examples of spatial strategy-making, particularly in terms of the format and content of the document itself. Like many spatial strategies, it does not provide a series of specific actions that can be simply read off from the strategy and implemented. Nevertheless, by comparison with the National Planning Framework for Scotland and the Wales Spatial Plan, its content is relatively well-developed as illustrated by its more specific identification of locations for the development of gateways and hubs. In spite of this and the rather different demographic and economic context prevailing in Ireland, a discernible 'style' of spatial planning has emerged in the Celtic periphery. Elements of this style or approach can be seen to differing extents in each of the three case studies. This can be characterised as a relatively broad-brush, strategic form of planning resulting in the formulation of an indicative framework for future development. In some quarters, this has led to questions about whether such documents actually do anything at all in terms of specific and concrete policies or actions. Certainly, anyone expecting to find such specific policies that they may be readily capable of implementation and monitoring will be disappointed. The documents are designed to act as frameworks for further work and discussion or dialogue between various stakeholders. Indeed, some work is now being progressed for example in Ireland and in Wales on taking forward the ideas and objectives contained in the strategies through the development of regional planning guidelines or the establishment of area-based priorities. In some ways, the process of spatial planning has only just started in these contexts. The Wales Spatial Plan expresses its role well in setting 'a direction of travel' over the longer term. The implication of this is that it is too early to evaluate the effectiveness of spatial planning initiatives in Scotland, Ireland and Wales. This is certainly true in relation to their capacity to influence spatial change and the future distribution of activities in space.

This apparent 'style' of spatial planning emerging in the Celtic periphery also has important process dimensions. The approach in each case has been broadly consensual, with attempts made to engage a range of stakeholders at various stages in the preparation of the strategy. The involvement of stakeholders has itself been dealt with relatively informally. Consultation has usually been based on early engagement and consultation on early versions of the documents finally issued. There have been opportunities for involvement and engagement, although this has not usually extended to formal and explicit opportunities to 'test' the contents of the strategy, such as through formal examination or hearing. Such mechanisms, it might be argued, are not appropriate to a strategic spatial strategy. It is though interesting to speculate on how the strategies would fare if subjected to a more formal and explicit examination. Some audiences have expressed concerns about the availability of sufficient quality spatial data on which to develop a strategy and whether the data that is available has been subjected to an appropriate depth of analysis. This has surfaced in the context of why certain places are identified, for example, as gateways or hubs while others have not, or why a territory has been organised around certain loosely-defined functional areas without any real 'evidence'. The style and approach emerging in the Celtic periphery therefore appears to be one based to some extent on the collection and interpretation of data, although not especially reliant upon it. One might even go so far as to question whether the spatial strategy as it stands might have been accomplished in similar form without any detailed or extensive data collection and analysis. Overall, the approach might be defined as a hybrid form of spatial planning that is characterised by both 'technical' and 'creative' or 'artistic' components.

The character of the spatial planning approaches in the Celtic periphery has been defined above as relatively informal. In embarking on the preparation of the various strategies, the responsible organisations have not been constrained to any great extent by legislation. In the United Kingdom in particular, the notion of spatial planning has been promoted as one that breaks out of a narrow, regulatory understanding of planning actions and processes. The relative informality of the various spatial planning exercises has been possible as a direct consequence of their being unencumbered by statutory processes and regulations. This provides opportunity for innovation and creativity in devising new approaches to planning, qualities that are increasingly rare in planning instruments and frameworks. Yet there are signs that the process of and context for spatial strategy-making is becoming increasingly formal and institutionalised. There are various forces and drivers promoting this. Some of these are domestic, and both the Wales Spatial Plan and the National Planning Framework for Scotland are increasingly being embedded in legislation and formality of process. The Welsh Assembly Government now has a statutory duty to prepare and revise the Wales Spatial Plan, whereas it started out as an initiative without any legislative basis. Such developments are presumably inspired by attempts to secure some increased status for the relevant strategies, or ensure that the strategies become more permanent features of the policy framework. The account of Scotland's National Planning Framework in this volume also highlights a European dimension to the increasing formality of strategy-making, such as through the European Union directive requiring 'strategic environmental assessment' of plans and programmes that have a significant impact on the environment. Some might argue that such requirements only provide appropriate checks and balances in devising spatial strategies. Others may argue that the increasing formality of spatial strategy-making processes will lead to the loss of some of their more valuable qualities, including their capacity for establishing a consensual vision and acting as frameworks for open dialogue between stakeholders. This will be a dimension of particular interest over the next generation of spatial strategies as attempts are made to formalise processes while maintaining a capacity for engagement and dialogue.

The case studies and experiences based on regional development and spatial planning in the Baltic States of Estonia, Latvia and Lithuania provide an especially valuable insight into how particular territories adapt over time to changing governmental, social and economic contexts. Although each of the stories is different, they highlight the difficulties of coming to terms with the social and economic effects of independence and the various legacies of the Soviet era. These processes have now been in effect for over a decade and the cases demonstrate that public policy instruments and legislative frameworks have taken a number of years to respond effectively. This is not particularly surprising as they have been designed within a rapidly changing and less stable context. The point has been made repeatedly that the particular legacy facing the Baltic States continues to actively shape the activity of planning, framing how it is perceived and defining the particular roles that it has to play. Interestingly, from an external perspective, the notion of planning seems to be one that is very much embedded in formal process and state regulations. The case studies highlight the significance of state laws and regulations in defining the objectives of regional development activity. Similarly, especially formal and detailed attempts at comprehensive planning exist at the national level. This is a form of 'planning' that might give rise to surprise in a western European context, given its incredible detail and formality. Yet the context prevailing in the Baltics suggests that more formal approaches to spatial planning and regional development are necessary in order to provide certain and specific requirements and ensure that such activities are implemented. Some of the difficulties in ensuring voluntary cooperation between different areas and actors require formalisation of processes and actions. However, the Estonian national government's experience in developing its National Spatial Plan demonstrates that less formal and institutionalised approaches to spatial planning are both practical and worthwhile in the context of the Baltics. Its style and approach relate more closely to, and indeed have provided inspiration for, some of the examples in the Celtic periphery.

The Dilemmas of Growth and the Pursuit of Balanced Regional Development

Some of the cases discussed demonstrate that regional disparities are enduring, long-standing and resilient to public policies designed to address or tackle them. Sustained policy interventions have in certain cases failed to turn regions around. One of the clearer messages to emerge from the various episodes of spatial strategy making and regional development activity presented in the preceding chapters is that these regional disparities have tended to increase rather than decrease. This increase in regional disparities could be read as simply a 'natural' extension and continuation of the forces driving the variable performance of regions; alternatively, it might be attributed in part to the latent contradictions in aspects of the European Union's policies and the very real pressures to realise domestic economic growth at the expense of concerns for how that growth is distributed. The fact that many of the contributors report an increase in regional or sub-regional disparities – often based on rapidly growing urban centres outstripping lagging, peripheral or more rural areas – should clearly be a cause for concern. Of course, it is in addressing these emerging or widening disparities in economic and social terms that many current regional development and spatial planning initiatives are initiated, with Ireland's National Spatial Strategy being one of the clearest in trying to confront this particular issue.

Practically all of the approaches to regional development and spatial planning included in this volume are to some extent based on the premise of promoting balanced regional development. Some of these are more explicit than others in highlighting balanced regional development as a stated objective of government policy in general and spatial or regional planning instruments in particular. However, the concept of balanced regional development can be interpreted in a number of different ways. For example, there is the issue of the scale and how this influences understanding of what constitutes balanced regional development. In the case study of the National Spatial Strategy in Ireland, the recent growth experienced and concentrated in the Greater Dublin Area could be argued as promoting a more balanced and polycentric pattern of growth in north-west Europe. Likewise, the promotion of development in Riga as a Baltic capital city might register at a certain scale as helping to deliver more balanced regional development within the context of European space. Yet, as these and other case studies make clear, these developments appear differently when framed within the context of national, domestic space. Scale therefore becomes an important contextual factor in how we interpret and understand the concept of balanced regional development. A second factor of importance in interpreting what balanced regional development can be taken to mean derives from how it is being formulated in some of the national contexts that have been addressed in the preceding chapters. This particular point has been addressed by Walsh (2002, p. 11) in commenting on the spatial strategy in Ireland, arguing that balanced regional development has been approached in terms of potential rather than redistribution. Such potential-based solutions are in many ways more pragmatic in recognising the difficulties of redistributing functions, investments and resources. New initiatives in strategic spatial planning recognise the weaknesses, shortcomings and indeed now inappropriate nature of earlier, traditional policies designed to actively redistribute activity from areas of pressure to areas of stagnation and decline. The capacity to implement a redistribution-based approach to balanced regional development is rather limited, constrained by a range of factors including limited resources, the competitive nature of cities and places, and the realities of policy development in a globalised context. So, to some extent, a potential-based approach to the issue of balanced regional development is a sensible one. Yet the capacity of a potential–based approach to address significant regional disparities, or even to prevent such disparities becoming even more marked, has to be questioned. Perhaps the best that such an approach can hope to deliver is an amelioration of some of the worst aspects of increasing economic and social disparities between different regions.

The Function and Effectiveness of Policy Instruments for Regional Development and Spatial Planning

Spatial strategies and regional development strategies of the kind assessed by the contributors of earlier chapters may perform a series of different functions. These include providing a platform for the geographic of spatial positioning of a particular territory, acting as a vehicle for the promotion of balanced regional development and addressing inter- and intra-regional disparities in economic, social and even environmental conditions. In this section, we identify a series of practical barriers to the more effective use of spatial plans and strategies. This starts with an account of some of the common or shared weaknesses of regional development plans and spatial strategies based on the sharing of experience in the GRIDS project. This is then followed by some more fundamental questions on the capacity for spatial planning exercises to bring about joined-up government and integrated solutions to a range of social, economic and environmental issues. Our assessment brings us to the conclusion that spatial planning as an activity offers a great deal of potential, yet there exists rather limited evidence that spatial planning can deliver on its various promises to promote more balanced regional development and integrated policies.

The sharing of experience of preparing regional development plans and spatial strategies allows us to draw out some of the common weaknesses and criticisms of the various approaches. The first of these is that many strategies engage in what might be described as the 'art of the possible' and manifests itself in the extensive production of spatial data and statistical information. Some approaches result in extensive and copious amounts of spatial data simply because the generation of that data is relatively straightforward and generally not too controversial. Such strategies tend to be a triumph of data collection and representation over vision, strategic thinking and action. The reality is that data collection can become an end itself and obscure the often more important aspects of strategy formation. The second weakness relates to the identification and involvement of stakeholders in strategy preparation. Many spatial strategy making processes place emphasis on the involvement of stakeholders in a consensual process, yet in many cases stakeholder engagement has been less successful than anticipated. Certain stakeholders have not been engaged in the process or have been difficult to involve. In some cases, this has arisen out of uncertainty as to what type and form of document might emerge from the process, especially where spatial planning frameworks are new forms of policy instrument. Yet it also raises questions as to the capacity of various stakeholders to engage at a regional level. Focusing engagement at a regional-level presumes that this is a meaningful and appropriate scale for a variety of different stakeholders and one at which they are sufficiently well resourced in order to become involved. These issues and concerns are amplified by other concerns on the profile enjoyed by spatial planning as one activity of government among a series of others enjoying much greater profile and political attention. The third in our common criticisms of regional development strategies and spatial plans is that they risk being interpreted as overly optimistic documents. This is based on a series of questions about whether spatial strategies are sufficiently well developed to be able to tackle and address the particularly difficult or 'wicked' issues facing a region. To some extent, this particular failing of certain strategies arises out of the consensual approach by which they have been prepared. The securing of consensus and the forging of agreement – essentially the design of a strategy that as many actors and agencies as possible can sign up to – can mean complex matters on which there may be disagreement are temporarily set aside. Yet it also derives from some of the wider factors surrounding the preparation of spatial strategies in particular. Strategies of a type that focus on the development of a strategic vision, the pursuit of more balanced regional development and developing the potential of different parts of a territory are inherently upbeat and optimistic in tone. The vocabulary of many spatial planning exercises – realising potential, future challenges, actions, vision, collaboration, stakeholders etc. – is itself an indicator of the terms on which the activity is premised. This in turn leads to questions on how effective spatial planning frameworks will be and to what extent they will be influential when it comes to making particularly difficult strategic choices and decisions. The fourth criticism that might be levelled at the various approaches to spatial planning is how they progress from data collection and analysis to the development of a strategy. Some of the comments above already allude to the question of whether the various strategies, visions and actions included in spatial strategy documents are especially well based on evidence. For many readers and users of spatial planning instruments, there appears to be a gap between evidence, understanding and strategy. The final criticism is related to implementation and incorporates a number of different issues. These issues are ones that are starting to be faced as various actors move from the devising of a strategy to its realisation and implementation. Many spatial strategies claim to be implemented or applied in a number of different and diffuse ways, from establishing frameworks for dialogue and discussion, through to influencing programmes and budgets for a range of sectors across different agencies. The concerns relate to the lack of specific actions in many strategies, through to the dedication of limited resources for implementation and the underdeveloped nature of frameworks for monitoring, evaluation and review.

The above paragraph relays a series of rather practical issues and concerns on the practice and effectiveness of spatial planning in practice. In addition to these, there is a wider set of concerns about the effectiveness of spatial planning as an activity that is designed to facilitate joined-up government, integrated policy development and combine economic, social and environmental concerns in arriving at more appropriate and effective solutions to regional problems. The first of these concerns is that the objective of joined-up government is not easily achieved. The contributors' sharing of experience within the context of the GRIDS project raised a number of instances where the policies of different arms of government appeared to conflict or pull in opposing directions. Some other concerns also surfaced on whether certain policy agendas, frequently those related to economic development policies, were driving issues forward and that any notion of 'joined-up government' (or indeed of securing more balanced regional development) was to a large extent a thin veil on an economic growth objective. Short-term political expediency, again centred around the facilitation of economic growth, also poses risks for the effectiveness of spatial planning with its longer-term objectives of spatial change. The capacity of spatial planning to facilitate joined-up government and successfully integrate a wide spectrum of sectoral policies appears to be as yet unproven. There seems to be very limited research or clear evidence of the effectiveness of spatial planning. Many of the spatial planning initiatives being progressed in the various parts of Europe could, at their worst, be portrayed as acts of faith based on an unproven capacity for spatial planning to deliver joined-up government. In effect, the promise of spatial planning needs to be realised. If it is not, then the current appeal and popularity of spatial planning in certain regions of Europe may fade. This does appear to be a rather pessimistic or negative conclusion to what has been an interesting and engaging collection of contributions from various parts of Europe. There are, of course, reasons to be optimistic, including the fact that a diversity of different regional development paradigms are available for exploring and trying to explain the various different issues addressed by the contributors. Research work within these different paradigms, if continued, may well come forward with valuable ideas for enhancing the effectiveness of both regional development and spatial planning activities. Like many others, we see the real value offered by the development of a spatial planning approach in its various guises, yet also recognise that it needs to be refined and subjected to further challenge and critique if it is remain a key feature in the landscape of regional planning and development.

References

Dabinett, G. and Richardson, T. (2005), 'The Europeanization of Spatial Strategy: Shaping Regions and Spatial Justice through Governmental Ideas', *International Planning Studies*, vol. 10, no. 3–4, pp. 201–218.

Pallagst, K. (2006), 'European Spatial Planning Reloaded: Considering EU Enlargement in Theory and Practice', *European Planning Studies*, vol. 14, no. 2, pp. 253–272.

Shaw, D. and Sykes, O. (2005), 'European Spatial Development Policy and Evolving Forms of Territorial Mobilisation in the United Kingdom', *Planning Practice and Research*, vol. 20, no. 2, pp. 183–199.

Walsh, J. (2002), 'The National Spatial Strategy as a Framework for Achieving Balanced Regional Development', in: McDonagh, J. (ed.) *Economy, Society and Peripherality: Experiences from the West of Ireland*, Arlen House: Galway, pp. 55–79.

Index